IET COMPUTING SERIES 34

AI for Emerging Verticals

Other volumes in this series:

AI for Emerging Verticals

Human-robot computing, sensing and networking

Edited by
Muhammad Zeeshan Shakir and Naeem Ramzan

The Institution of Engineering and Technology

Published by The Institution of Engineering and Technology, London, United Kingdom

The Institution of Engineering and Technology is registered as a Charity in England & Wales (no. 211014) and Scotland (no. SC038698).

The Institution of Engineering and Technology
Michael Faraday House
Six Hills Way, Stevenage
Herts, SG1 2AY, United Kingdom

www.theiet.org

British Library Cataloguing in Publication Data
A catalogue record for this product is available from the British Library

ISBN 978-1-78561-982-3 (hardback)
ISBN 978-1-78561-983-0 (PDF)

Typeset in India by MPS Limited
Printed in the UK by CPI Group (UK) Ltd, Croydon

Contents

17 Surface water pollution monitoring using the
Internet of Things (IoT) and machine learning   337
Hamza Khurshid, Rafia Mumtaz, Noor Alvi, Faisal Shafait, Sheraz Ahmed,
Muhammad Imran Malik, Andreas Dengel, and Quanita Kiran

About the editors

Muhammad Zeeshan Shakir is an associate professor at the School of Computing, Engineering and Physical Sciences, University of the West of Scotland, Paisley, Scotland, United Kingdom. He is an expert in networks, Internet of Things and machine-learning/artificial intelligence. He has won over 1.5 research funding for the UK/EU and international projects and has published over 150 research articles. He is a senior member of IEEE Communications Society and IEEE, a fellow of Higher Education Academy, and a chair of the IEEE ComSoc emerging technologies initiative on backhaul/fronthaul communications.

Naeem Ramzan is a full professor and director of the Affective and Human Computing for Smart Environment Research Centre at the University of the West of Scotland, Paisley, Scotland, United Kingdom. He has published nearly 200 highly cited publications and lead major national/EU/KTP projects worth over £10m. He is a senior member of the IEEE, a senior fellow of Higher Education Academy, a co-chair of MPEG HEVC verification (AHG5) group and a voting member of the British Standard Institution.

Preface

With a massive growth in data being generated by an ever-increasing emerging industrial application and an academic research and development, it is undoubtedly known that artificial intelligence (AI) and machine learning (ML) will play a major role in the digital transformation of our society, economy and industry. At the time of editing this book, several countries around the world have been affected by Covid-19 pandemic. The role of AI and ML for healthcare, industries and businesses has become more important than ever before. AI- and ML-enabled services can be formed from high-level intelligence and learning to automate the complex decisions particularly during such pandemic situations and leverage emerging analytical techniques; theoretic approaches and methodologies; automation and emerging algorithms, and applications. This book explores novel concepts and practices, cutting edge research and development and policy and regulations with a long-term and sustainable goal of fully automated advanced digital systems fostered by the technological advancements of AI and ML in a broad range of applications in the areas of robotics, human computing, sensing and networking.

Chapter 1: The field of robotics has been advancing with an ever-increasing pace during the last decades. Researchers are trying to create humanoid robots that will be able to perform several of the tasks that a normal human can perform, including the use of robotic hands for grasping. However, achieving stable and purposeful grasps with robotic hands is a challenging problem, especially for autonomous robots. In the first chapter, the authors examine the use of deep learning techniques in order to model human-hand behaviour and successfully translate it for robotic grasping of unknown items. Results for the proposed combination of convolutional neural networks and recurrent neural networks demonstrate the potential of this approach for modelling human behaviour and for translating this modelling for autonomous grasping with robotic soft hands.

Chapter 2: Affective computing is the computing that attempts to recognise, interpret, process or simulate human affect. One of the most notable applications of affective computing is the task of emotion recognition, and among the most promising proposed approaches for emotion recognition are the ones based on brain signals and ML. Chapter 2 offers an introduction to the field of emotion recognition based on electroencephalography (EEG) signals, presenting a feature extraction and feature selection approach combined with the Naïve Bayes (NB) classification algorithm. Results for detecting the emotional state, in terms of the valence and arousal dimensions, of users watching music videos demonstrate the potential of AI-based methods for emotion recognition, an application that can significantly benefit the fields of human–computer interaction (HCI) and of quality-of-experience (QoE).

Chapter 3: In addition to HCI, affective computing can potentially be beneficial for the field of animal-assisted intervention (AAI), a field that has gained a lot of attention in recent years as complement to conventional mental health treatment. The use of horses for AAI, also known as equine-assisted therapy (EAT), has long been considered as helpful for mental health treatment, finding applications in the treatment of children and adults suffering from PTSD, depression, symptoms related to combat trauma, and others. However, very few scientific studies on EAT have been based on analytical methods, with most of them relying on empirical observations. In Chapter 3, the authors propose the use of affective computing techniques for studying the emotional responses that horses seem to elicit in humans. A ML approach based on features from EEG, electrocardiography (ECG), and electromyography signals is used in order to assess the emotional state of humans during their interaction with horses. Experimental results demonstrate the suitability of the proposed approach that can potentially offer a quantitative method for assessing the emotional state of people undergoing EAT.

Chapter 4: Robots have merged with our day-to-day life and contributing to our society from different settings. They are not just the assembly of motors and electronics, rather they are also highly intelligent machines capable of doing difficult to hazardous jobs efficiently. Some applications of robots can be mentioned as industrial automation, military and defensive applications, decontamination of nuclear and highly radioactive material, space exploration and search and rescue operation. The development of robots is going to be safer and faster as the list of applications of robots will increase over the time. In particular, Chapter 4 reviews and analyses the state-of-the-art work in robotic locomotion, robotic manipulation with or without the assistance of humans and reviews significant robotic applications.

Chapter 5: Unmanned aerial vehicles (UAVs), commonly referred to as drones, have been successfully developed and deployed for multiple applications. ML plays a critical role in the success of UAVs, since real-time object detection is a crucial task for their operation. Chapter 5 describes a visual object tracking method that is based on artificial neural networks (ANNs) and was evaluated via simulation, as well as using a real quadcopter drone. The proposed method is based on the detection of a marker by the drones camera using the ANN approach and on the use of fuzzy logic for the marker's tracking. The experimental evaluation showed that the proposed approach was efficient in both the simulated and the real environment, demonstrating its potential.

Chapter 6: With the development of the cellular system, many people use mobile devices for different services while moving from one place to another. In a cellular network, the base stations provide services with voice and data to the users with mobility. Therefore, mobility management is a crucial function of the cellular network with aiming to provide services to the devices with mobility. This function is one of the key design challenges for cellular networks. In the era of the 5G network, it is even more challenging due to the heterogeneity nature of the network that has different types of technologies. In this context, predictive mobility management methods, which propose active handover process, have involved a significant amount of research motion in terms of latency, signalling overhead, etc. Chapter 6 discusses the mobility management briefly followed by the state of the art of predictive mobility management in detail. Then, the 3D transition matrix-assisted Markov chains-based predictive mobility management has been presented, which offers improvement in the prediction performances in the cases of revisits.

Chapter 7: 5G and beyond cellular networks have to be data intensive and service driven. The number of cellular-connected devices will rise from 5.6 billion in 2016 to more than 7.5 billion by the end of 2021. These devices will require data services of approximately 6.5 GB per device on average. Besides, the cellular network also needs to support diverse devices which will lead to huge growing traffic over the network. This will impose a challenge for the network with complexity in terms of design, management and scalability. The latest 5G technology has been designed in order to tackle all these challenges that will motivate the digital transformation to accomplish these requirements. AI will play a vital role in 5G while facing concerns of the scarce spectrum, multi-radio access technology, network virtualisation and many more. In Chapter 7, opportunities and development for AI-assist applications in 5G networks are reviewed. Some case studies are presented, which showed that AI could be a powerful tool to improve the performance of the 5G network. In addition, the crucial role of data analytics has been emphasised in this chapter.

Chapter 8: The cellular network needs to provide services to all the users by providing coverage. Any coverage hole will bring degradation to the reputation of the network operators. Coverage hole is a major issue from the beginning of the deployment phase until the maintenance phase. Traditionally, the drive test along with some propagation theory was considered in order to detect coverage hole. Afterwards, the minimisation of drive test (MDT) has been introduced, which reduces the cost of drive test for network operators. However, the MDT is still not able to provide information with accuracy. In Chapter 8, ML-assisted coverage hole detection mechanism has been discussed by using UAV or commonly known as drones. This mechanism will reduce the cost of network operators significantly and provide real-time information of the coverage with accuracy by exploiting the benefits of UAV. The mechanism can be used to deploy the temporary network quicker than using standard practices.

Chapter 9: Positioning means to estimate the location of an object or a person. Indoor positioning system is becoming more demanding with the application of position or location awareness. Out of many other technologies like Bluetooth, Radio Frequency Identification and ZigBee, Ultra-Wide Band (UWB) has more advantages in penetration ability, precise ranging, anti-multi-path and anti-interference due to its characteristics. Nevertheless, some factors such as environmental noise, non-line of sight (NLoS), high interferences from nearby devices, etc. may impose some challenges. These challenges can be resolved with the assistance of AI and ML. Hence, the accuracy of UWB can be achieved with fast speed covering larger distance and NLoS environments. Chapter 9 presents the indoor positioning accuracy of the UWB system by developing an NB classifier. Root mean square error is selected to characterise the received data in different levels followed by receiver operating characteristic curves which are plotted, and the area under the curves make it possible to visualise the accuracy of an NB classifier.

Chapter 10: Internet-of-Things (IoT) opened a new door in the field of telecommunication with remarkable applications such as smart cities, home automation, crowd surveillance, etc. Developing IoT applications may require the indoor tracking and positioning of sensors sometimes for the desired service. This indoor tracking and positioning of sensors perform differently with the type of indoor environment. Therefore, the classification of the indoor environment is very important since it leads to efficient power consumption. Chapter 10 demonstrates a novel method based on a cascaded two-stage ML techniques to achieve classification and localisation with high accuracy based on real-time measurement of the RF signal. In addition, several ML techniques such as decision trees, support vector machine (SVM), etc. have been studied for comparative study.

Chapter 11: EEG signals are commonly associated with medical applications, as well as with the field of affective computing. Recently, various researchers proposed their use as a biometrics modality due to their inherent characteristics and relation to the individual. These approaches commonly rely on ML for the subject identification task but rarely examine the issue of permanence of the EEG-based biometric signature, i.e. its stability over time. Chapter 11 examines the issue of permanence, also known as template ageing in EEG-based ML approaches for biometrics, when a consumer-grade EEG device is utilised. Experimental results show that EEG signals are heavily affected by session-specific noise and phenomena; thus identification performance degrades over time. The difference in performance between the examined approaches and other works in the literature that utilised medical-grade EEG devices suggests that consumer-grade EEG devices have poorer quality compared to medical-grade ones; hence more robust features are required for the training of the ML models when such devices are used.

Chapter 12: The continuously expanding video streaming industry seeks to offer enhanced QoE to its users by attempting to offer the best video quality possible under each user's network and hardware limitations. Efficient video quality assessment algorithms that successfully capture perceptual video quality, as experienced by human viewers, are necessary to achieve this aim. The industry relies on subjective quality metrics, like for example a peak signal-to-noise ratio and a structural similarity index, which have low computational complexity and thus are easy to compute. However, it is well established in the literature that such metrics do not accurately reflect the viewer's perception of visual quality and that viewer ratings in the form of mean opinion scores (MOS) remain the most accurate depiction of human-perceived video quality. The video multimethod assessment fusion (VMAF) metric attempts to address this issue by using ML to map objective quality metrics to MOS ratings, thus bridging the gap between objective metrics and user ratings. Chapter 12 examines the efficiency of the VMAF metric on three different video sequence data sets, demonstrating its superiority over commonly used objective metrics. Nevertheless, it is shown that performance suffers when the examined videos do not follow the design principles of the metric and that the data set used to train such metrics will significantly affect performance.

Chapter 13: Autonomous driving cars rely on a multitude of sensors for the acquisition of information about their surrounding environment which is then used for making driving-related decisions. Imaging sensors (cameras) and ML are commonly used for translating the visual input into driving parameters, such as steering angle, acceleration, braking, etc. Chapter 13 addresses this application as a multi-task learning problem and proposes a generalised multi-task learning framework for the estimation of various parameters needed for autonomous driving. Multiple ANNs, including various types of layers, are designed for the various tasks, with the relationship among tasks to be learned handled by including shared layers in the architecture, which later diverges into different branches in order to handle the difference in the behaviour of each task. An experimental evaluation on publicly available benchmark data sets showed that the proposed approach is able to predict primary driving parameters and vehicle localisation on the road regardless of road conditions.

Chapter 14: Potassium has a crucial role in the human body to maintain nerves, muscles and heart. However, high potassium in the blood is a medical problem, which is called hyperkalemia. People with renal/kidney diseases are highly likely to be developed hyperkalemia. Patients with renal impairment also have a high risk of developing other further health problems for instance heart failure, high blood pressure, electrolyte imbalance, metabolic acidosis. It is also possible to develop hyperkalemia without renal impairment; however, those with kidney disease are most at risk. Due to hyperkalemia, the potassium level fluctuates in the blood cause disturbance to the timing and pace of contractions within the heart, which has a negative effect such as cardiac arrest. There are higher chances of being cardiac arrest which is associated with hyperkalemia. With the increasing level of potassium, the cardiac arrest progressively worsens and urgent treatment is required by admitting the patients to the hospital. The cardiac activity can be observed by performing electrocardiogram (ECG) test in all clinics worldwide through traditional methods or through emerging mobile sensors. Chapter 14 investigates the use of remote ECG tests as a diagnostic instrument for the initial detection of hyperkalemia by using ML in order to predict blood potassium levels from ECG data.

Chapter 15: ML has been successfully used in the field of medicine, finding application in diagnosis, personalised health, smart health, connected health and others. In the case of connected health, portable and often wearable sensors are used in order to transmit health-related information and diagnose or predict pathologies. Chapter 15 examines the use of compressed sensing and ML for the transmission of electrocardiography (ECG) data and potential diagnosis of pathological situations. Compressed sensing is used to obtain a reduced representation of an ECG signal, which is then used to extract features used for the classification of the samples as pathological or healthy using an SVM classifier without the need to reconstruct the original ECG signal. Results demonstrate the potential of the proposed approach for ECG signal classification in the compressed domain, allowing for efficient and low-power consumption continuous monitoring and real-time decision-making in low power and low resources wireless devices.

Chapter 16: The proliferation of IoT networks has led to the continuous generation and collection of huge amounts of data. Acquiring, aggregating and processing these data put a lot of strain on the IoT network, both at the sensing nodes and the cloud level. Dimensionality reduction by means of clustering algorithms is commonly used in order to reduce the amount of data. Self-organising maps (SOMs) is an ideal candidate due to their inherent property of topology preservation and unsupervised learning, although at the cost of high computational complexity. In Chapter 16, the authors propose hardware, scalable and distributed SOM architecture based on the distribution of the SOM operation over a highly connected network of routers called network-of-chip. The experimental evaluation of the proposed architecture for different networks and cluster sizes on an image quantisation application demonstrated its potential for large-scale hardware SOM solutions.

Chapter 17: Water is one of the main basic requirements for humans to survive. Bad-quality water causes many diseases for instance diarrhoea, typhoid, hepatitis and many others which will lead to death in some cases. People living near industrial areas are more likely to consume polluted water. It is very important to monitor the quality of the water using an intelligent system for population, especially in countries with agronomic nature such as Pakistan. The traditional system to test the water quality is to take the sample to the lab and test it by using chemicals followed by manually controlled assessments which are very expensive and time-consuming. This system is non-real-time and not available in many countries worldwide. Chapter 17 demonstrates IoT- and ML-enabled real-time water quality monitoring and prediction system with water quality parameters such as temperature, pH, dissolved oxygen, conductivity and turbidity. These parameters are used to calculate the water quality index which is internationally recognised.

Part I

Human–robot

Chapter 1

Deep learning techniques for modelling human manipulation and its translation for autonomous robotic grasping with soft end-effectors

Visar Arapi[1], Yujie Zhang[1,2], Giuseppe Averta[1,2,3],
Cosimo Della Santina[4], and Matteo Bianchi[1,2]

One of the key enablers for the extraordinary dexterity of human hands is their compliance and capability to purposefully adapt with the environment and to multiply their manipulation possibilities. This observation has also produced a significant paradigm shift for the design of robotic hands, leading to the avenue of soft end-effectors that embed elastic and deformable elements directly in their mechanical architecture. This shift has also determined a perspective change for the control and planning of the grasping phases, with respect to (w.r.t.) the classical approach used with rigid grippers. Indeed, instead of targeting an accurate analysis of the contact points on the object, an approximated estimation of the relative hand-object pose is sufficient to generate successful grasps, exploiting the intrinsic adaptability of the robotic systems to overcome local uncertainties. This chapter reports on deep learning (DL) techniques used to model human manipulation and to successfully translate these modelling outcomes for enabling soft artificial hands to autonomous grasp objects with the environment.

1.1 Introduction

Achieving stable and purposeful grasps with robotic hands is a challenging problem, especially under the framework of autonomous operations. Classical approaches for grasp planning and execution targeted the exact definition of the contact points on the object (object-centric approach) [1]. These approaches defined a set of available contact points and then identified point locations and contact forces, relying on the

[1]Centro di Ricerca "Enrico Piaggio", University of Pisa, Pisa, Ital
[2]Department of Information Engineering, University of Pisa, Pisa, Italy
[3]Soft Robotics for Human Cooperation and Rehabilitation, Fondazione Istituto Italiano di Tecnologia, Genova, Italy
[4]Computer Science and Artificial Intelligence Laboratory, Massachusetts Institute of Technology, Cambridge, USA

knowledge of object properties. These methods were proven to work well with rigid robotic hands, but can be hardly applied to a new generation of end-effectors, which can deform and interact with the environment. The latter category of robotic end-effectors, which can be continuously deformable [2] or soft-articulated [3], envisions the purposeful introduction of elastic elements in their mechanical structure to allow the adaptation around different objects and with the environment, the increase of the device robustness and the reduction of the control burden (often capitalizing upon under-actuation schemes). The motivation for the design of these soft hands is the human example: everyday human hands purposefully leverage on their softness to exploit the environmental constraints [4] for multiplying grasping opportunities and degrees of freedom, while reducing the computational complexity needed for task execution. Lifting a coin from a table, pivoting the object around one or more fingers interacting with the surface represent some exemplary cases of this ability. Under a robotic point-of-view, soft manipulators have also produced a perspective shift in grasp planning problems, requiring only an approximated estimation of the relative hand-object pose is sufficient, letting the elasticity of the end-effectors and the inter-action with the environment doing the rest [5]. It is hence clear that this paradigm shift also requires new mathematical tools, to model human behaviour (which represents the golden standard for artificial manipulation) and to translate it in well-defined control laws for autonomous manipulators. Under this regard, machine learning (ML) and, especially, DL [6] have emerged as promising techniques to tackle the afore-mentioned twofold goal. Indeed, ML and DL allow one to overcome the modelling challenges that arise when dealing with soft bodies and their interaction with the external environment, targeting solutions close enough to the desired ones, rather than exact, leveraging on the adaptation capabilities of the soft hands to overcome local uncertainties.

However, so far only few works in the literature have applied learning methods for (i) studying human hands in everyday grasps with the environment and (ii) controlling soft hands, by suitably translating human observation outcomes on the robotic side. Regarding (i), pioneer work on convolutional neural network (CNN) applications to hand gesture recognition dates back to 1990s. Among the more recent examples, it is worth mentioning the EgoHands [7], a CNN-based framework trained on 15,000 segmented hands (obtained through a manually pixel-level process on 4,800 egocentric video frames – first person videos of people playing four game board activities). EgoHands detects accurately one or more hands from each video frame, with very robust performance w.r.t. changes in environment conditions, particularly during environmental constraint exploitation (ECE) [4] for grasping. Regarding (ii), in [8] authors introduced a mixed approach combining learning by demonstration with reinforcement learning to transfer grasping capabilities of known objects from a human operator to the robotic system. In [9], GRNN (generalized regression neural networks) and autoencoders were adopted to learn from human demonstration examples how to manipulate previously unseen thin objects with a soft gripper. In [5], a library of reactive strategies was collected from a subject operating a soft hand and successfully translated for robotic grasping of new items, in a human–robot handover scenario. In [10], a 3D convolutional neural network was trained with tens of thousands of labelled images. The network output provides the control input for the hand approaching direction.

All these papers are extremely promising, especially for the integration of DL with the intrinsic compliance of soft end-effectors, i.e. their embodied intelligence. However, they failed in terms of result generalization and in effectively grasping the full potentiality that the human example and the environment exploitation could represent for achieving autonomous grasps with soft hands.

In this chapter, we report on two successful applications of DL to the study of human hands and its translation for autonomous grasping with soft grippers. We will discuss the results and finally comment on future avenues and possibilities of these approaches.

1.2 Investigation of the human example

Everyday, humans purposefully take advantage from the interaction with the environment, to accomplish successful manipulation actions, relying on the intrinsic compliance of their hands. This is one of the key enablers for human extraordinary manipulation capabilities, which have not been yet matched on the robotic side. For these reasons, the observation and modelling of the human example could provide useful insights for the control of soft robotic hands, which can take advantage from the exploitation of the environmental constraints, similarly to human hands. In [11], authors modelled human grasping behaviour introducing transition probabilities for the identification of the conditions leading to the decision between one path of action w.r.t. another one. The outcomes of this investigation resulted in different action sequences w.r.t. different object shapes. Translation of these results for the control of soft robotic end-effectors could allow the robots to effectively evaluate the transition conditions, relying on suitable sensors and computational tools. Towards this goal, the first mandatory step is the recognition of human gestures, which is usually accomplished through wearable [12,13] or remote devices. Regarding remote systems, the most commonly used strategy is represented by video recordings. In the literature, there have been important examples for the extraction of features describing human gestures in video sources, which include methods based on k-means classification or Hidden Markov models [12,13].

At the same time, DL approaches have emerged as a promising tool for feature extraction, e.g. image classification [14], object detection [15], hand gesture recognition in video sources. Regarding the latter point, it is worth mentioning EgoHands [7], where four actions were recognized by a CNN – trained with 4,800 segmented hands – in a combination with windowing at fixed temporal size. CNNs can be synergistically used in a combination with recurrent neural networks (RNNs), which allow one to efficiently and robustly manage spatio-temporal features [16–18]. RNNs usually rely on long–short-term memory (LSTM) cells, which can put in memory a compressed representation of medium-range temporal relationships in the input sequence [19].

However, to the authors' best knowledge, there is currently no approach based on DL applied to videos, for the characterization of the dynamic and time-dependent content underpinning human hand pose evolution, during the interaction with the environment. To bridge this gap, we proposed a framework, named DeepDynamic-Hand presented in [20], which targets visual features related to the hand shape only (instead of considering the whole video frame) and dynamic video annotation encompassing both the pre-grasp and grasping actions. DeepDynamicHand consists of two neural architectures: the first one is a CNN for segmenting human hand in each video frame, enabling the extraction of a compressed and rich encoding of the hand posture; the second architecture is an RNN based on LSTM recurrent units [21].

The latter architecture takes the sequence of encodings as input provided by the CNN and generates a sequence of action primitives as output – i.e. a dictionary of meaningful behaviour components whose composition enables one to successfully interact with the environment in grasping tasks – performed by human hands in the videos.

1.2.1   Methods

Let us consider a set of videos

$$\langle \mathbf{V}_1, \mathbf{V}_2, \ldots, \mathbf{V}_T \rangle. \tag{1.1}$$

A single video $\mathbf{V}_j$ comprises a sequence of frames

$$\mathbf{V}_j = (\mathbf{I}_{j,1}, \mathbf{I}_{j,2}, \ldots, \mathbf{I}_{j,n}), \tag{1.2}$$

where $\mathbf{I}_{j,t} \in \mathbb{R}^{w \times h \times 3}$, w and h are the width and height of the video frame at time t, respectively. In general, the number of frames n composing the video varies from case to case. Our goal is to automatically convert each video into a sequence of labels:

$$\mathbf{Y}_j = (\mathbf{y}_{j,1}, \mathbf{y}_{j,2}, \ldots, \mathbf{y}_{j,n}), \tag{1.3}$$

where each label $\mathbf{y}_{j,t}$ (j refers to the actual video, while t is the temporal frame) is the *action primitive* – included in a pre-defined (finite) dictionary S – executed by the participant's hand in each frame. Moreover, considering that, in each video, actions performed by the participant are executed in a dynamic temporal sequence, implies that the label $\mathbf{y}_{j,t}$ associated with the action primitive at frame t depends on features observed both in prior and in the actual frames $(\mathbf{I}_{j,1}, \mathbf{I}_{j,2}, \ldots, \mathbf{I}_{j,t})$.

To address the aforementioned challenge, we propose a two-stage architecture (Figure 1.1). In the first stage (Figure 1.1(a)), we leverage on a CNN-based approach to recognize the hand in each video frame $\mathbf{I}_{j,i}$ and subsequently extract a condensed and, still, informative characterization of the hand pose. To this end, we employ two units, namely *window proposal* and *window classification*, respectively. The *window proposal* unit:

$$H_P : \mathbb{R}^{w \times h \times 3} \longrightarrow \mathbb{R}^{w_k \times h_k \times 3}, \tag{1.4}$$

where $w_k \leq w$ and $h_k \leq h$ is realized through the pre-trained four-dimensional Gaussian kernel density estimator fitted on the EgoHands data set [7]. The aim of such unit is to discover the most likely regions that enclose the hand within a probabilistic

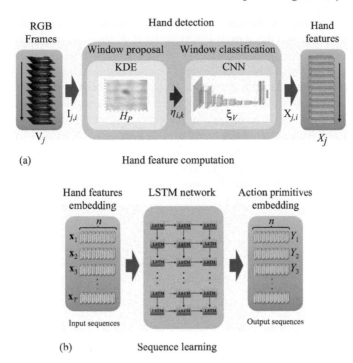

Figure 1.1   *General structure of the proposed architecture. In (a), we show a
CNN-based approach, used to detect hands in the frames extracted
from videos, encoding the associated bounding boxes into feature
vectors corresponding to the activation of the penultimate fully
connected layer of the CNN (hand feature computation). In (b), we
show an LSTM model, trained to learn to predict the sequence of n
input vectors, corresponding to the n video frames, into a sequence of n
hand action primitives (sequence learning).*

context. Accordingly, the output includes a set of candidate windows that are then
passed to the *window classification* unit:

$$\xi_V : \mathbb{R}^{w_k \times h_k \times 3} \longrightarrow (p, 1 - p) \in \mathbb{R}^2, \tag{1.5}$$

where $p \in [0, 1]$, whose target is to detect the presence of the hand in the candidate window (hereinafter, bounding box). For this purpose, we use the pre-trained CNN developed as part of the EgoHands framework [7]. The structure of the CNN is summarized
in Table 1.1. Convolutional layers – Conv$_i$ – extract input features through convolution
operations represented by the number of filters (kernels) b with spatial size $f \times f$,
applied to the input with stride s. The outcomes of convolutional layers are sequentially saturated by ReLU$_i$ layers (introducing nonlinearity into the CNN); down-
sampled by Pool$_i$ layers (which apply a mask on $f \times f$ input regions and stride s);
and normalized by Norm$_i$ layers. On the top of the CNN structure, there are two fully

Table 1.1   Description of the CNN structure. Each row describes a layer of the network, organized from input to output. Kernels (b) refer to the number of kernels (each of them is an $f \times f$ matrix, whose dimensions are determined by the spatial size (f) containing the convolutional parameters, stride (s) controls the shift step of the kernel (convolution layer) or the mask (pooling layer) around the input volume, and output size represents the output dimension (height, weight and depth in the case of a volume or the vector size).

Type	Kernels (b)	Spatial size (f)	Stride (s)	Output size
Conv_1	96	11	4	55×55×96
ReLU_1	–	–	–	55×55×96
Pool_1	–	3	2	27×27×96
Norm_1	–	–	–	27×27×96
Conv_2	256	5	1	27×27×256
ReLU_2	–	–	–	27×27×256
Pool_2	–	3	2	13×13×256
Norm_2	–	–	–	13×13×256
Conv_3	384	3	1	13×13×384
Conv_4	384	3	1	13×13×384
ReLU_4	–	–	–	13×13×384
Conv_5	256	3	1	13×13×256
ReLU_5	–	–	–	13×13×256
Pool_5	–	3	2	6×6×256
FC_6	–	–	–	4096
ReLU_6	–	–	–	4096
FC_7	–	–	–	4096

connected layers FC_6 and FC_7, respectively. These layers connect all neurons of the previous layer with 4096 nodes. Finally, the *Softmax* function capitalizes on the last FC_7 layer encodings to generate a probability distribution over two classes (*hand*, *no-hand*).

Supposing $\eta_{i,k} \in \mathbb{R}^{w_k \times h_k \times 3}$ be the most likely scored bounding box enclosing the hand. We leverage on FC_6 layer encodings to characterize hand pose features. This layer comprises less task-specific information than FC_7 layer, which is closer to the Softmax layer and, thus, more dedicated to the recognition of the hand rather than its high level information (i.e. edges, shapes, etc.). As a result, for each frame we represent the hand pose features as fixed vectorial encodings $x_{j,i} \in \mathbb{R}^g$, where $g = 4100$ (the first four components refer to the bounding box coordinates, while the remaining ones include the FC_6 layer encodings). Therefore, the whole video $\mathbf{V}_j$ is now represented as sequence:

$$\mathbf{X}_j = (x_{j,1}, x_{j,2}, \ldots, x_{j,n}), \tag{1.6}$$

of such hand-pose encodings.

In the second stage (Figure 1.1(b)), the *sequence learning* model is trained to process the input sequence $\mathbf{X}_j$ – hand pose encodings obtained by the CNN – to predict a related output sequence of action primitives:

$$\mathbf{Y}_j = (\mathbf{y}_{j,1}, \mathbf{y}_{j,2}, \ldots, \mathbf{y}_{j,n}). \tag{1.7}$$

Moreover, to model the dynamic temporal behaviour, we employ an RNN – implemented using LSTM recurrent units – in the *Sequence learning* component of our architecture. Specifically, LSTM is able to provide as output the prediction for the current frame, while taking into account the history of the poses and action sequences performed by the hand in the previous instants. To this end, the action primitives (which – as aforementioned – are symbols from a discrete and finite alphabet) are converted to a numeric vector using a *one-hot* encoding. The approach encodes the kth symbol of the action primitive alphabet as a vector of length equal to the alphabet size, where only the kth element is set to 1, while the rest is equal to zero. More formally, the one-hot encoding of the action label for frame $\mathbf{x}_i$ is the vector $\mathbf{y_i} \in \mathbb{R}^{|S|}$ defined as

$$\mathbf{y_i}^k = \begin{cases} 1, & \text{if } k = \text{ind}(\mathbf{y_i}) \\ 0, & \text{otherwise}, \end{cases} \tag{1.8}$$

where $\text{ind}(\mathbf{y_i})$ is the index of the current label in the dictionary S.

Moreover, the details of the LSTM network are specified by model selection, using validation data outside of the training and test samples for ensuring robustness and avoiding results biased towards high precision on the test set. Such details include, among others, the number of hidden layers and the number of LSTM units in each layer. The following experimental analysis provides details on the final configuration. More information and technical details can be found here [20].

1.2.2 Experiments

Videos were manually segmented and labelled by an experienced person using the action primitives described later. Each grasping video is represented by a combination of a subset of the following action primitives: *rest, approach, close, slide, flip, edge*.

Note that the CNN we leverage on to detect hands was trained on RGB images (hands), instead our videos are in black and white. In addition the participants wore a glove during the experiments. We thus apply a simple image segmentation filter using the *imbinarize* function in MATLAB® to convert each frame into RGB coding. In this way, we can select the pixels connected to the glove, which roughly represent the hand, and colorize them with the same colour, chosen as the mean value of EgoHands ground truth [7].

1.2.2.1 Evaluation on ECE data set

Training and testing procedures are executed on an NVIDIA Tesla M40 GPU with 12 GB of on-board memory. We propose two types of cross-validation: *hold out* and *leave one out* to verify the generalization and robustness of action primitive prediction. The goal of cross-validation is to estimate the expected level of model predictive accuracy in a way that is independent from the data used to train the model.

Considering that *hold out* approach requires less computation time compared to *leave one out*, we employed it to determine both network hyper-parameters (i.e. LSTM depth and width) and learning hyper-parameters (i.e. batch size, learning rate, number of epochs and dropout). We trained 30 different network configurations that were obtained by varying, respectively: the number of LSTM hidden-layers in $\{1, 2, 3\}$, the number of LSTM cells per layer in $\{64, 128, 256, 512\}$, batch size in $\{5, 10, 15, 20\}$, learning rate in $\{10^{-2}, 10^{-3}, 10^{-4}\}$, the number of epochs in $\{10, 20, 30, 40\}$ and dropout in $\{0.4, 0.5, 0.6\}$. Relying on the results of each simulation, we consider the configuration that provided both the highest *min-score* accuracy – the lowest accuracy w.r.t. the six classes – and *f1-score* [22] accuracy on the validation data set – which are 73% and 91%, respectively. In such configuration, we consider three hidden layers, with, respectively, 256, 256 and 128 dimensions for the size of the LSTM memory. We train the network for 30 epochs using RMSprop optimizer with a fixed learning rate of 10^{-3}, batch size 20 and dropout 0.5. Furthermore, with such architecture and such learning parameters, the network is able to predict the dynamic hand strategies in the test data set with an accuracy ranging from 75% up to 96%, depending on the action class. Normalizing scores w.r.t. the total number of classes, we obtain an accuracy of 85% – refer to [20] for details.

Results of the leave one out cross-validation analyses of network performance, which necessitate a longer computation time compared to hold out approach, but guarantee more robust validation results, are reported in Figure 1.2(b). We show the per class normalized confusion matrix index of the predictor of all six classes that were detected. What we can observe from Figure 1.2(b) is that there is a class (*approach*) with a precision of over 94%, three classes with a precision over 83% (*edge, close, rest*), one class (*slide*) with a precision of 73% and one (*flip*) that reaches a reasonable 62%. This is a very strong result given the fact that the predictor is trained on videos with poor quality – videos are in black and white format, and subjects wore gloves. Furthermore, we provide a comparison with a benchmark support vector machine (SVM) method in Figure 1.2(a). This approach is implemented with the purpose of noticing the accuracy discrepancy when action primitives are predicted without considering any temporal information. It is also evident from the results that LSTM outperforms SVM, confirming the crucial relevance of temporal information for an accurate classification of action primitives.

Figures 1.3 and 1.4 show some examples of action primitives predicted by our DeepDynamicHand model on ECE data set. In each video frame, we overlaid (i) the bounding box that likely encloses the hand, colour changes depending on the action primitive the hand currently performs, (ii) the predicted action label, and in case of failure, the true label and (iii) the level of confidence represented with a filled rectangle – the colour is green if the predicted action is true, red otherwise. We can observe that wrong classification usually happens when a transaction between primitives occurs. Figure 1.3(f) refers to such an example, showing that confusion may arise in situations where hand shapes are hardly distinguishable by a human as well.

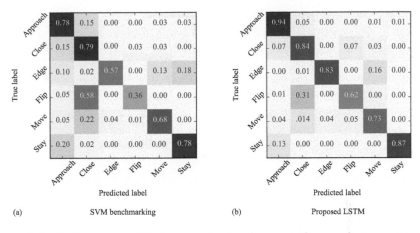

Figure 1.2   *Performance of the proposed network, reported as confusion matrices evaluated on (a) a benchmark SVM method and (b) the proposed LSTM. For each matrix, the true classes are reported on the y-axis and the predicted classes are reported on the x-axis. Optimal performances are represented by purely diagonal matrices. Results show significantly better performances for the LSTM case, confirming the crucial relevance of temporal information for an accurate classification of action primitives.*

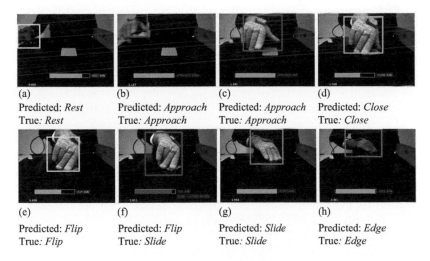

Figure 1.3   *Action primitives classified by the proposed network during reaching and grasping of a credit card. Each picture represents a time frame of the action execution. For each frame of (a)–(h), we show a bounding box around the hand with a colour dependent on the classified action, the label associated with the predicted action, a bar indicating the level of prediction confidence (green if the classification is correct, red otherwise).*

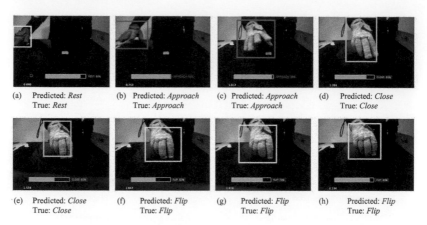

(a) Predicted: *Rest*   (b) Predicted: *Approach*   (c) Predicted: *Approach*   (d) Predicted: *Close*
     True: *Rest*   True: *Approach*   True: *Approach*   True: *Close*

(e) Predicted: *Close*   (f) Predicted: *Flip*   (g) Predicted: *Flip*   (h) Predicted: *Flip*
     True: *Close*   True: *Flip*   True: *Flip*   True: *Flip*

Figure 1.4   Action primitives classified by the proposed network during the reaching and grasping of a French chalk. Each picture represents a time frame of the action execution. For each frame of (a)–(h), we show a bounding box around the hand with a colour dependent on the classified action, the label associated with the predicted action, a bar indicating the level of prediction confidence (green if the classification is correct, red otherwise).

1.3   Autonomous grasping with anthropomorphic soft hands

In the previous section, we reported on how the human example can be investigated using DL techniques to identify common action primitives, which take into account the compliance of the hands for the exploitation of the environmental constraints during manipulation tasks. In this section, we describe the usage of DL to translate human observations on the robotic side, for autonomous grasping with soft hands [23]. More specifically, we considered a soft articulated robotic hand, the Pisa/IIT SoftHand [3], although the approach can be generalized to any soft end-effector. In our solution, which was presented in [23], the intelligence is distributed on three levels of abstractions, see Figure 1.5: (i) *high-level*: a classifier for planning the right action, choosing among a set of available ones, (ii) *medium level*: a set of human-inspired low-level strategies implementing both the approaching phase and the sensor-triggered reaction, and (iii) *low level*: a soft hand whose embodied intelligence mechanically manages local uncertainties. All the three levels are human inspired. We report the detailed description of these components in the next subsections.

1.3.1   High level: deep classifier

The target of the deep neural network is the association to an object, detected from the scene using an RGB camera, the primitive, intended as the temporal evolution of the hand pose, that humans would likely perform for grasping it. The object detection is implemented using the state-of-the-art detector YOLOv2 [24], which produces

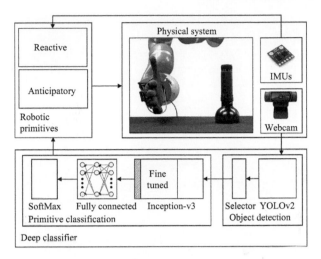

*Figure 1.5   General description of the proposed methodology, combining reactive
actions and anticipatory behaviour. A deep classifier observes the
scene and – given a specific object – predicts the approaching strategy
a human would implement to grasp the object. This semantic
description is used to select a corresponding motion primitive on the
robot, in terms of hand posture over time. IMUs fastened on the fingers
detect contact with the object and triggers a reactive grasp behaviour.*

as output a set of labelled bounding boxes containing all the objects in the scene
from the RGB input image. This output is fed to the second classifier, which is
built moving from Inception-v3 [25] trained on the ImageNet data set. The goal is
not to obtain a one-to-one signature of a particular object, but, on the contrary, to
achieve a semantic description that can be applied to objects with similar geometric
characteristics. We modified the Inception-v3 and added two fully connected layers
(2048 neurons each, with ReLU activation), which perform an adaptive nonlinear
combination and refinement of the features. The outcome of the last layer acts as
input to the Softmax, whose output is a probability distribution on the set of motion
primitives.

The deep classifier was trained using 6336 first person RGB videos (single-
object, table-top scenario), which were collected from 11 right-handed subjects
grasping 36 objects, see Figure 1.6 – which cover most of grasping possibilities in
everyday life – from different points of view (4), see Figure 1.7. Videos were visually
inspected to extract and label the main strategies, resulting in a set of ten primitives,
i.e. *Top, Top Left, Top Right, Bottom, Pinch, Pinch Right, Slide, Flip* and *Lateral*. For
more details on primitive description, refer to [23]. The choice of these primitives
was done taking inspiration from literature [4,26] and to provide a representative yet
concise description of human behaviour, without any claim of exhaustiveness. Note
that the selection of the action primitive is also object-configuration dependent.

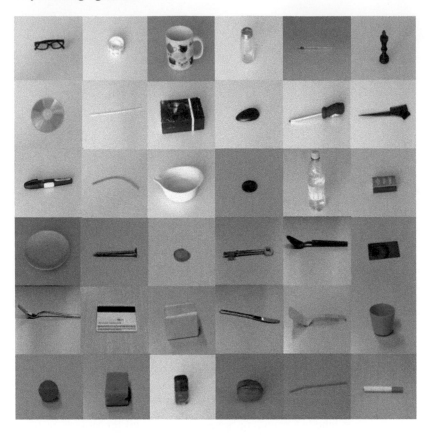

*Figure 1.6   Set of objects (36) used during the experiments with human
participants (pictures are not in scale)*

1.3.1.1   Object detection

The activity of object detection is achieved through a YOLOv2 detector [24]. More
specifically, given an RGB image as input, YOLOv2 is able to provide as output a
series of labelled bounding boxes that contain all the objects in the scene. Among
all, we first discard all the ones labelled as person. Then, assuming that the target is
placed close to the centre of the picture, we select the bounding box closest to the
scene centre. Note that this is an arbitrary selection, made only for implementation
purposes, and can be easily generalized. After the identification of the particular
object, the picture is automatically cropped around the bounding box and resized to
416×416 pixels. The result of this procedure is then used as input for a second block
used for classification.

1.3.1.2   Primitive classification

Network architecture

The primitive classification is based on a transfer learning approach [27]. This
approach leverages on prior knowledge – learned from one environment – to solve a

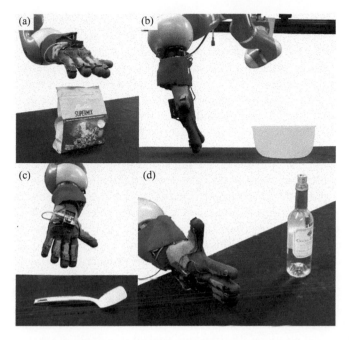

*Figure 1.7   Initial configuration of the hand w.r.t. the object at the beginning of
four different motion primitives: (a) top grasp, (b) bottom grasp,
(c) pinch grasp, and (d) lateral grasp. Moving from these initial poses,
the hand translates until the contact with the object is detected by the
IMUs. The contact triggers a reactive behaviour.*

new problem, typically related, but different in general. With this approach, a reduced
amount of samples is needed to train the model, thus resulting in shorter training
time while preserving high accuracy of results. To do this, we leveraged on Inception-
-v3 [25], trained on the ImageNet data set [28] to classify objects from images. We
keep the early and middle layers and remove the Softmax layer. This enables a direct
access to the informative, highly refined, neural features that Inception-v3 uses for
the classification. It is worth noticing that the object classification is not intended
as one-to-one, but rather it aims at extracting high level – semantic – descriptions
that can be easily transferred to objects with similar characteristics. On the top of
the original architecture we also included two fully connected layers containing 2048
neurons each (with ReLU activation function). These layers introduce a nonlinear,
adaptive, combination of the high-level features identified by the convolutional and
pooling layers, further refining the information. In this way, the geometric features
are implicitly linked each other to serve as the base for the classification. The output
of the last fully connected layer is thus fed into the Softmax layer, which produces
as output a probability distribution over the considered set of motion primitives. The
output of the overall network is then the motion primitive that shows the maximum
probability.

Training and validation

The network was trained using the labelled data set introduced earlier. More specifically, while the original parameters of the Inception-v3 were fine-tuned for the specific task, the parameters of the two fully connected layers placed at the top of the architecture were trained from scratch. This was achieved using a different learning rate for the layers. Indeed, the weights of the first 172 layers – which are more devoted to universal features, like curves and edges – were maintained unchanged, while the remaining 77 layers – used to capture features more related to the specific data set – were retrained in this implementation. Changes on the latter were limited by a relatively small learning rate λ_{ft}. Finally, the last two fully connected layers were randomly initialized and trained with a higher learning rate.

We minimized the risk of over-fitting by using a dropout policy [29]. More specifically, for every new training sample presented to the network, we randomly disconnected a set of neurons by masking their activation. Each neuron has a specific disconnection probability p_{drop}. This results in a new – different – topology of the network after each training, with the ultimate result to introduce variability and minimize the arising of unwanted co-adaptation of weights. Network design and training were performed through Keras library [30] leveraging on an NVIDIA Tesla M40 GPU with 12 GB of memory on-board.

A hold-out validation was then used to verify the robustness and the generalization capabilities of primitive classification. To do this, we split our samples into three data sets: 70% of samples used for the training phase; 20% of samples used for the validation phase; 10% of samples used for the testing phase. The three subdatasets were organized with a balanced representation of objects for each class we considered. We performed the training using 30 different configurations of the network, leveraging on *cross entropy* cost function to adjust the weights by calculating the error between the output of the Softmax layer and the label vector of the given sample category. Each configuration resulted from the variation of the most relevant hyper-parameters of the learning phase, i.e. probability of dropout $p_{\text{drop}} \in \{0.4, 0.5, 0.6\}$, learning rates $\lambda_{\text{ft}} \in \{10^{-3}, 10^{-4}, 10^{-5}, 10^{-6}\}$ and $\lambda_{\text{tr}} \in \{10^{-2}, 10^{-3}, 10^{-4}\}$, the number of epochs in $\{10, 20, 30, 40\}$ and batch size $\in \{10, 20, 30, 40\}$. The training time employed – for each network – was between 1 and 5 h. Among all the configurations trained, we selected the one that provided the highest $f1$-score accuracy [22] on the validation set. In our case, we had a maximum value of 97% with the following hyper-parameters: $p_{\text{drop}} = 0.5$, $\lambda_{\text{ft}} = 10^{-5}$, $\lambda_{\text{tr}} = 10^{-3}$, 30 epochs and batches size 20.

The network with these parameters resulted is able to correctly classify the motion primitives with an accuracy between 86% and 100%, depending on the primitive, with an average value equal to 95%. In Figure 1.8, we show the normalized accuracy of the proposed network for the ten classes considered in this work. It is worth noticing that the occasional failure of the network is related to two main reasons. First, the formulation of the problem itself makes intrinsically not possible an accuracy of 100%, since different subjects may use different grasping strategy for the same object in the same configuration. An example is the grasp of the coin, which is typically grasped through a flip strategy, but sometimes may be grasped leveraging on a sliding primitive

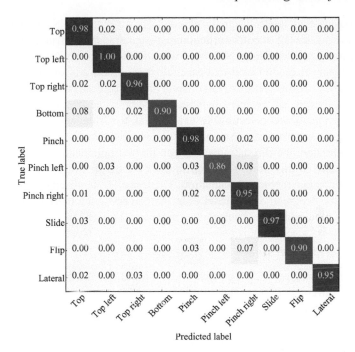

Figure 1.8   Performance of the proposed deep classifier, reported as confusion matrix evaluated on the test set. Each element of the matrix reports the percentage of cases in which the primitive identified (identified by the row label) is classified as the primitive associated with the column label. Optimal performances are represented by purely diagonal matrices. Numerical values are colour coded: white is low rate, dark green is high rate.

instead. Another reason for occasional failure is related to the experimental setup. Indeed, the usage of a single-RGB camera sometimes results in a misinterpretation of the object size which, for example, could lead to the prediction of a top grasp instead of a bottom grasp for a bowl. This particular problem can be solved through the usage of a stereo-camera; this extension is currently under evaluation and is left for future developments of this work.

1.3.2   Transferring grasping primitives to robots

In [31], Johansson and Edin hypothesized that the central nervous system (CNS)

monitors specific, more-or-less expected, peripheral sensory events and use these to directly apply control signals that are appropriate for the current task and its phase.

This means that control signals descending from the CNS are more likely computed in advance (i.e. feedforward/anticipatory actions). Motivated by this observation, our translation of human behaviour in a robotic framework was implemented leveraging mostly on feedforward actions. To do this, we moved from the observations discussed in the previous section of this chapter and defined a basis of human-inspired motion primitives, to be triggered by specific events. The first triggering event is associated with the object detection. To each object, the framework associates a corresponding grasping primitive. Among all the primitives included in this work, we do not consider here the flip, because this cannot be implemented by the particular end-effector used in this work. Motor primitives are divided into two main phases: (i) approaching and (ii) reactive adaptation. The transition between the two phases is triggered by the detection of a contact event perceived by the Inertial Measurement Units (IMUs) mounted on the back of the fingers of the soft hand.

1.3.3   Experimental setup

Even if the proposed approach is general and not limited to the specific robotic architecture, it is convenient to report here its description to increase clarity. The platform we used is composed by a Pisa/IIT SoftHand [32] mounted as end-effector on a KUKA LWR-IV arm. The particular end-effector used is an anthropomorphic soft robotic hand with 19 degrees of freedom, which are jointly (following synergistic covariation patterns) actuated by one single degree of actuation. It is worth noticing that the particular design and control of the end-effector represent a low-level *intelligence embodied*, an integral part of the control architecture itself. Video information are recorded through an RGB camera, fastened close to the robot base to generate a first-person point-of-view.

The soft hand is endowed with inertial sensors (IMUs) placed on the back of the fingertips. Measures recorded from IMUs (i.e. accelerations) are needed to detect contacts and trigger reactive grasping [5] strategies. Figure 1.9 shows the whole experimental setup, with reference frames for the global and end-effector reference systems.

1.3.3.1   Approach phase

Given the starting pose, the approaching phase towards the object position is encoded via the following Cartesian trajectory:

$$x(t) = x_0 + dtQ(t) = Q_0, \tag{1.9}$$

where $x \in \mathbb{R}^3$ represents the hand 3D Cartesian position and $Q \in \mathbb{R}^4$ is the quaternion that encodes its orientation (all w.r.t. the global reference system); $x_0 \in \mathbb{R}^3$ and $Q_0 \in \mathbb{R}^4$ refer to the initial position and orientation, and $d \in \mathbb{R}^3$ is the approaching direction. All these three quantities are defined by the selected primitive and dictated by the aim of heuristically reproducing as close as possible the human behaviour observed in the videos. Figure 1.7 depicts the initial configuration of the hand for four directions of approach, while Table 1.2 collects numerical values of initial orientations and approaching directions for all the primitives implemented in this work.

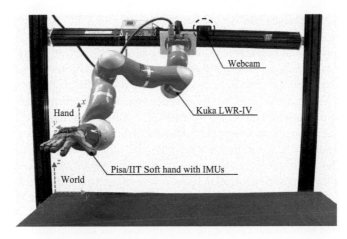

Figure 1.9   Robotic platform used for the experiments. A Kuka LWR is mounted on a rigid framework and equipped with a Pisa/IIT SoftHand as end-effector. The scene is recorded through a camera mounted at the robot base. Hand is sensorized through Inertial Measurement Units (IMUs) placed on the back of the fingertips. Local and global reference systems are also reported.

Table 1.2   Initial orientation Q_0 and normalized direction of approach $\hat{d}$ for each primitive

Strategy	Q_0^T	$\hat{d}^T$
Top	[0.0 0.711 0.0 0.703]	[0 0 −1]
Top left	[0.269 0.6570 −0.2721 0.6496]	[0 0 −1]
Top right	[0.269 −0.657 −0.272 −0.649]	[0 0 −1]
Bottom	[0.145 −0.696 0.701 0.030]	[0 1 0]
Pinch	[0.084 0.816 0.17 0.458]	[0 0 −1]
Pinch left	[0.116 0.733 0.483 0.463]	[0 0 −1]
Pinch right	[0.186 0.890 −0.110 0.400]	[0 0 −1]
Slide	[0.0 0.711 0.0 0.703]	[0 0 −1]
Lateral	[0 −1 0 0]	[0 1 0]

1.3.3.2   Grasp phase

Following the approaching phase, the action is intended to proceed with the grasp of the detected object. This is the phase in which primitives differentiate more from each other. On the following, we will review the grasping strategies implemented in this work. Note that, when not differently specified, hand movements are intended in local coordinates.

Top and lateral grasps

The local wrist/hand adaptation around the object leverages on the reactive grasp framework [5], moving from a set of 13 basis adaptation movements of the end-effector w.r.t. the contacted object. A detailed description of these strategies is reported in [5], on the following we will recall some concepts, useful for the understanding of this chapter. In [33], a human participant was asked to reach and grasp a tennis ball placed on a table, while actively controlling the SoftHand through an interface endowed with a lever, which is used to accomplish a grasping task. The user was instructed to continuously move the hand until a contact with the object was perceived then adapt the hand orientation w.r.t. the object so to favour the grasp. Movements were replicated 13 times, considering different approaching direction. For each movement, the 3D pose of the hand was recorded via motion tracking (PhaseSpace) and synchronized with the recordings of fingers accelerations $\alpha_1, \ldots, \alpha_{13} : [0, T] \to \mathbb{R}^5$ from IMUs, and the hand motor current (to keep track of the hand closure). This resulted in the association between acceleration profiles and corresponding reactive adaptation movements of the hand w.r.t. the object. In [23], when the Pisa/IIT SoftHand touches an object, acceleration profiles $a : [0, T] \to \mathbb{R}^5$ are recorded through the IMUs. Then, one reactive strategy – defined by the local rearrangement – is selected as the one that maximizes the covariation of measured IMUs signals with the recorded ones:

$$j = \arg\max_i \int_0^T a^\mathrm{T}(\tau)\alpha_i(\tau)\mathrm{d}\tau. \tag{1.10}$$

When this adaptation w.r.t. the object is completed, the hand closes around the object. Preliminary experiments on top grasps, discussed in [33], proved the effectiveness of this approach, which is here extended to top right, top left and lateral strategies.

Bottom

In the case of large concave objects, to mimic human behaviour, when the contact is triggered, the hand rotates along the x-axis of an angle equal to $\pi/3$ and translate along the y-axis of 300 mm. This roto-translation is determined to let the palm move over and enables the thumb entering into the object concave part during hand closure.

Pinches

For pinch strategies, the hand is programmed to close without any change in relative pose. Note that the end-effector we used in this work is conceived for power grasps, but the interaction with the environment enables the execution of pinch grasping actions.

Slide

To account for objects difficult to be grasped via power of pinch strategies (e.g. a book), we implemented a multi-phase anticipatory strategy, triggered, as usual, by the contact with the object:

1. exert a normal force on the object (x-axis) to preserve the contact during sliding (commanding a ref. position 10 mm below the contact position);
2. translate towards the table edge (sliding);
3. remove the normal force (inverse of step 1);
4. translate (translation 100 mm along x and 50 mm along z) and rotate ($\pi/12$ radians around y) the hand to favour the grasp;
5. close the hand.

1.3.3.3 Control strategy

A Jacobian-based Inverse kinematic algorithm is used to map the Cartesian references provided by the motion primitives to the joint level q_r. Then, a joint impedance control is used to realize the movement, with stiffness $K = 10^3$ N m/rad and damping $D = 0.7$ N m s/rad. The resulting control law is $\tau(t) = Ke(t) + D\dot{e}(t) + \mathbb{D}(q, \dot{q})$, where τ is the vector of joint torques, while $e = q_r - q$ and $\dot{e} = \dot{q}$ are the joint tracking error and its derivative, respectively. $\mathbb{D}$ is a compensation of the robot dynamics evaluated by the KUKA embedded controller. Control and strategies implementation was developed in ROS.

1.3.4 Results

We evaluated the performances achieved by the proposed framework by performing a set of experiments in a table-top scenario. A flat surface is placed in front of the manipulator, as reported in Figure 1.9. One of the objects is placed by an operator approximatively in the centre of the table. RGB data extracted from the camera are used to classify through the proposed deep neural network. The classification outcome is then associated with the corresponding motion primitive. Each object is randomly proposed three times. Position and orientation of the object can vary at every time, taking a random position inside a circle of $\sim$100 mm centred in the table centre. Tests were performed with 20 different objects (see Figure 1.10). None of these was used during the training phase. The particular selection was made so as to consider all the grasping strategies included in the study. Note that for objects 5–10, 16 and 19, the classification can point to different strategy depending on the object position/orientation. The total amount of configurations tested is 111.

Table 1.3 collects the results of this study. We achieved an overall success rate equal to 81.1% (a grasp is labelled as successful if the closure is maintained for 5 s). It is worth noticing that objects 15 and 12 – which are rotationally symmetric – are classified as associated with top grasp primitives, regardless the specific orientation under testing. Regarding the success rate for each primitive, our results show the following: top 85.7% (Figure 1.11(a)–(h)), top left 73.3% (Figure 1.11(i)–(p)), top right 100% (Figure 1.11(q)–(x)), bottom 100% (Figure 1.12), pinch 55.6% (Figure 1.13(a)–(d)),

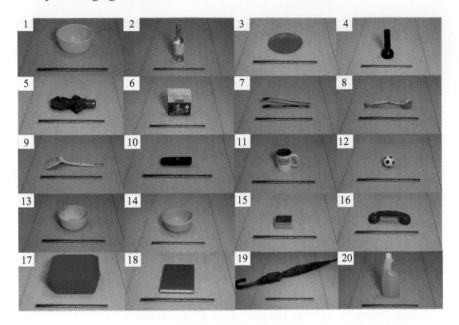

*Figure 1.10   Set of objects (20) used during the experiments with the robotic
             platform for the experimental validation. Note that all the selected
             objects are different w.r.t. those used during the training phase.
             A 30-cm ruler is placed in all the pictures to enable a qualitatively
             perception of the objects size.*

pinch left 55.6% (Figure 1.13(e)–(h)), pinch right 66.7% (Figure 1.13(i)–(e)), slide
83.3% (Figure 1.14), lateral 86.7% (Figure 1.15).

1.4   Discussion and conclusions

One of the key enablers for the extraordinary dexterity of human hands is their compliance and capability to purposefully adapt with the environment, to multiply their
manipulation possibilities. This observation has also produced a significant paradigm
shift for the design of robotic hands, leading to the avenue of soft end-effectors that
embed elastic and deformable elements directly in their mechanical architecture.
This shift has also determined a perspective change for the control and planning of
the grasping phases, w.r.t. the classical approach used with rigid grippers. ML and,
especially, DL can be promising tools to overcome the modelling challenges that arise
when dealing with soft bodies and their interaction with the external environment,
targeting solutions close enough to the desired ones, rather than exact, leveraging on
the adaptation capabilities of the soft hands to overcome local uncertainties.

    More specifically, in this chapter we report on how DL can be used to model
human behaviour and to translate this modelling for autonomous grasping with robotic

Table 1.3   *Strategy used, successes and failures for each grasp*

Object	Strategy	Successes	Failures
1	Bottom	3	0
2	Lateral	2	1
3	Slide	2	1
4	Lateral	3	0
5	Top	3	0
	Top left	2	1
	Top right	3	0
6	Lateral	3	0
	Top	3	0
	Top left	2	1
	Top right	3	0
7	Pinch	3	0
	Pinch left	2	1
	Pinch right	3	0
8	Pinch	2	1
	Pinch left	2	1
	Pinch right	2	1
9	Pinch	0	3
	Pinch left	1	2
	Pinch right	1	2
10	Top	3	0
	Top left	2	1
	Top right	3	0
11	Lateral	3	0
12	Top	2	1
13	Bottom	3	0
14	Bottom	3	0
15	Top	2	1
16	Top	2	1
	Top left	3	0
	Top right	3	0
17	Bottom	3	0
18	Slide	3	0
19	Top	3	0
	Top left	2	1
	Top right	3	0
20	Lateral	2	1
Total	–	90	21

soft hands. In the first section, we propose an approach that combines CNN and RNN and represents the first attempt to include also dynamic information for classifying different time-related action primitives, which are used by humans for grasping and manipulation tasks. This idea will be further explored and tested to extract an exhaustive description of human grasping and manipulation with the environment and to

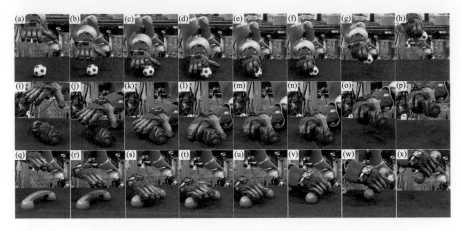

Figure 1.11   *Snapshot of power top grasps generated through the proposed*
architecture. Subfigures (a)–(h) show a top grasp performed on object
12; subfigures (i)–(p) show a top-left grasp performed on object 5;
subfigures (q)–(x) show a top-right grasp performed on object 16. For
each line, it is possible to observe an approaching phase (e.g.
subfigures (a) and (b)), a contact detection (e.g. subfigure (c)), a
reactive behaviour for posture adaptation (e.g. subfigures (c)–(f)) and
a firm grasp and lift of the object (e.g. subfigures (g) and (h)).

Figure 1.12   *Snapshot of a bottom grasp performed on object 14. Subfigure (a)*
shows the initial configuration of the primitive. In (b) the contact
triggers the reactive routine, and so on in (c)–(e). Finally, in subfigure
(f) the item is firmly lifted.

devise effective guidelines for the translation of human observations on the robotic
side [20]. In the second section, we report on how the human example can be used
for autonomous grasping of the soft hands using DL [23]. This work represents –
together with [10] – the first attempt to validate – over a large set of objects – the
combination of soft robotic hands and DL techniques for autonomous grasping, with
a success rate of 81%.

In the future, we will work to integrate the results from [20] within the framework
reported in [23]. The objective will be to increase the data set of the primitives to
be implemented with soft manipulators. On the other side, we aim at testing the DL
human-inspired approach with other robotic soft hands, e.g. continuously deformable
[2], and investigate sensing strategies to predict grasping failures. We do believe that

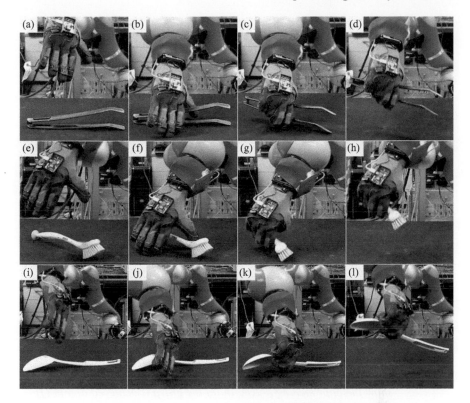

Figure 1.13 Snapshot of pinch grasps generated through the proposed architecture. Subfigures (a)–(d) show a pinch grasp performed on object 7; subfigures (e)–(h) show a pinch-left grasp performed on object 8; subfigures (i)–(l) show a pinch-right grasp performed on object 9. For each line, it is possible to observe an approaching phase (e.g. subfigures (a) and (b)), a contact detection (e.g. subfigure (b)), and a firm grasp and lift of the object (e.g. subfigures (c) and (d)).

DL can be an effective solution to devise control guidelines for soft end-effectors that autonomously perform manipulation and grasping tasks following the human example.

Acknowledgement

This work has received founding from the European Union's Horizon 2020 research and innovation programme under grant agreement no. 688857 (SoftPro), no. 732737 (Iliad) and no. 871237 (Sophia), and by the Italian Ministry of Education and Research (MIUR) in the framework of the CrossLab project (Department of Excellence). The

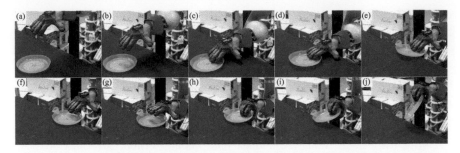

Figure 1.14   *Snapshot of slide grasp performed on object 3. Subfigures (a)–(c) show the approaching phase. Subfigures (d) and (e) show how the system exploits the environment towards the table edge. Subfigures (f) and (g) show the hand changing its relative configuration w.r.t. the object, established in subfigures (h) and (i). Finally, in subfigure (j), the item is firmly lifted.*

Figure 1.15   *Snapshot of lateral grasp performed on object 4. Subfigures (a)–(d) show the approaching phase. In (e) the grasp is achieved and in (f) the item is firmly lifted.*

content of this publication is the sole responsibility of the authors. The European Commission or its services cannot be held responsible for any use that may be made of the information it contains.

References

[1]   Prattichizzo D and Trinkle JC. Grasping. In: Springer handbook of robotics. Springer; 2016. p. 955–988.

[2]   Deimel R and Brock O. A novel type of compliant and underactuated robotic hand for dexterous grasping. The International Journal of Robotics Research. 2016;35(1–3):161–185.

[3]   Catalano MG, Grioli G, Farnioli E, *et al.* Adaptive synergies for the design and control of the Pisa/IIT SoftHand. The International Journal of Robotics Research. 2014;33(5):768–782.

[4]   Eppner C, Deimel R, Alvarez-Ruiz J, *et al.* Exploitation of environmental constraints in human and robotic grasping. The International Journal of Robotics Research. 2015;34(7):1021–1038.

[5] Bianchi M, Averta G, Battaglia E, *et al.* Touch-based grasp primitives for soft hands: Applications to human-to-robot handover tasks and beyond. In: 2018 IEEE International Conference on Robotics and Automation (ICRA). Brisbane, Australia: IEEE; 2018. p. 7794–7801.

[6] LeCun Y, Bengio Y, and Hinton G. Deep learning. Nature. 2015;521(7553): 436–444.

[7] Bambach S, Lee S, Crandall DJ, *et al.* Lending a hand: Detecting hands and recognizing activities in complex egocentric interactions. In: Proceedings of the IEEE International Conference on Computer Vision; 2015. p. 1949–1957.

[8] Gupta A, Eppner C, Levine S, *et al.* Learning dexterous manipulation for a soft robotic hand from human demonstrations. In: Intelligent Robots and Systems (IROS), 2016 IEEE/RSJ International Conference on. Daejeon, South Korea: IEEE; 2016. p. 3786–3793.

[9] Nishimura T, Mizushima K, Suzuki Y, *et al.* Thin plate manipulation by an under-actuated robotic soft gripper utilizing the environment. In: Intelligent Robots and Systems (IROS), 2017 IEEE/RSJ International Conference on. Vancouver, Canada: IEEE; 2017. p. 1236–1243.

[10] Choi C, Schwarting W, DelPreto J, *et al.* Learning object grasping for soft robot hands. IEEE Robotics and Automation Letters. 2018;3:2370–2377.

[11] Puhlmann S, Heinemann F, Brock O, *et al.* A compact representation of human single-object grasping. In: Intelligent Robots and Systems (IROS), 2016 IEEE/RSJ International Conference on. Daejeon, South Korea: IEEE; 2016. p. 1954–1959.

[12] Ong EJ and Bowden R. A boosted classifier tree for hand shape detection. In: Automatic Face and Gesture Recognition, 2004. Proceedings. Sixth IEEE International Conference on. Seoul, South Korea: IEEE; 2004. p. 889–894.

[13] Beh J, Han DK, Durasiwami R, *et al.* Hidden Markov model on a unit hypersphere space for gesture trajectory recognition. Pattern Recognition Letters. 2014;36:144–153.

[14] Simonyan K and Zisserman A. Very deep convolutional networks for large-scale image recognition. arXiv preprint arXiv:1409.1556. 2014.

[15] Girshick R, Donahue J, Darrell T, *et al.* Rich feature hierarchies for accurate object detection and semantic segmentation. In: Proceedings of the IEEE Conference on Computer Vision and Pattern Recognition. Columbus, USA; 2014. p. 580–587.

[16] Karpathy A, Toderici G, Shetty S, *et al.* Large-scale video classification with convolutional neural networks. In: Proceedings of the IEEE Conference on Computer Vision and Pattern Recognition; 2014. p. 1725–1732.

[17] Ng JYH, Hausknecht M, Vijayanarasimhan S, *et al.* Beyond short snippets: Deep networks for video classification. In: Computer Vision and Pattern Recognition (CVPR), 2015 IEEE Conference on. Boston, Massachusetts: IEEE; 2015. p. 4694–4702.

[18] Sudhakaran S and Lanz O. Convolutional long short-term memory networks for recognizing first person interactions. In: Computer Vision Workshop (ICCVW), 2017 IEEE International Conference on. Venice, Italy: IEEE; 2017. p. 2339–2346.

[19]   Nguyen A, Kanoulas D, Muratore L, Caldwell DG, and Tsagarakis NG. Translating videos to commands for robotic manipulation with deep recurrent neural networks. In: Robotics and Automation (ICRA), 2018 IEEE International Conference on. IEEE; 2018, p.1–9.

[20]   Arapi V, Della Santina C, Bacciu D, *et al.* DeepDynamicHand: A deep neural architecture for labeling hand manipulation strategies in video sources exploiting temporal information. Frontiers in Neurorobotics. 2018;12:86. Available from: https://www.frontiersin.org/article/10.3389/fnbot.2018.00086.

[21]   Hochreiter S and Schmidhuber J. Long short-term memory. Neural Computation. 1997;9(8):1735–1780.

[22]   Yang Y and Liu X. A re-examination of text categorization methods. In: Proceedings of the 22nd Annual International ACM SIGIR Conference on Research and Development in Information Retrieval. New York, USA: ACM; 1999. p. 42–49.

[23]   Della Santina C, Arapi V, Averta G, *et al.* Learning from humans how to grasp: A data-driven architecture for autonomous grasping with anthropomorphic soft hands. IEEE Robotics and Automation Letters. 2019;4(2):1533–1540.

[24]   Redmon J and Farhadi A. YOLO9000: Better, faster, stronger. In: Proceedings of the IEEE Conference on Computer Vision and Pattern Recognition; 2017. p. 7263–7271.

[25]   Szegedy C, Vanhoucke V, Ioffe S, *et al.* Rethinking the inception architecture for computer vision. In: Proceedings of the IEEE Conference on Computer Vision and Pattern Recognition. Las Vegas, USA; 2016. p. 2818–2826.

[26]   Feix T, Romero J, Schmiedmayer HB, *et al.* The grasp taxonomy of human grasp types. IEEE Transactions on Human-Machine Systems. 2016;46(1):66–77.

[27]   Thrun S and Pratt L. Learning to learn. Springer Science & Business Media; 2012.

[28]   Deng J, Dong W, Socher R, *et al.* ImageNet: A large-scale hierarchical image database. In: Computer Vision and Pattern Recognition, 2009. CVPR 2009. IEEE Conference on. Miami, USA: IEEE; 2009. p. 248–255.

[29]   Srivastava N, Hinton G, Krizhevsky A, *et al.* Dropout: A simple way to prevent neural networks from overfitting. The Journal of Machine Learning Research. 2014;15(1):1929–1958.

[30]   Charles PWD. Project Title. GitHub repository. 2013. Available from: https://github.com/charlespwd/project-title.

[31]   Johansson RS and Edin BB. Predictive feed-forward sensory control during grasping and manipulation in man. Biomedical Research – Tokyo. 1993;14: 95–95.

[32]   Della Santina C, Piazza C, Gasparri GM, *et al.* The quest for natural machine motion: An open platform to fast-prototyping articulated soft robots. IEEE Robotics & Automation Magazine. 2017;24(1):48–56.

[33]   Bianchi M, Averta G, Battaglia E, *et al.* Tactile-based grasp primitives for soft hands: Applications to human-to-robot handover tasks and beyond. In: Robotics and Automation (ICRA), 2018 IEEE International Conference on. Brisbane, Australia: IEEE; 2019.

Chapter 2

Artificial intelligence for affective computing: an emotion recognition case study

Pablo Arnau-González[1], Stamos Katsigiannis[1],
Miguel Arevalillo-Herráez[2], and Naeem Ramzan[1]

This chapter provides an introduction on the benefits of artificial intelligence (AI) techniques for the field of affective computing, through a case study about emotion recognition via brain (electroencephalography – EEG) signals. Readers are first provided with a general description of the field, followed by the main models of human affect, with special emphasis to Russell's circumplex model and the pleasure–arousal–dominance (PAD) model. Finally, an AI-based method for the detection of affect elicited via multimedia stimuli is presented. The method combines both connectivity- and channel-based EEG features with a selection method that considerably reduces the dimensionality of the data and allows for efficient classification. In particular, the relative energy (RE) and its logarithm in the spatial domain, as well as the spectral power (SP) in the frequency domain are computed for the four typically used EEG frequency bands (α, β, γ and θ) and complemented with the mutual information measured over all EEG channel pairs. The resulting features are then reduced by using a hybrid method that combines supervised and unsupervised feature selection. Detection results are compared to state-of-the-art methods on the DEAP benchmarking data set for emotion analysis, which is composed of labelled EEG recordings from 32 individuals, acquired while watching 40 music videos. The acquired results demonstrate the potential of AI-based methods for emotion recognition, an application that can significantly benefit the fields of human–computer interaction (HCI) and of quality-of-experience (QoE).

2.1 Introduction

Human–computer interfaces have evolved enormously in recent years, with new modalities for HCI becoming available at increasingly lower cost. The combination of these new HCI solutions with powerful AI algorithms is providing the means to add

---

[1] School of Computing, Engineering and Physical Sciences, University of the West of Scotland, Paisley, UK
[2] Departamento de Informatica, Universitat de Valéncia, Valencia, Spain

the *smart* tag to many solutions for everyday problems. Proof of this trend in the consumer market is the proliferation of devices that work as or embed smart-assistants, e.g. Google Home, Apple's Siri, Amazon's Alexa. Other examples of new HCI modalities are the recent developments on brain–computer interfaces (BCI). BCIs cover a wide spectrum of applications, spanning from medical purposes to educational uses, like, for example, detecting focus levels [1]. Furthermore, it has been suggested that the study of brain signals (EEG) could lead to the detection of the emotional state of individuals at any given moment [2]. The understanding and modelling of the user affective state could lead to huge advances in the fields of HCI and QoE, as already pointed out by Dr Rosalind Piccard [3]. Having computers that are aware of the user's emotional state would enable these computers to react to it, improving the user experience by providing more relevant content, in the case of a smart assistant, or help in one way or the other in the case of an intelligent tutoring system.

Regardless the application, it is clear that AI techniques, such as supervised classification, are essential for detecting different emotions from the acquired brain signals [2,4,5], while affect is key to improve the user experience in many different areas. Efficient affect detection from brain signals is currently an open problem with numerous research works being conducted every year. Apart from solutions based on brain signals, there are also video-based affect detection approaches [6,7]. However, weak emotions, i.e. emotions that are shown with very little intensity are difficult to capture from video sources [8]. Therefore, research is generally focused in recognising emotions from sources that are affected even when the emotion is not publicly shown, as is the case with brain signals. In this direction, AI techniques are vital to create user-specific models for recognising emotions.

2.2   Models of human affect

In order to measure or detect an emotion or the affective state of an individual, the literature proposes a number of human affect models. These models study emotion following two different approaches, either focusing on the emotion itself or on characteristics of the emotion. These models can be categorised as either discrete or continuous.

2.2.1   Discrete models of affect

Theorists have long discussed a small set of categories for describing emotional states. In 1962, Tomkins suggested that there are eight basic emotions [9]. Plutchik later proposed a different set of eight basic emotions: fear, anger, sorrow, joy, disgust, surprise, acceptance and anticipation [10]. More recently, Ortony, Clore and Collins collected a summary of lists of basic emotions [11].

2.2.1.1   Six basic emotions and FACS

Probably, the most prominent discrete model of emotions is the one proposed by Ekman. This model studies emotions via a discrete approach, suggesting that there is a reduced number of primary, or primitive, emotions, i.e. happiness, anger, fear, disgust, surprise and sadness [12,13], and that all the other emotional states are nothing but combinations of these primary emotions. Ekman defines each of the basic emotions as not a single affective state but a family of states [14], where each member of the family shares certain characteristics. The justification of this affirmation is sustained in his previous work [15], where 60 different expressions of anger were specified. In that study, all the identified anger expressions shared a specific muscular pattern that was different from the patterns specified in other families, such as for disgust or happiness. Ekman also related the intensity of the emotion with the strength of the muscular contractions [16]. Under these assumptions, a model for mapping facial expression to emotions was proposed. The resulting facial action coding system (FACS) [17] maps facial expressions, defined by fundamental contractions of facial muscles (action units or AUs). Table 2.1 provides a brief example of a FACS containing seven examples of emotions.

2.2.1.2 Plutchick's wheel of emotion

Plutchick [10] proposed an alternative model of human affect. In his approach, emotions are categorised in three different categories (primary, secondary and tertiary). The three categories are organised in a conical shape, turned upside down, where the emotions are located close, according to their relation (see Figure 2.1). Similarly to Ekman, Plutchik identified anger, disgust, sadness, surprise, fear and joy, as primary emotions, but he also added trust and anticipation.

2.2.2 Continuous (dimensional) models of affect

Continuous models treat emotional states as states characterised by continuous variables in an N-dimensional space. Most notable models are Russell's circumplex model of affect, the PAD model, and the Lövheim cube of emotions.

Table 2.1 Facial action coding system

Emotion	Activated AUs	Facial muscles contraction
Happiness	6+12	Cheek Raiser + Lip Corner Puller
Sadness	1+4+15	Inner Brow Raiser + Brow Lowerer + Lip Corner Depressor
Surprise	1+2+5+26	Inner Brow Raiser + Outer Brow Raiser + Upper Lid Raiser + Jaw Drop
Fear	1+2+4+5 +7+20+26	Inner Brow Raiser + Outer Brow Raiser + Brow Lowerer + Upper Lid Raiser + Lid Tightener + Lip Stretcher + Jaw Drop
Anger	4+5+7+23	Brow Lowerer + Upper Lid Raiser + Lid Tightener + Lip Tightener
Disgust	9+15+16	Nose Wrinkler + Lip Corner Depressor + Lower Lip Corner Depressor
Contempt	12+14	Lip Corner Puller + Dimpler

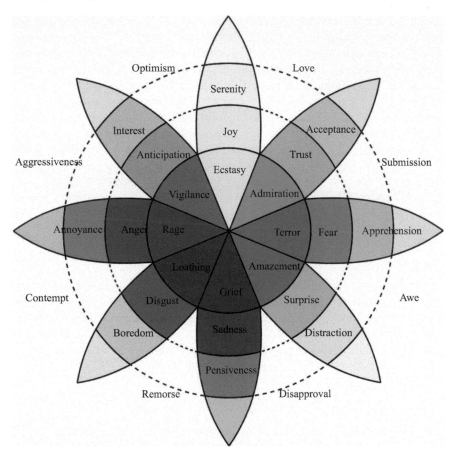

Figure 2.1   Plutchick's wheel of emotion, 2D projection. Source: Public domain image.

2.2.2.1   Russell's circumplex model of affect

Prior to Russell's proposal of a circumplex model of affect, other researchers had already proposed a similar system. Schlosberg [18] proposed that emotions are organised in a circular manner, meaning that emotions were better represented in a bipolar space rather than in six mono-polar spaces, an assumption on which Russell based his model of affect, along with previous studies about the affective structure of the English language. Supporting the hypothesis of Schlosberg that dimensions of evaluation, activity and potency are major components of the meaning of the language [19], Russell's model of affect proposed that emotion can be located in a two-dimensional space defined by two traits: arousal, ranging from inactivity to excitement, and valence (positiveness), ranging from unpleasantness to pleasantness (see Figure 2.2).

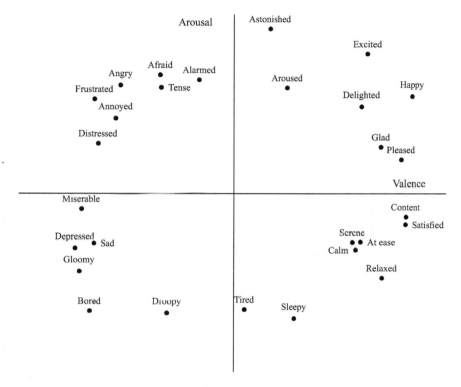

Figure 2.2   Russell's circumplex model of affect

2.2.2.2   The pleasure–arousal–dominance (PAD) model

The PAD model consists of a revision of 1979's Russell's circumplex model, representing a more modern version of it, with a few changes incorporated. Mehrabian and Russell [20] proposed that emotion can be located in a three-dimensional space. The new space is defined by the previously defined dimensions (arousal, valence) and includes a third dimension, dominance, which defines the control that the emotion has over the individual, i.e. low dominance values would apply to emotions such as calm or joy, while strong emotions, such as love or fury, would have a high dominance value.

2.2.2.3   Lövheim cube of emotion

A biochemistry-based model of affect was proposed by Lövheim [21] in 2011 that maps emotional states to a three-dimensional space defined by the combinations of the concentration levels of three mono-amines, i.e. dopamine, noradrenaline and serotonin. As discussed by the author in [21], the three dimensions do not match exactly with the ones described in Russell's model, but there are some common patterns observable (see Figure 2.3). This model, apart from being one of the newest ones in emotion theory, is very interesting since it explains emotion from a biochemical perspective.

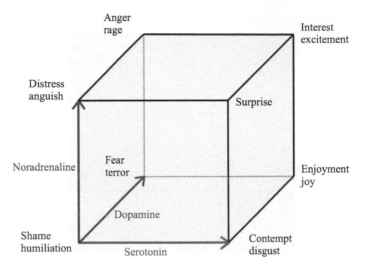

*Figure 2.3   Lövheim cube of emotion. Source: wikimedia.org. GNU Free
Documentation License.*

2.3   Previous work on emotion recognition

One major difficulty in dealing with the evaluation of emotion recognition methods
is related to the non-existence of a common ground truth that would allow a fair
comparison between different proposals. This has led many authors to test and report
their results on proprietary data sets, limiting the impact of their proposals because of
the intrinsic difficulty associated with assessing their performance in relation to other
existing or newly developed methods. One major contribution in this direction was
the DEAP data set [22], a multimodal data set specifically created for the analysis
of human-affective states. DEAP contains physiological recordings from 32 subjects
while watching 40 music videos, which were selected in order to elicit emotions
in each of the four quadrants of Russell's circumplex model [23]. Recordings were
annotated with the associated emotional state via self-reporting; thus DEAP can be
used as a baseline for benchmarking. The creators of DEAP performed an initial
classification experiment for establishing a baseline performance [22]. They used the
SP of single-EEG channels and the SP asymmetry from 14 pairs of electrodes and
selected the features according to a Fisher discriminant analysis with a threshold set
at 0.3.

Previous works on emotion recognition from EEG signals mostly focused on
channel-related features, e.g. [24]. As a first example, Liu *et al.* [25] proposed a single
fractal model based on their observation that higher levels of arousal were usually
related to higher values of the fractal dimension [26]; as much as valence levels relate
to fractal dimension differences between concrete electrodes located in the right and
left hemisphere of the scalp. This initial work was validated with their own data set

and later extended in [27] by using higher order crossings [28] and features from the general Higuchi fractal dimension spectra in order to understand EEG signals as multi-fractal signals. Other studies focused on a different type of features that considers the connectivity between the EEG electrodes. For example, Chen *et al.* [29] set a classification problem by extracting groups of such features and studied the performance of each set. In particular, they analysed Pearson's correlation [30], phase coherence [31] and mutual information, which led to the best results. Other works, such as Gupta *et al.*'s [32], used graph-theoretic features to classify emotional states through support vector machines (SVMs) and relevance vector machine classifiers.

2.4 Data sets for emotion recognition

Since EEG signals are very dependent on the individual, solutions proposed by different authors are potentially not generalisable for other individuals. For this reason, different benchmarking data sets have been made publicly available over time for providing a common ground for testing different proposals. Up to now, five major data sets have been publicly released: DEAP [22], MAHNOB [33], DREAMER [34], AMIGOS [35] and SEED [36].

These data sets have been created by recording EEG and other physiological signals of different individuals, while being exposed to different emotional stimuli in the form of video sequences. MAHNOB, DREAMER, SEED and AMIGOS used film excerpts, while DEAP used music videos. There is also difference in the EEG signal acquisition devices. DEAP and MAHNOB used the Biosemi Active II system, a non-medical-grade high performance EEG recording and monitoring device, SEED used a similar EEG recording system, the ESI NeuroScan, while DREAMER and AMIGOS used the Emotiv EPOC wireless EEG headset. A brief overview of these data sets is provided in Table 2.2.

As can be observed from Table 2.2, DEAP, MAHNOB and SEED have been recorded using high-quality EEG-recording devices, while DREAMER and AMIGOS data sets have been recorded using consumer-grade devices, namely the Emotiv EPOC. The experimental protocol applied for data acquisition was very similar for all data sets. The participant would watch the stimuli in random order and rate the felt emotion immediately after exposure to each stimulus. An exception to this protocol is found in the SEED data set, where participants did not provide the subjective ratings, rather the data set is annotated with the emotions each video is supposed to elicit and video sequences were presented in a specific sequence.

Since the main purpose of these data sets is to help researchers' model human emotions from EEG sources, the samples are annotated according to emotional models. Excluding SEED, the examined data sets contain recordings annotated according to Russell's model (see Section 2.2.2.1 for more details) or a revised version of the model, such as the PAD model (see Section 2.2.2.2). Annotations were acquired through self-reporting using a standard scale designed for the self-report of emotions, i.e. the Self-Assessment Manikin (SAM) scale [37]. SAM is composed by three different sets of five manikins each, with the central one corresponding to the neutral

Table 2.2   Overview of the different available data sets

Data set	Subjects	Video no.	Video content	Video duration (s)	Recording device	Channel no.	Sampling frequency (Hz)
DEAP	32	40	Music videos	60	Biosemi Active II	32	512 (downsampled to 256)
MANHOB	27	20	Excerpts from movies	34.9–117 ($\mu = 81$)	Biosemi Active II	32	512 (downsampled to 256)
DREAMER	23	18	Excerpts from movies	60	Emotiv EPOC	14	128
AMIGOS	40	16 + 4 (two protocols)	Excerpts from movies	45 Long videos	Emotiv EPOC	14	128
SEED	15	15	Excerpts from movies	240	ESI NeuroScan	63	1,000 (downsampled to 200 Hz)

emotion and the extremes corresponding to the highest and lowest possible value for each of the scales.

2.5   Proposed methodology

Our proposal is based on using both *connectivity features* and *energy features* simultaneously. While *energy features* provide information about how the energy is distributed across the EEG signal bands, *connectivity features* study the interactions between different EEG channels and enrich the data provided by the former. The combination of both types of features, along with the use of a feature reduction scheme that allows the classification to be applied in a low-dimensional space, endows the proposal with the ability to distinguish low and high levels of arousal and valence more accurately than other state-of-the-art methods recently reported in the emotion recognition literature.

2.5.1   Connectivity features

According to Chen *et al.* [29], *mutual information* is a good indicator of the connectivity between EEG channels. *Mutual information* measures how informative a random variable is to another. Its calculation is based in entropy, which is calculated as

$$H(X) = -\sum p_i \cdot \log p_i \tag{2.1}$$

where p_i is the probability of the ith element of time series X. This expression allows to compute the *mutual information* between two signals X and Y as

$$MI(X;Y) = H(X) - H(X|Y) \tag{2.2}$$

or alternatively as

$$MI(X, Y) = -\sum p_{ij}^{XY} \cdot \log\left(\frac{p_{ij}^{XY}}{p_i^X p_j^Y}\right) \tag{2.3}$$

where p_{ij}^{XY} is the joint probability of the ith element of time series X and jth element of time series Y.

In this work, we have used *mutual information* as implemented by Moddemeijer [38], and for the replication of Chen's experiment [29], we have used the same toolbox [39]. In particular, we have applied the floor function on the original signals, which rounds each value to the nearest integer that is lower than or equal to it.

2.5.2 Energy features

For each EEG signal X and frequency band $f = \{ \alpha$ (8–13 Hz), β (14–30 Hz), γ (30–47 Hz), θ (4–7 Hz)$\}$, the energy was extracted as

$$E_f(X) = \sum_i X_i^2 \tag{2.4}$$

where X_i is the ith element of signal X filtered in the frequency band f.

The RE and the logarithmic relative energy (LRE) for each combination of channel and frequency band were then extracted using the following formulas:

$$RE_f(X) = \frac{E_f(X)}{E_\alpha(X) + E_\beta(X) + E_\gamma(X) + E_\theta(X)} \tag{2.5}$$

$$LRE_f(X) = \log(RE_f(X)) \tag{2.6}$$

where f represents the frequency band $(\alpha, \beta, \gamma, \theta)$.

2.5.3 Dimensionality reduction

Once the mutual information and energy features were extracted from the EEG signals, an ad-hoc feature reduction scheme was applied prior to classification. To this end, a number of dimensions d are initially selected, and a one-way analysis of variance (ANOVA) is performed in order to detect which features are significantly different across the available classes and discard features with a p-value above a threshold. This threshold was set to 0.01 in this work. When less than d features are retained, this threshold is iteratively incremented by 0.01 until more than d features have been selected. A principal component analysis (PCA) was then applied to further reduce the dimensionality of the remaining data to the established parameter d, which is set by integrating it within the grid search process required to tune the kernel-dependent SVM parameters, as explained in the following section.

2.6 Experimental results

Results obtained with the proposed method were compared to the ones obtained by using the Koelstra *et al.* [22] and the Chen *et al.* [29] methods, both implemented as indicated in their original publications. Koelstra *et al.* extracted the SP features for the different bands (alpha, slow alpha, beta, gamma and theta) and the asymmetry of 14 different pairs of those SP features and then applied the Fisher discriminant analysis to reject features with $J_i \leq 0.3$, J_i being the Fisher linear discriminant for the *i*th feature, before using a Naïve Bayes classifier. Similarly, Chen *et al.* computed the mutual information between all pairs of EEG channels, without applying any filter in the frequency domain. Then, they applied the same feature selection method as in [22] to discard the less correlated features.

To provide a fair comparison, all competing methods were tested on the DEAP data set and evaluated under the same experimental setting, namely a leave-one-out cross-validation scheme applied separately for each individual in the data set. This process yielded a total of 40 different trained models per user (one per video). At each iteration of the cross-validation procedure, one sample of an individual was used for testing the model and the rest of the individual's samples were used for training. Performance metrics were then averaged across all iterations in order to determine the classification performance for each individual. The class labels for each sample were computed as in the Koelstra *et al.* and Chen *et al.* works, by thresholding the original valence and arousal values to *Low* and *High* depending on whether the original value was less than 5 or equal to or higher than 5, respectively. Following this approach, the problem of predicting the valence and arousal values was converted to two binary classification problems. The SVM classifier with a radial basis function kernel was selected in the proposed work and was applied using the libSVM interface for MATLAB® R2014a [40]. For estimating the SVM parameters, we used a grid-search for obtaining the best C and γ. Furthermore, we also added to the grid the optimal number of dimensions d for the dimensionality reduction as an additional parameter. MATLAB R2014a was also used for applying the compared methods by employing the available implementation of Naïve Bayes (fitNaiveBayes).

The conversion of the valence and arousal values to binary values resulted in the data set being considerably unbalanced, for both valence and arousal. This makes the average classification accuracy a misleading measure of performance, given that a classifier that is biased towards the largest class may yield higher values. Hence, we have selected the average $F1$-score as the measure for evaluating the performance of the competing methods. The final $F1$-score was calculated by averaging the $F1$-scores obtained for each of the 32 individuals in the DEAP data set. Table 2.3 presents the average $F1$-scores and the standard deviations achieved for the proposed and the examined methods.

As seen in Table 2.3, the proposed approach performed better than the Koelstra *et al.* and the Chen *et al.* methods for both valence and arousal. Furthermore, average $F1$-scores for valence are higher than for arousal for all methods, independently from the features and classification method used. This indicates that the original EEG recordings may be better suited to predict this variable.

Table 2.3   F1-scores and standard deviation across individuals obtained with each method

	Koelstra *et al.* [22]	Chen *et al.* [29]	Proposed
Arousal	0.5333 (0.1009)	0.4167 (0.0860)	**0.5806 (0.1415)**
Valence	0.6122 (0.1262)	0.6219 (0.1158)	**0.6715 (0.1077)**

Note: Results in bold indicate the highest F1-score achieved for arousal and valence

For arousal, the proposed method reached an average $F1$-score of 0.5806, which is considerably higher than the one achieved by the second best method, which is Koelstra *et al.* It is noticeable that Chen *et al.* yielded an $F1$-score below 0.5, which indicates that the method performs worse than by systematically choosing the dominant class for each individual. Koelstra *et al.* perform only slightly higher than 0.5.

In terms of valence, all methods yield average $F1$-scores that are significantly higher than 0.5. The proposed method yielded an average $F1$-score of 0.6715, which is again significantly better than the next highest value, which is 0.6219 and corresponds to Chen *et al.* In this case, Koelstra *et al.* score only slightly below (0.6122). With regard to the variance of the results across different subjects, there is not much difference between the three approaches, and only a slight advantage is observed in the favour of the proposed method.

It is also worth mentioning that, apart from the lower $F1$-score compared to valence, the prediction of arousal using the proposed approach exhibited the highest variance across different subjects, out of all entries in Table 2.3. This indicates that the performance for predicting the level of arousal differed considerably between individuals, supporting the previous argument that the method performs worse at predicting arousal compared to valence.

In order to test the statistical significance of the results acquired for the proposed method, we computed the significance statistic p of two-sampled tests, comparing our proposal to each of the competing methods. Due to the fact that none of the pair of distributions followed were normal or homoscedastic, as they did not fit a normal distribution ($p > 0.05$ for Lilliefors test) or they did not have similar standard deviations ($p > 0.05$ for Bartlett's test), we used a non-parametric alternative to Student's t-test, the one-tailed Wilcoxon's signed-rank test to compute the significance statistic p of the $F1$-scores. The p-values obtained using the Wilcoxon test are displayed in Table 2.4, showing that the improvements in performance in relation to the compared methods were statistically significant and outperformed Chen *et al.*'s and Koelstra *et al.*'s approach, with a significance level $p < 0.05$ in both cases.

To further demonstrate the difference in performance between the three examined methods, Figure 2.4 shows the boxplots for the distributions of $F1$-scores obtained across the different individuals, for both valence and arousal. The horizontal line within each box represents the median $F1$-score m, across all individuals. The bottom and top edges of the box refer to the 25th and 75th percentiles, $q1$ and $q3$,

Table 2.4   *p-Values acquired using the one-tailed*
Wilcoxon's signed rank test

	Chen *et al.* [29]	Koelstra *et al.* [22]
Arousal	$<10^{-4}$	0.0280
Valence	0.0009	0.0073

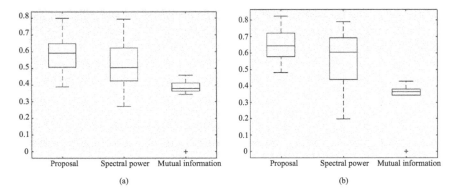

Figure 2.4   *F1-scores comparison: (a) arousal and (b) valence*

respectively. The whiskers represent the interval $[m - 1.57((q_3 - q_1)/\sqrt{(n)}), m + 1.57((q_3 - q_1)/\sqrt{(n)})]$. Any measurement outside this interval is considered as an outlier and is represented by using a cross.

Results presented on Figure 2.4 are consistent with the data shown in Table 2.3. Regarding arousal, the median $F1$-score for the proposed method appears significantly higher than for the other methods, but the bigger box indicates a higher variance. For valence, the three methods present different variances, and the median $F1$-score is again higher for the proposed approach, indicating a better overall performance.

2.7   Conclusions and discussion

The performance of classification-based approaches for emotion recognition depends on many different factors, such as feature extraction, feature selection or the classifier used. In emotion detection from EEG signals, it is common to have a small number of training samples with a relatively high dimensionality, making the problem difficult to address. In this chapter, we have proposed a feature combination method for emotion recognition from EEG signals that uses both connectivity and channel-based features. In particular, the distribution of the energy between EEG frequency bands and the connectivity between EEG electrodes have been combined under a unified classification approach. To compensate the increase in the dimensionality of the data, the proposed method employs a feature reduction method that selects features according to their significance level as computed by a one-way ANOVA and them applies PCA on the remaining set. Finally, classification takes place in a low-dimensional space. Overall, the proposed method resulted in a considerable increase in performance at predicting both the valence and arousal dimensions of an emotional state, in terms of the average classification $F1$-score.

As a shared limitation with most other existing methods, the classification instances are the entire EEG recordings. This limits the practical application of the approaches within a real setting where actions need to be triggered in response to an emotion. In these cases, the detection will suffer a delay that depends on the length of the recording, which may or may not be acceptable in each particular case. Windowed approaches have recently been attempted to solve this problem, e.g. [41]. This would allow a seamless integration with existing applications, including recommendation systems and intelligent tutors, e.g. [42].

Another limitation of the presented work is related to the reconstruction of the emotion by using two-dimensional mappings based on valence and arousal levels. This is also a challenging problem: first, because it requires a simultaneous correct prediction of the two variables in order to locate the emotion in the right quadrant; second, because different emotions in the same quadrant need to be distinguished by using quantifiable valence and arousal levels.

Finally, other works have already demonstrated the benefits of data fusion approaches for emotion recognition and used multimodal models to combine features and/or scores from different sources of information, e.g. [22]. We believe that the proposed feature reduction mechanism also has potential in such context.

Overall, the acquired results demonstrate the potential of AI-based methods for emotion recognition, an application that can significantly benefit the fields of HCI and of QoE.

Acknowledgements

We would like to thank Philippe Geril for allowing us to repurpose part of the materials previously presented by us [43] in the 30th European Simulation and Modelling (ESM) Conference. This chapter was partially supported by the Spanish Ministry of Economy and Competitiveness through projects TIN2014-59641-C2-1-P and PGC2018-096463-B-I00.

References

[1]   Huang J, Yu C, Wang Y, *et al.* FOCUS: Enhancing children's engagement in reading by using contextual BCI training sessions. In: Proceedings of the SIGCHI Conference on Human Factors in Computing Systems. New York City, NY, USA: ACM; 2014. p. 1905–1908.

[2]   Arnau-González P, Arevalillo-Herráez M, and Ramzan N. Fusing highly dimensional energy and connectivity features to identify affective states from EEG signals. Neurocomputing. 2017;244:81–89.

[3]   Picard RW. Affective computing. Cambridge, MA, USA: MIT Press; 2000.

[4]   Arnau-González P, Arevalillo-Herráez M, Katsigiannis S, *et al.* On the influence of affect in EEG-based subject identification. IEEE Transactions on Affective Computing. 2018; Early access. DOI: 10.1109/TAFFC.2018.2877986.

[5]   Arnau-Gonzalez P, Katsigiannis S, Ramzan N, *et al.* ES1D: A deep network for EEG-based subject identification. In: 2017 IEEE 17th International Conference on Bioinformatics and Bioengineering (BIBE). Piscataway, NJ, USA: IEEE; 2017. p. 81–85.

[6]   Dhall A, Goecke R, Joshi J, *et al.* Emoti W 2016: Video and group-level emotion recognition challenges. In: Proceedings of the 18th ACM International Conference on Multimodal Interaction. New York City, NY, USA: ACM; 2016. p. 427–432.

[7]   Noroozi F, Marjanovic M, Njegus A, *et al.* Audio-visual emotion recognition in video clips. IEEE Transactions on Affective Computing. 2017;10(1):60–75.

[8]   Le Ngo AC, Oh YH, Phan RCW, *et al.* Eulerian emotion magnification for subtle expression recognition. In: 2016 IEEE International Conference on Acoustics, Speech and Signal Processing (ICASSP). Piscataway, NJ, USA: IEEE; 2016. p. 1243–1247.

[9]   Tomkins S. Affect imagery consciousness: Volume I: The positive affects. New York City, NY, USA: Springer Publishing Company; 1962.

[10] Plutchick R. The nature of emotions. American Scientist. 2001;89:344–350.

[11] Ortony A, Clore GL, and Collins A. The cognitive structure of emotions. Cambridge, UK: Cambridge University Press; 1990.

[12] Ekman P. An argument for basic emotions. Cognition & Emotion. 1992; 6(3–4):169–200.

[13] Ekman P. Emotion in the human face. Malor books reprint edition. Malor Books; 2013. Available from: https://books.google.co.uk/books?id=F8r0mwEACAAJ.

[14] Ekman P and Friesen WV. Measuring facial movement. Environmental Psychology and Nonverbal Behavior. 1976;1(1):56–75.

[15] Ekman P, Friesen W, and Hager J. Facial action coding system: A technique for the measurement of facial movement. Mountain View, CA, USA: Consulting Psychologists Press; 1978.

[16] Ekman P, Freisen WV, and Ancoli S. Facial signs of emotional experience. Journal of Personality and Social Psychology. 1980;39(6):1125.

[17] Friesen WV and Ekman P. EMFACS-7: Emotional facial action coding system; 1983.

[18] Schlosberg H. The description of facial expressions in terms of two dimensions. Journal of Experimental Psychology. 1952;44(4):229–237. Available from: http://dx.doi.org/10.1037/h0055778.

[19] Russell J. A circumplex model of affect. Journal of Personality and Social Psychology. 1980;39:1161–1178.

[20]   Mehrabian A. Pleasure–arousal–dominance: A general framework for describing and measuring individual differences in temperament. Current Psychology. 1996;14(4):261–292.

[21]   Lövheim H. A new three-dimensional model for emotions and monoamine neurotransmitters. Medical Hypotheses. 2012;78(2):341–348.

[22]   Koelstra S, Muhl C, Soleymani M, *et al.* DEAP: A database for emotion analysis using physiological signals. IEEE Transactions on Affective Computing. 2012;3(1):18–31.

[23]   Russell JA. Affective space is bipolar. Journal of Personality and Social Psychology. 1979;37(3):345–356.

[24]   Valenza G, Greco A, Bianchi M, *et al.* EEG oscillations during caress-like affective haptic elicitation. Psychophysiology. 2018;55(10):e13199.

[25]   Liu Y, Sourina O, and Nguyen MK. Real-time EEG-based human emotion recognition and visualization. In: International Conference on Cyberworlds (CW). Piscataway, NJ, USA: IEEE; 2010. p. 262–269.

[26]   Higuchi T. Approach to an irregular time series on the basis of the fractal theory. Physica D: Nonlinear Phenomena. 1988;31(2):277–283.

[27]   Liu Y and Sourina O. EEG-based subject-dependent emotion recognition algorithm using fractal dimension. In: IEEE International Conference on Systems, Man and Cybernetics (SMC). Piscataway, NJ, USA: IEEE; 2014. p. 3166–3171.

[28]   Kedem B and Yakowitz S. Time series analysis by higher order crossings. IEEE Press, New York; 1994.

[29]   Chen M, Han J, Guo L, *et al.* Identifying valence and arousal levels via connectivity between EEG channels. In: IEEE International Conference on Affective Computing and Intelligent Interaction (ACII). Piscataway, NJ, USA: IEEE; 2015. p. 63–69.

[30]   Pearson K. Note on regression and inheritance in the case of two parents. Proceedings of the Royal Society of London. 1895;58(347–352):240–242.

[31]   Pikovsky A, Rosenblum M, and Kurths J. Synchronization: A universal concept in nonlinear sciences. vol. 12. Cambridge, UK: Cambridge University Press; 2003.

[32]   Gupta R, Laghari KuR, Falk TH. Relevance vector classifier decision fusion and EEG graph-theoretic features for automatic affective state characterization. Neurocomputing. 2016;174:875–884.

[33]   Soleymani M, Pantic M, and Pun T. Multimodal emotion recognition in response to videos. IEEE Transactions on Affective Computing. 2012;3(2):211–223.

[34]   Katsigiannis S and Ramzan N. DREAMER: A database for emotion recognition through EEG and ECG signals from wireless low-cost off-the-shelf devices. IEEE Journal of Biomedical and Health Informatics. 2018;22(1):98–107.

[35]   Correa JAM, Abadi MK, Sebe N, *et al.* Amigos: A dataset for affect, personality and mood research on individuals and groups. IEEE Transactions on Affective Computing. 2018.

[36]   Zheng WL and Lu BL. Investigating critical frequency bands and channels for EEG-based emotion recognition with deep neural networks. IEEE Transactions on Autonomous Mental Development. 2015;7(3):162–175.

[37]   Morris JD. Observations: SAM: The self-assessment manikin; an efficient cross-cultural measurement of emotional response. Journal of Advertising Research. 1995;35(6):63–68.

[38]   Moddemeijer R. On estimation of entropy and mutual information of continuous distributions. Signal Processing. 1989;16(3):233–246.

[39]   Brown G, Pocock A, Zhao MJ, *et al.* Conditional likelihood maximisation: a unifying framework for information theoretic feature selection. The Journal of Machine Learning Research. 2012;13(1):27–66.

[40]   Chang CC and Lin CJ. LIBSVM: A library for support vector machines. ACM Transactions on Intelligent Systems and Technology. 2011;2:27:1–27:27.

[41]   Salmeron-Majadas S, Arevalillo-Herráez M, Santos OC, *et al.* Filtering of spontaneous and low intensity emotions in educational contexts. In: International Conference on Artificial Intelligence in Education (AIED 2015). Madrid, Spain, Springer, Cham; 2015. p. 429–438.

[42]   Arnau D, Arevalillo-Herráez M, and González-Calero JA. Emulating human supervision in an intelligent tutoring system for arithmetical problem solving. IEEE Transactions in Learning Technologies. 2014;7(2):155–164.

[43]   Arnau-González P, Ramzan N, and Arevalillo-Herráez M. A method to identify affect levels from EEG signals using two dimensional emotional models. In: 30th European Simulation and Modelling Conference-ESM'2016. Ostend, Belgium: EUROSIS; 2016.

Chapter 3

Machine learning-based affect detection within the context of human–horse interaction

Turke Althobaiti[1], Stamos Katsigiannis[2], Daune West[2], Hassan Rabah[3], and Naeem Ramzan[2]

This chapter focuses on the use of machine-learning techniques within the field of affective computing, and more specifically for the task of emotion recognition within the context of human–horse interaction. Affective computing focuses on the detection and interpretation of human emotion, an application that could significantly benefit quantitative studies in the field of animal-assisted therapy. The chapter offers a thorough description, an experimental design, and experimental results on the use of physiological signals, such as electroencephalography (EEG), electrocardiography (ECG), and electromyography (EMG) signals, for the creation and evaluation of machine-learning models for the prediction of the emotional state of an individual during interaction with horses.

3.1 Introduction

Affective computing is a field within computing that focuses on emotion recognition and interpretation, entailing a variety of methods that allow the use of affect information according to user-specific needs [1]. Among the available approaches for emotion recognition, the analysis of physiological signals has gained prominence in human–computer interaction applications. Various physiological signals originate from the central nervous system, as well as from the peripheral nervous system, and studies have shown that they contain information associated with the affective state of an individual [2]. Such information can be further exploited for the task of emotion recognition, with various studies having linked physiological signals to the valence and arousal dimensions of emotion [2–4]. Apart from human–computer interaction, the detection of the affective state of an individual could potentially benefit various other fields, such as the field of animal-assisted intervention (AAI). The use of AAIs

[1] Faculty of Science, Northern Borders University, Arár, Saudi Arabia
[2] School of Computing, Engineering and Physical Sciences, University of the West of Scotland, Paisley, UK
[3] Institut Jean Lamour, University of Lorraine, Nancy, France

as complement to conventional mental health treatment has gained a lot of attention in recent years [5,6], although the lack of sufficient research on the effectiveness of such techniques has hindered their acceptance. However, more and more sophisticated studies are being conducted [7].

A widely documented case of AAI is the use of horses for mental health treatment. Equine-assisted therapy (EAT) has many forms, including therapeutic riding, hippotherapy, equine-facilitated therapy, and equine-assisted learning therapy [8]. Evidence of the recognition of horses as agents of healing can be found in early mythology, with physicians suggesting that horse riding would "raise spirits" in people suffering from conditions that could not be treated [9]. Similar examples can be found throughout history. For example, reports from the eighteenth century indicate that the Pope's physician suggested horse riding as a remedy to the Pope's health problems [10], while Mayberry [11] reported a recommendation by a Scottish physician from 1870 that the riding of a spirited horse "stimulated life forces" and should thus be recognised as a treatment for people suffering from depression. The assertion that horse riding may have therapeutic benefits for people with disabilities has been gaining momentum since the mid-twentieth century [12].

It should be noted that riding horses for therapy differs from recreational or sports horse riding as it incorporates activities that are equine-orientated and designed to promote some of the following positive outcomes: physical, emotional, behavioural, social, cognitive, and educational objectives. The methods used by organisations which provide EAT and therapeutic treatment involving horses varies considerably. The belief that horses have therapeutic benefits for humans derives from historical observations of the emotional and physical health gains that relationships between the two entities have brought to human lives [8]. According to Kendall *et al.* [8], the sensitivity of horses to non-verbal communication of humans and other animals in their environment and their natural lack of socio-cultural standards and restrictions that communication between humans abides to, offers an environment where a sense of safety, security and trust can be fostered in people, especially those who suffer from disabilities. Based on these observations, EAT is being increasingly introduced in the treatment of both children and adults who suffer from PTSD [13,14], depression [15], symptoms related to combat trauma [16], etc.

Scientific studies on EAT have been carried out by several researchers, for example, [17–19]. However, few of these research studies have concentrated on gaining deeper knowledge of the complex emotions that horses seem to elicit in their riders and handlers. Although evidence of this emotional response in humans during human–horse interaction has been recorded in historic documents on horsemanship [20–22], these sources offer conclusions drawn from evidence based on subjective experiences and empirical observations. The capabilities of modern computing technology and health sensors have been fundamental in facilitating the measurement and quantitative examination of emotional reactions triggered in humans during activities or interactions. Drawing on analytical methods to assess human–horse interactions quantitatively could potentially be an effective way to gain insightful data which could demonstrate the benefits of EAT.

The aim of this chapter is to examine physiological signal-based affect recognition techniques as a potential solution for assessing the emotional response of humans to interactions with horses. To this end, following a predefined procedure, EEG, ECG, and EMG signals were captured while humans were interacting with horses. During a variety of activities involving horses, participant emotional states were recorded using a method of self-reporting that required them to identify and select, from a list, the relevant emotions based on their experience during each activity. The emotions reported by the participants were then mapped to their respective valence and arousal values according to Russell's circumplex model of affect [23]. The acquired physiological signals and the associated emotion-related labels were used in order to train machine-learning models for the task of predicting the respective valence and arousal values, thus predicting the emotional state of the respective participant.

The rest of this chapter is divided into six sections. Section 3.2 gives a brief overview of several recent studies within the field of affect recognition and human–horse interaction. Section 3.3 presents a comprehensive description of the experimental approach followed in this study, while Section 3.4 provides a description of the acquired data analysis process and the machine-learning approach followed. Experimental results are provided in Section 3.5 and finally the results are discussed in Section 3.6 and conclusions are drawn in Section 3.7.

3.2   Background

Emotion recognition is one of the main applications in affective computing and has attracted of lot of attention from the research community. The use of physiological signal analysis for emotion recognition has shown great potential and thus has been and still is extensively studied [24,25]. The use of features extracted from physiological signals with the aim of training machine-learning models for the prediction of the valence and arousal dimensions of an emotion is one of the most promising solutions. The performance of support vector machines (SVM) using features extracted from peripheral physiological signals and eye gaze data was studied by Soleymani *et al.* [26] for affect recognition when film clips are used for affect elicitation. Peripheral physiological signals along the Naïve Bayes classifier were also examined by Koelstra *et al.* [2] using music video clips as stimulus, while the performance of connectivity- and channel-based EEG features was examined on the same data by Arnau-González *et al.* [27]. The performance of features extracted from various physiological signals was studied by Abadi *et al.* [28], while the use of EEG- and ECG-based features, and EEG, ECG, and galvanic-skin-response-based features when film clips are used as stimulus and low-cost portable devices used for signal acquisition were examined by Katsigiannis and Ramzan [3] and Correa *et al.* [29], respectively.

While the use of physiological signals for affect recognition has been studied extensively, very limited research has been conducted for the use of physiological signals for assessing the emotional responses associated with human–horse interaction. Hama *et al.* [30] concluded in an early study that grooming horses leads to a reduction in tension both for the human subjects and the horses. Many years after that study, Chen *et al.* [31] examined the relationship between autism spectrum disorder (ASD) and resting frontal EEG brain activity in young children when interacting with a horse. Results showed that children with ASD exhibited higher left frontal dominance during the baseline condition, but right frontal dominance while grooming the horse, indicating that this change was a result of the interaction with the horse. The reliability of wearable physiological signal sensors for monitoring physiological signals in horses for the purpose of assessing human–horse interaction was examined by Guidi *et al.* [32], concluding that it was viable to quantitatively assess human–horse interaction in such a manner. In another study, Lanata *et al.* [33] examined the use of ECG signals for assessing human–horse interaction before the interaction, during visual–olfactory interaction and while grooming the horse, with the purpose of using machine learning to detect the interaction activity, achieving an accuracy of 70.87% using the nearest mean classifier and 90.95% using an SVM classifier on the same data during a later study [34]. Machine-learning approaches and ECG-based features were also employed by Althobaiti *et al.* [35] for distinguishing between negative and positive emotions during human–horse interaction, reporting an accuracy of 74.21%. In another study, Althobaiti *et al.* [36] examined the use of ECG, EMG, and EEG-based features in combination with various classification algorithms for the detection of the valence and arousal dimensions of the emotional state of humans during human–horse interaction.

Despite the aforementioned approaches for examining human–horse interaction via physiological signals and machine learning, it is evident that more extensive studies are required in order to establish robust methods for the evaluation of human–horse interaction.

3.3   Experimental protocol

In this work, the emotional responses elicited though human–horse interaction were studied through an experiment designed to accommodate such interaction while physiological signals were recorded. Participants were selected and participated in activities involving interaction with horses, while their emotional responses were documented via self-reporting.

3.3.1   Field experiment setting

A small livery yard situated in the county of Ayrshire, Scotland, United Kingdom was selected as the location for data acquisition, with the experiments taking place from late May until early August 2018. Prior to the experiment taking place, a consent form was signed by participants who were also briefed on the experimental procedure and were given instructions about the experiment. During the briefing, they were given an opportunity to ask questions about the processes involved, to ensure that they were not in any doubt of what would be required of them. Instructions on the handling of the horses and personal safety were also provided by the horse handler. After the physiological sensors were attached to the participants by the supervising researcher and the quality of signal acquisition was verified, the experiment commenced.

Two healthy horses, Max, which was 20-year old, and Braga, which was 8-year old, were selected by the handler based on their history of having a calm and friendly temperament in the company of humans who were both familiar and unfamiliar to them. The experimental procedure was repeated two times by each participant, one time interacting with Max and one time interacting with Braga, and was divided in three activities conducted in consecutive order within a small indoor sanded arena:

1. *Observing.* Observing was the first activity which lasted for a period of 4 min. During this activity, the participants were required to sit on a chair within the sanded arena while the horse freely moved around. The aim of this activity was to provide conditions where a sense of familiarity could be created between the participant and the horse, as well as to give the horse an opportunity to become acquainted with the surroundings which also included the research team and their equipment [32].

2. *Grooming.* Grooming was the second activity, lasting for a period of 2 min, which required the participants to groom the horse with a brush. Previous research has reported a reduction in heart rate in both humans and horses during similar activities when they are both comfortable [30]. It should, however, be noted that the horse was tied to a pole throughout the duration of this activity.

3. *Leading.* Leading was the third and final activity of the experiment, during which the participants were required to lead the horse around a predetermined route within the sanded arena. The time frame of this particular activity was determined by the experience of the individual participant and their ability to control the horse, although a maximum duration of 4 min was set.

On completion of the three activities, the participants were asked to complete a questionnaire regarding their emotional state during each activity.

A 10-min interval between the experiments with each horse was factored into the experiment and provided the handler with sufficient time to escort the next horse into the arena. This also allowed sufficient time for physiological sensors to be placed on participants, if required.

3.3.2   Experimental data acquisition

EEG, ECG, and EMG signals were captured throughout the whole duration of the experiment using wireless, portable low-cost and low-weight sensors, while a laptop computer was utilised for signal recording and visualisation. The portable sensors were selected for their convenience during outdoor use as other types that require cables may restrict user movement during interaction with the horses. Furthermore, the small form-factor of the sensors and being wearable made them invisible to the participants. This fact, along with setting the laptop used for signal recording to not emit any sounds or show movement in the screen, ensured that there was minimal external interference due to the presence of equipment, thus avoiding bias.

ECG signals were captured at a 256-Hz sampling rate using a SHIMMER v2 [37] sensor that utilised four standard electrodes positioned on both lower ribs and clavicle. EMG signals were also captured at a 256-Hz sampling rate using a SHIMMER v2 sensor that utilised three standard electrodes positioned on the upper trapezius muscles. A 14-channel EEG signal was captured at a 256-Hz sampling rate using the Emotive EPOC+ wireless headset [38] that utilises 16 gold plated contact sensors which are fixed to flexible plastic arms placed against the head of the user in areas aligned with the AF3, F7, F3, FC5, T7, P7, O1, O2, P8, T8, FC6, F4, F8, AF4, M1, and M2 locations of the international 10–20 system [39], with the M1 and M2 electrodes used as reference. Furthermore, all the recorded ECG, EMG, and EEG samples were accompanied by timestamps with millisecond precision

In addition to the captured physiological signals, a video recording of the experimental procedure was captured for all the participants in order to provide reference material for validation and for allowing the researchers to accurately trace and record the timestamps associated with each activity.

3.3.3   Self-reporting of emotional state

On completion of the three activities with each horse, participants were given a questionnaire to provide an assessment of their emotional state during the activities they conducted. In that questionnaire, participants were asked to report the emotions they felt during each activity out of a list of 28 emotions, shown in Table 3.1. These 28 emotions were selected due to their available mapping in the valence and arousal dimensions, as proposed by Russell in the *circumplex model of affect* [23] and is shown in Figure 3.1. According to Russell's valence/arousal model [40], the valence and arousal dimensions correspond to the main aspects of human emotion, with valence being a measurement of the positiveness of an emotion and arousal a measurement of the excitement associated with an emotion. This model allows for each perceived emotional state to be depicted on a 2-dimensional plane, with valence and arousal at each axis, respectively, as shown in Figure 3.1. It must be noted that participants were only instructed to select the emotions that they felt and did not have to use the valence/arousal scale, thus ensuring that any bias due to a misunderstanding of the rating scale was avoided.

Table 3.1   The emotions listed in the self-reporting questionnaire arranged in terms of valence and arousal

Low-arousal Negative valence	Low-arousal Positive valence	High-arousal Negative valence	High-arousal Positive valence
Miserable	Content	Alarmed	Astonished
Sad	Satisfied	Afraid	Excited
Depressed	At ease	Angry	Aroused
Gloomy	Serene	Tense	Happy
Bored	Calm	Frustrated	Delighted
Droopy	Relaxed	Annoyed	Glad
	Sleepy	Distressed	Pleased
	Tired		

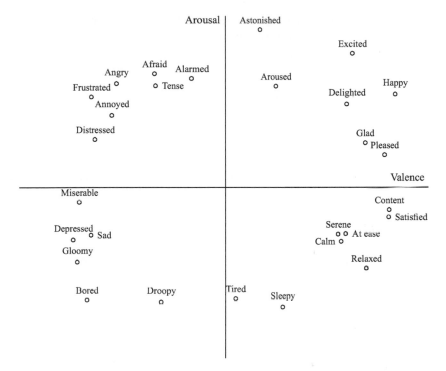

Figure 3.1   *Positioning of emotions in the valence/arousal space according to*
Russell's circumplex model of affect [23]

3.3.4   Participants

Out of the 23 participants recruited for the field experiments, only the data from 19
were considered for further analysis, as the captured data for four participants were
unusable due to erroneous data recording. These 19 participants consisted of 12 males
and 7 females who reported having normal health and were between 19 and 64 years
old, with the average age being 38.05 years with a standard deviation of 13.14 years.
Furthermore, eight participants reported having no prior experience with horses, six
participants reported having prior experience with the horses used in this study, and
five participants reported prior experience with other horses.

3.4   Analysis of captured data

3.4.1   Pre-processing of physiological signals

The video recordings of the experiments were used in order to extract the timestamps
referring to each activity and participant. Using these timestamps, the captured ECG,
EMG, and EEG signals for each participant were segmented into six segments, each
referring to a particular activity and horse. Then, the following denoising procedures

were applied to the acquired segments in order to reduce the effects of noise and artefacts that originate from the participants' movement during signal capturing:

- **ECG:** Baseline wander is a common artefact in ECG signals, originating from body movement, respiration, and high-frequency noise [41]. The effects of baseline wander in the captured ECG signals were reduced as proposed in [42], by first applying a median filter with a 200-ms window, then a median filter with a 600-ms window, followed by the subtraction of the filtered signal form the original signal. Baseline wander reduction was then followed by a bandpass filter (0.7–20 Hz) in order to further reduce noise.
- **EMG:** The Augsburg biosignal toolbox (AuBT) [43] was used for the pre-processing of EMG signals. The process followed consisted of cutting the peaks in the EMG signal with values within the 3% of the lowest or highest signal values, applying a third-order Butterworth FIR lowpass filter with a 0.4-Hz cut-off frequency, and finally the normalisation of the filtered signal to the range [0, 1].
- **EEG:** A Butterworth bandpass filter (0.4–65 Hz) was first applied to the EEG signal, followed by the PREP EEG data pre-processing pipeline [44] applied using the EEGLAB toolbox [45].

3.4.2   Extraction of features from physiological signals

Each segment of the pre-processed physiological signals was used in order to extract features that would later be used for the training of machine-learning models. It must be noted that only the last 30 s of each segment were used for feature extraction in order to remove any bias stemming from the varying duration of each activity. Inconsistent duration of activities is a common issue in affective computing studies that is usually addressed by either analysing signals using a moving window of fixed duration (e.g., [46]) or by only considering a fixed-length window from the beginning or ending of the signal (e.g., [2,3,28]). The latter option was used in this study since the moving window approach is more suitable for real-time applications. The following features were extracted from the captured physiological signals:

- **ECG:** 84 ECG-based features, commonly used in affect recognition studies [2,3, 35,36], were extracted using the AuBT [43]. The extracted features consisted of the maxima, minima, mean, median, standard deviation, and range from the raw signal and the derivative of PQ, QS, and ST complexes of the ECG signal, the maxima, minima, mean, median, standard deviation, and range from the heart rate variability (HRV) histogram, the number of intervals with latency >50 ms from HRV, and the power spectral density (PSD) from HRV between the intervals [0 , 0.2], [0.2 , 0.4], [0.4 , 0.6], and [0.6 , 0.8]. The computed features were then concatenated in order to create the final feature vector.
- **EMG:** 21 EMG-based features, commonly used in affect recognition studies [35,36], were extracted using the AuBT [43]. The following seven features were extracted from each of the raw EMG signals, its first derivative and its second derivative: mean, median, standard deviation, minima, maxima, and the number of times per time unit that the signal reached the minima and the maxima.

The 21 computed features were then concatenated in order to create the final feature vector.

- **EEG (spectral):** Five spectral features were computed from each of the theta (θ), alpha (α), beta (β), and gamma (γ) bands of each of the 14 EEG signal's channels, as described in [47], resulting in a total of 280 features. The computed features were consisted of the *spectral flatness*, the *spectral bandwidth*, the *ratio f50 vs f90*, the *spectral crest factor*, and the *spectral roll-off*. Finally, the 280 computed features were concatenated in order to create the final feature vector.
- **EEG (MFCC):** Mel frequency cepstral coefficients (MFCCs) have been used for EEG-based affect detection in various studies [48–50]. In this study, 12 MFCC features were extracted, as proposed in [48], from each EEG channel using 18 filterbanks that led to 12 cepstral coefficients. The 168 computed features were then concatenated in order to create the final feature vector. Four different MFCC feature vectors were computed over the following frequency bands of the EEG signal: [0.5–40 Hz], [4–40 Hz], [0.5–30 Hz], and [4–30 Hz].
- **EEG (PSD):** PSD-based EEG features have been extensively utilised for the detection of patterns in EEG signals that relate to human emotion [2,26,36,49,50]. In this study, the logarithm of the PSD of the theta (θ), 4–8 Hz, low alpha ($\tilde{\alpha}$), 8–10 Hz, alpha (α), 8–13 Hz, beta (β), 13–30 Hz, and gamma (γ), 30–64 Hz, bands of each of the 14 EEG signal's channels were computed using Welch's estimate of spectral power, leading to five features per channel. The 70 computed features were then concatenated in order to create the final feature vector.
- **Feature fusion:** The performance of feature fusion was also examined by creating feature vectors via concatenating individual feature vectors after normalising them to the range [0, 1], thus compensating for the variability in numerical range across different types of features.

3.4.3 Emotion labels

The questionnaire answered by each participant of this study was used in order to extract the valence and arousal values associated with each activity. The mapping of the emotions included in the questionnaire to their associated valence and arousal values followed the one proposed in Russell's *circumplex model of affect* [23], as shown in Figure 3.1. To this end, the vector (V, A), with V referring to the valence value and A referring to the arousal value, was computed for each emotion within the questionnaire. V and A took values within the range $[-1, 1]$ with negative values referring to negative valence or low arousal, respectively, and positive values referring to positive valence or high arousal, respectively. Since participants were allowed to select multiple emotions for each activity, the final vector (V, A) that referred to a participant's emotional state during a specific activity with a specific horse was computed as the sum of the vectors (V_k, A_k), $k = 1, 2, \ldots, N$, with k being the kth reported emotion and N being the number of different emotions reported. Finally, thresholding was used in order to convert the numerical V and A values to emotion labels. Valence was set to *positive* for $V > 0$ and to *negative* for $V < 0$, while arousal was set to *low* for $A < 0$ and *high* for $A > 0$. As a consequence, the problems of predicting the valence and arousal dimensions of the emotional state of a participant were converted to binary problems. As a result, each feature vector in this study was associated with a valence and an arousal label.

After computing the valence and arousal labels, their distribution was examined in order to establish the class balance of the created data set. From Figure 3.2, it is evident that the data set is moderately unbalanced for arousal since 70.2% of the samples refer to high arousal and only 29.8% to low arousal. Furthermore, the data set is highly unbalanced for valence as only 12.3% of the samples refer to negative valence, while 87.7% refer to positive valence. The distribution of valance labels in this study is consistent with the outcomes of the Hama *et al.* study [30] which suggested that human–horse interaction is usually a pleasant experience for humans that leads to positive emotions.

The distribution of valence and arousal labels was also examined in relation to the participants' prior experience with horses. As can be seen in Figure 3.3, the distribution of arousal labels was similar for both participants with and without prior experience with horses, with ~70% reporting high arousal and ~30% low arousal. Contrary to that, participants with prior experience reported a higher percentage of ratings referring to positive valence (92.4%) compared to participants without prior experience (81.2%).

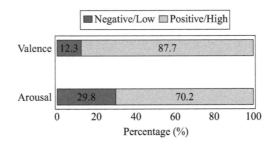

Figure 3.2   Distribution of valence and arousal labels

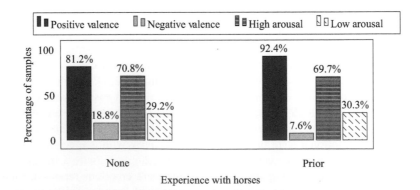

Figure 3.3   Distribution of valence and arousal labels in relation to the participants' prior experience with horses

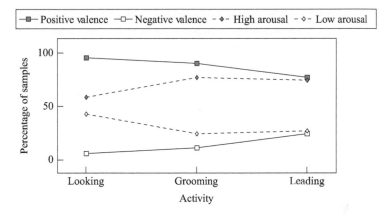

Figure 3.4   Distribution of valence and arousal labels in relation to the performed activity

Figure 3.4 shows the distribution of valence and arousal labels in relation to the horse-related activity in order of occurrence. As shown in that figure, the vast majority of participants (94.74%) reported emotions with positive valence for the first activity, Looking. The percentage of samples referring to positive valence decreased gradually for the next two activities, reaching 89.47% for the second activity, Grooming, and 76.32% for the third activity, Leading. It is evident that the first two activities (Looking and Grooming) elicited mostly pleasant emotions to the participants. However, the percentage of reported pleasant (positive valence) emotions decreased for the third activity, Leading. This can be attributed to the fact that "handling" a horse can be a challenging or even scary task for inexperienced people. Contrary to valence, arousal exhibited the opposite behaviour. For the first activity, Looking, the percentage of low and high arousal ratings was almost balanced (42.11% vs 57.89%), with the percentage of high arousal ratings increasing for the next two activities, reaching 76.32% for Grooming and 73.68% for Leading.

3.5   Experimental results

The computed feature vectors and their respective valence and arousal labels were used for the creation of machine-learning models in order to evaluate whether the extracted features are able to characterise the emotional state of the participants when they interacted with the horses. Supervised classification experiments were conducted for the prediction of the valence and arousal labels using the following classification algorithms: k-nearest neighbour (kNN), $k = 1, 3, 5$, linear discriminant analysis (LDA), decision trees (DT), linear SVM (LSVM), and SVM using a radial basis function kernel. To ensure that the trained models would not be overfitted and that the performance comparison would be fair, the trained models were evaluated by following a *leave-one-out* (LOO) cross-validation process. During the application of the LOO cross-validation, one sample is used for testing the trained model and the rest of the samples for training the model. This process is repeated until all the samples have been used for testing and the overall performance is computed as the average performance across all iterations. Furthermore, due to the unbalanced data set, classification accuracy would not be suitable as a performance metric. To compensate for the class imbalance, the classification $F1$-score was selected as a performance metric since it is more suitable in cases of uneven class distribution. Furthermore, the value of the $F1$-score metric depends on the class that is considered as positive. To this end, the reported $F1$-scores in this study correspond to the average $F1$-score between the two classes.

The performance results of the supervised classification experiments for the prediction of valence and arousal when using the best performing classifier for each feature set are reported in Table 3.2 in terms of classification $F1$-score. Apart from the single-modality features, results for some feature fusion approaches, as well as results for voting randomly (50% probability for each class), voting according to the majority class in the training data (100% probability of the majority class), and voting according to the class ratio (the probability of each class is equal to its ratio of samples within the training set), are also reported in Table 3.2. It is evident that the highest classification $F1$-scores for both valence and arousal were achieved using single-modality features, with fusion approaches performing slightly worse. Classification $F1$-score for valence reached 78.27% using the 1-NN classifier, while an

Table 3.2   *Valence and arousal classification F1-score (%) for the best performing classifier for each set of features*

Features	Valence		Arousal	
	Classifier	**$F1$-score (%)**	**Classifier**	**$F1$-score (%)**
ECG	LSVM	58.09*†‡	1NN	44.62*†‡
EMG	LDA	52.33*	5NN	50.75*†
EEG (PSD)	1NN	**78.27***†‡	DT	56.71*†‡
EEG (spectral)	1NN	71.50*†‡	DT	64.38*†‡
EEG (MFCC 4–40 Hz)	DT	68.49*†‡	LSVM	63.75*†‡
EEG (MFCC 0.5–40 Hz)	LSVM	68.49*†‡	LDA	**65.49***†‡
EEG (MFCC 4–30 Hz)	LSVM	55.21*†‡	LDA	55.88†‡
EEG (MFCC 0.5–30 Hz)	DT	68.27*†‡	LDA	61.99*†‡
All	LSVM	65.91*†‡	LSVM	59.29*†‡
ECG/EMG/EEG (PSD)	1NN	76.72*†‡	5NN	54.52*†
ECG/EMG/EEG (spectral)	1NN	76.72*†‡	3NN	55.02*†‡
ECG/EMG	5NN	59.67*	3NN	49.71*†‡
EEG (ALL)	LSVM	67.40*†‡	LSVM	61.62*†‡
	Random	41.71	Random	47.88
	Majority	46.73	Majority	41.24
	Class ratio	50.00	Class ratio	50.00

* Statistically significant difference compared to random voting ($p < 0.05$).
† Statistically significant difference compared to majority voting ($p < 0.05$).
‡ Statistically significant difference compared to class ratio-based voting ($p < 0.05$).
Results in bold refer to the highest $F1$-score achieved for valence and arousal.

$F1$-score of 65.49% was achieved for arousal using the LDA classifier. The best performing fusion approach for valence yielded an $F1$-score of 76.72% using the 1-NN classifier using the fusion of the ECG, EMG, and EEG (PSD) features, as well as the fusion of the ECG, EMG, and EEG (spectral) features. Furthermore, the best performing fusion approach for arousal yielded an $F1$-score of 61.62% using the LSVM classifier and the fusion of all the computed EEG features.

Considering the class imbalance within the data set and to ensure that the acquired results were significantly different from the results for random voting, majority voting, and class ratio-based voting, the acquired results were compared to the analytically computed results for these three cases, reported in Table 3.2. An unpaired Kruskal–Wallis test was used to test for significance against the predicted class labels for random voting and for class ratio-based voting, whereas a paired Wilcoxon signed-rank test was used to test for significance against majority voting since the predicted class labels could be computed definitely on a one-by-one basis. As shown in Table 3.2, all settings performed significantly better than random voting ($p < 0.05$) for both valence and arousal. Regarding majority voting, all settings performed significantly better for arousal, whereas for valence, only the EMG-based features and the fusion of ECG and EMG features failed the significance test ($p \geq 0.05$). Regarding class ratio-based voting, for valence, only the EMG-based features and the fusion of ECG and EMG features failed the significance test ($p \geq 0.05$), while for arousal, only the EMG-based features and the fusion of ECG, EMG, and EEG (PSD) features failed the significance test ($p \geq 0.05$). It must be noted that the best performing settings for both valence and arousal performed significantly better than all the three examined cases.

3.6 Discussion

The classification performance achieved in this study was compared with the results reported in other studies [2,3,26–29] that used physiological signals for the task of predicting valence and arousal. From Table 3.3, it can be seen that the reported

Table 3.3   Classification F1-scores (%) reported in the literature for valence and arousal when physiological signals are used

Approach	Stimulus	Brain signal device	Valence F1-score	Arousal F1-score
AMIGOS [29]	Film clips	Emotiv EPOC (EEG)	56.40	57.70
Arnau *et al.* [27]	Music videos	Biosemi Active II (EEG)	69.20	66.70
DEAP [2]	Music videos	Biosemi Active II (EEG)	60.80	58.30
DECAF [28]	Film clips	ELEKTA Neuromag (MEG)	59.00	58.00
DREAMER [3]	Film clips	Emotiv EPOC (EEG)	53.05	57.98
MAHNOB [26]	Film clips	Biosemi Active II (EEG)	56.00	42.00
This study	Horses	Emotiv EPOC+ (EEG)	78.27	65.49

Note: $F1$-scores refer to the highest performance achieved when using only physiological signals.

results are consistent with the ones reported in the literature, providing evidence that the utilised physiological signal-based features are suitable for the task of emotion recognition during human–horse interaction and are able to provide performance on par with the state-of-the-art. Furthermore, the fact that this performance was achieved using low-cost portable devices for signal acquisition indicates that such devices are potentially a suitable alternative to expensive non-portable medical-grade devices such as the ones used in [2,26,27], a finding that is also consistent with the findings of [3,29]. The use of portable wearable low-weight sensors is of utmost importance for applying affective computing techniques within EAT studies, since in most cases, the study of human–horse interaction requires that the ability of the users to move is not restricted. Being able to monitor the emotional responses of people interacting with horses can potentially be highly beneficial to quantitative studies on EAT, by providing the means to study such complex emotional responses.

3.7   Conclusion

This chapter provided an experimental approach for the task of emotional state detection via physiological signal analysis and machine learning. Experimental results showed that the described approach is suitable for the detection of the emotional state of an individual during interaction with horses, as it achieves performance on par with the state-of-the-art in emotion recognition literature. The described methodology can potentially benefit the field of EAT as it constitutes a quantitative method for assessing the emotional state of people undergoing EAT, thus providing the means to measure its effects.

References

[1] Picard RW. Affective computing: From laughter to IEEE. IEEE Trans Affective Comput. 2010;1(1):11–17.
[2] Koelstra S, Muhl C, Soleymani M, *et al.* DEAP: A database for emotion analysis using physiological signals. IEEE Trans Affective Comput. 2012; 3(1):18–31.
[3] Katsigiannis S and Ramzan N. DREAMER: A database for emotion recognition through EEG and ECG signals from wireless low-cost off-the-shelf devices. IEEE J Biomed Health Inf. 2018;22(1):98–107.
[4] Ramzan N, Palke S, Cuntz T, *et al.* Emotion recognition by physiological signals. In: Proc. IS&T International Symposium on Electronic Imaging. Springfield, VA, USA: Society for Imaging Science and Technology; 2016.
[5] Morrison ML. Health benefits of animal-assisted interventions. Complement Health Pract Rev. 2007;12(1):51–62.
[6] Amiot CE and Bastian B. Toward a psychology of human-animal relations. Psychol Bull. 2015;141(1):6.

[7]   Acri M, Hoagwood K, Morrissey M, *et al.* Equine-assisted activities and therapies: Enhancing the social worker's armamentarium. Soc Work Educ. 2016;35(5):603–612.

[8]   Kendall E, Maujean A, Pepping CA, *et al.* Hypotheses about the psychological benefits of horses. Explore. 2014;10(2):81–87.

[9]   Haskin MR. Therapeutic horseback riding for the handicapped. Arch Phys Med Rehabil. 1974;55:473–474.

[10] Woods D. Horseriding catching on as a therapy for the disabled. Can Med Assoc J. 1979;121(5):631–650.

[11] Mayberry RP. The mystique of the horse is strong medicine: Riding as therapeutic recreation. Rehabil Lit. 1978;39(6–7):192–196.

[12] Masini A. Equine-assisted psychotherapy in clinical practice. J Psychosoc Nurs. 2010;48(10):30–34.

[13] Yorke J, Nugent W, Strand E, *et al.* Equine-assisted therapy and its impact on cortisol levels of children and horses: A pilot study and meta-analysis. Early Child Dev Care. 2013;183(7):874–894.

[14] Earles JL, Vernon LL, and Yetz JP. Equine-assisted therapy for anxiety and posttraumatic stress symptoms. J Trauma Stress. 2015;28(2):149–152.

[15] Kemp K, Signal T, Botros H, *et al.* Equine facilitated therapy with children and adolescents who have been sexually abused: A program evaluation study. J Child Fam Stud. 2014;23(3):558–566.

[16] Schroeder K and Stroud D. Equine-facilitated group work for women survivors of interpersonal violence. J Spec Group Work. 2015;40(4):365–386.

[17] Benda W, McGibbon NH, and Grant KL. Improvements in muscle symmetry in children with cerebral palsy after equine-assisted therapy (hippotherapy). J Altern Complement Med. 2003;9(6):817–825.

[18] Klontz BT, Bivens A, Leinart D, *et al.* The effectiveness of equine-assisted experiential therapy: Results of an open clinical trial. Soc Anim. 2007;15(3):257–267.

[19] Selby A and Smith-Osborne A. A systematic review of effectiveness of complementary and adjunct therapies and interventions involving equines. Health Psychol. 2013;32(4):418.

[20] Xenophon. The Art of Horsemanship (Translation by Morris H. Morgan). Mineola, NY, USA: Dover Publications Inc.; 2006.

[21] Duarte D. The Royal Book of Jousting, Horsemanship, and Knightly Combat: A Translation Into English of King Dom Duarte's 1438 Treatise Livro Da Ensinança de Bem Cavalgar Toda Sela (The Art of Riding in Every Saddle). Preto AF, editor. Highland Village, TX, USA: The Chivalry Bookshelf; 2010.

[22] de Pluvinel A. Le Maneige Royal (Translated by Hilda Nelson from a 1626 edition). Franktown, VA, USA: Xenophon Press; 2010.

[23] Russell JA. A circumplex model of affect. J Pers Soc Psychol. 1980;39(6):1161–1178.

[24] Zeng Z, Pantic M, Roisman GI, *et al.* A survey of affect recognition methods: Audio, visual, and spontaneous expressions. IEEE Trans Pattern Anal Mach Intell. 2009;31(1):39–58.

[25]   Gunes H and Schuller B. Categorical and dimensional affect analysis in continuous input: Current trends and future directions. Image Vision Comput. 2013;31(2):120–136.

[26]   Soleymani M, Lichtenauer J, Pun T, *et al.* A multimodal database for affect recognition and implicit tagging. IEEE Trans Affective Comput. 2012;3(1): 42–55.

[27]   Arnau-González P, Arevalillo-Herráez M, and Ramzan N. Fusing highly dimensional energy and connectivity features to identify affective states from EEG signals. Neurocomputing. 2017;244:81–89.

[28]   Abadi MK, Subramanian R, Kia SM, *et al.* DECAF: MEG-based multimodal database for decoding affective physiological responses. IEEE Trans Affective Comput. 2015;6(3):209–222.

[29]   Correa JAM, Abadi MK, Sebe N, *et al.* AMIGOS: A dataset for affect, personality and mood research on individuals and groups. IEEE Trans Affective Comput. 2018;(Early Access).

[30]   Hama H, Yogo M, and Matsuyama Y. Effects of stroking horses on both humans' and horses' heart rate responses. Jpn Psychol Res. 1996;38(2):66–73.

[31]   Chen CCJ, Crews D, Mundt S, *et al.* Effects of equine interaction on EEG asymmetry in children with autism spectrum disorder: A pilot study. Int J Dev Disabil. 2015;61(1):56–59.

[32]   Guidi A, Lanata A, Baragli P, *et al.* A wearable system for the evaluation of the human-horse interaction: A preliminary study. Electronics. 2016;5(4):63.

[33]   Lanata A, Guidi A, Valenza G, *et al.* Quantitative heartbeat coupling measures in human-horse interaction. In: Proc. IEEE EMBC. Orlando, FL, USA; 2016.

[34]   Lanata A, Guidi A, Valenza G, *et al.* The role of nonlinear coupling in human-horse interaction: A preliminary study. In: Proc. IEEE EMBC. Seogwipo, South Korea; 2017.

[35]   Althobaiti T, Katsigiannis S, West D, *et al.* Affect detection for human-horse interaction. In: Proc. 21st Saudi Computer Society National Computer Conference (NCC). Riyadh, Saudi Arabia: IEEE; 2018. p. 1–6.

[36]   Althobaiti T, Katsigiannis S, West D, *et al.* Examining human-horse interaction by means of affect recognition via physiological signals. IEEE Access. 2019;7:77857–77867.

[37]   Burns A, Greene BR, McGrath MJ, *et al.* SHIMMER – A wireless sensor platform for noninvasive biomedical research. IEEE Sens J. 2010;10: 1527–1534.

[38]   Badcock NA, Mousikou P, Mahajan Y, *et al.* Validation of the Emotiv EPOC EEG gaming system for measuring research quality auditory ERPs. PeerJ. 2013;1(e38).

[39]   Wijayasekara D and Manic M. Human machine interaction via brain activity monitoring. In: Proc. IEEE HSI. Sopot, Poland; 2013.

[40]   Russell JA and Mehrabian A. Evidence for a three-factor theory of emotions. J Res Pers. 1977;11(3):273–294.

[41] Blanco-Velasco M, Weng B, and Barner KE. ECG signal denoising and baseline wander correction based on the empirical mode decomposition. Comput Biol Med. 2008;38(1):1–13.

[42] Kannathal N, Acharya UR, Joseph KP, *et al.* Analysis of electrocardiograms. In: Advances in Cardiac Signal Processing. Berlin, Heidelberg: Springer; 2007. p. 55–82.

[43] Wagner J. Augsburg Biosignal Toolbox (AuBT). Augsburg: University of Augsburg; 2005.

[44] Bigdely-Shamlo N, Mullen T, Kothe C, *et al.* The PREP pipeline: Standardized preprocessing for large-scale EEG analysis. Front Neuroinf. 2015;9:16.

[45] Delorme A and Makeig S. EEGLAB: An open source toolbox for analysis of single-trial EEG dynamics including independent component analysis. J Neurosci Methods. 2004;134(1):9–21.

[46] AlZoubi O, D'Mello SK, and Calvo RA. Detecting naturalistic expressions of nonbasic affect using physiological signals. IEEE Trans Affective Comput. 2012;3(3):298–310.

[47] Monge-Álvarez J, Hoyos-Barceló C, San José-Revuelta LM, *et al.* A machine hearing system for robust cough detection based on a high-level representation of band-specific audio features. IEEE Trans Biomed Eng. 2019;66(8):2319–2330. DOI: 10.1109/TBME.2018.2888998.

[48] Piciucco E, Maiorana E, Falzon O, *et al.* Steady-state visual evoked potentials for EEG-based biometric identification. In: Proc. BIOSIG. Darmstadt, Bonn, Germany: Gesellschaft für Informatik; 2017.

[49] Arnau-González P, Arevalillo-Herráez M, Katsigiannis S, *et al.* On the influence of affect in EEG-based subject identification. IEEE Trans Affective Comput. 2018;(Early Access).

[50] Arnau-González P, Katsigiannis S, Arevalillo-Herráez M, *et al.* Image-evoked affect and its impact on EEG-based biometrics. In: 2019 IEEE International Conference on Image Processing (ICIP). Piscataway, NJ, USA: IEEE; 2019. p. 2591–2595.

Chapter 4

Robot intelligence for real-world applications

Eleftherios Triantafyllidis[1], Chuanyu Yang[1],
Christopher McGreavy[1], Wenbin Hu[1], and Zhibin Li[1]

4.1 Introduction

The rise of the machines, in popular science fiction movies such as The Matrix, has given us an exaggerated vision of what robots may be capable of doing in the future if humans recklessly ignore their capabilities. This may raise a fundamental question of whether robots are truly just machines. Certainly, recent advancements in the field of artificial intelligence would signify and support the aforementioned via the admittedly impressive capabilities of these systems in a multitude of different settings and applications.

On the other hand, robots in the classical industrial settings are thought more of as robotic labours: machines that obey without questioning or reasoning the commands of humans without hesitation or second thoughts. Perhaps there is a trade-off of making highly intelligent systems and highly obedient systems. It should be of no surprise that the proliferation of autonomous machines should even be expected in the coming decades.

In practical applications, robots are undoubtedly widespread and used for good reasons. They are highly efficient in handling tasks that are either too difficult, impossible, dangerous or all of the aforementioned together for humans. This is why robots have been widely used in settings that would have been otherwise too hazardous for humans. These include and are not limited to military and defensive applications [1], decontamination of nuclear and highly radioactive materials [2], space exploration [3,4], and search and rescue operations [5].

This tight entanglement between the human and robot has naturally led to significant focus by researchers, particularly due to robots being able to operate where humans cannot. Whether these robots operate separately, i.e. fully autonomously or in collaboration with humans, it should come of no surprise that the field itself encompasses a wide spectrum of robotic sub-fields that have grown to such an extent that robotics itself is rather an interdisciplinary endeavour.

[1]School of Informatics, The University of Edinburgh, UK

In this chapter, we will look into how robots can, have and will benefit the wider human community in tasks that perhaps were taken for granted. More specifically, we review and analyse state-of-the-art work in robotic locomotion, robotic manipulation with and without human supervision. We hope to assist readers in having a thorough related work as a basis of their research with the current state-of-the-art approaches in the aforementioned fields as well as the importance of robots today.

4.2   Novel robotic applications in locomotion

Humanoid robots have morphology similar to humans and are designed to possess the ability to traverse complex and dynamic terrains easily accessible by humans. Humanoid robots generally exhibit high manoeuverability and flexibility thus are capable of achieving stable locomotion while navigating through uneven terrain and stepping over obstacles. Considering the physical limitations of a wheeled robot, there are many advantages in choosing bipedal locomotion over wheeled locomotion, as bipedal robots are able to traverse complex terrains such as stairs, gaps and obstacles. Moreover, our knowledge of bipedal locomotion can also help us design better prosthetic limbs and exoskeletons that will greatly benefit the lives of people with gait pathologies. There is also demand for humanoid robots in the service industry, as people feel more comfortable with robots with a human-like appearance. As a result, humanoid robots and bipedal locomotion have been attracting increasing attention in recent years.

Bipedal locomotion is a very difficult problem to tackle as it takes a lot of efforts for a humanoid to maintain stability and not fall over. Currently, bipedal locomotion is mainly done using analytical engineering approaches. Engineering-based analytical approaches require a lot of human knowledge in designing the controllers and additional effort in tuning, which is a disadvantage. Researchers need a substantial understanding of locomotion before designing a system and need to spend effort in tuning parameters. A majority of analytical approaches produce unnatural behaviours such as keeping the knee bent and foot constantly flat on the ground. This is due to an engineering attempt to avoid singularity caused by straight knee and underactuation caused by foot tilting. Usually, walking gaits that exhibit these behaviours use more energy compared to more human-like walking gaits.

Honda's ASIMO humanoid robot had a large impact on robotic locomotion. Research on humanoid locomotion has boomed since the first unveiling of ASIMO in 2000. Now, there are multiple well-known humanoid robots developed by different universities and institutions, such as Valkyrie, iCub and Atlas, as seen in Figure 4.1.

4.2.1   Deep reinforcement learning for dynamic locomotion of bipedal robots

Machine-learning approaches, e.g. reinforcement learning (RL), require less human effort compared to analytical approaches. Though RL also requires a certain amount of human knowledge, the main effort is in the construction of the RL agent and reward, instead of structuring explicit controllers. Once the proper agent and reward

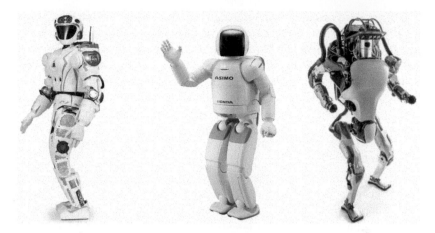

*Figure 4.1   Humanoid robots, from left to right, NASA Valkyrie, Asimo and Atlas.
Image courtesy, with the copyright holders of NASA, Asimo and Atlas
respectively. Images retrieved and adapted from [https://www.nasa.
gov/feature/r5], [https://asimo.honda.com/gallery/] and [https://www.
bostondynamics.com/atlas] respectively*

are constructed, the agent will be capable of learning the optimal policy by itself. The
effort spent on designing learning agents and reward is relatively less than the effort
spent on designing controllers using analytical approaches. Regarding the issue of
unnatural and inefficient motion behaviours, for RL, as long as the reward is designed
properly, RL will be able to learn a diverse set of human-comparable behaviours that
are more natural through exploration.

The success of AlphaGo has jump-started the robotics research communities
interest in deep RL (DRL), as it has demonstrated the capabilities of DRL algorithms in
solving complex tasks by winning over professional GO players. The recent announce-
ment of the success of AlphaGo Zero has further proven the potential of DRL. Various
works regarding novel DRL algorithms capable of working in continuous state and
action spaces done by researchers from OpenAI and DeepMind have also demonstrated the capability of DRL in solving highly complex and dynamic motor control
tasks. Given the increasingly more powerful DRL algorithms, an increasing number
of research works have used DRL to solve control tasks, as the recent progress in DRL
algorithms designed for continuous action domain has brought forward the possibility
of applying RL continuous control tasks that involve complicated dynamics.

4.2.1.1   Background: deep reinforcement learning

Recent breakthroughs in RL and deep learning have given rise to DRL, which is a
combination of RL and deep neural networks. Within DRL, deep neural networks are
utilized to approximate value function, $V(s)$ or $Q(s)$, policy $\pi(s, a)$ and model (state
transition and reward) [6].

DRL has been popularized in recent years due to its capability as a nonlinear state
abstraction tool which deals with action decision as well as evaluation. A great deal

of progress has been made in the development of DRL since it was first proposed by Mnih *et al.* [7]. The rise of DRL has enhanced the capability of agents to perform more complex and dynamic tasks in high-dimensional continuous state and action spaces. There are a wide variety of algorithms dedicated to solving high-dimensional continuous state and action space problems, such as the trust region policy optimization [8], soft actor critic (SAC) [9], proximal policy optimization (PPO) [10], asynchronous advantage actor-critic [11] and deep deterministic policy gradient method [12].

4.2.1.2   Related work: bipedal balancing with deep reinforcement learning

Humans efficiently make use of underactuated motions, such as toe tilting and heel rolling, for keeping balance while standing and walking. A biomechanical study of human walking has discovered the advantage of rolling around the heel and toe during walking phase [13]. From a biomechanical point, foot tilting creates better foot-ground clearance allowing the maximum ankle torques to be exploited [14,15].

Ankle push-off creates a control problem as an underactuated degree of freedom (DoF) is introduced. Once foot tilting occurs, the edge of the foot, namely the heel or toe becomes the only contact point between the foot and the ground which the robot pivots around. The physical feasible range of centre of pressure (COP) reduces to a singular boundary line on the edge of the foot. This new pivot is an underactuated DoF as zero torque can be applied on the pivoting axis, thus being unable to be controlled by the controller.

Many humanoid robots are designed to closely resemble the human morphology to perform human-comparable behaviours. However, their control mainly produces flat-footed locomotion, which is unnatural and inefficient. The reason does not lie in the physical capabilities, but rather the limitation in the control paradigm. Most zero moment point (ZMP)-based balance and walking controls assume the foot is placed flat on the ground creating a large size of support polygon as a fixed base. Most ZMP-based methods will fail during the underactuation, as they require the restriction of the ZMP or COP to be within a support polygon.

Some works have explored active foot tilting for balance recovery. More specifically, the work in [15] analysed thoroughly the dynamics of foot tilting and successfully designed a control strategy for underactuated ankle push-off with an implementation on a real robot. The underlying mechanism of foot tilting and the concrete mathematical proof in [15] suggest that foot tilting balance strategy is more robust against force perturbations than a flat-footed balance strategy.

Yang *et al.* have demonstrated that human-like knee lock and toe-tilt balancing behaviours naturally emerges from DRL in a 2D simulation within the sagittal plane [16]. From Figure 4.2, it can be seen that the humanoid actively adjusts the ankle joint angle during toe tilting in response to different pushes. It can also be seen that the humanoid has also learned a knee-lock configuration that provides more stability by exploiting the biomechanical constraint, very similar to what humans do. Yang *et al.* later extended upon the work in and achieved 3D balancing in both the sagittal and lateral plane [17]. The learned 3D balancing policy exhibits different behaviours depending on the amount of disturbance applied as shown in Figure 4.3. Different

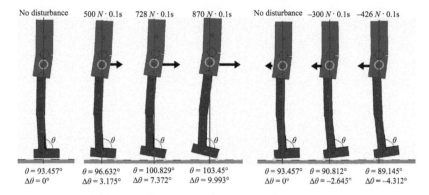

No disturbance	500 $N \cdot$ 0.1s	728 $N \cdot$ 0.1s	870 $N \cdot$ 0.1s	No disturbance	$-300 N \cdot$ 0.1s	$-426 N \cdot$ 0.1s
$\theta = 93.457°$	$\theta = 96.632°$	$\theta = 100.829°$	$\theta = 103.45°$	$\theta = 93.457°$	$\theta = 90.812°$	$\theta = 89.145°$
$\Delta\theta = 0°$	$\Delta\theta = 3.175°$	$\Delta\theta = 7.372°$	$\Delta\theta = 9.993°$	$\Delta\theta = 0°$	$\Delta\theta = -2.645°$	$\Delta\theta = -4.312°$

Figure 4.2   Responses generated by the policy upon pushes: (a) nominal standing without push, (b) forward push, (c) backward push. Images adapted from [16]

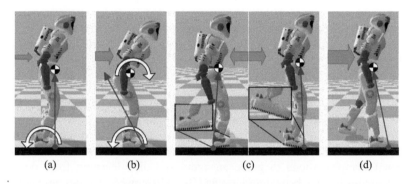

(a)   (b)   (c)   (d)

Figure 4.3   Responses generated by the policy upon pushes: (a) nominal standing prior to forward push, (b) forward push (c) backward push and response to the force and (d) forward push. Images adapted from [17]

0.0s   0.6s   1.0s   3.4s   4.4s

Figure 4.4   Snapshot of foot tilt strategy under impulse of 72 N s

control strategies emerge and range from generating ankle torque to shift the COP (ankle strategy), generating angular momentum (hip strategy), over tilting the foot to dissipate the disturbance (foot tilt strategy Figure 4.4), to taking a step to recover from the large push (stepping strategy Figure 4.5).

Figure 4.5   Snapshot of stepping strategy under impulse of 240 N s. Valkyrie robot takes two steps to stabilize.

4.2.1.3   Bipedal walking with deep reinforcement learning

Steady locomotion gait patterns can emerge without any gait phase information provided as input or reward for the DRL algorithm as shown by various researches [18]. However, most of the locomotion policies generate asymmetric jerky gaits that look unnatural and inefficient with a lot of unnecessary movements.

Researchers have come up with various solutions to solve those problems. The solutions can be roughly divided into three categories: (1) learning from demonstration, (2) periodic network architecture, (3) feedback control of predefined trajectory.

Learning from demonstration
The artificial agent can be guided to learn periodic and symmetric walking behaviours by providing human walking motion as expert demonstration for the agent to learn from. Such a technique that extracts information from the reference motion generated by expert demonstrations to guide an agent is called learning from demonstration. Examples include behaviour cloning (BC) [19], inverse reinforcement learning (IRL) [20] and generative adversarial imitation learning (GAIL) [21], and imitation by tracking (IT) [22]. BC minimizes the difference between the student and expert behaviour in a supervised learning fashion through the loss function. IRL fits a reward function to describe the demonstration and uses it as the objective to maximize. GAIL learns a discriminator to measure the similarity between expert demonstrations and behaviours generated by the policy, and the objective of the agent is to learn a policy that is indistinguishable from the demonstration. IT involves designing a tracking reward dedicated to measuring the similarity between the agent's state and the demonstration data [23–25].

Furthermore, there are a few works in the field of character animation that have utilized learning from demonstration to learn impressive human-like behaviours for humanoids. Jonathan Ho and Stefano Ermon implemented GAIL [21] to train the neural network policy to produce human-like walking and standing-up behaviours from human motion capture data [26]. Peng *et al.* implemented tracking reward to imitate various motions like walking, backflip, running and ball throwing on a simulated humanoid [23].

Periodic network architecture

Locomotion is periodic in nature; therefore, many locomotion controllers have structures that produce rhythmic outputs such as central pattern generator (CPG). CPG is commonly used to construct the bio-inspired neural network control policy for bipedal locomotion due to its ability to produce coordinated rhythmic and periodic gaits [27]. However, CPG is not necessary for designing a periodic controller, and other periodic structures can be used. Holden *et al.* proposed a special architecture named phase-functioned neural networks (PFNN) to generate locomotion animations from motion capture data for computer graphics and have successfully synthesized various human motions. Sharma and Kitani incorporated the PFNN architecture with DRL and developed a phase-parametric action-value function and a phase-parametric policy to learn locomotion policies in simulation [28].

Feedback control of predefined trajectory

Instead of training the agent to directly learn a natural-looking locomotion gait, a trajectory generator can be used to provide a periodic and symmetric locomotion trajectory and allow the agent to learn a feedback control loop that fine-tunes the trajectory to adapt to external disturbance. Usually, the trajectory generator is a separate entity and can function individually without the learning agent. Xie *et al.* learned a feedback controller on top of a predefined joint trajectory to control the bipedal Cassie robot in simulation [29]. Their method is shown to be able to generalize towards different velocity and terrain slope features. Tan *et al.* have come up with a similar approach for the quadrupedal Minotaur robot using a trajectory generator that generates a fixed trajectory [30], and the structure of the control framework is shown in Figure 4.6. Iscen *et al.* improved upon the work of Tan *et al.* and developed a framework that consists of an adaptive trajectory generator and a learned feedback controller that not only modulates the output of the trajectory generator and also the parameters of the trajectory generator [31], improving the generalization capability of the policy. This is illustrated in Figure 4.7.

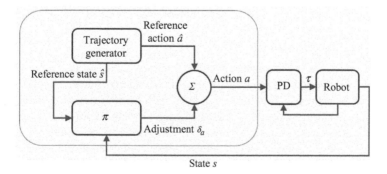

Figure 4.6   Learning feedback control policies with trajectory generators: feedback control with fixed trajectory generator

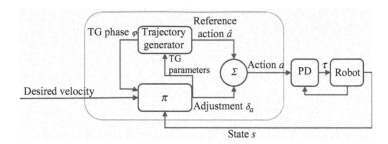

Figure 4.7   Learning feedback control policies with trajectory generators: feedback control with adaptive trajectory generator

4.2.2   Learning from humans

RL offers numerous advantages for designing locomotion controllers, which allows the robot to learn its own method of performing actions. We can also approach this problem from the opposite direction by looking at examples of experts in walking control. Humans have an exceptional ability to walk on flat ground, gradients, rough terrain and adapt to almost anything they encounter. If we can extract the controllers used by humans to walk and balance and transfer this to robotics, we would have a highly adaptable, robust walking robot. This section will explore these advantages, explore some of the methods of achieving this and discuss some drawbacks of designing controllers.

4.2.2.1   How to learn from humans

Much like in RL, our goal when we look at transferring human control into robotics is to find the policy π which maps an input state into an output action. Doing this typically requires three steps, as illustrated in Figure 4.8:

1.   Data collection: Measure human behaviour during the desired motion.
2.   Interpretation: Decide on how the collected data will be used.
3.   Implementation: Implement a robot controller based on the results shown earlier.

4.2.2.2   Data collection

When transferring characteristics from humans to robotics, it is important to think about what it is that we want to transfer and this will dictate how the data is collected. Humans are experts at many things which are still being developed in robotics and AI: reasoning, emotion, vision, movement among many more. It is impossible to improve all these areas at once, so when we want a robot to behave like a human, we have to think about exactly what problem will be solved. Identifying the problem will determine what data needs to be collected and how it will be collected.

In this section, we will be looking at how we can control the movement of robots so they move correspondingly to humans. When looking at movement, naturally we need a way of recording how human moves their bodies and a way to turn that into data. There are many quantities to measure in human movement and as many ways

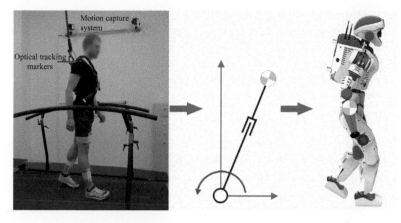

Figure 4.8 An example of the steps involved in designing a human-inspired controller: data collection, interpretation and implementation

to measure them, for example, measuring the activation of a group of muscles using electromyography (EMG) sensors can help mimic human actuation policies during impedance control [32]. Muscle activation can also be measured invasively, or via low-cost consumer devices. However, when measuring muscle activation, signals are often noisy and the correct measurement can be hard to obtain. For a more external view, human joint angles can be measured directly using flexible sensors [33], which tend to be much less noisy and fairly easy to work with. Joint angles can also be measured indirectly using inertial measurement units [34], video streams [35] or optical motion tracking [36], but since these methods capture more data than the other sensors, it is also possible to infer much more information from these methods.

Let us look at our example of making robots balance like humans when pushed. Here, we use optical motion tracking to measure the movement of humans in our study. This is accomplished by placing reflective markers on the body of subjects and tracking their movement using precise infrared cameras. Since we know where we placed the markers, we can reconstruct the dimensions and dynamics of the human body using tools such as OpenSim [37], which can calculate quantities such as joint angles, joint torques, limb positions, centre of mass (CoM) motion, inertia matrices and many more.

When choosing a method, it is important to consider the quantities that are going to be important for the robot controller, for example, there is no point in recording muscle activation if we are only worried about how the hand moves in space in response to some stimulus. Whichever method is chosen, the data we collect is worth little unless it is interpreted and put to use for the robotic system. We will look at the methods of interpreting the data in the next section.

4.2.2.3 Interpreting the data

Once the data has been collected, it needs to be processed from its raw form into something useful. There are many ways to interpret the collected data. Some controllers use real-time online remapping, which interprets data coming from humans directly into movement at the robot using robot joints [34] or from human end-effector positions to robot end-effector positions [38]. In this case, data interpretation involves filtering these positions and finding a transformation from the dimensions of the humans and approximating the motions to place directly onto a robot.

The collected data can be used similarly in machine-learning algorithms. Information we get from humans can be given directly to learning implementations, which act as a demonstration of the desired motion. As we saw in the previous section, this can lead to better learning output. By providing a learning algorithm, for example access to the joint angles and end-effector positions that humans use during walking, a robot can learn to walk faster than it would if it learned from scratch [39]. In the case of online retargeting and learning from demonstration, the level of interpretation does not need to be very deep, as the methods do not require it.

An alternative method of interpretation is much more involved but can yield interesting results. By looking more closely into the data, the fundamentals of human motion can be explored more explicitly. This exploration aims to find some approximation of the policy π used by humans to produce a particular motion. Such a policy can then be used as the basis of a classical controller. Finding underlying policies can be difficult, as humans are complex organisms, and there are many ways of searching for this.

The learning processed can be reversed using IRL [40], to estimate the reward function of human motion. Fitting regression models to data is another powerful tool for finding this policy [41]. The output of these methods is an estimate of the human policy in the form of a reward function or an analytical model. Once that model has been found it can act as an approximation of the policy humans use to control their behaviour.

If we go back to our example of transferring balancing behaviour, we can look at human behaviour across subjects and conditions and try to extract the common elements between them. In this section concerned with robotic balancing, we looked at the CoM of humans and how it behaved after they were pushed. Since many whole-body controllers focus on the CoM, it would be useful if we could find a way to transfer the behaviour at this level. There are many distinct motions in balance recovery, so we tried to find a single model which could map the current CoM position to the desired position so as the system would become stable. We found that a single model was able to explain human behaviour well using principles of minimum jerk [42]. To do this, we used regression techniques to try a set of candidate models which had elements resembling the human motion. By trying to fit increasingly more complex polynomials to the CoM motions of humans in both the X and Z direction, we could gradually see the fit becoming more accurate and with the increase in complexity, we can infer which aspects of the function are important to human motion. But it is important to know when to stop. If the order of the polynomial to too high, the model will overfit. Finding a model that fits means we can make the robot move in a similar way to humans in our experiments, which we hope would make them more robust. We can also infer a little about how humans might produce this behaviour, though this must be measured, as human motion is very complex with many possible factors in play at a given time.

4.2.2.4 Implementation

After identifying the behaviour that is to be transferred to a robot, collecting and interpreting the data, it is now time to put it to use.

In the case of real-time retargeting methods, once the data has been adjusted to fit the needs of the robot, it can be directly played onto the robot with a few adjustments [34]. These methods are useful since the robot can move real-time without too much focus on control and can use human sensing ability but also introduce their own problems in that the retargeting can be tricky since human dimensions do not match the robot dimensions and are difficult to extract a policy to be used when the human is removed. Here, the implementation is quite direct if low-level tracking controllers already exist on the robot.

In learning methods, the implementation tends to be done during training, and policies are learned using the data from the human. Depending on the structure of the agent, this may lead to a whole-body controller which outputs joint commands [34], or controllers which control specific movements and interface with other classical controllers [43].

The output from analytical models can be used in a similar way and will depend on how the data was collected and used. For simple cases, such as in the EMG example [32], the model can be directly transferred to the motor of the robot using input from the robot's sensor. Models can also be used to control exoskeletons and prostheses [44] while being used by humans.

A particularly useful aspect of analytical models is that they can be edited to account for the capabilities of the target system; because robots can react more quickly than humans, we can tune the model to increase performance.

Returning to our example, when we found CoM motion model, we then tuned the controller to account for the increased actuation capability of the robot, thus allowing the robot to recover more quickly than a human whilst using the same controller and maintaining the associated benefits of the learning. Since this model described CoM motion, it is already suitable to be used in classical whole-body controllers, since most take CoM state as input. To use this controller, we then only need to take the CoM state as input and the model we have produced through the above process then output a new desired CoM control to the whole-body controller, which moves the body to the new position. Since the model was derived from humans, the combination of our model and the whole-body controller will produce motions similar to that in humans, but optimized for the robot of our choosing.

Implementation of human-like behaviour is the goal for any human-inspired controller, and there are many ways of performing this step. The most suitable method is likely to be that which is most compatible with the behaviour we humans are trying to convey.

In conclusion, this process offers some advantages over other methods of control design but also has its disadvantages. Human-inspired control has a well-founded place in modern robotics in its own right and can also be useful in supplementing other methods such as machine learning.

4.3   Novel robotic applications in human-guided manipulation

When we think of an environment in which we are not physically present, we ask ourselves subconscious questions. Are we really immersed in the remote virtual or even physical location? Do we feel physically present? In the further extreme, we might even ask ourselves a fundamental question, can we inhabit a foreign body?

Embodying another organism or even machine is potentially the first step towards this vision. An appropriate analogy would be the homunculus argument, in which a supposedly little man is looking through a person's eye and controlling their actions [45,46]. If we assume a telepresence or a teleoperation scenario, the little man would be us, the human operators.

Autonomous robotic systems are mimicking humans in many ways and are expected to interpret high-level commands and plan and execute actions that will accomplish their given goal with an often high success rate. Naturally, the similarities between a humanoid robot and a human have led to the idea of inhabiting with the further extreme of embodying a machine [47].

While we are still far from accomplishing true embodiment, which would eliminate the doubt of feeling immersed in the remote location, the growth of virtual reality, robotics, networking technologies and mostly the advances in research concerning multi-modal interfaces would be the first building blocks towards that vision. Humans utilize a wide range of stimuli to perceive their surroundings, including vision, audition, touch, smell and taste [48,49]. It would thus seem natural to include ways to effectively maximize these senses. Research in multi-modal interfaces aims to provide solutions to increase the feeling of body ownership, namely embodiment, to the further extent of increasing immersion and overall human performance [50–52]. When an operator embodies a robot or avatar, the control signals they make are physically detached from the resultant actions, which is unusual for humans. Multi-modal interfaces, however, aim to mitigate this break in immersion by maximizing the perceived 'amount' of immersion and by extent leading to improved task performance when controlling a foreign body in a virtual environment [53,54].

4.3.1   Background, trends and challenges

Extensive research has been conducted in the field of remote piloting concerned with manipulation, with the hopes of robots imitating human-like dexterity in the future. In this section, we highlight state-of-the-art research in the field of robotics, particularly remote piloting, immersive object interaction and manipulation techniques, as well as multi-modal interfaces within the scope of human–computer interaction and human perception sciences. Finally, we also mention the popular state-of-the-art approaches used in robotic manipulation and beyond, via the use of machine-learning approaches, in particular, imitation learning (IL).

4.3.1.1 Telepresence vs teleoperation

Remotely piloted robotic systems can fall into two major categories: telepresence and teleoperated robots. While their differences may not be so apparent and it would almost feel like that these two terms are tightly entangled, their uses and applications are widely different. They do however have one important aspect identical to each other: the human in the loop.

The term telepresence is attributed to Minsky [55], describing a set of technologies used by a human operator to feel physically present at a remote location by mimicking his or her appearance via a robotic surrogate of themselves. Consequently, telepresence can be defined as the use of a set of technologies to achieve the feeling of being physically present at a remote location via the use of telerobotics.

Teleoperation, however, delegates the fine control of a robotic system via the physical controls from a human operator, to effectively manipulate any kind of objects in the remote location [56,57]. While teleoperation shares the same idea as telepresence, achieving the highest DoF is of key importance and can be quantified via the use of both quantitative and qualitative approaches. Teleoperation by definition is concerned with the 'operation' of robotic end-effectors to achieve manipulation.

Telepresence systems are primarily associated with communication technologies such as videoconferencing which is currently being redefined as telepresence videoconferencing part of a set of technologies also known as videotelephony.

In contrast to telepresence systems, teleoperated systems are mostly associated with applications concerning manipulation tasks. These can range from space exploration, military and defensive applications to search and rescue missions associated with hazardous environments [47,58–60]. Robots, however, do not operate only in environments where machines are present, robot–human collaboration is a very promising area to benefit humans in tasks that would otherwise be too difficult or dangerous without assistance [61]. However as easy as it may sound for a robot to hand objects or manipulate these in conjunction with a human at the same time, it remains a difficult task with numerous challenges [62–65].

Both telepresence and teleoperation categories share in their core structure the same underlying theories of tele-embodiment and tele-existence, both highly influenced by immersion and aiming to increase operator awareness [66]. Numerous studies have confirmed that an increase in the situational awareness of a human operator has a strong correlation with a respective increase in overall performances [67,68]. It is thus highly advisable to shed light on what constitutes immersion and what the influencing factors really are, these are further along analysed in Section 4.3.1.4.

4.3.1.2 Types of remote piloting

Now that we are familiar with the discrepancies between telepresence and teleoperation system and the main aspects of a remote robotic system, it is important to mention the types of remotely piloted robotic systems.

Remote manipulation of a robotic system has been introduced at the end of the 1940s, in which a slave manipulator was handling chemical and nuclear materials with direct visual feedback, constructed and developed by the Argonne National Laboratory [69]. The first, however, remote-controlled system was by Nicola Tesla in New York in 1898 demonstrating a radio-controlled boat. A remote manipulation system consists in essence of two parts, the robot itself, as well as a human in the loop, also known as an operator who controls the robotic system. As such, teleoperation is defined as 'to operate a vehicle or a system over a distance' [56].

Remotely piloted robotic system can in essence be classified into the following:

- Closed-loop control
- Coordinated teleoperation
- Supervisory control

Closed-loop control, also known as direct manipulation, includes the user directly controlling the robotic system through the use of actuators with no autonomy on the robotic side [70].

Coordinated teleoperation is the same as the aforementioned one; however, there is an implementation of some internal control loop.

Finally, supervisory control includes most of the control part, i.e. the autonomous procedures, on the side of the robotic system. The operator in this case only performs high-level tasks. This type of classification includes a double loop in which a human–machine interface is needed to transmit the double-flow of information back and forth [71]. This human–computer interface can include a virtual model, different sensory information, alert messages and more [70].

In all instances, however, a minimal delay is critical in preserving a smooth or even feasible teleoperation experience [70], as further highlighted in an intercontinental remote-piloting experiment between Germany and Japan [72].

4.3.1.3   Object interaction and manipulation

When we search for keys or coins in our pockets or bags, we tend to take for granted the dexterity necessary to not only find these via pure haptic exploration [73], but also the high complexity of grasping these. For a human, such a task seems to be quite simple. It almost seems a ubiquitous activity, which we forget how hard it is to master and acquire as children. For a robot, it is an entirely different setting.

Robots are fairly efficient in handling objects of various shapes and sizes, able to learn via basic human movements, such as poking [74], slicing [75] or even throwing items [76]. However, most robots still struggle with deformable objects, which is further aggravated as it is task-oriented and specific to the environment these operate [49]. While researchers have invested a lot of time and effort in designing efficient robotic end-effectors, controlling an entire a humanoid robot, also requires effectively controlling the arm, shoulder, torso and ultimately every joint available, thus further increasing the challenge of locomotion and by extent manipulation [49,77–79]. Our review, however, will be focused exclusively on the robotic end-effector as we are not investigating either locomotion or navigation scenarios but rather manipulation of rigid-bodies.

The complexity of a task and mostly the approach of grasping is highly dependent upon both the software and hardware of the robotic system. Concerning the latter, a multitude of robotic end-effectors exists and designing effective robotic end-effectors has been well researched for the past years [80,81]. Perhaps those of the most widely used ones in industry settings are suction approaches, providing an almost excellent solution to rigid-body objects, however with deformable objects, particularly cables, being of significant challenge [49,82]. In the simplest scenario, a robotic end-effector would consist of the widely used parallel jaw gripper, most probably with the addition of force sensing [49]. A gripper is a simple yet efficient solution to grasping rigid objects but is not efficient for more complex tasks and further aggravated by non-rigid objects, let alone coins or cables [49]. Researchers and engineers have even gone as far as designing from scratch, robotic end-effectors based on the task and driven by the objects at play [83,84].

Human-inspired hands have been well researched and efforts in constructing anthropomorphic end-effectors have been a primary goal for many researchers, including robotics engineers and material scientists [49,85]. However, this proved to be by far from an easy task, primarily attributed to the absence of soft-materials for the construction of such a robotic hand and also hard to imitate the DoFs mechanically [49,85,86]. Recent advances in human-inspired robotic end-effectors, particularly the Shadow Dexterous robotic hand by Shadow partially mitigated this by achieving a remarkable 24 DoF [87], very close to the total of 27 actual DoFs of a human hand. To achieve human-level dexterity, perhaps the best way to approach that goal is by using human-like hands [87].

Regardless of the robotic end-effector, it is of crucial importance to include sensing regarding the forces at play during manipulation. Disregarding careful exertion of forces from the robotic hand to an object can result in unpredictive behaviour and even destroy the object by crushing it under high forces [88]. This is why we need sensing as of forces during manipulation. To capture contact points and forces exerted from a robotic hand to an object, most researchers have thus far relied on vision-based approaches for both rigid [89] and deformable objects [90]. Even directly measuring the forces on the robotic hand via stretchable artificial skin has been well researched [91]. As we identified however previously, during embodiment, stimulating the senses of a human operator controlling, a robot is of crucial importance due to increased perception correlating to higher task performance [50–52]. By extent, the best way to approach the problem of sensing forces as identified earlier is by directly stimulating the respective senses of a human via for example haptic feedback; more details are provided in Section 4.3.1.4.

4.3.1.4   Multi-modal interfaces for perception

Manipulation is multi-modal, requiring more than one senses to be active to effectively control, approach and grasp an object with success [49]. In an even broader spectrum, the very interactions as humans initiate with the world are multi-modal [92–94]. In the ideal case, a multi-modal interface would be able to stimulate all human senses. Vision, haptics and auditory stimuli are to date focused by most researchers due to being more developed [48,54,95,200]. However, recent work in olfaction or even gustation has shown promising potential in robotics [96,97]. One study even estimated that the five human senses have a different contribution with sight, hearing, smell, touch and taste contributing to 70%, 20%, 5%, 4% and finally 1%, respectively, [48]. Immersion is nonetheless a subjective sensation with the influencing factors being subject to each individual's previous exposure to technologies, personality-related absorption and cognitive ability [57,98–100].

Visual interfaces and dominance

However, implementing these sensory devices to effectively stimulate each respective sense is not straightforward. Sensory conflict can arise when a multi-modal pipeline is unable to stimulate the senses in a synchronized way, resulting into a reduced spatial and temporal immersion, effectively nullifying the benefits of using multi-modal interfaces [95,101]. In addition to the discrepancies between the sensory conflicts, further findings indicate the dominance of vision, to the extent of outperforming haptic as well as vestibular cues [102,103]. Another study also found that vision is dominating proprioception [104], also referred to as kinaesthesia, which is defined as the sense of self-movement and the relative joint position of one's body [105]. For remote piloting, however, there is evidence that visual perception of spatial layout between a real world and a virtual world is indistinguishable [106].

Audiovisual interfaces

The importance of auditory cues in conjunction with visual information has been supported by numerous studies representing these as a useful supplement to just using visual feedback. This has been well documented in scenarios where visual channels were heavily loaded, in which auditory cues constituted a useful supplement increasing operator awareness of the surrounding environment [53,107]. Furthermore, there is evidence of reduced workload demand in simulated space robot teleoperation scenarios, signifying a reduction and prevention of potential accidents during actual space operations [108]. Using auditory feedback to complement vision instead of superimposing secondary visual information has also shown a decrease in distraction due to a less need of focusing attention to visual stimuli in a robot-assisted movement training [109]. Lastly, especially in scenarios where an Field of View (FoV) is limited, one study supports that auditory cues are of significant benefit due to the operator being able to localize the position of sounds even when not directly gazing at them, in unmanned aerial vehicle operation [110]. Furthermore, in a first-person-view manipulation of a humanoid robot, operators were able to intuitively control the teleoperation procedure when presented with an audiovisual interface [111].

Visuohaptic interfaces

With vision being of dominant presence in comparison to our other senses as identified earlier [102–104], it has led to the advances in visuohaptic interfaces. The entanglement between vision and haptics has shown a promising increase in human performance in tasks associated with nano-robotics by implementing both haptic feedback and the use of virtual reality [112], as well as in micro-manipulation scenarios [113–115]. As such, visuohaptic interfaces have been studied extensively, due to their promising significance in teleoperation scenarios through the use of pressure and vibration feedback [116]. As with auditory cues, somatosensory cues share the same usage that is being supplementary to visual information when the superimposition of visual information is already heavily loaded or limited [117]. Examples include haptic warning feedback regarding spatial properties as well as velocities of a remotely piloted robot [118,119]. In one study, the importance of somatosensory stimulation was signified when higher performance was observed in a pick-and-place task with the presence of haptic feedback, particularly contributing to lesser mean completion time and faster performance overall than without [120]. In another study, electro-tactile feedback in conjunction with a virtual reality head-mounted display was used to remotely manipulate a robotic arm [121]. Furthermore, in a planetary and space exploration setting, a visuohaptic interface for remote manipulation was used by communicating contact between a robot gripper and an object with vibration intensity controlling the proximity, to the extent of increasing spatial accuracy for the user [122]. In addition, tangible user interfaces have also been well researched, providing an alternative to the aforementioned methods via somatosensory stimulation directly from actual real-world objects providing a substantial experience by carefully aligning virtual and real-world object shapes into one [123,124].

Audiovisuohaptic interfaces
Perhaps, the true goal in increasing immersion is by combining all of the aforementioned ones [125]. One study highlights the potential of an audiovisuohaptic multi-modal interface in motor learning and how it can potentially affect functional task with an increased amount of complexity [53]. They hypothesize but do not confirm that an audiovisuohaptic multi-modal interface becomes more effective as the task complexity increases. In another study, different combinations of visual, auditory and somatosensory through vibrotactile feedback did not make a significant contribution in a telerobotic navigation task; however, operator spatial ability during manipulation, as well as subjective performance, did increase by combining the aforementioned modalities in one interface [126].

Overcoming cognitive overload
In Section 4.3.1.3, we briefly mentioned vision approaches to measure the forces and contact points exerted from a robotic hand. However, recklessly superimposing all that visual information disregarding the potential of heavily loading the visual sensory channel can result in overwhelming information leading to severe distraction [127], also known as cognitive overload [128]. Cognitive overload also arises when a user, in this case, an operator is constantly monitoring and commanding tasks that could otherwise be autonomous, thus building up to his or her stress levels [127,129]. This takes us back to Section 4.3.1.2, indeed providing more evidence from the current literature that a supervisory-control multi-modal interface may limit the accumulation of cognitive workload if integrated correctly.

The uncanny valley of stimuli
One study proposed the term 'Uncanny Valley of Haptics', whereby they confirmed that an enhanced somatosensory i.e. haptic stimulation without the corresponding stimulation of other sensory cues, such as visual or auditory, reduces the subjective feeling of realism and by extent immersion in teleoperation and virtual reality experiences [130]. Their study concludes that a multi-modal approach incorporating

multiple human sensory channels may be of significant benefits in increasing spatial and temporal immersion in remote manipulation scenarios. This sheds further light into the importance of using multi-modal interfaces and multi-sensory integration to increase human performance and by extent useful human demonstration data.

Overlapping stimuli

Neuroscience studies, primarily neuroimaging research, indeed confirm that the simultaneous presence of both visual and somatosensory sensory cues are of critical importance primarily due to both modalities activating, i.e. overlapping, in the same brain region [131–134]. The implication of the aforementioned is that both modalities should be simultaneous present. According to other studies, however, during sensory conflict, sensory signals are weighted by their reliability [135].

4.3.1.5   Immersive manipulation via learning

Humans are incredibly dexterous concerning manipulation. Even as children, complex, highly dexterous tasks seem to become significantly easier when our parents or adults illustrate i.e. demonstrate the tasks we as children initially found impossible. Why should this differ for intelligent robotic agents?

Explicitly programming a robot to do the aforementioned would be suboptimal as it would be task-specific and not transferable to a wide range of tasks. Generalizing would, in essence, be impossible. This is where learning is of particular interest. On the other hand, creating a human-like brain for robots to solve a variety of complex manipulation tasks has and still is a long-standing frontier [49].

There are in total three machine-learning paradigms: supervised, unsupervised and RL. In the latest, RL, the agent has three major attributes, observation, action and reward and has been widely implemented in a multitude of different settings [10,136,137], particularly in robotic control with the hope of autonomously completing in the near future a wide range of decisions for manipulation tasks [138]. More specifically, recent progress in manipulation via the use of RL has proven beneficial in solving dexterous in-hand manipulation [87,139]. A popular approach in training robotic systems is prior training in simulation environments and transferring that model to the respective real robot to avoid potential damages that would result from real-life training, this transition is also known as Sim-to-Real [87,140–142]. However, to achieve realistic simulation of physics entailing realistic friction forces and physical properties is not possible as of yet. Real experimentation is thus unavoidable in machine learning for robots and is highly recommended to acquire useful data [49].

The most popular algorithms to date in RL are PPO [10] and SAC [143]. Conventional approaches however such as the PPO [10] due to being on-policy are expensive regarding their sample complexity and by extent require substantial, often in millions, time steps of data collection to converge to a stable solution. Furthermore, PPO is highly dependent upon the hyper-parameters used and often requires tuning these carefully [143].

IL on the other hand focuses on imitating expert demonstrations. RL by itself is often not very stable and not easy to converge [144]. IL compensates this via supervised learning to an almost near-optimal behaviour where the agent attempts to replicate that behaviour [144–147].

IL is applied in situations where either conventional approaches of RL are unable to solve the problem or to reduce overall training times by providing a baseline of some demonstrations, in particular for PPO approaches where usually millions of time steps are required [143]. This is especially the case in robotic learning, where the reproduction of complex grasp motions is applied via human demonstration to mitigate the aforementioned drawbacks by using only and exclusively conventional RL methods [147,148]. While IL seems to be a promising approach, the trained policy is only as good as the demonstrations provided by the human expert, this is explicitly why we have focused on maximizing human perception.

Some approaches of IL include for example behavioural cloning (BC) [149], to imitate the demonstrations provided by human experts, which however severely suffer from drifting errors resulting into actions that were not as demonstrated. This is particularly due to out of distribution states that were encountered by the agents, consequently, agents never converge back to the actual states as demonstrated [144, 150]. Recent methods based on RL, however, mitigate this by training an agent (via RL), to effectively match human demonstration data over a period also known as a horizon, example of these include IRL, GAIL as well as soft Q IL [144,145,151].

Now that we know that maximizing immersion via the use of multi-modal interfaces translates in increased human performance we hypothesize that through such interfaces lies in the true human performance to allow effective demonstrations.

4.3.2 Discussion and frontiers in human-guided manipulation

As we have identified in this section, human–robot collaboration is of crucial importance not only in situations where both the human instinct and the computational and physical capabilities of robots are needed but also in more classical settings such as industry [57,152,153]. In a collaborative environment, however, where close proximity between humans and robots is necessary, it is of vital importance to enable safe physical interactions between the two – this still remains an industrial challenge [49]. Perhaps, by closing the gap between a robot and a human either via direct immersive teleoperation, i.e. demonstration, we would be able to achieve the aforementioned.

In Section 4.3.1.4, we mentioned the benefits of multi-modal interfaces for increased human performance either in direct teleoperation or learning approaches. However, maybe in the future robots can be controlled directly, via the human brain. Advances in brain–machine interfaces (BMIs), also known as a brain–computer interface, have investigated the direct communication between a human brain and a computer system. There are two major approaches in which a BMI can be achieved, non-invasive entailing functional magnetic resonance imaging as well as electroencephalogram [154–156] and invasive [157]. This would be the ultimate interface between a human and a computer. A BMI can potentially be thought of as 'full dive', in which 'full' immersion is achieved. While this would be a breakthrough of substantial magnitude, actual studies show limitations in incorporating these in remote piloting [158].

4.4   Novel robotic applications in fully autonomous manipulation

Manipulation is one of the major functions of robots. Nowadays robots have enormously promoted the manufacturing automation, but for robots to replace human in daily life manipulation tasks, there is still a long way to go. The most essential step to achieve that goal is enabling robots to acquire human-level manipulation abilities. With the rapid technological breakthrough in the past two decades, we now have powerful vision and tactile devices, stable robotic arms and multi-finger hands. However, the autonomous control of complex manipulation tasks remains difficult. Therefore, the Achilles' Heel of robotic manipulation at present is a 'robotic brain' for reasoning, planning and controlling.

Machine-learning approaches shed new light on autonomous manipulation in an end-to-end manner. Compared with analytical methods, the learning paradigm releases the tediousness of manually designing the task-relevant framework and reduces the heavy requirement of human prior knowledge. Recently DRL has shown the strong capability of solving continuous high-dimensional problems such as playing Go or video games. In the DRL context, the agent gathers training data through interaction with the environment and learns the optimal policy from trials and errors. Inspired by the previous success, some researchers start to explore the potential in solving complex manipulation tasks with DRL and obtain promising results.

A fine example of the state-of-the-art work in deep learning for robust grasping is the work of Mahler *et al.* [159]. Their work, named Dex-Net 2.0, uses a synthetic data set of approximately 6.7 million point clouds to effectively plan a robust grasping approach, by analytically measuring the grasp quality from thousands of 3D models from its predecessor, Dex-Net 1.0. The data set is not limited to rigid objects but also contains articulated as well as deformable objects which still pose a challenge in robotic manipulation. In Figure 4.9, we see the potential of fully autonomous, i.e. deep learning robots, more specifically the robotic system ABB YuMi, effectively grasping objects in real-world applications such as an order fulfilment settings.

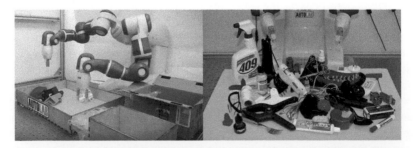

Figure 4.9   Dex-Net 2.0. Left image: A set of 40 household objects serving the purpose of evaluating the performance of the robotic grasp. Right image: Illustrating the experimental set-up for accomplishing an order fulfilment by grasping and moving objects to a shipping container. Image courtesy [159].

4.4.1 *Background*

During the execution of most robotic manipulation tasks, grasping is an essential and fundamental step. Given a robotic hand and a target object, in order to achieve a grasp with desired properties, one has to finely control the fingers before and during the grasp, including positions and forces of fingertips and joints. Such methods to compute the aforementioned finger parameters are referred to as grasp synthesis algorithms [160].

4.4.1.1 Robotic grasping and manipulation: grasp synthesis

'Synthesis' means generating the finger configuration to acquire some desired grasp properties. Several properties that a 'good' grasp should possess have been identified by researchers, e.g. equilibrium, and force-closure. Equilibrium is most basic and necessary to a grasp. A grasped object is in equilibrium if all the forces and moments applied on it have the sum of zero. Compared with equilibrium, force-closure is a step forward: a grasp verifies the force-closure property if the fingers are capable of resisting disturbing forces in any arbitrary direction.

4.4.1.2 Robotic grasping and manipulation: grasp quality evaluation metrics

This section introduces metrics to evaluate the quality of a given grasp in deep learning settings in manipulation. Combining the analytical quality evaluation with learning already presents some promising results [161]. Roa and Suárez [162] classified the major measures of grasp quality into two groups: measures related to the location of contact points and measures related to the configuration of the robotic hand.

In this part, we introduce a representative metric in DRL-based grasp planning. Largest minimum resisted wrench [163] is one of the commonly used metrics to measure the quality of a grasp. It represents the maximum wrench a grasp can resist in every direction, within the limits of finger force. For simplification the max finger force is normalized to 1, so that the metric only relates to the contact point. A wrench is a six-dimensional vector consisting of force and torque $\omega = [F, \tau]^T$. The friction cone is approximated as an m-edged pyramid, so that the contact force is expressed as $f_i = \sum_{j=1}^{m} \alpha_{ij} f_{ij}$. Therefore, the total wrench from n fingers acting on the object is

$$\omega = \sum_{i=1}^{n} \omega_i = \sum_{i=1}^{n} \sum_{j=1}^{m} \alpha_{ij} \omega_{ij}, \text{ with } \alpha_{ij} \geq 0, \sum_{j=1}^{m} \alpha_{ij} \leq 1 \tag{4.1}$$

All the possible wrenches on the object form a convex hull W of the Minkowski sum of ω_{ij}, where the W is known as *grasp wrench space* [164]:

$$W = ConvexHull\left(\bigoplus_{i=1}^{n} \omega_{i1}, \ldots, \omega_{im}\right) \tag{4.2}$$

4.4.1.3   Robotic grasping and manipulation: deep reinforcement learning

The recent development in DRL has opened new possibilities for robotics research. It has shown promising capabilities of solving continuous control tasks with high-dimensional spaces, such as pouring liquids [165], multi-finger grasping [166], in-hand manipulation [167] or bipedal locomotion tasks [39].

When strictly defining RL, an agent learns a policy in that framework from scratch by maximizing the expected cumulative return from autonomous interactions with the environment. In contrast to other machine-learning techniques, such as unsupervised and supervised learning, no pre-collected training data is required as the agent autonomously generates the training data by interacting with the environment and infers the quality of its state and actions through reward signals. Not requiring pre-generated training data is especially useful in large continuous action and state spaces, because labelling whether one action under the current state is good or bad is infeasible due to the infinite amount of possible combinations.

The task in RL is considered as a finite-horizon discounted Markov decision process, consisting of a state space S, an action space A, a distribution of initial states $p(s_0)$, the state transition dynamics $T : S \rightarrow S$, a reward function $r : S \rightarrow \mathbb{R}$ and a discount factor $\gamma \in (0, 1]$. Every learning episode starts with a sampled initial state s_0. Thereafter, at every time step, the agent chooses one action based on current state and the policy $\pi(s_t)$ to be executed. After execution, the agent will receive a reward $r(s_t, a_t)$ and the state observation s_{t+1} from the environment. The goal of the agent is to maximize the expected discounted sum of the rewards.

4.4.2   Related work

Recently there is a downward tendency of the emphasis on the grasp properties related to stability. There are three main reasons: first is that the computation requires complete knowledge of the object surface; second is that usually, the planned grasp is impossible or hard for the hand to execute; third is that mostly the grasp just needs to be relatively stable, which is enough and acceptable for the task. Therefore, recently many grasp synthesis algorithms start to focus more on the task compatibility and scalability, which requires a bit more robot 'intelligence'. Task compatibility represents how well a grasp can accomplish the specified task, which involves some high-level reasoning and the concept of graspable affordance [168].

4.4.2.1   Data-driven grasp synthesis

In the past two decades, much progress has been achieved in grasp synthesis. Sahbani *et al.* [169] have divided the mainstream of grasp synthesis algorithms into two parts: analytical approaches and empirical approaches. Analytical approaches generate the grasp configuration through the computation of kinematics and dynamics formulations. These kinds of approaches usually focus on the force closure property of a grasp and require a complete geometry model of the target object [170,171]. Heavy computation requirements and the difficulty of modelling a specific task limit the effectiveness of analytical approaches. Empirical approaches avoid the aforementioned drawbacks through learning mechanisms. IL [172] is applied in some researches where a human demonstration is provided and the robot learns to reproduce the grasp motion [173,174]. With the development of computer vision and deep learning, a promising path is to generate the grasp location directly from the visual input, such as depth image or a point cloud. These kinds of approaches often involve the design of the learning framework and CNN architecture and require a large amount of training data.

Vision-based data-driven methods show prominent performance in robotic grasping [175]. Compared with classical grasp synthesis, data-driven approaches improve the performance of grasping unknown objects [161,176–178].

However, training of the model requires very large data, either collected from simulation [176] or self-supervised real robot experiment which is time-consuming [177]. Furthermore, sampling and ranking of grasp candidates often take long computation time [161,177], which limits the capability of reactive control. The success of a grasp strongly relies on precise object perception and accurate hardware control. In the case of a grasp failure, no recovery strategy is being deployed, and the whole pipeline is simply reset and another attempt is repeated instead of an online, reactive adjustment [176].

4.4.2.2   From grasping to manipulation

Grasping itself is not the goal, instead, it is a stepping stone towards any subsequent manipulation task [49]. Besides the basic stability requirements, to determine an optimal grasp, one has to consider the purpose of that grasp as well as any manipulation afterwards. In other words, one has to consider grasping as a part of holistic robotic manipulation task. Some work has been done using neural networks to learn the semantic reasoning about the target objects or tools to generate the task-orientated grasping [179,180].

Vision and haptic information are important in grasping and manipulation [92]. Primarily, these two kinds of sensor information are processed individually and sequentially: vision input dominates before the grasp happens and tactile input guides the contact and re-grasp adjustment. Integration of multiple sensors remains however a problem [181]. There is still room to improve the robot's ability to decide what sensor to use when to switch between them, or even how to use them at the same time, and where humans come into play. Enabling robots to accomplish human-level tasks, remains a particularly challenging topic to date. Advances have nonetheless led to robots already being able to perform some primitive manipulation tasks like throwing [182], cutting [183] and poking [184]. Since these tasks are inherently different, the proposed methods lack generalization ability. An ambitious goal is to present a learning framework for all kinds of manipulation tasks.

4.4.2.3   DRL-based autonomous grasping and manipulation

In the paradigm of grasping, DRL has recently shown powerful capability. Compared with other machine-learning and data-driven approaches, the DRL's inherent property of learning from trial and error results in a more robust policy with some emergent untrained behaviours. Kalashnikov *et al.* [185] utilized DRL to enable closed-loop vision-based pick-and-place task from a cluttered bin. The learned policy continuously updates the grasp strategy based on the most recent vision input, in order to maximize the long-horizon grasp success. The success rate on unseen objects is dramatically high, up to 96%. Moreover, the policy automatically learns re-grasping, probing, re-positioning objects and other non-prehensile pre-grasp manipulations. Apart from learning grasping, synergy between pushing and grasping [186], re-grasping after failure [187] can also be generated with DRL. In addition, different off-policy RL algorithms have been evaluated and compared in vision-based grasping tasks in a simulation benchmark study [188].

DRL also offers a promising way of generating complex manipulation tasks, which typically relies on hand-engineered policy representations or human demonstrations beforehand. Normalized advantage function has been applied for learning manipulation tasks like door opening and pick-and-place [189]. The manipulation of deformable objects like cloth can also be achieved with a combination of imitation and DRL [190,191]. James *et al.* [192] have proposed a useful robotic learning simulation benchmark for different manipulations.

Dexterous in-hand manipulation has been a tough challenge for years due to high-dimensional configuration space and complex contact interactions. DRL provides an end-to-end solution to tackle these problems. Zhu *et al.* [193] learn different manipulation tasks on two low-cost multi-finger robotic hands. OpenAI has conducted many explorations in learning complex manipulation skills with Shadow Hand, a high-dimensional 24-DoF hand. With demonstration-augmented DRL, the hand learns a wide range of skills in simulation [194]. Moreover, on a physical platform, they achieved complex in-hand manipulation tasks of a cube rotating [167] and Rubik's cube solving [195].

4.4.3   Reaching, grasping and re-grasping

From the perspective of traditional planning approaches, reaching and grasping are inherently different and usually planned separately and deployed sequentially. For grasping of a moving ball, vision and proximity sensors have been used from a top-view [196]. Marturi *et al.* developed an approach of planning pre-grasp posture on-line and tracking a moving object, where the grasp motion was determined by a human operator [197]. Planning of the complete reaching and grasping motion is quite time-consuming and is often implemented in an open-loop or partially reactive controlled manner [198]. Current planning based methods have provided good results in solving reaching [196] or grasping problems [199] individually, but the switch between controllers is designed manually. As a next-level performance with increased robustness, reaching, grasping and even re-grasping should be addressed simultaneously in one unified control policy.

Part of the focus of our chapter is to study a unified control policy for reaching, grasping and re-grasping, which requires synergistic behaviours, more specifically, fine coordination between the hand and fingers. We are neither aiming to benchmark with the reaching ability of planning methods nor with the grasp quality of cutting-edge data-driven methods. Instead, the goal is to learn a unified policy with coordinated motor skills for the entire grasping loop.

4.5 Conclusion

We can conclude that robots have integrated into today's society to such an extent and their capabilities have been showcased in such a multitude of different settings that it would be safe to assume that this will only further continue to develop. While robots may be perceived as 'just machines', in our chapter we saw that this does not hold true. Robots are more than just an assembly of motors and electronics, they can become our surrogate selves, an alternative body which we may operate in situations where pure artificial intelligence has yet not solved or to just be able to retain in part the human instinct.

Remotely piloted robotic systems that integrate a human in the loop undoubtedly combine by their nature the instinct of a human operator and the computational complexity of a robot. As we identified in this chapter, these novel approaches will be of utmost importance in applications that involve time-sensitive and high-risk tasks. Perhaps, to enhance the cooperation between a human and the robot, the key element future researchers may have to investigate further is just one, immersion.

As such, we anticipate that the list of robotic applications will only grow in the future. We believe, the true use of robots, perhaps the only ones that are able to accomplish such tasks, are settings where it is either demeaning for humans to work in or outright dangerous situations threatening biological lifeforms. An important challenge that we believe is yet to be solved is robots that can work in close collaboration with other humans. Whether these would operate fully, semi or without autonomy, the obstacles that have separated humans and machines this long will gradually fade away, opening new roads and constitute previously thought challenges as solved.

References

[1] Satava RM. Virtual reality and telepresence for military medicine. Computers in Biology and Medicine. 1995;25(2):229–236. Virtual Reality for Medicine. Available from: http://www.sciencedirect.com/science/article/pii/001048259400006C.

[2] Bimbo J, Pacchierotti C, Aggravi M, *et al.* Teleoperation in cluttered environments using wearable haptic feedback. In: 2017 IEEE/RSJ International Conference on Intelligent Robots and Systems (IROS). Vancouver, BC, Canada: IEEE; 2017. p. 3401–3408.

[3] Li HZ, Liang YS, He T, *et al.* Research on Space Robot Shared Control System Based Augmented Virtual Reality. In: Advanced Materials Research. vol. 468. Switzerland: Trans Tech Publ; 2012. p. 1403–1409.

[4] Britton N, Yoshida K, Walker J, *et al.* In: Mejias L, Corke P, and Roberts J, editors. Lunar Micro Rover Design for Exploration through Virtual Reality Tele-operation. Cham: Springer International Publishing; 2015. p. 259–272. Available from: https://doi.org/10.1007/978-3-319-07488-7_18.

[5] Martins H and Ventura R. Immersive 3-D teleoperation of a search and rescue robot using a head-mounted display. In: 2009 IEEE Conference on Emerging Technologies Factory Automation. Mallorca, Spain: IEEE; 2009. p. 1–8.

[6]   Li Y. Deep reinforcement learning: An overview. Computing Research Repository (CoRR), preprint arXiv:170107274. 2017.

[7]   Mnih V, Kavukcuoglu K, Silver D, *et al*. Playing Atari with deep reinforcement learning. Computing Research Repository (CoRR), preprint arXiv:13125602. 2013.

[8]   Schulman J, Levine S, Moritz P, Jordan M, and Abbeel P. Trust region policy optimization. In: Proceedings of the 32nd International Conference on International Conference on Machine Learning – Volume 37 (ICML'15). Lille, France: JMLR 2015. p. 1889–1897.

[9]   Haarnoja T, Zhou A, Abbeel P, Levine, S. Soft actor-critic: Off-policy maximum entropy deep reinforcement learning with a stochastic actor. In: Proceedings of the 35th International Conference on Machine Learning. Stockholmsmässan, Stockholm Sweden: PMLR 2018. p. 1861–1870.

[10]   Schulman J, Wolski F, Dhariwal P, *et al*. Proximal policy optimization algorithms. Computing Research Repository (CoRR), preprint arXiv:170706347. 2017.

[11]   Mnih V, Badia AP, Mirza M, *et al*. Asynchronous methods for deep reinforcement learning. In: Proceedings of the 33rd International Conference on Machine Learning. New York, NY, USA: PMLR; 2016. p. 1928–1937.

[12]   Lillicrap TP, Hunt JJ, Pritzel A, *et al*. Continuous control with deep reinforcement learning. Computing Research Repository (CoRR), preprint arXiv:150902971. 2015.

[13]   Adamczyk PG, Collins SH, and Kuo AD. The advantages of a rolling foot in human walking. Journal of Experimental Biology. 2006;209(20): 3953–3963.

[14]   Li Z, Zhou C, Zhu Q, *et al*. Active control of under-actuated foot tilting for humanoid push recovery. In: Proc. IEEE/RSJ Int. Conf. Intell. Robots and Syst. Hamburg, Germany: IEEE; 2015. p. 977–982.

[15]   Li Z, Zhou C, Zhu Q, *et al*. Humanoid balancing behavior featured by under-actuated foot motion. IEEE Transactions on Robotics. 2017;33(2):298–312.

[16]   Yang C, Komura T, and Li Z. Emergence of human-comparable balancing behaviours by deep reinforcement learning. In: 2017 IEEE-RAS 17th International Conference on Humanoid Robotics (Humanoids). Birmingham, UK: IEEE; 2017. p. 372–377.

[17]   Yang C, Yuan K, Merkt W, *et al*. Learning whole-body motor skills for humanoids. In: 2018 IEEE-RAS 18th International Conference on Humanoid Robots (Humanoids). Beijing, China: IEEE; 2018. p. 270–276.

[18]   Heess N, Sriram S, Lemmon J, *et al*. Emergence of locomotion behaviours in rich environments. Computing Research Repository (CoRR), preprint arXiv:170702286. 2017.

[19]   Pomerleau DA. Efficient training of artificial neural networks for autonomous navigation. Neural Computation. 1991.

[20]   Ng AY, and Russell SJ. Algorithms for inverse reinforcement learning. In: Proceedings of the 17th International Conference on Machine Learning (ICML '00). San Francisco, CA, USA: Morgan Kaufmann Publishers Inc.; 2000. p. 663–670.

[21] Ho J and Ermon S. Generative adversarial imitation learning. In: Advances in Neural Information Processing Systems. Barcelona, Spain: Curran Associates, Inc.; 2016. p. 4565–4573

[22] Atkeson CG and Schaal S. Robot learning from demonstration. In: ICML. vol. 97. San Francisco, CA, USA: Citeseer; 1997. p. 12–20.

[23] Peng XB, Abbeel P, Levine S, *et al.* DeepMimic: Example-guided deep reinforcement learning of physics-based character skills. ACM Transactions on Graphics. 2018.

[24] Merel J, Ahuja A, Pham V, *et al.* Hierarchical visuomotor control of humanoids. Computing Research Repository (CoRR), arXiv:181109656. 2018.

[25] Yang C, Yuan K, Shuai H, *et al.* Learning natural locomotion behaviors for humanoid robots using human bias. IEEE Robotics and Automation Letters. 2020.

[26] Merel J, Tassa Y, Srinivasan S, *et al.* Learning human behaviors from motion capture by adversarial imitation. Computing Research Repository (CoRR), preprint arXiv:170702201. 2017.

[27] Endo G, Morimoto J, Matsubara T, *et al.* Learning CPG-based biped locomotion with a policy gradient method: Application to a humanoid robot. The International Journal of Robotics Research. 2008;27(2):213–228.

[28] Sharma A and Kitani KM. Phase-parametric policies for reinforcement learning in cyclic environments. In: Thirty-Second AAAI Conference on Artificial Intelligence. New Orleans, USA: AAAI Conference on Artificial Intelligence; 2018.

[29] Xie Z, Berseth G, Clary P, *et al.* Feedback control for Cassie with deep reinforcement learning. In: 2018 IEEE/RSJ International Conference on Intelligent Robots and Systems (IROS). Madrid, Spain: IEEE; 2018. p. 1241–1246.

[30] Tan J, Zhang T, Coumans E, *et al.* Sim-to-real: Learning agile locomotion for quadruped robots. Computing Research Repository (CoRR), arXiv preprint arXiv:180410332. 2018.

[31] Iscen A, Caluwaerts K, Tan J, *et al.* Policies modulating trajectory generators. In: Proceedings of The 2nd Conference on Robot Learning. USA: PMLR; 2018. p. 916–926.

[32] Howard M, Braun DJ, and Vijayakumar S. Transferring human impedance behavior to heterogeneous variable impedance actuators. IEEE Transactions on Robotics. 2013;29(4):847–862.

[33] Park JW, Kim T, Kim D, *et al.* Measurement of finger joint angle using stretchable carbon nanotube strain sensor. PLoS One. 2019;14(11).

[34] Yang Y, Ivan V, and Vijayakumar S. Real-time motion adaptation using relative distance space representation. In: 2015 International Conference on Advanced Robotics (ICAR). Istanbul, Turkey: IEEE; 2015. p. 21–27.

[35] Mehta D, Sridhar S, Sotnychenko O, *et al.* VNect: Real-time 3d human pose estimation with a single RGB camera. ACM Transactions on Graphics (TOG). 2017;36(4):1–14.

[36]   Gordon DF, Henderson G, and Vijayakumar S. Effectively quantifying the performance of lower-limb exoskeletons over a range of walking conditions. Frontiers in Robotics and AI. 2018;5:61.

[37]   Delp SL, Anderson FC, Arnold AS, *et al.* OpenSim: Open-source software to create and analyze dynamic simulations of movement. IEEE Transactions on Biomedical Engineering. 2007;54(11):1940–1950.

[38]   Tosun T, Mead R, and Stengel R. A general method for kinematic retargeting: Adapting poses between humans and robots. In: ASME 2014 International Mechanical Engineering Congress and Exposition. Montreal, Quebec, Canada: American Society of Mechanical Engineers Digital Collection; 2014.

[39]   Yang C, Yuan K, Merkt W, *et al.* Learning whole-body motor skills for humanoids. In: 2018 IEEE-RAS 18th International Conference on Humanoid Robots (Humanoids). Beijing, China: IEEE; 2018.

[40]   Hadfield-Menell D, Russell SJ, Abbeel P, *et al.* Cooperative inverse reinforcement learning. In: Advances in Neural Information Processing Systems. Red Hook, NY, USA: NIPS (ACM); 2016. p. 3909–3917.

[41]   Vijayakumar S and Schaal S. Locally weighted projection regression: An o (n) algorithm for incremental real time learning in high dimensional space. In: Proceedings of the Seventeenth International Conference on Machine Learning (ICML 2000). USA: ACM (ICML). vol. 1; 2000. p. 1079–1086.

[42]   Flash T and Hogan N. The coordination of arm movements: an experimentally confirmed mathematical model. Journal of Neuroscience. 1985.

[43]   Tsounis V, Alge M, Lee J, *et al.* DeepGait: Planning and control of quadrupedal gaits using deep reinforcement learning. Computing Research Repository (CoRR), arXiv preprint arXiv:190908399. 2019.

[44]   Azimi V, Shu T, Zhao H, *et al.* Robust control of a powered transfemoral prosthesis device with experimental verification. In: 2017 American Control Conference (ACC). Seattle, WA, USA: IEEE; 2017. p. 517–522.

[45]   Gregory R. The Oxford Companion to the Mind. Oxford, UK: Oxford University Press; 2005.

[46]   Lipton JI, Fay AJ, and Rus D. Baxter's homunculus: Virtual reality spaces for teleoperation in manufacturing. IEEE Robotics and Automation Letters. 2018;3(1):179–186.

[47]   Stone RJ. Haptic feedback: A brief history from telepresence to virtual reality. In: Brewster S and Murray-Smith R, editors. Haptic Human-Computer Interaction. Berlin, Heidelberg: Springer Berlin Heidelberg; 2001. p. 1–16.

[48]   Heilig ML. EL Cine del futuro: The cinema of the future. Presence: Teleoperators & Virtual Environments. 1992;1:279–294.

[49]   Billard A and Kragic D. Trends and challenges in robot manipulation. Science. 2019;364(6446). Available from: https://science.sciencemag.org/content/364/6446/eaat8414.

[50]   Yanco Ha and Drury J. "Where am i?" acquiring situation awareness using a remote robot platform. In: 2004 IEEE International Conference on Systems, Man and Cybernetics (IEEE Cat No04CH37583). The Hague, Netherlands: IEEE; 2004. p. 2835–2840.

[51]   DeJong BP, Colgate JE, and Peshkin MA. Improving teleoperation: reducing mental rotations and translations. In: IEEE International Conference on Robotics and Automation, 2004. Proceedings. ICRA'04. vol. 4. New Orleans, LA, USA: IEEE; 2004. p. 3708–3714.

[52]   Jennett C, Cox AL, Cairns P, *et al.* Measuring and defining the experience of immersion in games. International Journal of Human-Computer Studies. 2008;66(9):641–661. Available from: http://dx.doi.org/10.1016/j.ijhcs.2008.04.004.

[53]   Sigrist R, Rauter G, Riener R, *et al.* Augmented visual, auditory, haptic, and multimodal feedback in motor learning: A review. Psychonomic Bulletin & Review. 2013;20(1):21–53. Available from: https://doi.org/10.3758/s13423-012-0333-8.

[54]   Chen JYC, Haas EC, and Barnes MJ. Human performance issues and user interface design for teleoperated robots. IEEE Transactions on Systems, Man, and Cybernetics, Part C (Applications and Reviews). 2007;37(6): 1231–1245.

[55]   Minsky M. Telepresence. New York, USA: Omni; 1980. p. 45–51.

[56]   Fong T and Thorpe C. Vehicle Teleoperation Interfaces. Netherlands: Kluwer; 2001.

[57]   Mcglynn SA and Rogers WA. Considerations for presence in teleoperation. In: Proceedings of the Companion of the 2017 ACM/IEEE International Conference on Human–Robot Interaction – HRI'17. New York, NY, USA: ACM/IEEE; 2017.

[58]   Sheridan T. Teleoperation, telerobotics and telepresence: A progress report. Control Engineering Practice. 1995;3(2):205–214.

[59]   Sgouros NM and Gerogiannakis S. Robot teleoperation environments featuring WAP-based wireless devices. Journal of Network and Computer Applications. 2003;26(3):259–271. Available from: http://www.sciencedirect.com/science/article/pii/S1084804503000171.

[60]   Álvarez B, Iborra A, Alonso A, *et al.* Reference architecture for robot teleoperation: Development details and practical use. Control Engineering Practice. 2001;9(4):395–402. Available from: http://www.sciencedirect.com/science/article/pii/S0967066100001210.

[61]   Ajoudani A, Zanchettin AM, Ivaldi S, *et al.* Progress and prospects of the human–robot collaboration. Autonomous Robots. 2018;42(5):957–975. Available from: https://doi.org/10.1007/s10514-017-9677-2.

[62]   Huber M, Knoll A, Brandt T, *et al.* Handing over a cube spatial features of physical joint-action. Annals of the New York Academy of Sciences. 2009;1164:380–382.

[63]   Cakmak M, Srinivasa SS, Lee MK, *et al.* Using spatial and temporal contrast for fluent robot-human hand-overs. In: 2011 6th ACM/IEEE International Conference on Human–Robot Interaction (HRI). Lausanne, Switzerland: IEEE; 2011. p. 489–496.

[64]   Huang CM, Cakmak M, and Mutlu B. Adaptive Coordination Strategies for Human–Robot Handovers. In: Robotics: Science and Systems. USA: RSS; 2015.

[65]   Mainprice J, Gharbi M, Siméon T, *et al.* Sharing effort in planning human–robot handover tasks. In: 2012 IEEE RO-MAN: The 21st IEEE International Symposium on Robot and Human Interactive Communication. Paris, France: IEEE; 2012. p. 764–770.

[66]   Lichiardopol S. A Survey on Teleoperation. DCT Rapporten. Eindhoven, Netherlands: Technische Universiteit Eindhoven; 2007. DCT 2007.155.

[67]   Burke JL, Murphy RR, Coovert MD, *et al.* Moonlight in Miami: Field study of human–robot interaction in the context of an urban search and rescue disaster response training exercise. Human–Computer Interaction. 2004;19(1–2): 85–116. Available from: https://www.tandfonline.com/doi/abs/10.1080/073 70024.2004.9667341.

[68]   Drury JL, Scholtz J, and Yanco HA. Awareness in human–robot interactions. In: SMC'03 Conference Proceedings. 2003 IEEE International Conference on Systems, Man and Cybernetics. Conference Theme – System Security and Assurance (Cat. No.03CH37483). vol. 1. Washington, DC, USA: IEEE; 2003. p. 912–918.

[69]   Vertut J and Coiffet P. Teleoperation and Robotics: Evolution and Development. NJ, USA: Studentlitteratur; 1985.

[70]   Lichiardopol S. A Survey on Teleoperation. Technische Universiteit Eindhoven, Netherlands: Semantic Scholar; 2007.

[71]   García CE, Carelli R, Postigo JF, *et al.* Supervisory control for a telerobotic system: A hybrid control approach. Control Engineering Practice. 2003;11(7):805–817. Available from: http://www.sciencedirect.com/science/article/pii/S096706610200206X.

[72]   Buss M and Peer A. Design and Control of Admittance-Type Telemanipulation Systems. Munich, Germany; 2008.

[73]   Okamura A, Turner ML, and Cutkosky M. Haptic exploration of objects with rolling and sliding. vol. 3; 1997. p. 2485–2490.

[74]   Agrawal P, Nair A, Abbeel P, *et al.* Learning to poke by poking: Experiential learning of intuitive physics. In: Proceedings of the 30th International Conference on Neural Information Processing Systems. NIPS'16. Red Hook, NY, USA: Curran Associates Inc.; 2016. p. 5092–5100.

[75]   Zhang K, Sharma M, Veloso M, *et al.* Leveraging Multimodal Haptic Sensory Data for Robust Cutting. USA: IEEE; 2019.

[76]   Zeng A, Song S, Lee J, *et al.* TossingBot: Learning to Throw Arbitrary Objects With Residual Physics. USA: IEEE; 2019.

[77]   Mason MT. Toward robotic manipulation. Annual Review of Control, Robotics, and Autonomous Systems. 2018;1(1):1–28. Available from: https://doi.org/10.1146/annurev-control-060117-104848.

[78]   Bouyarmane K, Chappellet K, Vaillant J, *et al.* Quadratic programming for multirobot and task-space force control. IEEE Transactions on Robotics. 2019;35(1):64–77.

[79]   Li Z, Zhou C, Castano J, *et al.* Fall Prediction of legged robots based on energy state and its implication of balance augmentation: A study on the humanoid. In: 2015 IEEE International Conference on Robotics and Automation (ICRA). Seattle, WA, USA: IEEE; 2015. p. 5094–5100.

[80] Bicchi A. Hands for dexterous manipulation and robust grasping: A difficult road toward simplicity. IEEE Transactions on Robotics and Automation. 2000;16(6):652–662.

[81] Grupen RA, Henderson TC, and McCammon ID. A survey of general-purpose manipulation. The International Journal of Robotics Research. 1989;8(1):38–62. Available from: https://doi.org/10.1177/027836498900800103.

[82] Bernardin A, Duriez C, and Marchal M. An interactive physically-based model for active suction phenomenon simulation. In: SWS19 – SOFA Week Symposium. Paris, France; 2019. Available from: https://hal.inria.fr/hal-02419381.

[83] Rahman N, Carbonari L, D'Imperio M, *et al.* A dexterous gripper for in-hand manipulation. In: 2016 IEEE International Conference on Advanced Intelligent Mechatronics (AIM). Banff, AB, Canada: IEEE; 2016. p. 377–382.

[84] Bircher WG, Dollar AM, and Rojas N. A two-fingered robot gripper with large object reorientation range. In: 2017 IEEE International Conference on Robotics and Automation (ICRA). Singapore: IEEE; 2017. p. 3453–3460.

[85] Chalon M, Grebenstein M, Wimböck T, *et al.* The thumb: Guidelines for a robotic design. In: 2010 IEEE/RSJ International Conference on Intelligent Robots and Systems. Taipei, Taiwan: IEEE; 2010. p. 5886–5893.

[86] Chang LY and Matsuoka Y. A kinematic thumb model for the ACT hand. In: Proceedings 2006 IEEE International Conference on Robotics and Automation, (ICRA). Orlando, FL, USA: IEEE; 2006. p. 1000–1005.

[87] Andrychowicz OM, Baker B, Chociej M, *et al.* Learning dexterous in-hand manipulation. The International Journal of Robotics Research. 2020;39(1):3–20. Available from: https://doi.org/10.1177/ 0278364919887447.

[88] Homberg BS, Katzschmann RK, Dogar MR, *et al.* Haptic identification of objects using a modular soft robotic gripper. In: 2015 IEEE/RSJ International Conference on Intelligent Robots and Systems (IROS). Hamburg, Germany: IEEE; 2015. p. 1698–1705.

[89] Pham T, Kyriazis N, Argyros AA, *et al.* Hand-object contact force estimation from markerless visual tracking. IEEE Transactions on Pattern Analysis and Machine Intelligence. 2018;40(12):2883–2896.

[90] Yuan W, Dong S, and Adelson E. GelSight: High-resolution robot tactile sensors for estimating geometry and force. Sensors. 2017;17(12):2762.

[91] Gerratt AP, Sommer N, Lacour SP, *et al.* Stretchable capacitive tactile skin on humanoid robot fingers – First experiments and results. In: 2014 IEEE-RAS International Conference on Humanoid Robots. Madrid, Spain: IEEE; 2014. p. 238–245.

[92] Turk M. Multimodal interaction: A review. Pattern Recognition Letters. 2014;36:189–195. Available from: http://www.sciencedirect.com/science/article/pii/S0167865513002584.

[93] Bunt H, Beun RJ, and Borghuis T. Multimodal human-computer communication: systems, techniques, and experiments. vol. 1374. Germany: Springer Science & Business Media; 1998.

[94] Quek F, McNeill D, Bryll R, *et al.* Multimodal human discourse: Gesture and speech. ACM Transactions on Computer-Human Interaction.

2002;9(3): 171–193. Available from: https://doi.org/10.1145/568513. 568514.

[95]   Popescu GV, Burdea GC, and Trefftz H. Multimodal Interaction Modeling. In: Handbook of Virtual Environments: Design, Implementation, and Applications. USA: Taylor & Francis Group; 2002. p. 435–454.

[96]   Keshavarz B, Stelzmann D, Paillard A, *et al.* Visually induced motion sickness can be alleviated by pleasant odors. Experimental Brain Research. 2015;233(5):1353–1364.

[97]   Narumi T, Nishizaka S, Kajinami T, *et al.* Augmented reality flavors: Gustatory display based on edible marker and cross-modal interaction. In: Proceedings of the SIGCHI Conference on Human Factors in Computing Systems. CHI'11. New York, NY, USA: ACM; 2011. p. 93–102. Available from: http://doi.acm.org/10.1145/1978942.1978957.

[98]   Barfield W. Virtual Environments and Advanced Interface Design. New York, NY, USA: Oxford University Press; 1995.

[99]   Sacau A, Laarni J, and Hartmann T. Influence of individual factors on presence. Computers in Human Behavior. 2008;24(5):2255–2273.

[100] Menchaca-Brandan MA, Liu AM, Oman CM, *et al.* Influence of perspective-taking and mental rotation abilities in space teleoperation. In: Proceeding of the ACM/IEEE International Conference on Human–Robot Interaction – HRI'07. Arlington, Virginia, USA: ACM; 2007.

[101] Richard P, Burdea G, Gomez D, *et al.* A comparison of haptic, visual and auditive force feedback for deformable virtual objects. In: Proceedings of the International Conference on Automation Technology (ICAT). vol. 49. USA: Semantic Scholar; 1994. p. 62.

[102] Rock I and Victor J. Vision and touch: An experimentally created conflict between the two senses. Science. 1964;143(3606):594–596. Available from: https://science.sciencemag.org/content/143/3606/594.

[103] Klatzky RL, Loomis JM, Beall AC, *et al.* Spatial updating of self-position and orientation during real, imagined, and virtual locomotion. Psychological Science. 1998;9(4):293–298. Available from: http://www.jstor.org/stable/40063340.

[104] Burns E, Razzaque S, Whitton MC, *et al.* MACBETH: The avatar which I see before me and its movement toward my hand. In: 2007 IEEE Virtual Reality Conference. Charlotte, NC, USA: IEEE; 2007. p. 295–296.

[105] LaValle SM. Birds-Eye View, In Virtual Reality. Cambridge University Press; 2019. Available from: http://vr.cs.uiuc.edu/vrch2.pdf.

[106] Arthur EJ, Hancock PA, and Chrysler ST. The perception of spatial layout in real and virtual worlds. Ergonomics. 1997;40(1):69–77.

[107] Shilling RD and Shinn-Cunningham B. Virtual Auditory Displays. In: Handbook of Virtual Environments. USA: CRC Press; 2002. p. 105–132.

[108] Nagai Y, Tsuchiya S, Iida T, and Kimura S. Audio feedback system for teleoperation experiments on engineering test satellite VII system design and assessment using eye mark recorder for capturing task. In: IEEE Transactions on Systems, Man, and Cybernetics – Part A: Systems and Humans. 2002;32(2):237–247. doi: 10.1109/TSMCA.2002.1021111.

[109] Secoli R, Milot MH, Rosati G, *et al.* Effect of visual distraction and auditory feedback on patient effort during robot-assisted movement training after stroke. In: Journal of NeuroEngineering and Rehabilitation. USA: Pubmed (NIH); 2010.

[110] Simpson BD, Bolia RS, and Draper MH. Spatial audio display concepts supporting situation awareness for operators of unmanned aerial vehicles. In: Human Performance, Situation Awareness, and Automation: Current Research and Trends HPSAA II, vols. I and II. Netherlands: Springer; 2013. p. 61.

[111] Tachi S, Komoriya K, Sawada K, *et al.* Telexistence cockpit for humanoid robot control. Advanced Robotics. 2003;17(3):199–217. Available from: https://doi.org/10.1163/156855303764018468.

[112] Ferreira A and Mavroidis C. Virtual reality and haptics for nanorobotics. IEEE Robotics Automation Magazine. 2006;13(3):78–92.

[113] Xie H, Onal C, Régnier S, *et al.* Atomic Force Microscopy Based Nanorobotics: Modelling, Simulation, Setup Building and Experiments. vol. 71. Germany: Springer; 2011.

[114] Salcudean SE and Yan J. Towards a force-reflecting motion-scale system for microsurgery. In: Proceedings of the 1994 IEEE International Conference on Robotics and Automation. vol. 3. San Diego, CA, USA: IEEE; 1994. p. 2296–2301.

[115] Fukuda T, Tanie K, Mitsuoka T, *et al.* Dual mode control method of micromanipulator with visual feedback. IFAC Proceedings Volumes. 1988;21(16): 377–382. 2nd IFAC Symposium on Robot Control 1988 (SYROCO'88), Karlsruhe, FRG, 5–7 October. Available from: http://www.sciencedirect.com/science/article/pii/S147466701754639X.

[116] Gemperle F, Ota N, and Siewiorek D. Design of a wearable tactile display. In: Proceedings Fifth International Symposium on Wearable Computers (ISWC '01). Zurich, Switzerland: IEEE; 2001. p. 5–12.

[117] Bolopion A and Régnier S. A review of haptic feedback teleoperation systems for micromanipulation and microassembly. IEEE Transactions on Automation Science and Engineering. 2013;10(3):496–502.

[118] Cholewiak RW and Collins AA. The generation of vibrotactile patterns on a linear array: Influences of body site, time, and presentation mode. Perception & Psychophysics. 2000;62(6):1220–1235. Available from: https://doi.org/10.3758/BF03212124.

[119] Rochlis JL and Newman DJ. A tactile display for international space station (ISS) extravehicular activity (EVA). Aviation, Space, and Environmental Medicine. 2000;71(6):571–578.

[120] Brickler D, Babu SV, Bertrand J, *et al.* Towards evaluating the effects of stereoscopic viewing and haptic interaction on perception-action coordination. In: 2018 IEEE Conference on Virtual Reality and 3D User Interfaces (VR). Reutlingen, Germany: IEEE; 2018. p. 1–516.

[121] Pamungkas DS and Ward K. Tele-operation of a robot arm with electro tactile feedback. In: 2013 IEEE/ASME International Conference on Advanced Intelligent Mechatronics. Wollongong, NSW, Australia: IEEE; 2013. p. 704–709.

[122] Aleotti J, Bottazzi S, and Reggiani M. A Multimodal User Interface for Remote Object Exploration in Teleoperation Systems; 2002. Available from: https://pdfs.semanticscholar.org/98bd/ce82196ecb7e2f8f0f1a6a480f0a2a00e 80d.pdf.

[123] Azmandian M, Hancock M, Benko H, *et al.* Haptic retargeting: Dynamic repurposing of passive haptics for enhanced virtual reality experiences. In: Proceedings of the 2016 CHI Conference on Human Factors in Computing Systems. CHI '16. New York, NY, USA: Association for Computing Machinery; 2016. p. 1968–1979. Available from: https://doi.org/10.1145/2858036.2858226.

[124] Ullmer B and Ishii H. Emerging frameworks for tangible user interfaces. IBM Systems Journal. 2000;39(3–4):915–931. Available from: https://doi.org/10.1147/sj.393.0915.

[125] Cizmeci B, Xu X, Chaudhari R, *et al.* A multiplexing scheme for multimodal teleoperation. ACM Transactions on Multimedia Computing, Communications, and Applications. 2017;13(2):21:1–21:28. Available from: http://doi.acm.org/10.1145/3063594.

[126] Lathan CE and Tracey M. The effects of operator spatial perception and sensory feedback on human–robot teleoperation performance. Presence: Teleoperators & Virtual Environments. 2002;11(4):368–377. Available from: http://dx.doi.org/10.1162/105474602760204282.

[127] Martins H and Ventura R. Immersive 3-D teleoperation of a search and rescue robot using a head-mounted display. In: 2009 IEEE Conference on Emerging Technologies & Factory Automation. Mallorca, Spain: IEEE; 2009.

[128] Arkin RC and Ali KS. Integration of reactive and telerobotic control in multi-agent robotic systems. In: Proceedings of the 3rd International Conference on Simulation of Adaptive Behavior: From Animals to Animats 3: From Animals to Animats 3 (SAB94). Cambridge, MA, USA: MIT Press; 1994. p. 473–478.

[129] Cheng G and Zelinsky A. Supervised autonomy: A paradigm for teleoperating mobile robots. In: Proceedings of the 1997 IEEE/RSJ International Conference on Intelligent Robot and Systems. Innovative Robotics for Real-World Applications. IROS'97. vol. 2. Cambridge, MA, USA: ACM; 1997. p. 1169–1176.

[130] Berger C, Gonzalez-Franco M, Ofek E, *et al.* The uncanny valley of haptics. Science Robotics. 2018;3:eaar7010.

[131] Ghazanfar AA and Schroeder CE. Is neocortex essentially multisensory? Trends in Cognitive Sciences. 2006;10:278–85.

[132] Amedi A, Malach R, Hendler T, *et al.* Visuo-haptic object-related activation in the ventral visual pathway. Nature Neuroscience. 2001;4:324–330.

[133] James T, Keith Humphrey G, Gati S, *et al.* Haptic study of three-dimensional objects activates extrastriate visual areas. Neuropsychologia. 2002;40: 1706–1714.

[134] Sathian K and Zangaladze A. Feeling with the mind's eye: Contribution of visual cortex to tactile perception. Behavioural Brain Research. 2002;135:127–132.

[135] Helbig HB and Ernst M. Optimal integration of shape information from vision and touch. Experimental Brain Research. 2007;179:595–606.

[136] Mnih V, Kavukcuoglu K, Silver D, *et al.* Human-level control through deep reinforcement learning. Nature. 2015;518(7540):529.

[137] Espeholt L, Soyer H, Munos R, *et al.* Impala: Scalable distributed deep-RL with importance weighted actor-learner architectures. Computing Research Repository (CoRR), arXiv preprint arXiv:180201561. 2018.

[138] Schulman J, Levine S, Abbeel P, *et al.* Trust region policy optimization. In: International Conference on Machine Learning. Lille, France: ACM; 2015. p. 1889–1897.

[139] Rajeswaran A, Kumar V, Gupta A, *et al.* Learning Complex Dexterous Manipulation With Deep Reinforcement Learning and Demonstrations. USA: RSS; 2017.

[140] Peng XB, Andrychowicz M, Zaremba W, *et al.* Sim-to-real transfer of robotic control with dynamics randomization. In: 2018 IEEE International Conference on Robotics and Automation (ICRA). Brisbane, QLD, Australia: IEEE; 2018. p. 1–8.

[141] Sadeghi F and Levine S. CAD2RL: Real Single-Image Flight Without a Single Real Image. USA: RSS; 2016.

[142] Kumar V and Todorov E. MuJoCo HAPTIX: A virtual reality system for hand manipulation. In: 2015 IEEE-RAS 15th International Conference on Humanoid Robots (Humanoids). Seoul, South Korea: IEEE; 2015. p. 657–663.

[143] Haarnoja T, Zhou A, Abbeel P, *et al.* Soft actor-critic: Off-policy maximum entropy deep reinforcement learning with a stochastic actor. Computing Research Repository (CoRR), arXiv preprint arXiv:180101290. 2018.

[144] Reddy S, Dragan AD, and Levine S. SQIL: Imitation Learning via Reinforcement Learning With Sparse Rewards. USA: DBLP; 2019.

[145] Ziebart BD, Maas A, Bagnell JA, *et al.* Maximum entropy inverse reinforcement learning. In: Proceedings of the 23rd National Conference on Artificial Intelligence. AAAI'08. vol. 3. Chicago, IL, USA: AAAI Press; 2008. p. 1433–1438.

[146] Frith CD, Wolpert DM, Schaal S, *et al.* Computational approaches to motor learning by imitation. Philosophical Transactions of the Royal Society of London Series B: Biological Sciences. 2003;358(1431):537–547. Available from: https://royalsocietypublishing.org/doi/abs/10.1098/rstb.2002.1258.

[147] Argall BD, Chernova S, Veloso M, *et al.* A survey of robot learning from demonstration. Robotics and Autonomous Systems. 2009;57(5):469–483. Available from: https://doi.org/10.1016/j.robot.2008.10.024.

[148] Ekvall S and Kragic D. Interactive grasp learning based on human demonstration. In: IEEE International Conference on Robotics and Automation, 2004. Proceedings. ICRA'04. vol. 4. New Orleans, LA, USA: IEEE; 2004. p. 3519–3524.

[149] Pomerleau DA. Efficient training of artificial neural networks for autonomous navigation. Neural Computation. 1991;3(1):88–97.

[150]   Ross S, Gordon G, and Bagnell J. A reduction of imitation learning and structured prediction to no-regret online learning. Journal of Machine Learning Research – Proceedings Track. 2010;15.

[151]   Ho J and Ermon S. Generative Adversarial Imitation Learning. Barcelona, Spain: NIPS; 2016.

[152]   Cherubini A, Passama R, Crosnier A, *et al.* Collaborative manufacturing with physical human–robot interaction. Robotics and Computer-Integrated Manufacturing. 2016;40:1–13. Available from: http://www.sciencedirect.com/science/article/pii/S0736584515301769.

[153]   Krüger J, Lien TK, and Verl A. Cooperation of human and machines in assembly lines. CIRP Annals. 2009;58(2):628–646. Available from: http://www.sciencedirect.com/science/article/pii/S0007850609001760.

[154]   LaValle SM. Robotic Interfaces, Frontiers, In Virtual Reality. IL, USA: Cambridge University Press; 2017.

[155]   Lebedev MA and Nicolelis MAl. Brain–machine interfaces: Past, present and future. Trends in Neurosciences. 2006;29(9):536–546. Available from: sads.

[156]   Lecuyer A, George L, and Marchal M. Toward adaptive VR simulators combining visual, haptic, and brain-computer interfaces. IEEE Computer Graphics and Applications. 2013;33(5):18–23.

[157]   Burwell S, Sample M, and Racine E. Ethical aspects of brain computer interfaces: a scoping review. BMC Medical Ethics. 2017;18(1).

[158]   Wolpaw JR, Birbaumer N, Mcfarland DJ, *et al.* Brain–computer interfaces for communication and control. Clinical Neurophysiology. 2002;113(6): 767–791.

[159]   Mahler J, Liang J, Niyaz S, *et al.*. Dex-Net 2.0: Deep Learning to Plan Robust Grasps With Synthetic Point Clouds and Analytic Grasp Metrics. USA: RSS; 2017.

[160]   Shimoga KB. Robot grasp synthesis algorithms: A survey. The International Journal of Robotics Research. 1996.

[161]   Mahler J, Liang J, Niyaz S, *et al.* Dex-Net 2.0: Deep learning to plan robust grasps with synthetic point clouds and analytic grasp metrics. CoRR. 2017.

[162]   Roa MA and Suárez R. Grasp quality measures: Review and performance. Autonomous Robots. 2015.

[163]   Ferrari C and Canny J. Planning optimal grasps. In: Proceedings 1992 IEEE International Conference on Robotics and Automation. Nice, France: IEEE; 1992.

[164]   Pollard NS. Synthesizing grasps from generalized prototypes. In: Proceedings of IEEE International Conference on Robotics and Automation. Minneapolis, MN, USA: IEEE; 1996.

[165]   Hangl S, Ugur E, Szedmak S, *et al.* Reactive, task-specific object manipulation by metric reinforcement learning. In: 2015 International Conference on Advanced Robotics (ICAR). Istanbul, Turkey: IEEE; 2015.

[166]   Merzic H, Bogdanovic M, Kappler D, *et al.* Leveraging contact forces for learning to grasp. In: 2019 IEEE International Conference on Robotics and Automation (ICRA). Montreal, QC, Canada: IEEE; 2019.

[167] OpenAI, Andrychowicz M, Baker B, *et al.* Learning dexterous in-hand manipulation. CoRR. 2018.

[168] Chemero A. An outline of a theory of affordances. Ecological Psychology. 2003.

[169] Sahbani A, El-Khoury S, and Bidaud P. An overview of 3D object grasp synthesis algorithms. Robotics and Autonomous Systems. 2012.

[170] Ponce J and Faverjon B. On computing three-finger force-closure grasps of polygonal objects. IEEE Transactions on Robotics and Automation. 1995.

[171] Zhu X and Wang J. Synthesis of force-closure grasps on 3-D objects based on the Q distance. IEEE Transactions on Robotics and Automation. 2003.

[172] Schaal S, Ijspeert AJ, and Billard A. Computational approaches to motor learning by imitation. Philosophical Transaction of the Royal Society of London, Series B. 2003.

[173] Ekvall S and Kragic D. Interactive grasp learning based on human demonstration. In: IEEE International Conference on Robotics and Automation, 2004. Proceedings. ICRA'04. New Orleans, LA, USA: IEEE; 2004.

[174] Argall BD, Chernova S, Veloso M, *et al.* A survey of robot learning from demonstration. Robotics and Autonomous Systems. 2009.

[175] Bohg J, Morales A, Asfour T, *et al.* Data-driven grasp synthesis: A survey. IEEE Transactions on Robotics. 2014.

[176] Kappler D, Bohg J, and Schaal S. Leveraging big data for grasp planning. In: 2015 IEEE International Conference on Robotics and Automation (ICRA). Seattle, WA, USA: IEEE; 2015.

[177] Pinto L and Gupta A. Supersizing self-supervision: Learning to grasp from 50K tries and 700 robot hours. CoRR. 2015.

[178] Levine S, Pastor P, Krizhevsky A, *et al.* Learning hand-eye coordination for robotic grasping with deep learning and large-scale data collection. CoRR. 2016.

[179] Kokic M, Stork JA, Haustein JA, *et al.* Affordance detection for task-specific grasping using deep learning. In: 2017 IEEE-RAS 17th International Conference on Humanoid Robotics (Humanoids). Birmingham, UK: IEEE; 2017.

[180] Detry R, Papon J, and Matthies L. Task-oriented grasping with semantic and geometric scene understanding. In: 2017 IEEE/RSJ International Conference on Intelligent Robots and Systems (IROS). Vancouver, BC, Canada: IEEE; 2017.

[181] Hang K, Li M, Stork JA, *et al.* Hierarchical fingertip space: A unified framework for grasp planning and in-hand grasp adaptation. IEEE Transactions on Robotics. 2016.

[182] Zeng A, Song S, Lee J, *et al.* TossingBot: Learning to throw arbitrary objects with residual physics. CoRR. 2019.

[183] Kevin Z, Mohit S, Manuela V, *et al.* Leveraging Multimodal Haptic Sensory Data for Robust Cutting. Toronto, ON, Canada: Humanoids; 2019.

[184] Agrawal P, Nair A, Abbeel P, *et al.* Learning to poke by poking: Experiential learning of intuitive physics. CoRR. 2016.

[185] Kalashnikov D, Irpan A, Pastor P, *et al*. QT-Opt: Scalable deep reinforcement learning for vision-based robotic manipulation. CoRR. 2018.

[186] Zeng A, Song S, Welker S, *et al*. Learning synergies between pushing and grasping with self-supervised deep reinforcement learning. CoRR. 2018.

[187] Chebotar Y, Hausman K, Su Z, *et al*. Self-supervised regrasping using spatio-temporal tactile features and reinforcement learning. In: 2016 IEEE/RSJ International Conference on Intelligent Robots and Systems (IROS). Daejeon, South Korea: IEEE; 2016.

[188] Quillen D, Jang E, Nachum O, *et al*. Deep reinforcement learning for vision-based robotic grasping: A simulated comparative evaluation of off-policy methods. CoRR. 2018.

[189] Gu S, Holly E, Lillicrap TP, *et al*. Deep reinforcement learning for robotic manipulation. CoRR. 2016.

[190] Balaguer B and Carpin S. Combining imitation and reinforcement learning to fold deformable planar objects. In: 2011 IEEE/RSJ International Conference on Intelligent Robots and Systems. San Francisco, CA, USA: IEEE; 2011.

[191] Matas J, James S, and Davison AJ. Sim-to-real reinforcement learning for deformable object manipulation. CoRR. 2018.

[192] James S, Ma Z, Arrojo DR, and Davison AJ. RLBench: The Robot Learning Benchmark & Learning Environment. USA: ARXIV (Cornell University); 2019.

[193] Zhu H, Gupta A, Rajeswaran A, *et al*. Dexterous manipulation with deep reinforcement learning: Efficient, general, and low-cost. CoRR. 2018.

[194] Rajeswaran A, Kumar V, Gupta A, *et al*. Learning complex dexterous manipulation with deep reinforcement learning and demonstrations. CoRR. 2017.

[195] Akkaya I, Andrychowicz M, Chociej M, *et al*. Solving Rubik's Cube With a Robot Hand. USA: ARXIV (Cornell University); 2019.

[196] Suzuki Y, Koyama K, Ming A, *et al*. Grasping strategy for moving object using net-structure proximity sensor and vision sensor. In: 2015 IEEE International Conference on Robotics and Automation (ICRA). Seattle, WA, USA: IEEE; 2015.

[197] Marturi N, Kopicki M, Rastegarpanah A, *et al*. Dynamic grasp and trajectory planning for moving objects. Autonomous Robots. 2019.

[198] Kroemer OB, Detry R, Piater J, *et al*. Combining active learning and reactive control for robot grasping. Robotics and Autonomous Systems. 2010.

[199] Hang K, Stork JA, Pollard NS, *et al*. A framework for optimal grasp contact planning. IEEE Robotics and Automation Letters. 2017.

[200] Triantafyllidis E, Mcgreavy C, Gu J, and Li Z. Study of Multimodal Interfaces and the Improvements on Teleoperation. IEEE Access. 2020;8:78213–78227. Available from: doi: 10.1109/ACCESS.2020.2990080.

Chapter 5

Visual object tracking by quadrotor AR.Drone using artificial neural networks and fuzzy logic controller

Kamel Boudjit[1] Cherif Larbes[2] and Naeem Ramzan[3]

5.1 Introduction

Visual object tracking is a very critical issue in computer vision and video processing [1]. Real-time object detection is crucial as well for many applications of unmanned aerial vehicles (UAVs). These latter have a huge number of real-time applications that include surveillance, navigation, search-and-rescue, robotics, and so on. Despite the efforts and achievements that were made during the last decades, real-time object tracking remains a very challenging problem due to the loss of information caused by the projection of the 3D world on a 2D image, to the complex object motion, to the illumination changes and the real-time processing requirements [2]. A considerable progress has been made in recent years to address these visual object tracking issues in UAVs. The use of artificial intelligence (AI) has given a new impetus and new directions to the visual tracking research [3,4]

In this study, we consider the visual object-tracking problem in order to find an efficient and useful method for UAV. The aim of this study is to demonstrate the feasibility and the potential of incorporating AI into autonomous target tracking for UAVs applications. A proof-of-concept prototype was developed based on the UAV platform Parrot AR.Drone 2.0 and by using the Robot Operating System (ROS) and the package ardrone_autonomy simulated in Gazebo simulator.

In the first section of this work, a fuzzy logic controller (FLC) is used for visual object tracking by using the AR.Drone 2.0 and visual information feedback. Fuzzy logic is used for its ability to shape the control surfaces generated by the rules of the fuzzy inference system. In order to guarantee a correct recognition of the target by the AR.Drone 2.0, a quick response (QR) code and ar_track_alvar package in ROS have been used as target marker. Visual feedback is provided by identification of visual tags, using open-source software FuzzyLite to calculate the tag identification match and

[1] Department of Instrumentation and Automation, University of Science and Technology Houari Boumediene USTHB, Algiers, Algeria
[2] Department of Electronic, Ecole Nationale Polytechnique, ENP, Algiers, Algeria
[3] Department of Computing Engineering, University of the West of Scotland, UWS, Paisley, UK

orientation. The proposed algorithm is based on a small number of input parameters, which reduces the requirements for high computing power. The developed algorithm was validated by simulation studies and in-flight tests.

A new solution based on artificial neural network (ANN) technology is proposed in the second section of this work. In the last few years ANNs have emerged as a powerful class of models for image recognition and are widely considered in the computer vision community to be de facto the standard approach for most problems. However, ANN-based object detection is an extremely demanding task in terms of computation, usually necessitating high-end graphics processing units (GPUs) that involve too much power and weight, major drawbacks for a lightweight drone. The ANN technology provides a number of tools that could form the basis for a potentially fruitful approach to the object-tracking problem. To overcome the previous problems, multilayer perceptron (MLP) is used for this purpose in this work. Simulation and experimental results are presented to demonstrate the feasibility of the proposed method for visual object tracking.

The overall aim of this project is to research and investigate into methods using AI for autonomous tracking target and navigation, also determine the best solutions and to implement these solutions with the use of an AR.Drone that the drone can navigate itself and find a target. The key contributions of this chapter are as follows:

- Object detection based on AI fuzzy logic and neural network is extremely computationally demanding, typically requiring high-end GPUs. In our application, experiments on real data show promising results obtained on a standard CPU and pave the way toward future research in this direction.
- We present a method for supervising the training of an ANN, aiming to reduce the computational complexity of an algorithm for target tracking based on fuzzy Mamdani logic. This method avoids human interpretation errors and reduces the work needed to create a functional set of classes while maintaining the characteristics and intelligence of the original controller.
- Target tracking is based on an intelligent system that can be easily generalized to track any visual pattern in dynamic scenes.
- This work aims to use a visual-based control mechanism to control a quadrotortype aerial robot, which is in pursuit of a target. The nonlinear nature of a quadrotor, on the one hand, and the difficulty of obtaining an exact model for it, on the other hand, constitute two serious challenges in designing a controller for this UAV.
- Both simulated and experimental studies have been carried out, and based on the results of these studies it has been argued that the fuzzy logic and neural network controllers can be applied effectively to the target tracking using a drone.

5.2   System overview

This chapter addresses the autonomous target tracking by UAV using vision-based method and AI since they show a potential capability to solve robotics problems [5–8]. In this study, AR.Drone 2.0 developed by Parrot has been chosen as the research platform due to its low cost and easily availability. Two different control algorithms, FLC and neural network, have been developed for the target tracking control. The positions of the target relative to the location of the drone were used as input signals [8].

As previously mentioned, the quadrotor is programmed to have three operating modes: the identification, target tracking, and keep the position of the drone in front of the target.

The developed using Artificial Intelligence (AI) controllers are implemented in the AR.Drone UAV by using a dynamic look-and-move serving architecture as presented in Figure 5.1. In this scheme, the velocity references generated by the controller (running onboard drone) are used as input references for the quadrotor [9].

The platform runs under Robot Operating System (ROS) [10]. ROS is an open-source framework for developing robotic control systems [11]. The framework facilitates communications between different modules by using a centralized message-passing interface. Multiple modules can be used as components for a larger system.

The advantage of this system is the multithreading processing capability associated with real-time operation system. The computer, attached to the AR.Drone, makes the high-level processing. Embedded in the computer are the operating system Ubuntu, ROS Indigo framework and the Gazebo simulator for data exchange between computer and UAV. The ar_track_alvar is responsible for visual pattern recognition of the target spot. Therefore, a fully onboard system is used [12].

5.2.1 Control system

The first assumption made when implementing the controller is: if the quadrotor is correctly oriented toward the target, the tracking control resumes to a distance control (the distance control is calculated by considering that the quadrotor is always well oriented to the target, making the range correction independent of any angular variable). Figure 5.2 describes this situation, especially when the orientation has also to be corrected.

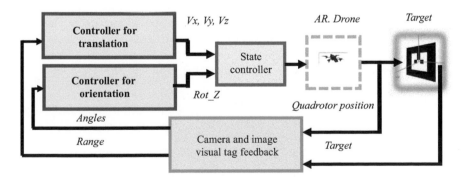

Figure 5.1   Block diagram of the target tracking using intelligent control system

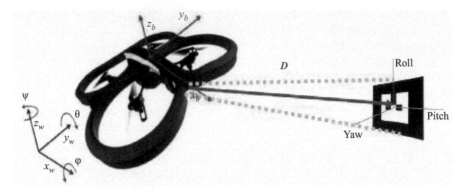

Figure 5.2 Depiction of control tasks

Figure 5.2 shows that, for a fixed target, the angle relative to the quadrotor longitudinal axis decreases as the distance to it increases. When D tends to infinity, the orientation angle correction tends to zero.

The variable T is the desired target position. The coordinates (X_T, Y_T, Z_T) are related to the target. D is the distance between the quadcopter center and the center of the target. The tracking task is to control the quadcopter in order to maintain a minimum orientation angle and positional error on track a visual marker. For that purpose, the quadcopter needs to translate across both the x- and y-axes to reduce the positional error and rotate along the z-axis to reduce the orientation error.

5.2.2 *Quadrotor dynamic model*

Drones have relatively simple structure, yet they are capable of performing a wide variety of movement patterns and exhibiting high maneuverability. They have six degrees of freedom, which consist of three translational and three rotational components. Pitch is corresponding to a rotational movement along y-axis and generates a translational movement along the x-axis. Similarly, roll is corresponding to a rotational movement along x-axis, which results in a translational movement along the y-axis. Figure 5.3 shows the quadrotor coordinate frames based on the Newton–Euler approach.

The dynamic model is presented as follows [13]:

$$
\begin{cases}
\ddot{x} = u_1(\cos\varphi \sin\theta \cos\omega + \sin\varphi \cos\omega) \\
\ddot{y} = u_1(\cos\varphi \sin\theta \cos\omega - \sin\varphi \cos\omega) \\
\quad \ddot{z} = u_1(\cos\varphi \cos\theta) - g \\
\quad\quad \ddot{\varphi} = u_2 l \\
\quad\quad \ddot{\theta} = u_3 l \\
\quad\quad \ddot{\omega} = u_4
\end{cases}
\tag{5.1}
$$

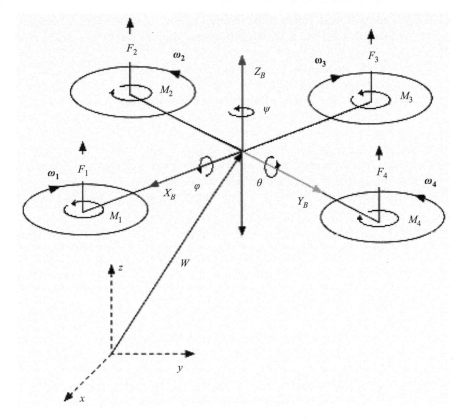

Figure 5.3   Quadrotor coordinate frames

where $(x, y, z)^T$ is the relative position of the mass center of the quadrotor with respect to an inertial coordinate frame, g is the gravitational acceleration, and l is the length from the mass center to the rotor. $(\varphi, \theta, \psi)^T$ are the three Euler angles that represent the attitude of the quadrotor, namely, the roll–pitch–yaw of the quadrotor. These angles are limited by

$$-\pi/2 < \varphi < \pi/2, -\pi/2 < \theta < \pi/2 \text{ and } -\pi < \psi < \pi$$

u_1 is the thrust force vector in the body system, u_2, u_3, and u_4 are, respectively, the control inputs of roll, pitch, and yaw moments.

5.3   Fuzzy-logic-based identification and target tracking

Our research is concerned with search target and obstacle avoidance for autonomous quadrotor. Some methods use mathematical models, which may cause an increase of calculations. The workload of the computer will hold up the calculation speed so the running UAV will receive data far on in time. Hence, the completed, refined, and succinct AI method is needed if we want to pursuit a good target-tracking system [14–16].

In order to manage uncertainty and imprecision, we used FLC (see Figure 5.1) that can be implemented successfully to manage complex systems. The advantage to using fuzzy systems is the possibility of using approximation in cases where analytical functions are not very useful or do not exist at all. An FLC system gives the possibility of closely monitoring every step, and even switching the mode given a certain context [17–19]. The fact that fuzzy logic can be fault tolerant is especially useful in environments where the degree of uncertainty is high, such as when autonomously landing. All constraints and factors are calculated and taken into account by the FLC before making the final decision, which makes this controller a good choice for unknown, dangerous environments.

5.3.1   Simulation studies

The aim of the controller is to generate desired yaw commands for the vehicle based on the location of the target in the image plane. This section will describe the details of this controller.

To develop the fuzzy controllers, we used a combination of Robot Operating System (ROS), ROS Gazebo [20] with the tum_ardrone simulator [21], ROS package ar_track_alvar, and tools from FuzzyLite. ROS is a software package that allows for the transport of sensor and control data via "topics" using the publisher/subscriber message-passing model. The tum_ardrone simulator is a package for ROS Gazebo

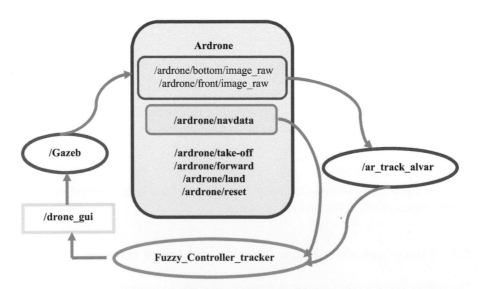

Figure 5.4   Interaction between all the active processes from Gazebo and ROS during the simulator tests

that allows for simulation of the AR.Drone in 3D environments. FuzzyLite is an open-source FLC library, written in C++, which has a graphical user interface (GUI) [22], called QtFuzzyLite, for designing FLCs. Figure 5.4 shows the configuration of nodes in ROS for performing tracking control.

In Figure 5.4, the green node is the target-tracking controller node named "fuzzy_tracker." As inputs, the node takes a calculated pose relative to the center of the detected target and the target identity descriptor (ID). With the inputs, the node creates a control vector based on the ID and calculated pose of the target. ROS Gazebo (blue node) was used for simulating the image streams coming from the AR.Drone. Scenes from the simulator were extracted using camera-emulating nodes built into the "tum_simulator." With the image streams, the "ar_track_alvar" (red node) is able to process the images and provide feedback to the "fuzzy_tracker."

The rxgraph tool in ROS, which can inspect and monitor any ROS graph at runtime, automatically generated the previous graph. Its output renders nodes as ovals, topics as squares, and connectivity as arcs.

The workflow of the design of the FLC by using both software and hardware is listed as follows:

1.   Modify membership functions and/or rules in FuzzyLite GUI.
2.   Export FLC C++ code using FuzzyLite GUI.
3.   Insert generated code into simulated controller in ROS and compile.
4.   Run controller ROS node with Tum_simulator (Gazebo).
5.   Go to step 6 if controller is ready, if not repeat step 4.
6.   Run controller ROS node with Ardrone_autonomy drivers and AR.Drone 2.0 hardware.
7.   Repeat steps 1–6, if the hardware test of the controller exhibits unwanted behavior.

The defuzzification algorithm should be clear, and the process that determines the output signal should be identified clearly. In addition, the defuzzification should be logical and should have high membership degree. It should correspond to approximately the middle of the graph. For the reasons discussed previously, we have selected the center of gravity method for the FLCs. This can be calculated using the following equation:

$$C \cdot G = \frac{\sum_{i=1}^{n} o_i \cdot \mu_i}{\sum_{i=1}^{n} \mu_i} \tag{5.2}$$

where n represents the number of elements of the sampled membership functions. The maximum value of n is equal to the number of fuzzy rules in the fuzzy logic system. μ_i represents the weights of the n rules and is the output variable of the fuzzy set.

To reach the coordinate of the desired target (desired tag), a roll control loop and one fuzzy input are designed, which are the desired coordinates of y and the y-position from the NavData. The range of the fuzzification is -1 to 1 m, which is stated in five Gaussian membership functions. Meanwhile, the fuzzy output is the roll value in the range of -1 to 0, which is stated in two Gaussian membership functions. Table 5.1 shows names of I/O membership functions for translation motion along x-axis.

Table 5.1   Names of inputs/outputs membership functions for translation motion along x-axis

Input	Input MF	Output	Output MF
Ar_pose_x	Close	Cmd_y_vel	Left_1
Ar_pose_x	Close_1	Cmd_y_vel	Left_2
Ar_pose_x	Close	Cmd_y_vel	Right_1
Ar_pose_x	Close_1	Cmd_y_vel	Right_1
Ar_pose_x	Close_1	Cmd_y_vel	Right_2
Ar_pose_x	Close	Cmd_y_vel	Right_2

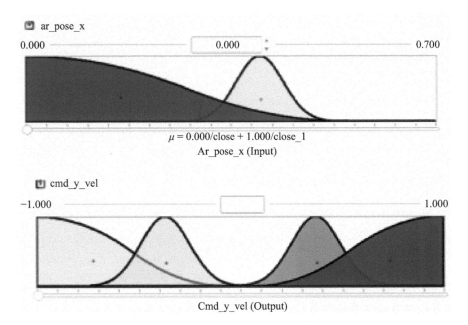

Figure 5.5   Membership functions for translation along x-axis using QtFuzzyLite

Figure 5.5 shows membership functions for all the inputs and the outputs for translation along x-axis using FuzzyLite.

Table 5.2 lists the names of inputs/outputs membership functions for translation motion along y-axis.

Figure 5.6 shows membership functions for all the inputs and the outputs for translation along y-axis using FuzzyLite.

After applying the fuzzy rules that were set to the fuzzified input variables, the results must be defuzzified in order to get a crisp output for the quadrotor's actuators. Overall, there are four outputs corresponding to the direction of spin and amount of thrust that each actuator must apply in order for the quadrotor to complete a stabilized

Table 5.2   Names of inputs/outputs membership functions for translation motion along y-axis

Input	Input MF	Output	Output MF
Ar_pose_y	Left_2	Cmd_x_vel	Forward
Ar_pose_y	Left_1	Cmd_x_vel	Forward_1
Ar_pose_y	Center	Cmd_x_vel	Forward_1
Ar_pose_y	Center	Cmd_x_vel	Forward
Ar_pose_y	Right_1	Cmd_x_vel	Forward_1
Ar_pose_y	Right_2	Cmd_x_vel	Forward

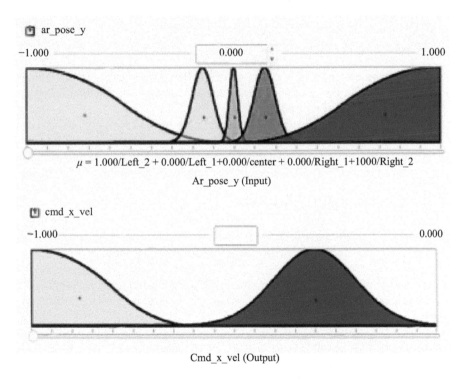

Figure 5.6   Membership functions for translation along y-axis using QtFuzzyLite

point-to-point movement. Finally, defuzzifier is performed using the center of gravity method. It performs defuzzification by finding the center of the area encompassed by all the rules. The rules for the translation motion controller along *y*-axis and *x*-axis are as follows:

✓ if ar_pose_y is Left_2 and ar_pose_x is close then cmd_x_vel is forward and cmd_y_vel is left_1

✓   if ar_pose_y is Left_1 and ar_pose_x is close_1 then cmd_x_vel is forward_1 and cmd_y_vel is left_2
✓   if ar_pose_y is center and ar_pose_x is close then cmd_x_vel is forward_1 and cmd_y_vel is right_1
✓   if ar_pose_y is center and ar_pose_x is close_1 then cmd_x_vel is forward and cmd_y_vel is right_2
✓   if ar_pose_y is Right_1 and ar_pose_x is close_1 then cmd_x_vel is forward_1 and cmd_y_vel is right_2
✓   if ar_pose_y is Right_2 and ar_pose_x is close then cmd_x_vel is forward and cmd_y_vel is right_1

Figure 5.7 represents generated plot of the output surface of a fuzzy inference system using the first two inputs and the two outputs.

The algorithm of the FLC is implemented in the AR.Drone, which is flown autonomously in a closed space using ROS, the procedures for testing are as follows:

1.   Through the ROS software, the AR.Drone is flown in hover mode 1 m from the ground. That point is called the initial position with the coordinates value (0,0,1), for 5 s, before the search for the target.
2.   By switching off the hovering mode, the AR.Drone will fly autonomously with the designed FLC controller toward the desired target spot.
3.   After activation of the automatic mode the AR.Drone heads straight for the first target, if it is not the desired target, the AR.Drone will avoid this target by turning left.
4.   For the second, third, and fourth targets, the quadrotor will avoid these targets to reach the desired target.
5.   Once the desired target is in the quadrotor's field of view, the AR.Drone will recognize the target and move toward it, with a safety distance of 1 m.

In this work, an FLC-based path planning was designed to avoid obstacles and search target while the quadrotor is in motion. Assumptions have been made to verify the effectiveness of the proposed controller.

Figure 5.8 shows the environment in Gazebo simulator, consisting of five targets. The quadrotor must avoid the first, second, third, and fourth targets and at the end, it must position itself in front of the desired target; the line in yellow shows the path that the quadrotor must go. Navigation using FLC is the process of directing and controlling the movement of an AR.Drone from one target to another. It requires the determination of the direction in which it has to go to reach the desired destination.

In this section, we show the simulation result utilizing our FLC algorithm. In the simulation, the drone task is to reach the desired position and target. Figure 5.9 shows the different sequences of simulation with obstacle avoidance and target tracking.

In this test, the quadrotor moves toward each target, after identification if the target is not desired the drone avoids it. At the end, the quadrotor goes directly to the desired target.

Figure 5.10 illustrates the path traveled by the quadrotor.

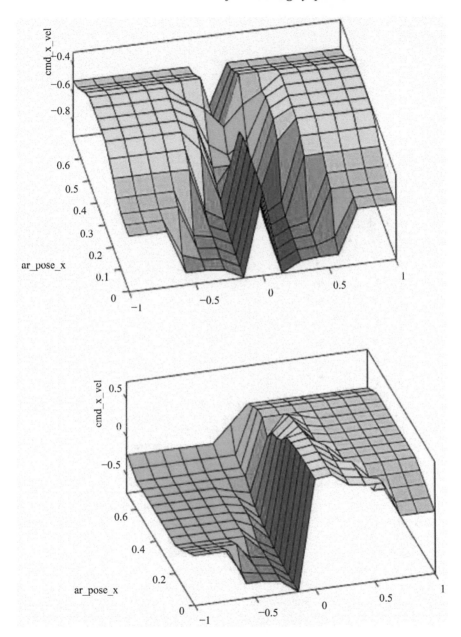

Figure 5.7   Sample fuzzy logic control surface

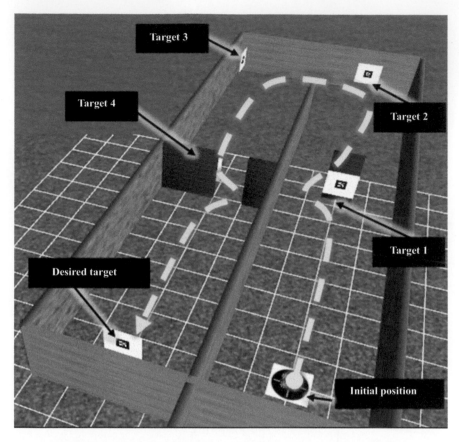

Figure 5.8   General view of the simulation environment in Gazebo

The image received from the quadrotor is reformatted to a binary image. ar_track_alvar searches for the defining features of a QR-code; if found it determines the location of the three corner squares. The AR.Drone can calculate the dimensions of the QR-code as observed by its camera. Combining the size and the location of its corner squares, a bounding box is drawn around the QR-code. This bounding box is passed on to the ardrone_fuzzy_controller for initiating its tracking functions. After doing so ar_track_alvar attempts to decode the QR-code; if successful its contents will be displayed in the interface Gazebo. The video related to the tests presented in this section is available in https://www.youtube.com/watch?v=JI0rSwWIC_I.

In this second simulation test, three targets have been introduced. The quadrotor must avoid the first and the second targets to reach the desired one. Figures 5.11 and 5.12 show the scenario of the simulation using ROS Gazebo.

In this test, the quadrotor moves to the first target. If the target is not desired, the quadrotor avoids it. In the second step, the quadrilateral moves toward the second target and avoids the same, if it has the undesired marker In the third step of this test,

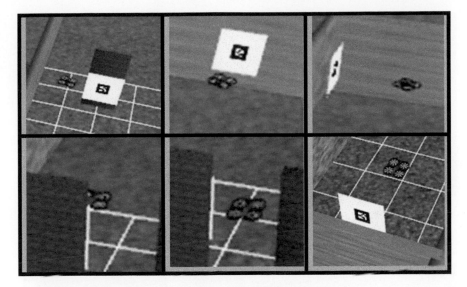

Figure 5.9 Different sequences of simulation

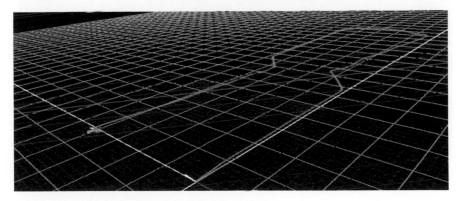

Figure 5.10 Illustration of the trajectory traveled by the quadrotor under RViz–Gazebo

the quadrotor goes directly to the desired target. Figure 5.13 shows the path traversed by the quadrotor to reach the target.

5.3.2 Experimental setup

In the hardware setup achieved for the experiments, a laptop was used for both communication and control of the AR.Drone 2.0 quadrotor. ROS was used to control the drone in the same way as for the simulation studies. For testing the developed FLCs on the hardware, the configuration presented in Figure 5.14 was used.

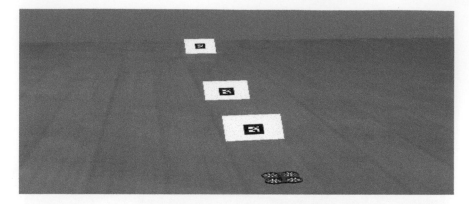

Figure 5.11   The scenario of the second simulation test under Gazebo ROS

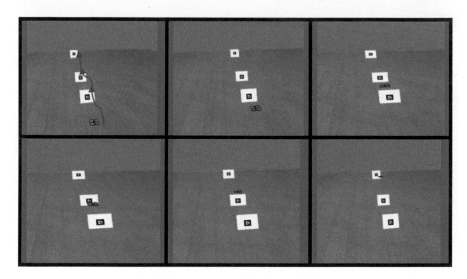

Figure 5.12   Simulation results with obstacle avoidance

Controllers from red node (Ardrone_Driver) and blue node (Fuzzy_Tracker) were used on the hardware for hovering and tracking target respectively. The Ardrone_autonomy node displays the raw camera feed and the telemetry data coming in from the drone. Other nodes for path planning and navigation use this information.

After the connection has been established, the application immediately starts streaming the video obtained from the front camera of the quadrotor. When the target (tag) is visible to the quadrotor, a red frame appears around the target. This will freeze the video stream so that it is possible to draw a bounded box and as precisely as possible, so that it does not contain a lot of background, but only the desired object.

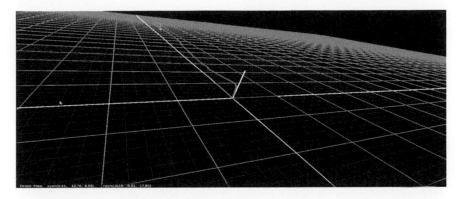

Figure 5.13   Illustration of the trajectory recorded by the RViz–Gazebo

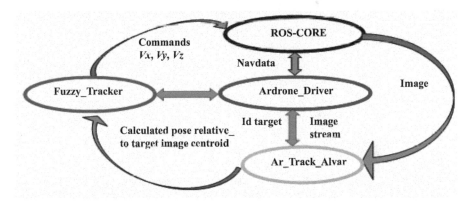

Figure 5.14   ROS software configuration for hardware experimentation

After pressing the Start tracking button, it is recommended to move the quad-copter or the object slightly for about 10–15 s, so that the algorithm initiates the target tracking process. If the target-tracking algorithm is capable of tracking the selected object, it displays a red square around the target. In addition, a line connecting the current center of the bounded box and the center of the image will reveal the horizontal and vertical displacement of the quadcopter. Then, after pressing the Take-off button, the quadcopter will take off and start following the object autonomously. Then, the FLC process is activated. During the next 5 s, the controller sends commands to the AR.Drone. Figure 5.15 shows some images captured by the camera during the execution of this test whereas parts (a) and (b) of Figure 5.15 show the beginning of the test and parts (c) and (d) show the captured image at the middle of the test. Figure 5.15(e) shows the quadrotor near the target.

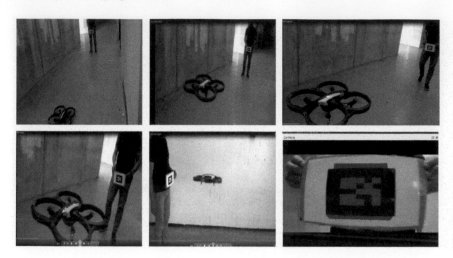

Figure 5.15   Real-time experiments show the performance of the proposed target-tracking system: (a) initial position, (b) take-off, (c) location, (d) target tracking, (e) safety distance, and (f) camera capture

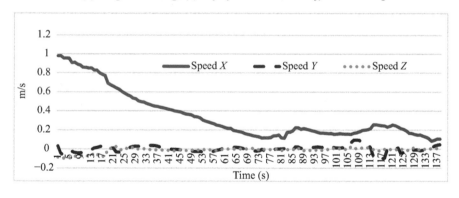

Figure 5.16   Evolution of the speed of the quadrotor along the axes X, Y, and Z

One notes from Figure 5.15(e) that the AR.Drone follows the object with a fixed safe distance and retains the image of the target centered on its front camera. From Figure 5.15 and all the experimental results, it can be concluded that the quadrotor follows perfectly the target.

Figure 5.16 illustrates the speed evolution along the three axes X, Y, and X. We notice that the quadrotor moves rapidly toward the target with a starting speed of 1 m/s, but once the target gets close to the quadrotor, the speed decreases and reaches 0.1 m/s. This is justified by the fact that the quadrotor must maintain a safe distance of 1 m from the target.

Figure 5.17 shows the speed error evolution according to the three axes x, y, and z.

From Figure 5.17, one notes that the speed error along the x-axis is very large at takeoff. It reaches 0.7 m/s and thereafter decreases gradually to almost zero. For the

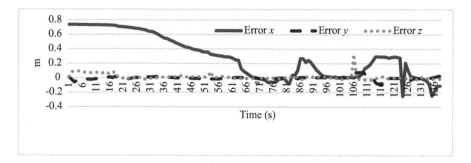

Figure 5.17   Evolution of the speed error along axes x, y, and z

errors along the axes *y* and *z*, their values oscillate around zero. The video related to the tests presented in this section is available in https://www.youtube.com/watch?v= IwdetPYuv0g.

In this section, fuzzy controllers were designed and implemented for target tracking using the AR.Drone quadrotor. Simulation based demonstration of the controllers was provided using the combination of open-source tools FuzzyLite, ROS Gazebo and "ar_track_alvar" with Tum_ardrone simulator. For different tests, the obtained simulation results are promising. They showed acceptable performances of the tracking. The control variables have been successfully tested, following the inevitable compromise between stability, precision and speed of the system response.

Once the optimal fuzzy controller was obtained, we proceeded with real flight tests using an AR.Drone. The QR of the controller and the small errors during these tests demonstrate the excellent behavior of the controller.

The tests showed that the fuzzy logic controller can be used to solve the target-tracking problem using AR.Drone. In addition, from the tests, which were carried on different initial positions, the quadrotor tracked the target perfectly.

5.4   Artificial neural networks (ANN) for target identification and tracking using a quadrotor

Object tracking is performed to track an object over a sequence of images. Object tracking is defined as the process of segmenting an object of interest from a video scene and keeping track of its motion, orientation, occlusion, etc. in order to extract the useful information [23]. Difficulties in tracking objects can arise due to abrupt object motion, changing appearance patterns of both the object and the scene, nonrigid object structures, object-to-object and object-to-scene occlusions, and camera motion. Tracking is usually performed in the context of higher level applications that require the location and/or shape of the object in every frame [24]. Realtime object tracking is recently becoming more and more important in the field of video analysis and processing. The technique of motion detection and object tracking can be applied to video surveillance system to prevent against threats [25,26].

The proposed artificial vision system in this section is based on computational intelligent techniques inspired by biological neural model of human beings. Known as ANNs, these techniques are mainly characterized by their ability to learn through experiences to adapt to adverse conditions. These features make the ANN a great field of study and drive it to reach success in solving real problems such as identification, classification, digital image processing, and control. In our study, the target's position information can aid the UAV to determine what constitutes its surroundings and what actions if necessary are to be taken [27,28]. The potential applications of such visual target tracking systems are autonomous UAV navigation, target localization, path planning, obstacle avoidance, surveillance systems, and so on.

The tracking system presented in this section was developed by using the Robot Operating System (ROS) framework. The ANN algorithm was written as a ROS node that receives the information from the target's position at every moment using the front camera of the drone, the controller based on ANN sends the commands of speed and translations to the AR.Drone [29,30].

The simulation environment Gazebo was used to evaluate the behavior of the ANN algorithm in a physical simulation. The RViz package was used to visualize the current environment state during simulation, including the identification and localization of the markers. Figure 5.18 illustrates the development process of the achieved system.

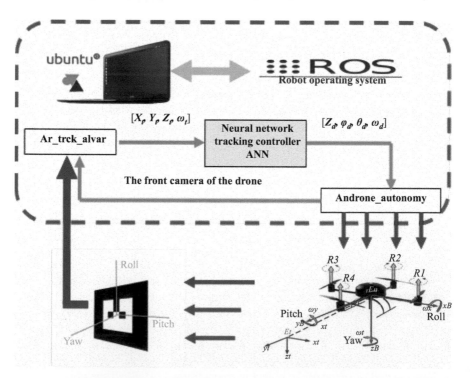

Figure 5.18　Block diagram of the target tracking neural network ANN control system

The hardware used in our project are as follows:

- AR.Drone 2.0
- Laptop with Ubuntu 14.04 and ROS Indigo

The software used in our project are as follows:

- ROS Indigo
- Ubuntu 14.04
- AR.Drone 2.0 onboard drivers
- AR tag ROS package ar_track_alvar
- ROS package ardrone_autonomy Lab, AR.Drone 2.0 driver ROS wrapper
- ROS package Tum_ardrone

5.4.1   Design of the neural network

In ANNs, the learning is realized by the adaptation of the network weights based on the input data and the corresponding desired outputs. At each iteration, the parameters are updated such that the output of the network will match with the desired value.

Different algorithms for the adaptation of the weights have been proposed in the literature. Among those, gradient descent method is the most widely used one, in which the gradient of a cost function utilizing the difference between the desired and network outputs has been determined, and then the weights are updated in the opposite direction of this gradient to minimize the cost function. The main drawback of this method is that the network can stuck at a local minimum, and as a result, the network output will not converge to the desired value. To alleviate this problem, back-propagation-based learning algorithms can be employed. The main advantage of this method is that it guarantees the robustness, stability and fast convergence of the overall system. For our work, we use a neural-network-type MLP. Thus, for our work a Back-Propagation Neural Networks (BPNN) is selected for the application at hand, and it consists of three

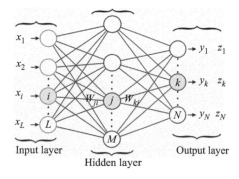

Figure 5.19   Global scheme of a multilayer neuron network MLP

layers: one input layer (of source nodes), one hidden layer (with sigmoid activation function), and one output layer. Figure 5.19 shows scheme of a multilayer neuron network MLP.

For our application, the learning algorithm has two phases:

- First, a training input pattern is presented to the network input layer. The network propagates the input pattern from layer to layer until the output layer generates the output pattern.
- If this pattern is different from the desired output, an error is calculated and then propagated backward through the network from the output layer to the input layer. The weights are modified as the error is propagated.

5.4.1.1   Input layer

The input layer of a neural network is determined by the characteristics of the application inputs. In our work, the input layer is the information received by the front camera of the drone and represents the Euclidean position of the target with respect to the drone. These data are described by the following values:

- Pose.Position X: Represents the angle of orientation of the target with respect to the drone. This value is zero if the target is on the x line of the drone. It is negative if the target is to the left of the x line of the drone and it is positive if the target is to the right of the x line of the drone.
- Pose.Position Y: Represents the height of the target relative to the drone. This value is zero if the target is at the same height as the drone. It is negative if the target is above the drone, and it is positive if the target is below the drone.
- Pose.Position Z: Represents the distance that separates the target from the drone. This value is always positive. Its variation depends on the movements of the drone.

Figure 5.20 represents Euclidean reference points of the drone relative to the target.

- Pose.Orientation X: Represents the orientation of the target with respect to the drone, along the x-axis in a quaternion.
- Pose.Orientation Y: Represents the orientation of the target with respect to the drone, along the y-axis in a quaternion.

Figure 5.21 shows the rotation reference points of the drone.

Figure 5.20   The Euclidean landmarks of the drone

Figure 5.21   Rotational reference points of the drone

5.4.1.2   Output layer

The output layer of the network is designed according to the need of the application output. The output layer is the information related to the movement of the drone. These data are represented by the following variables:

- Linear Speed $X(V_X)$: Represents the linear velocity of the drone along the x-axis. It allows the drone to move forward or backward.
- Linear Speed $Y(V_Y)$: Represents the linear velocity of the drone along the y-axis. It allows the drone to make a lateral movement to the right or to the left.
- Linear Speed $Z(V_Z)$: Represents the linear velocity of the drone along the y-axis. It allows the drone to move upward or downward.
- Angular velocity $Z(Rot_Z)$: Represents the rotation of the drone along the z-axis in a quaternion. It allows the drone to rotate right or left.

5.4.1.3   Data collection and training phase

The AR.Drone is operated and controlled manually in the Gazebo ROS simulator to follow the target with different initial starting positions and orientations. During the data collection, data synchronization is applied to ensure that every state change is caused by the captured control command. During training, the network is presented with a large amount of input patterns (training set). The desired corresponding outputs are then compared to the actual network output nodes. The error between the desired and actual response is used to update the weights of the network interconnections. This update is performed after each pattern presentation.

For our learning, we used a learning method containing 644 examples. The partitioning of collected data was done according to a ratio of 0.8 that is to say 80% for learning and 20% for the test of learning.

In our application, we started with a learning step equals to 0.1 and we varied this value until we found a good compromise between speed and convergence. Table 5.3 shows the possible configurations for the learning process.

Let us note that the learning is good if the error rate is less than 0.020. In neural network training results the mean square error would result different values; thus we have done nine experiment trainings to find optimal result.

Figure 5.22 shows the results chosen for the learning process. They are presented by a learning curve (in blue) and a learning test curve (in red).

Table 5.3   The different configurations for learning process

Experiment	Maxnumber of iterations	The learning step	Number of hidden layers
Conf 1	100	0.1	120
Conf 2	600	0.01	80
Conf 3	100	0.01	105
Conf 4	400	0.01	120
Conf 5	500	0.5	50
Conf 6	400	0.8	50
Conf 7	250	0.2	80
Conf 8	350	0.3	25
Conf 9	100	0.6	85

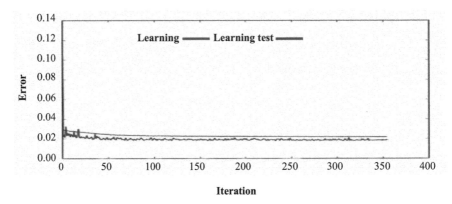

Figure 5.22   Mean square error curve of the training of configuration 8

For configuration 8, one notes that the learning curve of the MLP converges successfully toward a final solution. The test curve also converges without fluctuations. For our application, we have selected this configuration.

To perform the training process, the neural network requires some parameters that are listed as follows:

1. The architecture of the neural network is composed of three layers (input, hidden and output layers).
2. The input layer has 5 neurons, the hidden one has 25 neurons and the output one has 4 neurons.
3. The sigmoid activation function is used.
4. The weight initialization is achieved with Widrow and Ho.
5. 350 maximum epoch.
6. The learning rate is equal to 0.3.
7. The error target is equal to 0.02.

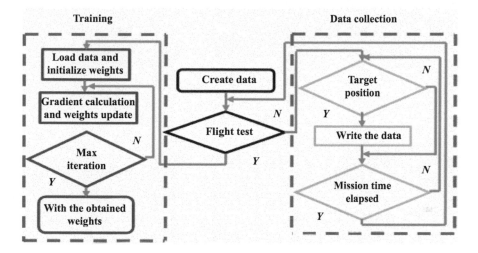

Figure 5.23 The neural network training phase flowchart

Figure 5.23 illustrates the data collection and training phases of the neural network controller.

5.4.2 Simulation results

In this section, the simulation scenario and results are presented. The Robotics Operating System (ROS) framework was used with Gazebo simulator to simulate the developed neural network controller. The workstation specifications were a PC with Ubuntu Linux 14.04 operating system that has I5 2.4 GHz processor, 8 GB RAM. In ROS, multiple codes, defined as nodes, can run simultaneously to control the system with topics and messages passing between different codes as a feedback and attributes that can be used in one another. Figure 5.24 shows a hierarchical multitask control system constructed by simply instantiating multiple navigation nodes.

Hence, the simulation software can be divided into the following code packages:

- NNController package: Contains the neural network controller forward propagation implementation.
- Data collection package: To perform data logging and synchronization of the captured data.
- Training package: Trains the neural network model with the collected data and obtains the weight matrices.
- Drone gui: Drives the quadrotor manually using the keyboard to tracking on targets for data collection.
- Ardrone_autonomy package: An open-source package used to receive the input commands from the control package and sends it to the AR.Drone model plugin used by the Unified Robot Description File (URDF) format inside the Gazebo simulator.

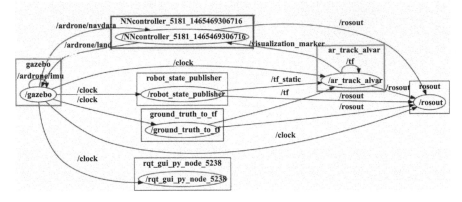

Figure 5.24   Interaction between all the processes from Gazebo and neural network in ROS

- Ar_track_alvar package: An open-source package used to estimate the position of the object with the markers using the front camera in which it calculates the distance to the marker and the defined *xyz*.
- Tum_simulator package: A package contains the AR.Drone URDF, sensors plugin, Inertial Measurement Unit (IMU), cameras, and sonar of the AR.Drone.

All the previous packages are implemented as ROS nodes that can communicate with each other using specified topics in a publisher–subscriber pattern.

For the experimental part, all the previous packages will be used except the Tum_simulator package, which is replaced by the ardrone_autonomy that communicates with the laptop via a Wi-Fi link.

As previously mentioned, the quadrotor is programmed to have three operating modes: the identification, target tracking, and keep the position of the drone in front of the target. In this simulation scenario, the quadrotor takes off from an initial starting position and then starts the identification mode with a predefined search pattern until a target is detected. Once the target markers are identified, the quadrotor starts the tracking mode with the Ar_Track_alvar package to estimate the position and orientation of the target and, hence, the neural network controller, the autonomous hovering phase uses the published target positions to drive the drone at a distance of 1 m near the target. Figure 5.25 shows that the quadrotor is positioned on the right at the same level of the target.

Figure 5.26 illustrates the flight sequences for target tracking.

From the simulation results, one notes that after takeoff of the drone detects the target and goes to the target by doing maneuvers on the right and on the left to adjust its trajectory. Once the drone is close to the target, it maintains a distance of 1 m from the tag. In all the period of the flight, the drone uses its frontal camera, when the target is visible, it draws red square. Figure 5.27 shows the path crossed by the drone to follow the target.

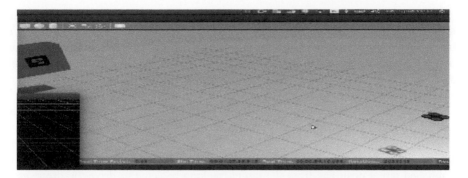

Figure 5.25   General view of the quadrotor's flight plan to follow the target

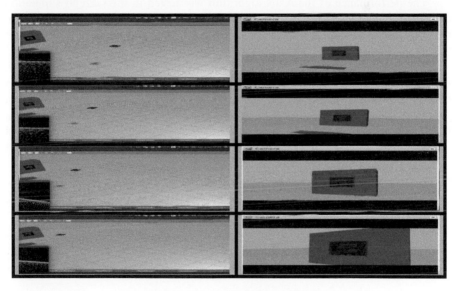

Figure 5.26   Simulation results

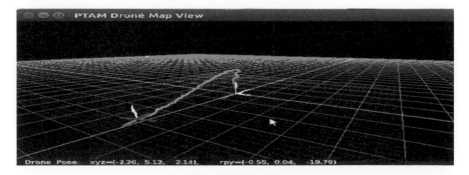

Figure 5.27   The trajectory traveled by the drone recorded by the RViz–Gazebo

The simulation of the system resulted in a successful target tracking as shown in Figure 5.26. The resulting simulation 3D exploration trajectory of the quadrotor is illustrated in Figure 5.26 proving the controllability of the system and the ability of the controller to drive the quadrotor to the defined reference angles. The video related to the tests presented in this section is available in https://www.youtube.com/watch?v=Y9oAPj2TYkc

Furthermore, Figure 5.28 presents the convergence of the X–Y positions respectively to the target position after the detection of the target.

The convergence of the quadrotor altitude is illustrated in Figure 5.29 that shows the tracking of the target. Hence, the designed intelligent controller has used the published target positions from the target-tracking package to drive the drone at a safe distance from the target.

The performance of the ANN algorithm was tested in the Gazebo simulation environment. The visual camera data were used for detecting markers (tag) placed in the 3D world. The camera data of AR.Drone were used to generate state inputs for the neural network.

The simulated roll and pitch angles are presented in Figures 5.28 and 5.29, respectively, and show that the angles are bounded and the coupling phenomena of the gyroscopic effect have been successfully eliminated. It can be observed that the ANN controller maintains the system angles brought back to equilibrium rapidly, thus demonstrating the agility of the drone with the proposed controller for target tracking.

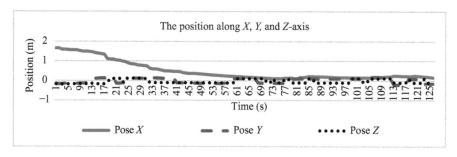

Figure 5.28   Evolution of the position of the drone along the three axes

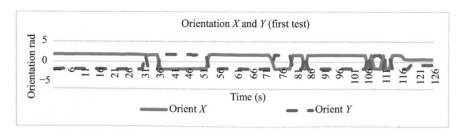

Figure 5.29   The evolution of the orientations along the two axes X and Y

5.4.3   Experimental validation and results

The UAV we used for our experiments is the Parrot AR.Drone 2.0. It is equipped with a 1 GHz ARM Cortex-A8 as the CPU and an embedded version of Linux as its operating system. In addition, the quadrotor has two cameras: an HD camera facing forward and another Quarter Common Intermediate Format (QCIF) camera facing down, a sonar height sensor, and an onboard computer. Communication between the AR.Drone and a host machine is performed via Wi-Fi connection. In order to realize our experience, a ROS application has been developed.

After takeoff, we control the quadrotor using the computer's keyboard. The ANN is activated and the AR.Drone changes to the autonomous flight mode. ANN-based controllers already tested in simulation under Gazebo ROS will be downloaded directly into the real platform. After the connection has been established, the application immediately starts streaming video obtained by the front camera of the quadrotor. When the target (tag) is visible to the quadrotor, a red frame appears around the target. This will freeze the video stream so that it is possible to draw a bounded box similar to that of simulation results and as accurate as possible, so that it does not contain a lot of background, but only the desired object. We primarily focus on the tracking accuracy and execution efficiency of the proposed neural network ANN, as well as the performance comparison against the software-based implementation under ROS. Figure 5.30 illustrates a general view before takeoff of the drone.

Figure 5.31 shows the tracking results for a moving tag (red marker), where we show eight consecutive frames. It is observed that the tracking window (red marker) is constantly enclosing and following the target during the entire moving process. Such observation results indicate that the proposed ANN is able to effectively track the object's movement in the current circumstance.

According to the results obtained one notes that the quadrotor follows perfectly the target (tag). We observed after takeoff, the drone goes directly to the target. Once the target is identified, a red square around the target is drawn. The neural network algorithm acts then on the quadrotor to correct its trajectory and to transmit the necessary commands to tracking the target. From the experimental tests, we conclude

Figure 5.30   General view of the experimental test

Figure 5.31   Real experiments to demonstrate the performance of the proposed target-tracking system

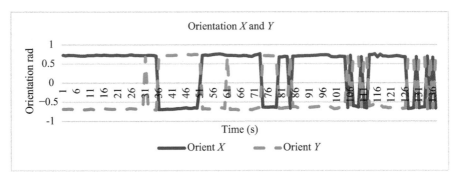

Figure 5.32   The evolution of the orientations along the two axes X and Y

that the experiments produce good results. A video of this experiment can be seen at the following URL: https://www.youtube.com/watch?v=YHxuejER5Pk

Figure 5.32 shows the evolution of the target orientation relative to the drone along the axes X and Y, called respectively Pose.Orientation X and Pose.Orientation Y. These two parameters were used as inputs for the neural network controller.

Figure 5.33 illustrates the three positions of the drone relative to the target. Three positions were used as inputs for the achieved neural network controller.

According to the figure, we see that the drone moves forward quickly along the X axis. The evolution of the position of the drone along the other two axes Y and Z varies forward slowly and remains unchanged compared the X axis.

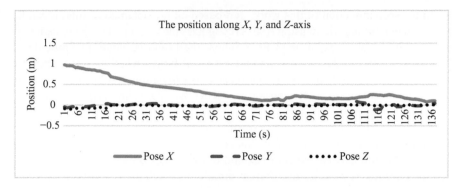

Figure 5.33   Evolution of the position of the drone along the three axes

At the end of the experiment, the quadrotor executed a maneuver that could not have been commanded by the ANN. We believe that the drone's unproductive behavior may have been caused by disruption of the movement commands that need to be sent every 5 ms. Additional tests are needed to determine if problems such as Wi-Fi connection disturbances or lag caused by the image processing cause the behavior observed in that experiment.

Overall, it can be seen that the obtained simulation and experimental results are very promising. The proposed ANN-based controller identifies and tracks the targets efficiently.

5.5   Conclusion

In this work, a vision system for identification and target-tracking using a Parrot AR.Drone 2.0 quadrotor UAV is presented. The proposed technique is based on the detection of a marker by the camera using two intelligent controllers; the first based on fuzzy logic FLC and the second an ANN. Then the distance between the quadrotor and the target is estimated and AI-based algorithms will be used to fly toward the marker.

In the first section of this work, simulation-based demonstration of the controllers was provided using the combination of open-source tools FuzzyLite, ROS Gazebo and "ar_track_alvar" with Tum_ardrone Simulator. For different tests, the obtained simulation results are promising. They showed acceptable performances of the tracking using a controller based on fuzzy logic. The control variables have been successfully tested, following the inevitable compromise between stability, precision and speed of the system response.

Once the optimal fuzzy controller was obtained, we proceeded with real flight tests using an AR.Drone. The QR of the controller and the small errors during these tests demonstrate the excellent behavior of the controller.

The tests showed that the FLC can be used to solve the target-tracking problem using AR.Drone. In addition, from the tests performed for different initial positions, the quadrotor has perfectly followed the target.

In the second section of this work, and based on the obtained results, it can be concluded that the algorithm using ANNs recognizes the target just as the recognition module used by ar_track_alvar in ROS. Thus, the proposed algorithm provides a better performance in the recognition process of the target, which is very important for realtime drone applications. Experiment and simulation results show that the implementation of image processing and neural network algorithm for object detection and tracking has been successful.

Future work includes an extensive set of experimental trials of the vision approach using a variety of visual features to be tracked and its integration with the intelligent controller. Additionally we expect to extend the strategies presented in this chapter, with the purpose of working in different conditions, such as targets with different shapes. Pattern recognition methods, like machine learning, will be tested with the main task of providing a more robust estimation of the form and location of the target.

References

[1]   W. Yeugkwon, K. Seyoug, and K. Eunjin, "Real-time visual tracking and remote control application for an aerial surveillance robot", Journal of Automation and Control Engineering, Vol 3, No. 6, 2015.

[2]   L. Mejias, S. McNamara, J. Lai, and J. Ford, "Vision-based detection and tracking of aerial targets for UAV collision avoidance", Intelligent Robot and Systems (IROS), 2010 IEEE/RSJ International Conference, Taipei, Taiwan, pp. 87–92. 2010.

[3]   S. Lange, N. Sunderhauf, and P. Protzel, "A vision based onboard approach for landing and position control of an autonomous multirotor UAV in GPS-denied environments", 2009 International Conference on Advanced Robotics, Munich, Germany, 22–26 June, 2009.

[4]   P. Linci and A. Vinyojita Mohanraj, "Target identification and tracking using UAV", International Journal of Engineering Research & Technology, Vol 4, No. 4, pp. 353–356, 2015.

[5]   C. H. El Houssein, F. Guérin, F. Guinand, *et al.*, "Vision based target tracking using an unmanned aerial vehicle", 2015 IEEE International Workshop on Advanced Robotics and Its Social Impacts, July 2015, Lyon, France, July 2015.

[6]   K. Boudjit and C. Larbes, "Detection and implementation autonomous target tracking with a quadrotor AR.Drone", 2015 12th International Conference on Informatics in Control, Automation and Robotics (ICINCO), Colmar, France, 21–23 July 2015.

[7]   F. Arifin, R. Arifandi Daniel, and D. Widiyanto, "Autonomous detection and tracking of an object autonomously using AR.Drone quadrotor", Journal of Computer Science and Information, Vol 7, pp. 11–17, 2014.

[8]   K. Alisher, K. Alexander, and B. Alexandr, "Control of the mobile robots with ROS in robotics courses", 25th DAAAM International Symposium on Intelligent Manufacturing and Automation, Vienna, Austria, 2014.

[9]   A. Prayitno, V. Indrawati, and G. Utomo, "Trajectory tracking of AR.Drone quadrotor using fuzzy logic controller", TELEKOMNIKA, Vol 12, No. 4, pp. 819–828, 2014.

[10] M. A. Olivares-Mendez, S. Kannan, and H. Voos, "V-REP & ROS tested for design, test, and tuning of a quadrotor vision based fuzzy control system for autonomous landing", 2014 International Micro Air vehicle Conference and Competition (IMAV 2014), Delft, Netherlands, 2014.

[11] W. Garage, "Documentation Robot Operating System", 2016. available: http://www.ros.org/wiki/.

[12] S. Niekum, "ar_track_alvar – ROS Wiki", 2012. available: http://www.ros.org/ wiki/ar_track_alvar.

[13] J. Meyer, A. Sendobry, S. Kohlbrecher, U. Klinganf, and O. Stryk, "Comprehension simulation of quadrotor UAVs using ROS and Gazebo", Springer Berlin Heidelberg, Berlin Heidelberg, pp. 400–411, 2012.

[14] K. Boudjit and C. Larbes, "Detection and target tracking with a quadrotor using fuzzy logic", 2016 8th International Conference on Modelling, Identification and Control (ICMIC), Algiers, Algeria, 15–17 November 2016.

[15] P. Benavidez, J. Lambert, A. Jaimes, and M. Jamshidi, "Landing of an ARDrone 2.0 quadrotor on a mobile base using fuzzy logic", International Journal of Complex Systems-Computing, Sensing and Control, Vol 1, No. 1–2, pp. 5–25, 2013.

[16] K. E. Wenzel, A. Masselli, and A. Zell, "Automatic take off, tracking and landing of a miniature UAV on a moving carrier vehicle", Journal of Intelligent & Robotic Systems, Vol 61, pp. 221–238, 2011.

[17] J. W. Tweedate, "Fuzzy control loop in an autonomous landing system for unmanned air vehicles", WCCI 2012 IEEE World Congress on Computational Intelligence, June 10–15, 2012, Brisbane, Australia, June 10–15, 2012.

[18] C. Fu, M. A. Olivares-Mendez, P. Campoy, and R. Suarez-Fernandez, "UAS see-and-avoid strategy using a fuzzy logic controller optimized by Cross-Entropy in scaling factors and membership functions", 2013 International Conference on Unmanned Aircraft Systems (ICUAS), Atlanta, USA, May 28–31, 2013.

[19] L. Doitsidis, K. Valavanis, N. Tsourveloudis, and M. Kontitis, "A framework for fuzzy logic based UAV navigation and control", 2004 IEEE International Conference on Robotics and Automation, 2004, Proceeding ICRA'04, New Orleans, LA, USA, Vol 4, pp. 4041–4046, 2004.

[20] A. H. N. Koenig, "Gazebo – ROS Wiki", 2019. available: http://www.ros.org/ wiki/gazebo.

[21] J. Engel. (2013). "tum_ardrone – ROS Wiki". Available: http://www.ros. org/wiki/tum_ardrone/

[22] J. Rada-Vilela. (2013). "FuzzyLite – A Fuzzy Logic Control Library and Application in C++", available: http://code.google.com/p/fuzzylite/

[23] K, Boudjit, C. Larbes, and N. Ramzan, "ANN design and implementation for real-time object tracking using quadrotor AR.Drone 2.0", Journal of Experimental & Theoretical Artificial Intelligence, Vol 30, No. 6, pp. 1013–1035, 2018.

[24]   R. V. Badu, S. Suresh, and A. Makur, "Online adaptive radial function net-works for robust object tracking", Computer Vision and Image Understanding, pp. 297–310, 2010.

[25]   L. Jangwon, J. Wang, D. Crandall, *et al.*, "Real-time object detection for unmanned aerial vehicles based on cloud-based convolutional neural net-works", Journal Concurrency and Computation: Practice and Experience, Vol 29, No. 6, 2017.

[26]   H. K. Kavith and S. C. P. Kumar, "Study on object tracking using neural network functions", International Journal of Advanced Research in Computer and Communication Engineering, Vol 3, No. 5, pp. 6424–6427, 2014.

[27]   A. Borji, S. Frintrop, D. N. Sihite, *et al.*, "Adaptive object tracking by learn-ing background context", Proc. IEEE Conf, Computer Vision and Pattern Recognition Workshops (CVPRW), Rhode Island, USA, pp. 23–30; 2012.

[28]   A. D. Mengistu and D. M. Alemayehu, "Robot for visual object tracking based on artificial neural network", International Journal of Robotics Research and Development (IJRRD), Baltimore, Maryland, USA, Vol 6, No. 1, 2016.

[29]   W. Yang, Z. Jin, C. Thiem, *et al.*, "Autonomous target tracking of UAVs based on lower-power neural network hardware", Machine Intelligence and Bio-inspired Computation: Theory and Applications VIII, Proc of SPIE, Vol 9119, 2014.

[30]   J. Ahmed, M. N. Jafri, and M. I. Khan, "Design and implementation of neural network for real-time object tracking", International Journal of Computer, Electrical, Automation, Control and Information Engineering, Vol 1, No. 6, pp. 1816–1819, 2007.

Part II
Network

Chapter 6

Predictive mobility management in cellular networks

Metin Öztürk[1], Paulo Valente Klaine[1], Sajjad Hussain[1], and Muhammad Ali Imran[1]

Future cellular networks are expected to see enhancements that will change their operation with the advent of new technologies, such as millimetre-wave (mmWave) communications, new physical layer waveforms, and network densification, to name a few. However, despite all the benefits that these concepts will bring to future networks, other challenges will arise. One issue that has gained attention in recent years is the problem of mobility management, which is expected to become even more challenging in future networks. This occurs due to the network densification process and the short-range coverage provided by mmWaves, which will lead to more frequent and an exponential number of handovers (HOs) by end users, generating a tremendous amount of signalling which cannot be handled by conventional means. To tackle these challenges, a proactive mobility-management concept, where HO events are triggered in advance with the help of intelligent tools that are able to predict the future behaviours of users and the network have been proposed recently. Results have shown that this proactive approach helps eliminating certain steps of the HO phase, resulting in less latency and signalling overhead, leading to a better network optimisation. On the other hand, if the accuracy of the predictions is not enough, this proactive approach can provide worse results than the reactive one. As such, the accuracy of the algorithm plays a vital role in ensuring the predictive management applicable. In this chapter, both traditional and proactive mobility managements in cellular networks are presented, and a Markov-chain-based proactive HO process is proposed.

6.1 Introduction

A cellular system is a type of wireless communication networks, where base stations (BSs) are deployed over wide geographical areas to connect user equipments (UEs)

---

[1]James Watt School of Engineering, University of Glasgow, Glasgow, UK

with each other. The name *cellular* comes from the fact that the considered geographical areas are split into *cells*, at which BSs are deployed in order to provide the required connectivity for all the UEs. As such, each BS, which is equipped with at least one antenna to emit wireless electromagnetic (EM) radiation, serving the UEs located under its coverage. However, only a small portion of the EM spectrum is allocated for cellular communications by the International Telecommunication Union (ITU). Thereby, the BSs need to use their radio resources as efficiently as possible in order to provide the requested content to users in an efficient manner [1,2].

6.1.1   The path towards 5G

Since the early 1980s, when the first generation of cellular networks (1G) was introduced, the cellular communication has evolved significantly. 1G used frequency division multiple access (FDMA) technology and it was completely analogue, meaning that the voice signals were modulated to the higher frequency channels instead of being converted to digital bit streams. Therefore, due to the nature of analogue communications, 1G had limited capabilities, which led to its disappearance soon after the introduction of the digital-based second generation of cellular networks (2G). 2G encodes the analogue voice signal to a digital signal, which is extremely more advantageous, as it can produce not only a less erroneous transmission but also a more efficient resource management. The first 2G system was Global System for Mobile Communications, which was developed in 1991, and it consisted of a time-division multiple access. In addition to being fully digital, another difference from its predecessor, 1G, was the introduction of short message services. In the further new versions of 2G, starting from 2.5G, packet switching was also included in the system, which helped to reach 144 kbps data rate [3].

The development of international mobile telephony by the year 2000 (IMT-2000) by ITU in the early 1990s paved the way for the first commercial release of third generation of cellular networks (3G) in the early 2000s. Two major standards, called Universal Mobile Telecommunications System (UMTS) – also referred to as Wideband Code-Division Multiple Access – and Code-Division Multiple Access (CDMA) 2000, were developed with different characteristics. Even though a 2-Mbps minimum downlink (DL) data rate was expected from 3G in the beginning, with its further versions, such as 3.5G and 3.75G, the peak data rate was able to reach up to several Mbps, which subsequently enabled some new applications, such as video conferencing, to emerge. However, the ever-increasing data demand, a growing number of connected users, and the need for higher data rates made 3G networks insufficient due to the nature of underlying CDMA technology being employed in 3G [4]. Besides, the operational cost of 3G is also high [5], making it challenging for the mobile network operators. These limitations led to the emergence of the fourth generation of cellular networks (4G). ITU Radiocommunication Sector released the requirements for 4G network in 2009; the peak data rate for low-mobility users should be of 1 Gbps, while a 100 Mbps for high-mobility users was expected [6]. Long-Term Evolution (LTE) is the standard developed by the 3G Partnership Project (3GPP) for 4G networks. With 4G, circuit switching was completely abandoned, and all-internet protocol-based communication system was adopted. In addition, in order to increase the peak data rate, orthogonal FDMA and multiple-input–multiple-output (MIMO) technologies were also introduced in 4G.

Nevertheless, with the introduction of emerging concepts, including internet of things (IoT) and machine-type communication (MTC), 4G would be no more sufficient due to its inherent human-type traffic-based design [7]. Furthermore, new applications, such as augmented reality and remote surgery, are quite demanding in terms of either bandwidth or latency, or both. In remote surgery, for example reliable and minimal latency is required, since any fault and/or delay in the communication system would result in undesired consequences. Therefore, the aforementioned new types of applications necessitate better cellular communication networks with regard to latency, data rates, reliability, etc., which, in turn, paved the way for the development of the fifth generation of cellular networks, 5G. Because of its promising offers and high expectations, 5G has been perceived as not only an evolution for cellular networks but a revolution also [8–10]. 5G is not an imagination any more, since it has already been deployed in several countries as of 2019, such as South Korea, China, and the United Kingdom, while it looms on the horizon for many other countries, envisioned to be deployed by 2020.

6.1.2 5G enablers and challenges

3GPP has been working on the standardisation for 5G New Radio (NR) and published Release 15, which is the first set of standards for 5G NR, in 2018. As such, 5G arises as a strong candidate to address all the aforementioned issues with the three main envisioned deployment scenarios: enhanced mobile broadband, massive MTCs, and ultra-reliable and low-latency communications, which are included in 5G for different objectives [11]. Nonetheless, each scenario comes with stringent requirements, such as 20 Gbps DL and 10 Mbps uplink (UL) target peak data rates, and 0.5 ms DL and UL latency. In this regard, in order to meet these requirements and address other near-future challenges, several new technologies have been proposed in 5G NR, such as the utilisation of mmWave frequencies [12]. For capacity enhancement, increased bandwidth, massive MIMO, and network densification are some of the possible solutions listed in [13], and it is mentioned that all these solutions should be considered together in order to satisfy the requirements of 5G in terms of data rates.

As mentioned earlier in this section, mmWave frequencies have already been designated in 5G NR [12] as frequency range (FR)-2, along with traditional sub-6 GHz frequency bands. Nevertheless, albeit the huge bandwidth availability, mmWave communication comes with its inherent problems, since it is more prone to suffer from severe penetration losses and blockages, owing to propagation characteristics of higher frequencies [14–16]. This subsequently reduces the coverage area of mmWave BSs, leading to more BS deployments to compensate the coverage holes [17]. Given that the antenna size is proportional to the wavelength of the transmitted signal, the use of mmWave frequencies facilitates the deployment of multiple antennas, which, in turn, puts MIMO-based communication at the heart of 5G. The primary benefits of MIMO over traditional single-input–single-output systems, where both the serving BS and the receiving equipment only have one transmitting antenna, are shortlisted in [18,19], and some of them are as follows: better capacity, enhanced reliability, improved energy efficiency, etc. Better capacity is provided by the reduced interference due to beams being more directive, which also helps in better frequency reuse, boosting the spectral efficiency. Moreover, reliability comes in the form of diversity, where the receiver gets multiple copies of the transmitted signal [19]. However, despite all of these benefits theoretically expanding with increasing the number of antennas [19], there are some issues, due to the increased complexity of these systems. Research challenges include channel reciprocity, pilot contamination, and orthogonality of channel responses, re-upper-bounding the amount of antennas to be deployed [20].

Network densification is another candidate to enhance network capacity, which subsequently improves the spectral efficiency of the system [21,22]. The idea of network densification is to deploy a large amount of small cells (SCs), which are compact and low-powered BSs, under the coverage area of conventional macro cells (MCs). As such, by bringing the BSs closer to the users, higher data rates can be achieved. Owing to the low transmit power of SCs [21,22], their coverage areas are much smaller than that of the MC, enabling frequency reuse and improving the network capacity. While, on the one hand, it is better to increase the number of SCs in order to obtain more capacity, on the other hand, it will make the effect of interference more significant, which would eventually undermine the obtained capacity gain [13].

6.1.3   Issues from new technologies

However, despite the benefit that all these new technologies and solutions will bring to the future wireless networks, several other issues arise. The dense deployment of SCs, for example despite increasing network capacity and improving users QoS, will generate more network signalling. This is due to the coverage area of SCs being quite limited, causing many more HOs to occur in the network, increasing signalling. Thus, if current HO methods are employed, it can be seen that future mobile networks will have to handle a huge amount of traffic just from this increased signalling [23].

Furthermore, in order to meet the stringent requirements of future wireless networks, especially in terms of latency, these novel techniques are not sufficient, as the control plane of networks also plays an important role [2]. Current cellular networks are heavily centralised and hierarchical, which, despite their simplicity, acts as a bottleneck in terms of signalling exchange, forcing data, and control traffic to traverse the whole network, all the way to the core [23]. Thus, it can be seen that current models of wireless networks are not scalable, and several issues will arise if current techniques are employed when the dense deployment of SCs is implemented. As such, one way to overcome these issues is by shifting the paradigm of current wireless networks, from reactive to proactive. By proactively deciding about their processes, especially in terms of signalling exchange, wireless networks should be able to reduce not only the overheads associated to it, but also latency (one of the key parameters envisioned to transform 5G networks). This, by its turn, guarantees a better performance from the user perspective both in terms of latency as well as other QoS parameters.

6.1.4 Chapter objectives

In this chapter, a brief overview of current mobility-management techniques in the context of 5G wireless networks is presented. The new radio resource control (RRC) inactive state, which is introduced in 5G, is also covered. More particularly, the mobility in cellular networks is divided into two categories, according to the RRC state of the user during the mobility: idle/inactive state and connected state mobility. This taxonomy is important, since each has distinctive challenges that should be addressed individually. For the idle/inactive state, for example the main challenge is cell selection/re-selection and paging. On the other hand, for the connected state mobility, the main issue is HO management.

After a brief discussion on mobility management in cellular networks, a predictive mobility-management approach is elaborated followed by recent research activities. The primary objective of this chapter, however, is the introduction of the 3D transition matrix concept for Markov-chain-based predictive mobility management. In this regard, first, the limitations of Markov chains, which rely on 2D transition matrices, are identified, and then the 3D transition matrix, which distinguishes the order of HOs and builds a separate 2D transition matrix for each HO, is presented. The superiority of the proposed model in cases of re-visits is confirmed through extensive simulations, whose results reveal that the 3D transition matrix-based predictions are more immune to re-visits in the trajectory than that of its 2D counterpart.

6.1.5 Organisation of the chapter

This chapter is organised as follows. Section 6.2 provides a brief discussion on the mobility management in cellular networks through a broad category of idle/inactive state mobility (location management) and connected state mobility (HO management). In Section 6.3, predictive mobility management is presented with a brief state-of-the-art review, while in Section 6.4 the advanced version of Markov-chain-based mobility prediction, which uses 3D transition matrix instead of conventional 2D one, is introduced. Lastly, Section 6.5 concludes the chapter.

6.2 Mobility management in cellular networks

3GPP has defined mobility as *the ability for a user to communicate whilst moving independent of location*, while mobility management has a definition of *a relation between the mobile station and the UTRAN (UMTS Terrestrial Radio Access Network) that is used to set-up, maintain and release the various physical channels.* [24]. Although these definitions are from Release 4, 3GPP sticks with them in Release 15 for 5G [25]. The aforesaid definition of mobility yields that the connection for the users are supposed to be maintained when they are mobile, and mobility management is the concept that ensures this connection. Therefore, mobility management plays a crucial role in cellular networks, since it is a challenging task to provide services to the users with diverse mobility profiles, such as stationary, low-mobility, and high-mobility.

Moreover, there are two different RRC connection states in legacy networks, idle and connected. However, a new type of RRC connection state has been introduced in 5G NR: inactive [26]. Before going in detail about the inactive state, it is better to give the 3GPP definitions for conventional idle and connected modes [24]. If the UE has no RRC connection with any radio access network (RAN) while being turned on, it is referred to as in the idle state. This means that the UE is tractable (in connection with the network) but is unable to transfer data. The connected state, on the other hand, refers to the case when the UE is not only turned on and tractable but also has an active RRC connection established with a RAN. The UE is able to transfer data when it is in connected mode. In this regard, there is a trade-off in switching between connected and idle modes: from the UE perspective, it switches to idle state in order to save energy, since measurement reporting drains its battery. However, in order to transmit data, the UE then needs to switch back to the RRC-connected mode, which results in latency and signalling overhead [27].

With the introduction of the inactive state, now the UE in the connected mode can be classified as either active or inactive, depending on the data-transferring activity; i.e. inactive if there is no data-transferring session, or active when it has an ongoing data transfer. Then, the inactive UE in connected mode can be switched to the inactive state rather than the idle state by releasing the RRC connection while keeping the core network connectivity [26–28]. As such, by entering the inactive mode, the UE can save energy while avoiding the heavy signalling that arises from the switch between the connected and idle states.

Moreover, from a mobility perspective, the mobility of the UE in the idle or inactive states is controlled by the UE itself, whereas the network becomes responsible for the mobility if the UE is in the connected state [26]. As reported in [29], mobility management in cellular networks can be broadly divided into two categories as idle/inactive state and connected state mobility. A similar fashion was followed in [30] with a slightly different terminology, namely location and HO management. In the following paragraphs, these different mobility concepts are investigated in a more detailed way.

- **Idle/inactive state mobility (location management):** Corresponds to the procedure taken just after the UE is powered on, as defined by 3GPP in [26,28]. Upon powered on, the UE is first supposed to select a public land mobile network, and it performs a cell selection based on current measurements and the 'S' criterion defined in [28]. When it selects a cell to camp on, it needs to continuously search for better cells, which is called as cell re-selection. The UE also requires to execute location registration, which helps the network to have an approximate location of the UE in order to perform a paging process. Therefore, in idle/inactive state mobility, location registration, cell selection, cell re-selection are the primary tasks to be carried out, and the procedures for idle and inactive modes are individually and comprehensively elaborated in 3GPP Release 15 [31].

- **Connected state mobility (HO management):** Corresponds when the UE is in the connected mode and has an ongoing data transmission. As such, the user is regarded as active and its mobility management becomes more challenging when compared to the aforementioned idle/inactive state mobility. Moreover, unlike the idle/inactive state mobility, connected state mobility is network controlled, but UE assisted. In particular, the UE keeps carrying out measurements on the signal quality from both the serving BS and neighbouring BSs in order to ensure that it is connected to the best cell around it [29,30,32,33]. When the UE is mobile, meaning that it changes its geographic location, it is quite likely that the signal qualities that it receives through measurements would vary continuously. This, by its turn, results in some neighbouring BSs providing better signal qualities than the serving one. Therefore, in these kind of cases, the UE would require its connection to be switched from the current serving cell to a neighbouring cell that is better than the serving cell in terms of signal quality. In this regard, HO is defined as the change of a serving cell of the UE while being active; i.e. having an ongoing data transmission.

Moreover, in terms of measurement reporting, it can be divided into two categories, periodic reporting or event triggered [29]. In periodic reporting, the UE performs measurements at regular intervals. On the other hand, in the case of event-triggered reporting, the UE sends its measurement reports to the serving BS only upon the occurrence of certain event conditions [29]. In other words, the UE assists the HO process in the following ways:

- by making measurements on signal strength from serving and neighbouring BSs;
- sending the measurement reports to the serving BS through one of the aforementioned strategies (periodic or event triggered).

After this point, the network control starts, in which the serving BS communicates with the target BS, selected as the best cell, to check its availability. Once the target cell admits the UE by ensuring that it has enough resources for it, the HO process is executed and completed through multiple signalling exchanges between different entities (e.g. UE, serving BS, target BS, and core network). This means that the UE is handed over to the target cell, which is the new serving cell, and the resources, which were allocated for the user in the previous serving cell, are released.

HOs can also be put in different taxonomies, such as intra-frequency/inter-frequency, intra-RAT/inter-RAT [29–31]. Intra-frequency HOs occur when the UE switches to a BS that transmits in the same frequency with the previous serving cell, while the HO is referred to as an inter-cell HO if the carrier frequencies of the serving cell and the target cell are different. Provided that two different FRs are already introduced in 5G NR, FR-1 and FR-2 [12], HOs between FRs are possible, as well as HOs within the same FR. While FR-1 covers sub-6 GHz frequencies, FR-2 includes mmWave frequencies above 24 GHz. Even though the HOs between different FRs can only be performed as inter-frequency, HO, the HOs within the same FR can be done as either intra-frequency or inter-frequency HO [31].

This chapter focuses on the second type of mobility (i.e. HOs), since it is more important for 5G networks given that:

- The heterogeneous characteristics of 5G networks, in which different type of BSs, such as macro, micro, and SCs (pico, femto) are included, make the HO management a more challenging task [2,3,13,29,33].
- Future networks are expected to have more frequent HOs due to:
  - network densification, which is envisioned to increase the number of SCs dramatically;
  - mmWave communications, in which the coverage areas of BSs are reduced, given that higher frequency bands are subject to more penetration losses.
- The QoS requirements of emerging applications, such as tactile internet, remote surgery, ultra-high definition video streaming, are demanding. Considering that HOs cause a reduction in perceived quality [27,29,33], meeting the QoS requirements of applications becomes more challenging.
- The number of devices connected to the Internet has been increasing, but it is expected to grow drastically, due to IoT applications. A report published by Ericsson forecasts that the number of IoT connections will reach 22.3 billion by 2024, which represents a 17% increase when compared to that of 2018, and 4.1 billion of the connections will be cellular IoT [34]. Considering this alongside the ever-increasing number of global mobile communication subscriptions, which is predicted to strike 8.8 billion by 2025 [34], the scenario becomes even more chaotic. Given that a portion of the IoT devices are mobile, requirement for a proper and efficient HO management will grow fast.

6.3   Predictive mobility management

It has become a cliché the fact that mobility management in cellular networks can be made more efficient and agile with the help of mobility prediction [29,32,33]. Considering the cognitive cycle [35] and cognitive networking [36] concepts for wireless communication networks, predictive mobility management can be broadly explained in three steps:

- **Obtaining contextual information:** Mobility-related behaviour of users are obtained in this phase. Some examples of contextual information to be gathered are:
  - exact locations of users (e.g. geographic coordinates);
  - attraction points visited;
  - trajectories taken;
  - mode of transportation (e.g. walk, car, bicycle);
  - sojourn time;
  - identification of places visited (e.g. home, work); and
  - HOs.

While some contextual information, such as location, sojourn time, and HOs, can be directly obtained with the help of both UE and network, some of them, such as identification of places and attraction points visited, require additional processing/analysis. Considering the needs of the application and capabilities of the agents,[1] the information to be collected can be decided accordingly.

- **Analysing/learning:** The collected information can be analysed in order to exploit meaningful information. This phase is needed due to the fact that the raw data could be hard to understand and does not necessarily include useful information [37–39]. Moreover, there could be hidden patterns in the data, which is difficult to figure out without further analysis. A raw data set consisting of coordinates of a user with corresponding time stamps at certain time intervals would be not meaningful as it is; however, some additional processing, such as statistical analysis or machine learning algorithms, can reveal some correlations and patterns in the data. For example, a user always leaves their home at around 08.30 in the morning in weekdays and commutes to work. The user also stops by a certain café to have a cup of coffee before completing its route to work. However, the user does not have any regular pattern at weekends and takes different trajectories; e.g. sometimes stays at home whole day and some other times goes to various events, such as cinema and concert, at different locations. Therefore, it can be inferred that this specific user has certain patterns with almost strict timings in the weekdays, whereas no obvious patters/regularities are observed for weekends. In summary, this analysing/learning phase converts the obtained information to meaningful knowledge.
- **Future predictions:** After data collection and its corresponding analysis, the developed knowledge/model can now be utilised for various use cases. By analysing the HO occurrences for a specific user by taking into account the involved BSs and the time stamp, the next or multistep ahead HOs of the users can be predicted, which, in turn, help in achieving seamless HOs.

Figure 6.1 demonstrates the LTE X2-based HO flow diagram for both predictive and non-predictive HO cases [32,40]. Note that predictive HO refers to the case where the target BS for the next HO of the user is predicted, which subsequently helps reducing the number of steps taken during the HO by executing some of the HO steps in advance. Furthermore, HO predictions are divided into two categories, according to the accuracy of the prediction: correct predictions (CPs) and incorrect predictions (IP). While the former means that the target BS for the next HO is predicted accurately, the latter happens when the predicted and target BSs are not the same. In particular, steps 1–10 are performed during non-predictive HO; 4–12 are for predictive HO with CP; and IP-1, IP-2, and 1–10 (all inclusive) for predictive HO with IP. It is worth noting that steps CP-1–CP-3 are taken in advance of an HO for the CP case, meaning that steps 1–3 of non-predictive case are eliminated with the predictive HO management with CP.

Therefore, as it is obvious from Figure 6.1, the predictive HO with CP case is more profitable compared to the non-predictive case in terms of number of signalling during

---

[1]Agent can refer to the entities that are involved in the predictive mobility management. It can be an individual entity, such as UE, as well as cooperation of different entities, such as UE–BS pair.

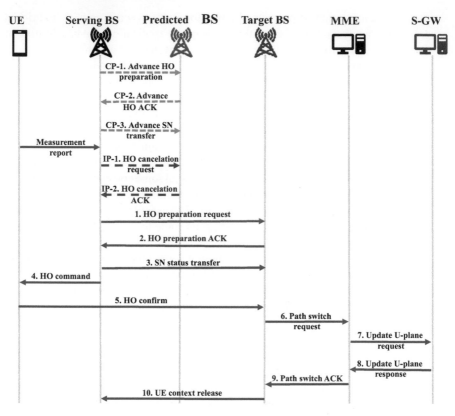

*Figure 6.1   LTE-X2-interface-based HO process (adopted from [32,40]). CP,
correct prediction; IP, incorrect prediction; SN, sequence number;
ACK, acknowledgement. Steps CP-1–CP-3 only apply to the CP case,
while steps IP-1 and IP-2 are only valid for IP case.*

an HO, whereas IP makes the predictive HO case more costly than the non-predictive
one. There are two primary takeaways from these phenomena:

- HO processes can be made less costly via predictive HO with CP, resulting in less
  signalling overhead and HO latency. This, in turn, promotes seamless HOs, which
  is envisioned to be one of the integral characteristics of 5G networks [41,42].
- Prediction accuracy plays a crucial role, since IPs can make the whole process less
  efficient by increasing the HO signalling and latency. Thus, more efficient mobility prediction algorithms should be developed given that the average gain from
  the predictive mobility-management process enhances with increasing prediction
  accuracy, such that [32,40]:

$$E[C_{HO}] = AC_{CP} + (1 - A)C_{IP}, \tag{6.1}$$

where $E[C_{HO}]$ is the expected HO cost, A is the prediction accuracy. C_{CP} and C_{IP} HO costs for CP and IP cases, respectively. Note that the HO cost can be any cost related to HO, such as signalling overhead and latency.

There are many studies available in the literature regarding the predictive mobility management for cellular networks, and they are discussed in the following paragraphs.

6.3.1 State of the art in predictive mobility management

In this section, recent predictive mobility-management approaches are presented in order to draw the state of the art. In [43], the authors aim to reduce ping-pong HOs as well as HO failures. Signal-to-noise-plus-interference ratio (SINR) is predicted in order to obtain knowledge on future-received power levels from the serving BS. In particular, with the help of future SINR – received from the serving BS – predictions, more informed HO decision can be made, which, in turn, helps minimising HO-related problems. To this end, HO margin and time-to-trigger (TTT) are considered as HO parameters; while HO margin is kept fixed, TTT is dynamically adjusted based on SINR predictions. First, when any candidate BS starts outperforming the serving BS in terms of received signal power, instead of waiting for a fixed TTT for this condition to be maintained, the authors propose to use predicted SINR values from the serving BS; such that the HO is only triggered if the SINR value of currently serving BS is found to be less than a certain threshold, which is basically an SINR value sufficient for healthy connection, for a certain time period. The authors evaluate the proposed algorithm by considering perfect predictions of the future SINR values – in order to obtain the upper bound for the potential gain – in addition to the developed recursive least squares algorithm, and the results revealed significant reductions in ping-pong HOs and HO failures.

Another similar work is proposed in [44], in which the authors introduce a comprehensive mobility prediction process. Two different types of memories, short-term and long-term, with different objectives are initially introduced. First, the UE performs signal quality and signal strength measurements from surrounding BSs,[2] which are stored in the short-term memory. Then, by utilising these stored measurements, future signal quality and signal strength predictions are carried out for both the serving BS and neighbouring BSs, followed by checking whether the predefined HO criteria are met. After that the output of this process is consolidated by statistical HO probability analysis with the help of historical HOs that are stored in the long-term memory. On the one hand, if the HO probability is above a certain threshold value, then the previously predicted HO is confirmed and predictive HO is triggered. On the other hand, in case the HO probability stays below that threshold, then the system backs off and triggers conventional non-predictive HO process. The location, speed, and direction of the UE are also investigated in order to save from storage and computational power, and the obtained results confirm that the proposed method is able to considerably reduce the HO latency.

---

[2]The control/data separated architecture is adopted in this work, and the HOs occur between data BSs. Therefore, for this work, BS refers to data BS.

The authors in [45] develop a predictive mobility prediction model for cellular networks. In particular, the objective of [45] is to make the resource utilisation more efficient with the help of proactive HO management. Semi-Markov renewal process was considered to model the user mobility, and corresponding HO predictions are performed through this model. In order to evaluate their model, the authors carried out data collection, where the HOs of selected users were recorded with corresponding time stamps for a period of 1 month. The developed semi-Markov model was trained with this collected data set. The authors evaluate their prediction accuracy performance, and promising results are obtained for specific cases, despite the model not working equally well for others. A numerical analysis on the gain for the resource utilisation is also performed, and the results confirm that the prediction accuracy plays a crucial role in making the predictive method more efficient than that of the conventional non-predictive process.

In [46], on the other hand, a recursive neural network (RNN)-based predictive mobility prediction approach is presented. In this regard, two different RNN architectures, long-short term memory (LSTM) and echo state network (ESN), are developed, and, as a benchmark, they are compared to a Kalman filter predictor. The trajectories used in training and testing phases were generated artificially, i.e. synthetic data, in order to evaluate the performance of the considered methods. The work mostly focuses on the prediction accuracy by investigating various parameters affecting it, such as RNN architecture and output structure. While the former refers to LSTM and ESN architectures, the latter refers to single and multiple output scenarios. The obtained results showcase that the benchmark method, Kalman filters, and ESN performed better with a single output owing to their linear characteristics, while LSTM predominantly performed better with multiple outputs due to its non-linear structure.

A probability suffix tree (PST)-based predictive mobility management is introduced in [47] by considering a cellular network with control-data separation. Moreover, the work considers ultra-dense wireless networks, and two different PST learning algorithms are developed (user specific and global). While the former is utilised when users have frequent visit patterns in the master eNodeB in question, the latter is for those who can be considered as random users, due to their insufficient presence in the area of the master eNodeB. Furthermore, during the execution phase of the developed mobility method, two different approaches are adopted: network controlled and user autonomous. Similar to the aforementioned work, which proposes a predictive HO management, the network-controlled one helps in shortening the HO process by executing some of the steps prior to the HO event. The user-autonomous one, on the other hand, is proposed to transfer some of the HO responsibilities to the user in order to reduce the network tasks.

In [48], the authors argue the importance of prediction accuracy, and reached a conclusion that it is not always profitable to perform a predictive HO. Then, a threshold mechanism is developed and the prediction accuracy of a predictor is assessed; such that if the prediction accuracy is above the threshold then the predictive HO process is triggered, otherwise if the threshold is not met, then the conventional non-predictive HO mechanism is executed.

6.4 Advanced Markov-chain-assisted predictive mobility management

As it can be seen, mobility management is expected to play a fundamental role in future networks. As such, several techniques, as shown in Section 6.2, have been applied to mobility management. One technique that has seen increased application in this context are Markov chains. Next, a brief overview on how Markov chains can be utilised in mobility prediction is presented, along with its disadvantages and possible ways to overcome them.

6.4.1 Markov-chain-based mobility prediction

Markov chain is a stochastic process that is used for time-variant probabilistic modelling. It is basically used for modelling the transition probabilities among states, which can be a condition that an agent is in. For an electronic device, for instance, the switching options can be defined as states, such that the device is in the *on* state when it is switched on and in the *off* state if it is switched off.

A formal definition of Markov chain, as described in [49], would be as follows: Let $(\mathcal{Y}, \mathcal{F}, P)$ be the probability space, where $\mathcal{Y}$, $\mathcal{F}$, and P are sample spaces that include all the possible outcomes; set of events; and measure function for the probabilities of the events, respectively. Moreover, let $(X, \mathcal{X})$ be a measurable space and $\mathcal{F}_i, i \in I$ be a filtration, where I is the index. Then, an adapted stochastic process $\{(X_i, \mathcal{F}_i), i \in I\}$ is said to be a Markov chain if

$$P(X_{i+1} \in \mathcal{G} | \mathcal{F}_i) = P(X_{i+1} \in \mathcal{G} | X_i), \tag{6.2}$$

for all $i \in I$ and $\mathcal{G} \in \mathcal{X}$ [49]. Therefore, the Markov property states that the outcome of any experiment depends only on the information available at the present time, which is i in this case.

Figure 6.2 demonstrates transitions among three different states, where $p_{i,j}$ is the transition probability from state i to state j, and $\sum_{j=1}^{N_{m,s}} p_{i,j} = 1$, where $N_{m,s}$ is the

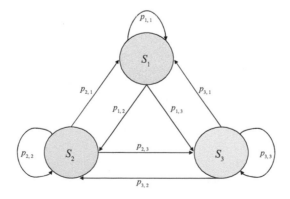

Figure 6.2   A sample Markov chain with three states, $N_{m,s} = 3$

number of available states. Markov-chain-based predictors define the transition probability from a current state to other states by building a transition matrix, which consists
of transition probabilities between the current state and all other possible states. One
of the main properties of Markov chains is that its predictions only dependent on the
current state of a user. The transition matrix can then be written as

$$\vec{\mathcal{T}} = \begin{bmatrix} p_{1,1} & \cdots & p_{1,N_{m,s}} \\ \vdots & \vdots & \vdots \\ p_{N_{m,s},1} & \cdots & p_{N_{m,s},N_{m,s}} \end{bmatrix}. \tag{6.3}$$

Then, the Markov-chain-based predictor makes a prediction by following a
model [50]:

$$\vec{p}_m = \vec{p}_0 \vec{\mathcal{T}}^m, \tag{6.4}$$

where $\vec{p}_m$ and $\vec{p}_0$ are the probability vectors belonging to the mth transition and the
initial distribution vector, respectively.

In the context of mobility management, the states of a Markov chain can be
seen as a user-cell association, in which the BS identification corresponds to the
state. Moreover, the transition matrix would then represent the probability of a user
transitioning from the current BS to one of its neighbours, and the initial distribution
can be given according to use mobility data, for example. In this context, the authors
in [40] propose a discrete-time Markov chain model in order to perform mobility
prediction and minimise the HO signalling cost of a control-data-separated network
scenario. Despite their simplicity, Markov chains are shown to be quite robust and are
able to predict the user's trajectory in terms of an HO sequence, decreasing signalling
costs.

6.4.2   Problem with the conventional Markov chains

However, despite their success, Markov chains have an inherit problem associated
to them, and that is of relying on a matrix in order to predict the next movement
of a user. Because this matrix is built based on a Markov process, it suffers from its
inherit memoryless property, which states that the conditional probability distribution
of future states depends only upon the present state [51]. Thus, it can be seen that due
to this property, issues can arise whenever there are re-visits (defined as whenever a
user visits the same BS more than once) in a given user's path. For example, given
that a user visits the same cell twice, but performs HO to different BSs, at the end
of the learning stage the probability of going to either one of the cells is of 50%.
As such, it can be seen that despite utilising a Markov chain to learn this transition
probability, there is no meaningful information learned and its performance would be
the same as of a random prediction. Based on that it is clear that whenever the path of

a given user does not include re-visits, Markov chain can work very well for mobility prediction. However, if re-visits occur, problems can arise and other solutions are necessary.

6.4.3   Introduction to 3D transition matrix

In order to mitigate the effects of re-visits in Markov-chain-based mobility prediction, two approaches can be considered, one is to include information about previous states, as in [52], while another is to include information about the order of states (i.e. the order in which each HO occurs), as in [53].

Considering the case of adding the HO order information to a conventional Markov chain. This can be done by building a 3D transition matrix, in which each row and column represent the probabilities between BSs, while the third dimension represents the order of the HO. In a more general manner, this idea can be described as a system that builds individual 2D transition matrices for each HO in a day, and then at the end of it, all matrices are combined, building a 3D transition matrix. Thus, whenever re-visits occur, a completely new 2D matrix is analysed, and since the same BS cannot be re-visited in a consecutive manner (otherwise there is no HO), the problem of re-visits is solved.

6.4.4   Performance evaluation

Based on this, a framework is proposed in which a 3D transition matrix is built in order to solve re-visit problems in Markov chains mobility-management-based algorithms. A simulation environment in MATLAB® is considered, in which 19 cells of a network are simulated and the movement of a single user through the system over a period of 100 days, with 10 HOs per day is considered. In order to analyse the effect of re-visits, two cases are considered, one in which the path of a user considers only different BSs (no re-visits), and another, in which a path having 50% re-visits is considered. Moreover, four scenarios with different route randomness are also investigated: 0% randomness, 15% randomness, 30% randomness, and 45% randomness. The accuracy of the two proposed methods are evaluated against a trajectory-dependent parameter, α, which basically acts as the learning rate of the system (i.e. a smaller value of α updates the transition matrix slowly, while a larger value of α updates it more quickly). Moreover, after choosing the most appropriate α for each scenario, the two methods are compared in terms of HO signalling cost, defined as the number of bytes exchanged during HO control messages, according to [40].

From Figures 6.3 and 6.4, it is clear that the performance of the proposed 3D transition matrix algorithm largely outperforms the performance of conventional 2D transition matrix Markov chains. It can be seen that when re-visits occur, 2D Markov chains are not able to make CPs, achieving its best performance of only around 42%, when no randomness is included in the user's route. On the other hand, when a 3D matrix is introduced, the performance approaches to 100% in the no randomness scenario.

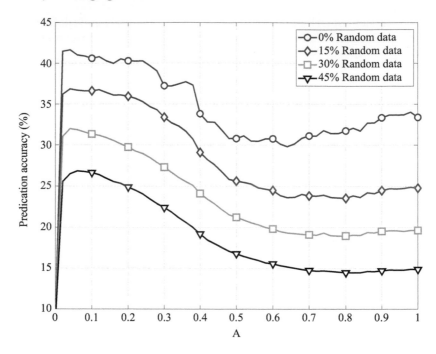

Figure 6.3   Prediction accuracy of the 2D Markov chain algorithm

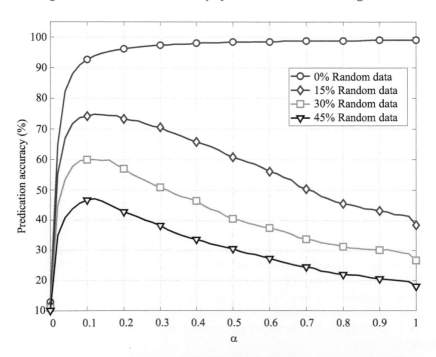

Figure 6.4   Prediction accuracy of the 3D Markov chain algorithm

Another interesting find is the effect of parameter α in the performance of the system. In general, it can be concluded that a larger α translates to a worse performance in the system, with the sole exception to this rule being the case of the 3D matrix and no randomness. This occurs because whenever α increases, the matrix remembers only the most recent transitions performed by the users, whereas when α is smaller, more transitions are taken into account. As such, whenever there is randomness in the user's route, more prediction errors are bound to be done for a larger α. On the other hand, if the route is fixed, a larger α definitely helps, as the matrix is able to converge faster to the learned values. Lastly, it can also be seen that α plays an important role in the system and should be chosen accordingly.

Based on that, for the evaluation in terms of HO signalling costs, the best values of α for each curve were chosen and results are shown in Figure 6.5.

From Figure 6.5, it can be seen that the proposed 3D matrix achieves a better performance than the conventional 2D approach in all considered scenarios. This occurs because the 3D matrix is able to make less mistakes in the mobility prediction, as such, it is able to allocate resources in advance in the correct BS, minimising the HO signalling costs. On the other hand, the conventional 2D Markov method, as seen from Figure 6.3, is not able to correctly predict the next cell of a user; thus, HO signalling is sent to the wrong BS, increasing its total cost. In addition, it can also be seen that due to the large amount of errors, even when predictions are done, the performance can be worse than a no prediction scenario. As such, the impact of CP and incorrect predictions plays an important role in the signalling exchange in mobility management.

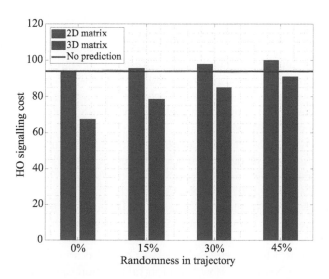

Figure 6.5   HO signalling cost for both 2D and 3D methods and different levels of trajectory randomness

6.5 Summary

Mobility management has already been identified as one of the key design challenges for cellular networks. Given the heterogeneous characteristics and new technologies, such as network densification, mmWave communication, it will be even more crucial and challenging for 5G networks. In this regards, predictive mobility-management techniques, which propose proactive HO process, have attracted a considerable amount of research activity owing to their efficiency in terms of latency, signalling overhead, etc. To this end, in this chapter, the predictive mobility management was discussed in detail with state of the art after a brief discussions on the mobility management in cellular networks. Then, the 3D-transition-matrix-assisted Markov-chain-based predictive mobility management, which offers enhancement in the prediction performances in the cases of re-visits, was introduced followed by performance evaluations in not only prediction accuracy but also HO costs.

References

[1]   Rappaport T. Wireless Communications: Principles and Practice. 2nd ed. Prentice Hall Communications Engineering and Emerging Technologies Series. Prentice Hall; 2002.

[2]   Aliu OG, Imran A, Imran MA, *et al.* A Survey of Self Organisation in Future Cellular Networks. IEEE Communications Surveys Tutorials. 2013 First;15(1):336–361.

[3]   Gupta A and Jha RK. A Survey of 5G Network: Architecture and Emerging Technologies. IEEE Access. 2015;3:1206–1232.

[4]   Evans BG and Baughan K. Visions of 4G. Electronics Communication Engineering Journal. 2000;12(6):293–303.

[5]   Stuckmann P and Zimmermann R. Toward Ubiquitous and Unlimited-Capacity Communication Networks: European Research in Framework Programme 7. IEEE Communications Magazine. 2007;45(5):148–157.

[6]   ITU-R. Requirements Related to Technical Performance for IMT-Advanced Radio Interface(s). International Telecommunication Union-Radio Communication Sector; 2008. M.2134.

[7]   Adeel A, Gogate M, Farooq S, *et al.* In: Durrani TS, Wang W, and Forbes SM, editors. A Survey on the Role of Wireless Sensor Networks and IoT in Disaster Management. Singapore: Springer Singapore; 2019. p. 57–66. Available from: https://doi.org/10.1007/978-981-13-0992-2_5.

[8]   Heath RW, Laus G, Quek TQS, *et al.* Signal Processing for the 5G Revolution [From the Guest Editors]. IEEE Signal Processing Magazine. 2014;31(6): 12–13.

[9]   Di Taranto R, Muppirisetty S, Raulefs R, *et al.* Location-Aware Communications for 5G Networks: How Location Information Can Improve Scalability, Latency, and Robustness of 5G. IEEE Signal Processing Magazine. 2014; 31(6):102–112.

[10] Kumar S, Gupta G, and Singh KR. 5G: Revolution of future communication technology. In: 2015 International Conference on Green Computing and Internet of Things (ICGCIoT). Noida, India: IEEE (USA); 2015. p. 143–147.

[11] 3GPP. 5G; Study on Scenarios and Requirements for Next Generation Access Technologies. 3rd Generation Partnership Project (3GPP); 2018. 38.913.

[12] 3GPP. 5G; NR; Base Station (BS) Radio Transmission and Reception. 3rd Generation Partnership Project (3GPP); 2018. 38.104.

[13] Shafi M, Molisch AF, Smith PJ, et al. 5G: A Tutorial Overview of Standards, Trials, Challenges, Deployment, and Practice. IEEE Journal on Selected Areas in Communications. 2017;35(6):1201–1221.

[14] Rappaport TS, Xing Y, MacCartney GR, et al. Overview of Millimeter Wave Communications for Fifth-Generation (5G) Wireless Networks—With a Focus on Propagation Models. IEEE Transactions on Antennas and Propagation. 2017;65(12):6213–6230.

[15] Busari SA, Mumtaz S, Al-Rubaye S, et al. 5G Millimeter-Wave Mobile Broadband: Performance and Challenges. IEEE Communications Magazine. 2018;56(6):137–143.

[16] Mesodiakaki A, Adelantado F, Alonso L, et al. Energy- and Spectrum-Efficient User Association in Millimeter-Wave Backhaul Small-Cell Networks. IEEE Transactions on Vehicular Technology. 2017;66(2):1810–1821.

[17] Torrieri D, Talarico S, and Valenti MC. Analysis of a Frequency-Hopping Millimeter-Wave Cellular Uplink. IEEE Transactions on Wireless Communications. 2016;15(10):7089–7098.

[18] Jameel F, Faisal F., Haider MAA, et al. Massive MIMO: A survey of recent advances, research issues and future directions. In: 2017 International Symposium on Recent Advances in Electrical Engineering (RAEE). Islamabad, Pakistan: IEEE (USA); 2017. p. 1–6.

[19] Albreem MA, Juntti M, and Shahabuddin S. Massive MIMO Detection Techniques: A Survey. IEEE Communications Surveys Tutorials. 2019;1: 3109–3132.

[20] Larsson EG, Edfors O, Tufvesson F, et al. Massive MIMO for Next Generation Wireless Systems. IEEE Communications Magazine. 2014;52(2): 186–195.

[21] Idachaba FE. 5G networks: Open network architecture and densification strategies for beyond 1000x network capacity increase. In: 2016 Future Technologies Conference (FTC). San Francisco, CA, USA: IEEE; 2016. p. 1265–1269.

[22] Romanous B, Bitar N, Imran A, et al. Network densification: Challenges and opportunities in enabling 5G. In: 2015 IEEE 20th International Workshop on Computer Aided Modelling and Design of Communication Links and Networks (CAMAD). Guildford, UK: IEEE (USA); 2015. p. 129–134.

[23] Giust F, Cominardi L, and Bernardos CJ. Distributed Mobility Management for Future 5G Networks: Overview and Analysis of Existing Approaches. IEEE Communications Magazine. 2015;53(1):142–149.

[24] 3GPP. Universal Mobile Telecommunications System (UMTS); Vocabulary for 3GPP Specifications. 3rd Generation Partnership Project (3GPP); 2003. TR 21.905.

[25]   3GPP. 5G; 5G System; Access and Mobility Management Services; Stage 3. 3rd Generation Partnership Project (3GPP); 2018. TS 29.518.

[26]   3GPP. 5G; NR; Radio Resource Control (RRC); Protocol Specification. 3rd Generation Partnership Project (3GPP); 2018. TS 38.331.

[27]   Khlass A, Laselva D, and Jarvela R. On the flexible and performance-enhanced radio resource control for 5G NR networks. In: 2019 IEEE 90th Vehicular Technology Conference (VTC2019-Fall). Honolulu, HI, USA: IEEE; 2019. p. 1–6.

[28]   3GPP. 5G; NR; User Equipment (UE) Procedures in Idle Mode and in RRC Inactive State. 3rd Generation Partnership Project (3GPP); 2018. TS 38.304.

[29]   Tayyab M, Gelabert X, and Jäntti R. A Survey on Handover Management: From LTE to NR. IEEE Access. 2019;7:118907–118930.

[30]   Sen J. Mobility and Handoff Management in Wireless Networks. In: Trends in Telecommunications Technologies. InTech; 2010. Available from: https://doi.org/10.5772%2F8482.

[31]   3GPP. 5G; NR; Requirements for Support of Radio Resource Management. 3rd Generation Partnership Project (3GPP); 2018. TS 38.133.

[32]   Ozturk M, Gogate M, Onireti O, *et al.* A Novel Deep Learning Driven, Low-Cost Mobility Prediction Approach for 5G Cellular Networks: The Case of the Control/Data Separation Architecture (CDSA). Neurocomputing. 2019; 358:479–489. Available from: http://www.sciencedirect.com/science/article/pii/S0925231219300438.

[33]   Zhang H and Dai L. Mobility Prediction: A Survey on State-of-the-Art Schemes and Future Applications. IEEE Access. 2019;7:802–822.

[34]   Ericsson. Ericsson Mobility Report; 2019. Available from: https://www.ericsson.com/49d1d9/assets/local/mobility-report/documents/2019/ericsson-mobility-report-june-2019.pdf.

[35]   III JM. Cognitive Radio Architecture. In: Cognitive Radio, Software Defined Radio, and Adaptive Wireless Systems. The Netherlands: Springer; 2006. p. 43–107. Available from: https://doi.org/10.1007%2F978-1-4020-5542-3_3.

[36]   Thomas RW, DaSilva LA, and MacKenzie AB. Cognitive networks. In: First IEEE International Symposium on New Frontiers in Dynamic Spectrum Access Networks, 2005 (DySPAN). Baltimore, MD, USA: IEEE; 2005. p. 352–360.

[37]   Cheng X, Fang L, Yang L, *et al.* Mobile Big Data: The Fuel for Data-Driven Wireless. IEEE Internet of Things Journal. 2017;4(5):1489–1516.

[38]   Wang J, Wu Y, Yen N, *et al.* Big Data Analytics for Emergency Communication Networks: A Survey. IEEE Communications Surveys Tutorials. 2016 Third quarter;18(3):1758–1778.

[39]   Liu Y, Kong L, and Chen G. Data-Oriented Mobile Crowdsensing: A Comprehensive Survey. IEEE Communications Surveys Tutorials. 2019 Third quarter;21(3):2849–2885.

[40]   Mohamed A, Onireti O, Hoseinitabatabaei SA, *et al.* Mobility prediction for handover management in cellular networks with control/data separation. In: 2015 IEEE International Conference on Communications (ICC). London, UK (USA): IEEE; 2015. p. 3939–3944.

[41] Huang X, Tang S, Zheng Q, *et al.* Dynamic Femtocell gNB On/Off Strategies and Seamless Dual Connectivity in 5G Heterogeneous Cellular Networks. IEEE Access. 2018;6:21359–21368.

[42] Zhang Z, Junhui Z, Ni S, *et al.* A Seamless Handover Scheme With Assisted eNB for 5G C/U Plane Split Heterogeneous Network. IEEE Access. 2019;7:164256–164264.

[43] Bastidas-Puga ER, Andrade G, Galaviz G, *et al.* Handover Based on a Predictive Approach of Signal-to-Interference-Plus-Noise Ratio for Heterogeneous Cellular Networks. IET Communications. 2019;13(6):672–678.

[44] Mohamed A, Imran MA, Xiao P, *et al.* Memory-Full Context-Aware Predictive Mobility Management in Dual Connectivity 5G Networks. IEEE Access. 2018;6:9655–9666.

[45] Farooq H and Imran A. Spatiotemporal Mobility Prediction in Proactive Self-Organizing Cellular Networks. IEEE Communications Letters. 2017;21(2):370–373.

[46] Zhang W, Liu Y, Liu T, *et al.* Trajectory prediction with recurrent neural networks for predictive resource allocation. In: 2018 14th IEEE International Conference on Signal Processing (ICSP). Beijing, China: IEEE (USA); 2018. p. 634–639.

[47] Sun Y, Chang Y, Hu M, *et al.* A Universal Predictive Mobility Management Scheme for Urban Ultra-Dense Networks With Control/Data Plane Separation. IEEE Access. 2017;5:6015–6026.

[48] Ozturk M, Klaine PV, and Imran MA. Improvement on the performance of predictive handover management by setting a threshold. In: 2017 IEEE 86th Vehicular Technology Conference (VTC-Fall). Toronto, ON, Canada: IEEE (USA); 2017. p. 1–5.

[49] Douc R, Moulines E, Priouret P, *et al.* Markov Chains. Springer International Publishing; 2018. Available from: https://doi.org/10.1007%2F978-3-319-97704-1.

[50] Mohamed A, Onireti O, Imran MA, *et al.* Predictive and Core-Network Efficient RRC Signalling for Active State Handover in RANs With Control/Data Separation. IEEE Transactions on Wireless Communications. 2017;16(3):1423–1436.

[51] Markov A and Nagorny N. Algorithm Theory. Trudy Matematicheskogo Instituta Akademiia nauk SSSR. 1954;42:1–376.

[52] Ozturk M, Klaine PV, and Imran MA. Introducing a novel minimum accuracy concept for predictive mobility management schemes. In: 2018 IEEE International Conference on Communications Workshops (ICC Workshops). Kansas City, MO, USA: IEEE; 2018. p. 1–6.

[53] Ozturk M, Klaine PV, and Imran MA. 3D transition matrix solution for a path dependency problem of Markov chains-based prediction in cellular networks. In: 2017 IEEE 86th Vehicular Technology Conference (VTC-Fall). Toronto, ON, Canada: IEEE (USA); 2017. p. 1–5.

Chapter 7

Artificial intelligence and data analytics in 5G and beyond-5G wireless networks

Maziar Nekovee[1,2], Dehao Wu[2], Yue Wang[3]
and Mehrdad Shariat[3]

5G technologies are expected to enable new verticals, services, and business models. Recently, the use of artificial intelligence (AI) and data analytics is shown to provide massive advantages in terms of reducing network complexity and enhancing its performance. In this chapter, we provide an overview of the recent studies on AI-assisted solutions in 5G wireless networks, followed by three case studies of our original work, including a *Q*-learning-assisted cell selection mechanism, an AI engine that enables intelligent 5G fronthaul slicing, and a beam management protocol for a multiple radio access technology (RAT) coexistence via learning. Realizing the vital role of data and data analytics in enabling AI for wireless networks in practice, we review data analytics in the current literature and discuss how data analytics and AI enable the applications in 5G networks. The recent industry and standardization activities of using AI in 5G networks are summarized. Finally, we give our insights on the research challenges and open questions.

7.1 Introduction

Future wireless networks are data intensive and service driven. Globally, the number of cellular-connected devices will rise from 5.6 billion connections in 2016 to more than 7.5 billion by year-end 2021, and monthly cellular usage across connected devices from an average of 2.1 GB per month, per device to more than 6.5 GB [1]. In addition to the growing traffic over the wireless links, future wireless networks are also required to support diverse services, i.e., verticals, with different and often diverging requirements, which has posed exponential growth of the networks in scale and complexity, as well as significant challenges on the design of networks.

[1]Quantrom Technologies Ltd., London, UK
[2]Centre for Advanced Communications Mobile Technologies and IoT, School of Engineering and Informatics, University of Sussex, Brighton, UK
[3]Network Standards and Research, Samsung R&D Institute, UK

5G, the latest generation of cellular technologies, will drive a significant digital transformation to fulfill these requirements. Data transmission over multiple radio interfaces and fast handover between them are required for mobile devices. Therefore, integration of multiple different RATs is considered as one of the most promising techniques. In addition, 5G networks are expected to operate over the conventional sub-6 GHz band, the new mmWave bands as well as unlicensed spectrum, including the 60 GHz mmWave frequencies [2]. In the context of 5G in unlicensed bands, the multi-standard and multi-operator spectrum sharing imposes significant challenges in terms of coexistence and efficient use of spectrum. A broad set of new technologies is being developed to enhance the emerging 5G capabilities, including network virtualization that combines hardware and software network resources and network functionality into a single, software-based administrative entity [2]. Network virtualization has posed great opportunities to enable the application of AI in the networks at the radio access network (RAN), edge, and the core network. The use of AI is envisaged to provide flexible and context-aware solutions to address the challenges in dynamic 5G wireless networks [3]. An artificial neural network (ANN)-based approach was proposed for tackling various challenges that arise in multi-RAT scenarios [4]. In [5], ANN was shown to allow multimode base stations (BSs) to steer their traffic flows between the mmWave, the microwave, and the unlicensed band based on the availability of a line-of-sight link, congestion on the licensed band, and the availability of the unlicensed band. Another application of deep learning (DL) ANNs in the context of Long-Term Evolution-Unlicensed (LTE-U) and Wi-Fi coexistence is presented in [6]. The proposed approach enables multiple small BSs to proactively perform dynamic channel selection, carrier aggregation, and fractional spectrum access while guaranteeing fairness with existing Wi-Fi networks and other LTE-U operators. Compared to an LTE network, 5G is required to provide ubiquitous connectivity by deploying a much denser network, and the number of available access points is much higher. Therefore, cell selection based on the measurements of the user equipment (UE) becomes more complicated. In the following case studies, we will address this issue by adopting an AI-assisted learning algorithm to optimize the network throughput. A holistic consideration of AI for 5G wireless systems should include not only access technologies but also wireless backhaul and fronthaul challenges and potential AI-assisted solutions. Therefore, in this work, we also address the implication of the 5G network slicing paradigm for fronthaul design. We describe the design of a novel AI-assisted 5G orchestrator that uses an AI engine to dynamically monitor and manage the very complex slicing operation at fronthaul level. In addition, at 5G fronthaul, the complexity of the network resource slicing is addressed in our case studies. An AI engine is proposed and incorporated as part of the fronthaul orchestrator, to govern different actions and optimize the system performance.

The rest of this chapter is organized as follows. Our case studies are presented in Section 7.2. In Section 7.3, we discuss the data analytics; we address how data analytics can be leveraged to facilitate the use of AI, and how data analytics and AI are convergence in 5G wireless networks. Then, recent industry and standardization of 5G networks are summarized in Section 7.4. Finally, in Section 7.5, research challenges and open questions are discussed, followed by conclusions in Section 7.6.

7.2   Case studies of AI in 5G wireless networks

There are variety of scenarios and vertical applications in 5G networks. Use cases are expected to drive 5G applications in smart mobility, smart wearables, e-Health, smart utility management, home automation, smart antenna, smart grids, and many more, with each requiring different levels of bandwidth, reliability, and latency. Data collected from various sources have different formats and exhibit complex correlations. AI algorithms are therefore proposed to uncover those unknown properties within the networks and to assist for optimizing network operations. In this section, we present a case study of a Q-learning-assisted cell selection scenario and demonstrate its enhanced performance. Following this, additional case studies covering the use of AI for 5G fronthaul slicing and 5G coexistence in mmWave bands are all presented.

7.2.1   Case study 1: AI for cell selection

In an LTE network, there may be only one or several BSs available to provide an acceptable level of connection to a UE. In contrast, in a 5G network, the number of available BSs can be much higher. This poses significant challenges for cell selection and reselection with a conventional LTE procedure based on the measurements of the UEs [7]. First, complexity of measurements and signalling overhead increases significantly as the number of possible connections increases. Second, the selection is made based on *instantaneous* measurement from a single UE, and therefore, it is not optimal when the entire network is considered.

In the example illustrated in Figure 7.1(a) and (b), we consider two UEs, and three surrounding BSs. Suppose UE2 is already connected to BS2, and UE1 enters

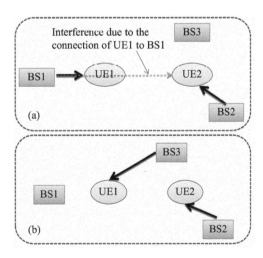

Figure 7.1   Cell selection scenarios: (a) UE1 associated with BS1 and (b) instead UE1 associates with BS3, and both UE1 and UE2 can maintain high SINR

the network and is searching for connection to a BS. In the conventional solution, the network would instruct UE to associate to a BS that has the highest measured signal strength. However, if UE1 connects to BS1, UE2 receives a high level of interference from the downlink transmission of BS1; therefore, the overall network throughput degrades significantly. Depending on the locations of the UEs and the context of the network, there exists a "best" association mechanism where high throughput of the entire network, rather than just the throughput of an individual UE, can be achieved.

Obtaining such an optimal solution is nontrivial. The dynamicity of the network combined with the large number of UEs and the highly dynamic nature of channels make it extremely difficult to model the environment. However, in this situation, the use of AI can greatly help with the cell selection and reselection process. Such autonomous and optimized BS–UE association can be achieved using, e.g., a Q-learning algorithm. Q-learning is a model-free reinforcement-learning algorithm. The goal of Q-learning is to learn a policy that tells an agent what action to take under what circumstances. It does not require a model (hence the connotation "model-free") of the environment, and it can handle problems with stochastic transitions and rewards, without requiring adaptations. The algorithm, therefore, has a function that calculates the quality of a state-action combination: $Q{:}S \times A \to R$. Before learning begins, Q is initialized to a possibly arbitrary fixed value. Then, at each time t, the agent selects an action $\mathbf{A}(t)$, observes a reward $\mathbf{R}(t)$, enters a new state $\mathbf{S}(t+1)$ (that may depend on both the previous state $\mathbf{S}(t)$ and the selected action), and Q is updated.

In our approach, the algorithm first collects data, including the UE locations, beam patterns, and the achieved throughput of individual UE. Then a Q-learning algorithm provides an estimate of the "reward," i.e., the average throughput of the network at a given time, t, according to the actions taken, which in this case is the immediate network throughput given the current environment and connection of BS–UE pair. Following this, the BS then instructs the UE on the optimal BS to connect to. The result of the actions, when applied to BS and UE, in turn, affects the current network throughput and the decision on which actions to take in the future, i.e., the next time instance.

We give an example of the procedure as follows:

1. The network collects data from the past UEs' experience. Examples of such data include the locations, beam patterns used for transmission, and the achieved throughput of individual UE (which requires the UEs to feed back to the network).
2. Each UE feed backs these data to a central network management unit as input to the network management algorithm.
3. The network management unit runs the proposed algorithm and outputs an "action" to the UE, where in our case the action here is specifically to instruct the UE to which BS it should be associated with.

In the proposed algorithm, we first collect data that include the locations, beam patterns used for transmission, and the achieved throughput of individual UE. In particular, the achieved throughput of each individual UE (e.g., the ith UE) is considered as a function of the SINR received by this UE, given by

$$R_i = B\log(1 + SINR_i) \tag{7.1}$$

where

$$SINR_i(\mathcal{L}_{BS}, \mathcal{L}_{UE}, \mathcal{B}, \mathcal{P}, \mathcal{H}) = \frac{P_t + G_{BF} - PL}{I + N} \tag{7.2}$$

In the previous equation, P_t is the downlink transmission power, G_{BF} is the beamforming gain, resulted from using a given beam pattern specified in a codebook, and PL is the path loss that is a random variable and a function of the relative locations between the UE and the serving BS. In addition, SINR of an individual UE is a function of $\mathcal{L}_{BS}, \mathcal{L}_{UE}, \mathcal{B}, \mathcal{P}, \mathcal{H}$ that are the locations of the BSs, the locations of the UEs, the beam patterns applied to each BS–UE pair, the path loss components, and the channels, respectively, which are all dynamically changing (expect for the BS locations) and are treated as random variables.

In addition, the noise term in the previous equation is given by $N = KTB$, where K is the Boltzmann constant, T is the noise temperature, and B is the bandwidth. Furthermore, the interference term I is given by aggregating the received signal from the interfering BSs, given by

$$I = \sum_{\substack{n=1 \\ n \neq i}}^{N} P_r \tag{7.3}$$

In step 2, the network management unit performs a Q-learning algorithm that provides an estimate of the "reward," i.e., the average throughput of the network at a given time t, according to the actions a_t, by

$$Q_{t+1} = Q_t + \alpha[R_t - Q_t] \tag{7.4}$$

where $0 \leq \alpha \leq 1$ is the learning rate, R_t is the immediate award, which in our case is the immediate network throughput given the current environment and connection of BS–UE pair, i.e., the actions a_t. The actions defined as a real-valued number, indicating which BS to be connected to. For example, $a_t = 3$ indicates the action of a UE connecting to the third BS.

The actions taken at a given time instant t are dependent on a parameter $0 \leq \epsilon < 1$. When $\epsilon = 0$, the network management unit always takes the optimal action, i.e., the connection that yields the maximum throughput at this time instant, given by

$$a_t^* = \text{argmax}\{Q_t(a_1), Q_t(a_2), \ldots, Q_t(a_N)\} \tag{7.5}$$

when $\epsilon \neq 0$, the algorithm would randomly choose one of the actions; therefore, it has a chance to sweep and evaluate all the possible actions, i.e., the so-called phase of exploration.

In step 3, the network management unit outputs the actions taken and instructs the UE/BS to act accordingly.

In a given example for the learning process in cell selection, the network can perform the simple Q-learning algorithm at a given time:

1. observes the current inputs from the UEs (e.g., location and channel information of the new UE);
2. selects and performs an action a_t^* for this time instant (in terms of which BS to connect to for the UE)
    i. if a randomly generated real-valued number is $<\mathcal{E}$, selects the action that maximizes the instantaneous network throughput of all UEs (exploitation);
    ii. otherwise, randomly makes a selection (exploration);
3. receives an immediate "reward" for this time instant R_t (in our case is the network throughput due to the selected action); and
4. computes average network throughput for the next time instant Q_{t+1} that is used for determining an action for the next time instant.

Simulated performance of the algorithm, where the learning phase lasts for about 200 runs (plays), is presented in Figure 7.2. The simulations leading to the result in Figure 7.1(b) used an example of a network with four BSs and four UEs, where the locations of BSs are fixed, whereas the locations of UEs are random. A clear advantage in terms of enhanced average network throughput can be observed when Q-learning is applied, where the network throughput is shown to have about 16% increase, compared to that using the conventional highest SINR criterion.

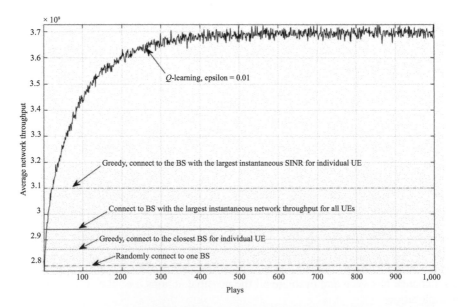

Figure 7.2   Average network throughput obtained using Q-learning, compared to that using greedy connection

7.2.2 Case study 2: AI for 5G fronthaul

Next-generation fronthaul interface (NGFI) [8] targets redefining interface flexibility and network functional split between remote and centralized units. Such an interface enables statistical multiplexing on fronthaul bandwidth, decoupling interface traffic from some radio frequency (RF)-level attributes (e.g., number of antennas) and results in more flexible remote unit connectivity to a centralized unit. One key challenge is how NGFI should support network slicing.

A system overview of the required fronthaul slicing is shown in Figure 7.3. It can be seen that slicing of network resource at fronthaul is extremely complex. The slicing is affected by multiple factors and their changing contexts—factors such as the clustering on the remote aggregation unit (RAU) [8], the functional split between RAU and radio cloud center (RCC) [8], and dimensionality of solution space on network resources to be reserved on fronthaul (power, processing capability, radio resources, buffering memory, route to be selected across multiple fronthaul nodes, etc.). The existing solutions that use simple radio resource reservation or abstracted end-to-end network management solutions are not directly applicable. In particular, the non-convex and highly dynamic nature of the optimization problem requires constant training with different iterative algorithms. We propose a new approach based on the AI engine which can be incorporated as part of a dedicated fronthaul orchestrator. This AI engine will learn through constant training and govern different actions: from predicting upcoming traffic load on the fronthaul to dynamic reservation of resources and load balancing between central and remote entities. The application of AI at the fronthaul is three-fold:

7.2.2.1 Fronthaul load prediction

Orchestrator Engine monitors data traffic load on Uplink (UL)/Downlink (DL) per RAU–RCC pair on the fronthaul, enabling intelligent prediction of upcoming load in either directions. This is done via incorporating multiple layers of data.

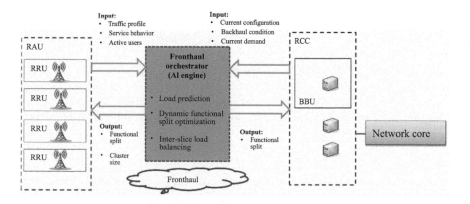

Figure 7.3   Concept of the fronthaul slicing with AI engine

7.2.2.2   Dynamic functional split optimization

Orchestrator Engine may dynamically split the traffic on UL (DL) per RAU across multiple fronthaul slices (toward different RCC entities) based on predicted levels of load, ensuring each slice of fronthaul network resources encompasses user traffic with similar service profiles and behavior. As an example, the functional split for fronthaul slices with lower predicted load (in terms of bandwidth/latency by-product) can be adjusted from a lower layer split (with stricter requirement) to an upper layer split (with relaxer requirement). This can be seen as an enhancement of currently envisioned multilevel (yet static) functional split between central and remote nodes in standardization roadmap.

7.2.2.3   Fronthaul inter-slice load balancing

On another level, the Orchestrator Engine can balance the bandwidth reservation versus latency provision across different fronthaul slices in an on-demand fashion taking into account real-time refinements in load predictions and dynamic functional split per RAU–RCC.

The optimization steps can be executed in the order given, or in parallel (via accumulating all information within Orchestrator Engine), or iteratively with a feedback loop (via incrementally moving the network resources from fronthaul slices in excess to fronthaul slices in shortage till the target key performance indicators (KPIs) in fronthaul network are met). In particular, when executed with a feedback loop, this may be carried out via state-of-the-art reinforcement learning (RL) algorithms.

7.2.3   Case study 3: AI for coexistence of multiple radio access technologies

5G New Radio (NR) is expected to support diverse spectrum bands, including the conventional sub-6 GHz band, the new licensed mmWave bands that are being allocated for 5G, as well as unlicensed spectrum [9]. Very recently 3rd Generation Partnership Project (3GPP) Release 16 [9] has introduced a new spectrum sharing paradigm for 5G in unlicensed spectrum. Furthermore, the recent DARPA Spectrum Collaboration Challenge is collaborative machine learning competition to overcome scarcity in the RF spectrum. MulteFire that was developed as an extension of Licensed-Assisted Access and LTE-U is now also working on technologies for sharing unlicensed spectrum for 5G. It is envisioned that AI and machine learning would play an important role in addressing new challenges of spectrum sharing for 5G and result in much better spectrum sharing paradigms than the existing ones.

As an example of such new challenges, the scenario of 60 GHz unlicensed spectrum sharing is shown in Figure 7.4(a), which depicts a beam-collision interference scenario in this band.

In this scenario, multiple 5G NR BSs belonging to different operators and different access technologies use mmWave communications to provide Gbps connectivity to the users. Due to high density of BS and the number of beams used per BS, beam-collision can occur where unintended beam from a "hostile" BS can cause server interference to a user. Coordination of beam scheduling to avoid such interference

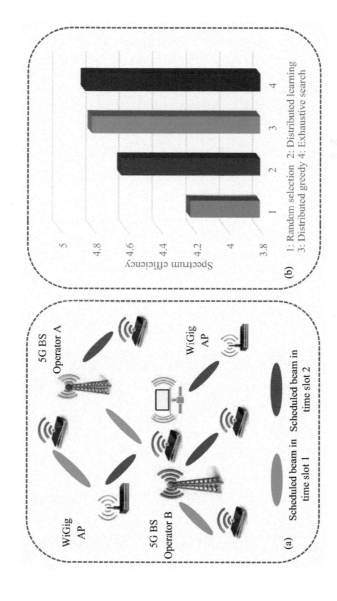

Figure 7.4 (a) Coexistence in 60 GHz with beamforming and (b) average spectrum efficiency (cell size = 200 m)

scenario is not possible when considering the use of 60 GHz band as different BSs. Operating in this band may belong to different operators or even use different access technologies, e.g., 5G NR versus WiGig.

To address this important challenge, we proposed in [10] a novel multi-RAT coexistence mechanism where neighboring BSs, each serving their own associated UEs, learn their own optimal beam scheduling in a distributed manner such that their own utility function, e.g., spectral efficiency, is maximized. Mathematically, the problem can be formulated as a combinatorial optimization problem for which an exhaustive search, which requires global learning among coexisting RATs, has an extremely high algorithmic complexity. In contrast, our proposed distributed learning protocol yields a comparable spectral efficiency for the entire networks to exhaustive search, at much lower computational complexity and without the need for coordination between adjacent BS.

The distributed learning algorithm works by assigning a probability, P_{a_i} to the time-ordered sequence of beams available to each BS, e.g.,

$$a_i = \{b_i^1, b_i^2, \ldots, b_i^M\} \quad b_i = \{b_i^2, b_i^1, \ldots, b_i^{Mi}\}, \tag{7.6}$$

etc. for base station i, where Mi is the number of UEs served by base station i. At the start of the learning process, these probabilities are initialized uniformly at $1/Mi!$ The corresponding probability for each beam sequence is then updated at each timestep based on the interference-level feedback received from the UEs served by the corresponding BS. This is achieved with RL, using a reward function, such as spectral efficiency, in the following way:

$$P_{a_i}(U(a_i)(t+1)) = P_{a_i}(U(a_i)(t) - \omega U(a_i)(t))/U^{\max}(t)P_{a_i}(U(a_i)(t)) \tag{7.7}$$

where ω is the weight factor, $U(a_i)(t)$ is the current reward function corresponding to the choice of beam sequence (a_i), and $U^{\max}(t)$ is the maximum reward function up to time t. A new beam sequence is then randomly selected according to the set of updated probabilities $\{P_{a_i}, P_{b_i}, P_{c_i}, \ldots\}$.

As an example, Figure 7.4(b) shows the system spectrum efficiency for the scenario with ten BSs operating in 60 GHz and a cell size of 200 m, with UEs randomly distributed in the service area, with BS using analog beamforming to serve their UEs. Further details of the simulations are provided in Table 7.1.

Table 7.1   Main system parameters

Parameter	Value
Carrier frequency	60 GHz
Bandwidth	500 MHz
Base station Tx power	30 dB m
Number of BS antennas	16
Number of UE antennas	1
Noise temperature	300 K

Results are obtained using two variants of distributed learning and are compared with random beam scheduling as well as an exhaustive search. It can be seen from this figure that distributed learning significantly improves system spectral efficiency as compared to random scheduling. The exhaustive searching algorithm gives the best spectrum efficiency. However, the value is very close to the one generated by distributed learning algorithms. We note that spectral efficiency with distributed learning algorithm is slightly worth than the greedy one but has lees complexity and converges faster.

7.3   Data analytics in 5G

Data analytics is becoming increasingly important to enable the use of AI for wireless communications. In fact, the acquisition of meaningful data, and the analysis of it, is fundamental for feeding the correct training set to the system, hence to perform AI correctly. In the following, we provide review and studies on how data analytics can be leveraged to facilitate the use of AI, and how data analytics and AI are convergence in 5G wireless networks. In the past decade, coverage and connection of the wireless networks have increased tremendously. Mobile network operators (MNOs) have access to a massive amount of data from the networks and subscribers, and data analytics not only employs a customer-centric, quality-of-experience-based approach from the data sources to optimize end-to-end network performance, which requires more effort than traditional optimization, but it also provides a unified and converged platform for multiple targets of optimization.

In 5G mobile and wireless networks, data generated by environments are heterogeneous, which are usually collected from various sources, having different formats and exhibit complex correlations. AI algorithms can help one to manage this complexity and turn it to advantage. The algorithms can help one to uncover unknown properties of wireless networks, identify correlations and anomalies that we cannot see by inspection, and suggest novel ways to optimize network deployments and operations. The versatile AI algorithms for the next-generation networks have drawn unparalleled research interest, which includes the problem solving from RAT selection to malware detection, and the development of networked systems [3]. However, finding the relevant data, extracting the valuable data, and mining the data by human experts are too complicated and time consuming. DL, as one of the most promising learning algorithms, has demonstrated the remarkable performance for solving problems in the complex networks [11]. Deep ANNs and deep RL can generate models that achieve an impressive level of accuracy. However, large amounts of data come with the curse of the need for scalability to be able to manage them. Distributed AI algorithms will have to be devised to be able to generate models without having to move the data far from its source [3]. Another challenge regarding data analytics for AI is to clean and correctly label the data to be fed for learning. Training data that are not classified correctly leads to a lousy classifier. In fact, this may go beyond being a technical problem, since it is possible to end up with models that reflect in their classification biases and prejudices, raising moral, and ethical concerns. This connects with a recurring issue with most models generated by AI. When the model produces outputs for given inputs, it is not possible for the AI expert to explain why and wherein these decisions are made.

AI is expected to assume the primary role in the development and evolution of analytics, but analytics will not reduce to either of them. AI offers tools to extract relevant information, suggestions, or predictions from data sets that are too large, too complex, or insufficiently understood to make predictions otherwise. AI has a wider scope that replicates (or improves on) human intelligence, and other cognitive functions in machines. In this context, functions such as learning, pattern matching, problem solving, and prediction are relevant to analytics.

Analytics covers a lot of ground, and the existing deterministic, rule-based algorithms are efficient and well suited. However, it is expected that AI may expand its reach; especially, when we move to more complex network architectures. For instance, we may not need AI to decide where to put a new macro station as constraints are many. However, when the network architectures become more complex, there will be more solutions available at a given location; then AI may become useful. AI can correlate multiple sources of data and find what is relevant within the entire data set. Going through this process manually is too labor intensive to get beyond a basic correlation and selection of data that gives only limited insight into network and service performance. AI may uncover correlations that were not previously recognized, because its automated processes can explore data more deeply and more systematically than humans can. Human expertise is still crucially valuable in narrowing the focus to find solutions and to keep complex problems manageable, but it can limit the ability to find novel solutions or insights.

7.4   Industry and standard activities

7.4.1   Open standards required

In a world where AI is widely used, open standards are needed for the data-driven approaches.

It is expected that data held by the private sector become more broadly available, and as open as possible. Second, rights and responsibilities are expected adequately distributed, and more control over the usage and sharing of data is given to the individual. However, significant concerns of individual and group privacy are caused. On the other hand, open data could be messy or erroneous, which makes AI systems risky and creates erroneous results. Therefore, making data open or available is necessary but is not alone sufficient for enabling machine-led analysis. Data need to be both accessible and machine ready.

Standards can help one to make sure that the meaning of data is retained, as they are transferred between systems, by setting out where the data came from and how they had been processed. Open standards are intended to make the exchange of data easier, and by allowing software systems, data sets, or documents to be interoperable, and put to a wide range of uses.

The standardization of interfaces, processes, and data formats is of high importance in communications as it increases the reliability, interoperability, and modularity of a system. Standardized formats may be needed to specify how to train, adapt, compress, and exchange individual AI algorithms, and to ensure that multiple algorithms correctly interact with each.

7.4.2   Achievements and activates of standardization

Besides the open standards requirements, several standardization and regulatory bodies have dedicated attention to develop data analytics and AI for the future 5G networks. Some significant activities of standardization are highlighted next.

The European Telecommunications Standards Institute (ETSI) launched the Industry Specification Group on Experiential Networked Intelligence (ENI) in February 2017 [12]. The Industry Specification Group (ISG) aims to define an architecture that uses AI techniques and context-aware, metadata-driven policies to adjust offered services based on changes in user needs, environmental conditions, and business goals, according to the "observe-orient-decide-act" control loop model. ENI is the first ETSI group that focuses on the standardization and specification of an architecture that uses AI to improve the operator's experience. The group specifications developed in ENI ISG include the use cases, requirements, and system architecture.

3GPP is currently standardizing what is known as service-based architecture (SBA) for the 5G core as part of system architecture for 5G systems in Release 15. In SBA, different network functions and associated services can directly communicate with each other as originator or consumer of a service via a common bus known as service-based interface. One key function envisioned within SBA is Network Data Analytics Function (NWDAF), enabling network access to the operator-driven analytics for different purposes, including intelligent slice selection and control [13]. In Release 16, 3GPP envisions to improve NWDAF scope via introducing use cases and solutions for supporting network automation deployment [14]. So far, several enhancements have been proposed from customized mobility management, 5G quality of service improvement to dynamic traffic steering and splitting, and service-classification-based resource management.

7.5   Challenges and open questions

AI is a vibrant field of research, with a range of areas for further development across different methods and applications. Recent advances in 5G networks have opened up further research challenges and questions that relate to both technical and societal issues. Technical challenges may include the following: to computationally scale to large data sets; do not require large amounts of labeled data; data, energy, and other resource-efficient methods and the improved hardware to support advanced learning algorithms. The societal challenges are addressed to ensure continued public confidence in AI-assisted systems. For instance, interpretability and transparency are expected for AI learning systems, whose workings and outputs can be understood or interrogated by human users. Others include algorithm robustness, privacy, and fairness, inference of causality, human–machine interactions, and security. From the technical point of view, we raise awareness of the following two open questions.

7.5.1   Big data or small data

A large amount of data are often regarded necessary in order to train the network and to build enough experience for the network to learn. Obtaining sufficiently large amount of data has been made possible with the explosion of the connected devices and IoT. However, as the volume grows, it becomes increasingly difficult to store the data, as well as to extract useful information from the massive data sets. Recently, AI algorithm using small data for assisting the learning has been investigated [15]. In particular, in highly structured data sets and for a short span of time, small data sets have been proven to be sufficient to produce the relevant features of the network and hence to train the network. In the case when actual data are not always available, the use of synthesized data is also possible, for example, for an initial proof of concept. Synthesized data are especially useful, in the case when a training set does not contain a specific required feature of the network, for example, when faulty data cannot always be efficiently collected in a reasonably reliable network.

The important question to note is that the balance between getting enough data for the network to be trained and to learn, while not overload the system, for example, by getting unnecessary data that bring complications to extract the meaningful information. In addition, specific data sets should be considered for specific problems and applications.

7.5.2   Centralized or distributed learning

Wireless networks are centralized as well as distributed. As data traffic on mobile networks continues to grow, Cloud-RAN architecture is proposed for MNOs to reduce capital expenditures and operating expenses, and to improve user experience through less interference. The centralization makes it possible to obtain a complete overview of all of the stations deployed and to coordinate signal processing and manage interference between cells and devices. On the other hand, with data usage patterns changing rapidly, distributed RAN (DRAN) is proposed for operators to boost coverage and capacity. DRAN greatly simplifies wireless infrastructure by replacing legacy expansive rack units with compact baseband units. It is a cost-effective and efficient way to get the most out of existing infrastructure while scaling operations to meet new requirements. The different RAN architecture poses an interesting question on where learning should be placed.

On the one hand, it is known that a localized learning may not always guarantee the same optimized solutions or results as when learning is performed globally. For example, a learning engine that is placed at one domain of the network may sufficiently address problems locally to that specific domain, while the solution may not be considered optimal anymore when the entire network is considered. On the other hand, for some network problems, e.g., network service assurance, effective solutions via learning may need an end-to-end view of the network. Such an end-to-end view of the network is not always possible, as the data obtained in one domain may not be available in the other domain. In such a case, local and distributed learning may be useful, in particular when some KPIs such as delays are taken into consideration. It is noted that distributed and centralized learnings are not exclusive to each other. The choice of where and how the learning should be performed depends on the specific problems to address, the network contexts, as well as the constraints of the learning.

7.6 Conclusions

This chapter has reviewed the recent development of AI-assisted applications in 5G wireless networks. A few case studies have been presented that have demonstrated AI as a powerful tool to enhance the performance and to efficiently assist the management of the complex heterogeneous networks. AI offers significant capabilities through data analytics. However, the importance of understanding the data and feeding the meaningful training set to the AI algorithms has not been fully recognized. Therefore, the vital role of data and data analytics has been highlighted in Section 7.3. Recent standardization activities have been summarized, followed by a discussion of the research challenges and open questions. The use of AI is envisaged to be a major digital transformation in wireless networks, with massive opportunities in the research community to innovate. It is the purpose of this work not only to present the benefits of using AI in wireless networks but also to help raise awareness and give insights of the challenges, in particular when considering the practical 5G wireless networks, and when bringing the research results to practice.

References

[1] N. Heuveldop, "Ericsson mobility report," *Ericsson, Stockholm,* 2017.

[2] ETSI Network Functions Virtualisation Standards [Online]. Available: https://www.etsi.org/technologies/nfv

[3] M. G. Kibria, K. Nguyen, G. P. Villardi, O. Zhao, K. Ishizu, and F. Kojima, "Big data analytics, machine learning and artificial intelligence in next-generation wireless networks," *IEEE Access,* vol. 6, pp. 32328–32338, 2018.

[4] M. Chen, U. Challita, W. Saad, C. Yin, and M. Debbah, "Machine learning for wireless networks with artificial intelligence: A tutorial on neural networks," *IEEE Communications Surveys & Tutorials,* vol. 21, no. 4, pp. 3039–3071, 2019.

[5] U. Challita and M. K. Marina, "Holistic small cell traffic balancing across licensed and unlicensed bands," in *Proceedings of the 19th ACM International Conference on Modeling, Analysis and Simulation of Wireless and Mobile Systems.* Malta: ACM. pp. 166–175, 2016.

[6] U. Challita, L. Dong, and W. Saad, "Proactive resource management in LTE-U systems: A deep learning perspective," *arXiv preprint arXiv:1702.07031,* 2017.

[7]   "Evolved Universal Terrestrial Radio Access (E-UTRA), user equipment (UE) procedures in idle mode," *3GPP, 36.304, Release 8.*

[8]   "Next generation fronthaul interface," *China Mobile White Paper,* no. Version 1.0, 2015.

[9]   S.-Y. Lien, S.-L. Shieh, Y. Huang, B. Su, Y.-L. Hsu, and H.-Y. Wei, "5G new radio: Waveform, frame structure, multiple access, and initial access," *IEEE Communications Magazine,* vol. 55, no. 6, pp. 64–71, 2017.

[10] M. Nekovee, Y. Qi, and Y. Wang, "Self-organized beam scheduling as an enabler for coexistence in 5G unlicensed bands," *IEICE Transactions on Communications,* vol. 100, no. 8, pp. 1181–1189, 2017.

[11] C. Zhang, P. Patras, and H. Haddadi, "Deep learning in mobile and wireless networking: A survey," *IEEE Communications Surveys & Tutorials,* vol. 21, no. 3, 2019 .

[12] The Experiential Networked Intelligence Industry Specification Group (ENI ISG) at ETSI. Available: https://www.etsi.org/technologies/experiential-networked-intelligence

[13] "Study on access traffic steering, switching and splitting support in the 5G system architecture," *3GPPP TR 23.793,* vol. V0.1.0, 2017.

[14] "Study of enablers for network automation for 5G," *3GPP TR 23.791, Release 16.*

[15] A. Mestres, A. Rodríguez-Natal, J. Carner, *et al.*, "Knowledge-defined networking," *SIGCOMM Computer Communication Review,* vol. 47, no. 3, pp. 2–10, 2017.

Chapter 8

Deep *Q*-network-based coverage hole detection for future wireless networks

Shahriar Abdullah Al-Ahmed[1],
Muhammad Zeeshan Shakir[1], and Qasim Zeeshan Ahmed[2]

Coverage hole is one of the notably important features which cannot be ignored from the start of the planning phase throughout the operational stage of the cellular network. Any coverage hole in this era of technological advancement will cause severe hamper to the communication system and the reputation of the network operators. Network operators always have to ensure the best quality of service (QoS) with the best key performance indicators (KPIs). Thus, the operators require an incomparable tool to detect coverage hole efficiently. In the past, drive test (DT) with propagation theory was used to detect coverage hole. Then, minimization of drive test (MDT) was introduced in order to eliminate the problems of DT. However, the MDT is not free from any problems either. The outdated user equipment (UE) report, user control over the device and inaccurate information could be problematic for the network operators to detect coverage hole. In this chapter, we demonstrate a mechanism of coverage hole detection by exploiting unmanned aerial vehicle (UAV) and deep *Q*-network (DQN) effectively. This system could be a part of self-organising networks (SON) and utilised by operators whenever required without the human in the system or human-in-the-loop (HiTL) model.

8.1 Introduction

Technologies have been utilised since the beginning of mankind for the welfare of humans and society. The innovation of these technologies has advantages and disadvantages which made the individuals to research and improve over time to reduce flaws. Sometimes the researchers combine more than one concept to create and apply in new or improved innovation. A similar approach has been taken when utilising machine learning (ML) in today's technological paradigm. The history of ML started around 300 BC by a great philosopher Aristotle [1] and established around 1950 [2].

[1]School of Computing, Engineering and Physical Sciences, University of the West of Scotland, Paisley, UK
[2]Department of Engineering and Technology, University of Huddersfield, Huddersfield, UK

Over time, this process has been improved and new algorithms have been created. Presently, the use of ML has become essential in today's technological flow to improve system efficiencies and to reduce the model of HiTL for the elephantine number of devices [3].

The huge number of devices and advancements in technologies has opened the new door of diverse communication services such as human-centric, machine-to-machine and human-to-machine. For these services, the next-generation SON requires to be more organised and powerful with better coverage and capacity while maintaining very low latency [4]. Thus, remarkably poor coverage or coverage hole could be a major concern for users and operators.

UAV is one of the novel inventions that has become the centre of attention for many researchers over the past decades. The UAVs have been studied and deployed due to its low cost, reaching capability to anywhere (i.e. flexibility and mobility) and above all, its low risks. UAVs have been utilised by military forces at first due to its many advantages and merit. Today, they can be used by civilians and commercial operators for numerous purposes while following the uses of UAV regulations from the relevant authorities. UAVs are currently being used for crowd surveillance, building smart cities, precise agriculture, remote condition monitoring, forest fire detection and so forth. One of the cellular uses of UAVs could be detecting coverage hole for cellular networks for future applications and services.

8.1.1 Motivation and background

Coverage hole forms when the signal-to-interference-plus-noise ratio (SINR) falls below a threshold level required to maintain standard QoS. There are many places in the United Kingdom and other countries where cellular coverage is extremely poor or no coverage available at all. These areas are mostly situated on the rural side of the country, for example, highlands, islands and national parks. Online magazines and other media are highlighting these uncovered areas with high importance. In one online magazine, Holyrood, it is mentioned that there are 16 sites identified as no 4G coverage in Scotland [5]. Besides, the Scottish Government and Scottish Future Trust are working in partnership to develop the Scottish 4G Infill Programme [6] to provide coverage to the uncovered areas.

Coverage hole is one of the important features which cannot be ignored from the planning phase of the network deployment. Also, operators throughout their operational stage need to make sure that there is no existence of coverage hole to provide the optimal services to the end users. Any coverage hole may hamper the services which will downgrade the reputation of the operators specially in the era of machine-to-machine and human-to-machine communication. Traditionally, an expensive DT with the propagation model has been used to detect any coverage hole by constructing a radio map with the aid of many radio parameters [7]. Usually, the radio map is not very accurate most of the time and causes more operating expenditure (OPEX). Thus, Third Generation Partnership Project (3GPP) has introduced the MDT to replace DT to be a part of SON [8]. This feature enables operators to reduce OPEX by collecting radio measurements and associated information from UEs to examine network performance and detect any coverage hole. However, the MDT has some concerns such as UEs are unable to give an immediate report and UE might not provide accurate geographical location due to many factors, including poor coverage [9]. In addition, UE battery power and location might not be available which are controlled by the user. The issue of General Data Protection Regulation (GDPR) also needs to be considered under which users might not be agreed to provide UE data [10]. Having discussed the issues of DT and MDT, there are some challenges for network operators to detect coverage hole in any radio environment:

- Cost: Coverage hole detection platform has to be cost-effective and reusable for several geographic scenarios. Operators should deal with very low capital expenditure (CAPEX) and OPEX.
- Cellular coverage: Densifying the network is one of the main goals of 5G and beyond networks. By using the coverage hole detection system, network operators can decide where and how to densify the network (e.g. fixed, small-cell base station or on-demand flying base station can be deployed).
- Hard-to-reach spots: Some difficult or hard-to-reach spots need to be regularly checked for cellular coverage where it is hard for humans to reach or less crowded or occasionally crowded to receive up-to-date UE report.

In this chapter, we will discuss coverage hole detection flexibly and cost-effectively. This mechanism will not only work for coverage hole detection but also for providing on-demand coverage to the mobile users and Internet of Things (IoT) data collection and monitoring.

8.2   Machine learning

ML is a branch of artificial intelligence that aids the machines to act from learning and improving from its past experiences without explicit programming [11]. ML focuses on the development of algorithms for computers to self-learn from data, pattern recognition and computational theory. There are mainly four types of ML which have been discussed below:

1. **Supervised learning**: Supervised learning is used to classify or predict the output based on input and model data. Some examples can be given as Gmail spam email filter system, movie or product recommendation to the consumer in e-commerce websites, weather prediction and so on [12]. This learning process can also be divided into classification and regression. Besides, this learning mechanism may be applied to analyse the radio link failure (RLF) report in order to predict coverage hole; however, it might not be suitable for real-time coverage hole detection.
2. **Unsupervised learning**: This type of learning does not require to supervise the model, and it is applied to unlabelled data sets to discover on singularly [12]. For

example, NASA uses this type of learning to create different clusters of heavenly bodies [13]. Unsupervised learning can be further divided into two categories: clustering and association. The algorithm of this type of ML may not be suitable for predicting coverage hole detection on real-time basis.

3. **Semi-supervised learning**: Semi-supervised learning is a hybrid mechanism that works on a large amount of data where some of the data is labelled. An example can be given as automatic face detection and tagging on Facebook from many photos of the same person [13]. Like an unsupervised learning mechanism, this type of ML also may not be suitable for detecting coverage hole; however, certain types of necessary data from RLF can be classified in order to detect coverage hole.

4. **Reinforcement learning**: This learning is about taking suitable action to get the highest reward in an environment. Robotic movement can be a good example where robot consistently learns from its mistakes and rewards from a stochastic environment. Therefore, this learning is suitable for detecting coverage hole in any radio environment by using the trial and error method and in the real-time manner.

8.2.1   Reinforcement learning

In reinforcement learning (RL), an agent interacts with the environment and solves problems through trial and error mechanism without any supervised signal in an unknown environment [14]. The RL agent takes actions in a situation where it receives positive or negative rewards and stores the experiences based on the reward. Depending on the learning of previous experiences, the agent fixes the error and makes the learning better than before in each iteration. A fundamental model of the RL has been shown in Figure 8.1. The RL can be continuous or episodic system while discovering a single or multi reward in an environment. Some classical algorithms of RL can be mentioned as temporal difference learning, Q-learning, SARSA and so on [15] among which, the Q-learning has been briefly discussed as follows.

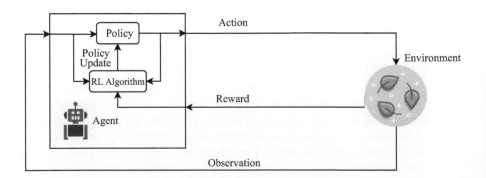

Figure 8.1   Reinforcement learning system

The traditional well-known Q-learning algorithm is a model-free RL which provides solving any RL problem. The Q-function which is the pair of state and action evaluates the gathered reward and can be given as:

$$Q(s_t, a_t) \leftarrow Q(s_t, a_t) + \alpha_Q \left[r_{t+1} + \gamma \max Q'(s', a') - Q(s, a) \right] \tag{8.1}$$

In the previous equation, r_{t+1} denotes the instantaneous reward, s_t and s' are the state of the agent as well as a_t and a' are the available actions that the agent picks at time t and $t + 1$, respectively. Parameter $(0 < \alpha_Q < 1)$ denotes the learning rate and parameter $(0 < \gamma < 1)$ denotes the discount factor. This algorithm also requires an epsilon-greedy policy which is a method of selecting random actions with uniform distribution for a set of available actions by picking exploration or exploitation strategy.

8.2.2 Deep reinforcement learning

Deep reinforcement learning (DRL) is an extension of RL where RL combines with the deep learning (DL) and enhances the learning for an agent [16]. In DRL, the agent still learns through trial and error by taking actions in state and observes the reward. The DL parameters are updated during the process of the learning which makes the learning more efficient. The main concept of combining RL and DL was attempted several years ago; however, Google DeepMind team published their result successfully in NIPT 2013 [17]. In that paper, DQN was introduced along with convolutional neural network (CNN) and afterwards the team presented modified and improved versions of DQN.

8.3   System model

It has been mentioned earlier that the coverage hole forms when the SINR falls below a threshold level. Particularly, these events occur due to many reasons such as obstruction or fading, while signal propagates through radio environment. For the system model, we consider a rural environment with M macro base stations (MBSs) which are distributed according to spatial Poisson point process in a geographical area. In this scenario, only the downlink of the mobile network has been considered that serves a range of users. All the MBSs have been considered using the same frequency band of LTE signal with omnidirectional antennas. This deployment environment has an UAV to act as an UE in order to calculate the SINR and find the signal level at various positions. The user association for load balancing has been ignored because the system is for coverage hole detection only. To calculate the SINR, we need to calculate the received power at the UAV by using an acceptable path loss (PL) model for the reason that the signal level is not the same at all heights due to many propagation factors.

A widely used alpha-beta (AB) path loss model [18,19] is considered for its simplicity in this environment. It is because the measurements below 5 m purely follows the terrestrial propagation [20]. Therefore, the PL can be calculated between the MBS and UAV at any position (x_{UAV}, y_{UAV}) based on [19] and can be given as:

$$PL(d) = \alpha \log_{10}(R) + \beta + X_\sigma \qquad [dB] \qquad (8.2)$$

In the above equation, R (in meters) is the 3D distance between the UAV and MBS and can be written as $R = \sqrt{d^2 + (h_{MBS} - h_{UAV})^2}$. Here, d is the ground distance between the UAV and MBS can be written as $d = \sqrt{(x_{UAV} - x_{MBS})^2 + (y_{UAV} - y_{MBS})^2}$ and h_{MBS} and h_{UAV} are the heights of the MBS and UAV, respectively. Other parameters in the equation such as α denotes the PL exponent, β represents the intercept point with the line $d=1$ m. The shadowing component X_σ is a random variable generally modeled as zero-mean Gaussian distribution with σ deviation (in dB). Again, this path loss model has been extended in [18] to be acceptable for airborne UAV by modifying α, β and σ based on heights according to the following equations:

$$\alpha(h_{UAV}) = \max(k_1\alpha + k_2\alpha \log_{10}(h_{UAV}), 2) \qquad (8.3)$$

$$\beta(h_{UAV}) = k_1\beta + k_2\beta \log_{10}(\min(h_{UAV}, h_{FSPL})) \qquad [dB] \qquad (8.4)$$

$$\sigma(h_{UAV}) = k_1\sigma + k_2\sigma \log_{10}(\min(h_{UAV}, h_{FSPL})) \qquad [dB] \qquad (8.5)$$

where h_{FSPL} is defined as free space propagation with $\alpha = 2.0$. The values of k_1 and k_2 are derived from the measurement presented in Table 8.1 in rural environment ranging from 1.5 m to 120 m [18]. The same PL model also applies for the received signal from interfering MBS to UAV. Then, we can calculate the SINR at (x_{UAV}, y_{UAV}) from serving MBS using [21]:

$$SINR_{(x_{UAV}, y_{UAV})} = \frac{P^{rx}_{i,k}}{\sum_{m=1, m \neq i}^{M} P^{rx}_{m,k} + N} \qquad [dB] \qquad (8.6)$$

where $P^{rx}_{i,k} = P^{tx}_{i,k} - PL(d)$, $P^{rx}_{i,k}$ denotes received signal power from i-th serving MBS on subcarrier k at the UAV at any position (x_{UAV}, y_{UAV}), $P^{tx}_{i,k}$ stands for the transmit signal power of i-th serving MBS on subcarrier k and $PL(d)$ denotes PL between the MBS and UAV at any given position. Furthermore, $\sum_{m=1, m \neq i}^{M} P^{rx}_{m,k}$ represents the sum of the individual interfering signal power received from interfering MBS at the UAV at any given position. It is to be noted here that we ignored the channel gain. Variable N denotes thermal noise power. Here, SINR level of more than 7 dB is assumed as fair to excellent signal, but the SINR level below 7 dB is considered as a weak signal and may cause a coverage hole [22]. Figure 8.2 presents a graphical model of the mechanism to detect coverage hole by UAV.

Table 8.1   Path loss model simulation parameters

Parameter	k_1	k_2
α	3.9	−0.9
β	−8.5	20.5
σ	8.2	−2.1

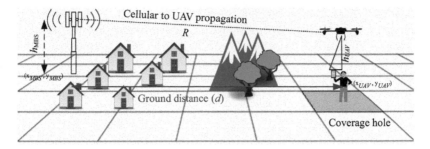

Figure 8.2   Graphical description of UAV detecting coverage hole

8.4   DQN-based coverage hole detection

DQN has drawn attention to many researchers and academia and industry profession-als. In this section, we discuss the navigation of the UAV based on DQN to detect coverage hole. In particular, first we create the environment for UAV as an RL agent then the UAV needs to navigate through the environment using an RL algorithm which is DQN in this case.

In our approach, we would like to exploit the controlling power of UAV to find out the coverage hole or poor coverage while considering all the challenges. UAVs are very flexible which can reach anywhere. If the UAV can act as UE which is UAV-UE, then it would be possible to collect the signal statistics in a certain area or hard-to-reach areas. In the past, we had DT and at present, we have MDT to collect the information of the cellular signal. Having discussed the issues of DT and MDT, we can take advantage of UAV to collect the radio signal information at various positions. However, there are still some challenges that need to be taken care, including navigation of the UAV in different areas.

To navigate the UAV in a certain area, for example 20 km × 20 km geograph-ical grid, we can use the grid system similar to the Earth grid system. This grid can be generated over a geographical map and feed into the algorithm inside the UAV. The grid system will help us to locate the coverage hole area in the grid eas-ily and use Cartesian coordinates (x, y) from the plane for UAV manoeuvring rather than going anywhere like a self-driving UAV. ML can be employed here for many reasons. First of all, ML will help to eliminate the HiTL model. If any UAV is deployed with ML, we do not need any HiTL for a large set of work. Besides, DT costs huge money where ML will reduce OPEX to deploy cellular networks. Addi-tionally, UAV with ML will help to be a part of SON and operators do not need to worry about the GDPR to get data from UE about the radio environment and coverage.

In our approach, we selected RL for many advantages. RL is very suitable for autonomous robots in an unknown environment and uncertain situation. In RL, an agent takes actions and interacts with environment to get the maximum reward. The UAV can be an agent where the agent will interact with the radio environment and collect many parameters, for example signal strength and get a reward for discovering a poor coverage area. After implementing the Q-learning algorithm to detect coverage hole in one of our articles [10], we selected to use DQN for the coverage hole detection. The prime reason for using DQN is the calculation strategy and less complexity if there is increased number of grids or a larger area to scan that will bring large table of states and actions to compute Q-values accurately. The concept of the proposed method can be found in Figure 8.3 where it has the environment as well as the graphical concept of the mechanism.

8.4.1 DQN components to detect coverage hole

To understand the mechanism of DQN to detect coverage hole, we need to be familiar with the components of the DQN:

DQN structure: The structure of the DQN can be found in Figure 8.3 where we can say that the main structure can be divided into three parts, namely, target network, policy network and experience replay memory. The target neural network (NN) and policy NN are the same two networks that are used to update and optimise the training.

State: Each grid is taken as state s which will represent the SINR. The UAV will move along the state space and calculate SINR under the considered radio environment. Following the state space, we have action selection in the action space.

Action selection: The important function of this proposed scheme is to take the best action by the UAV. That is to say, the input of the function of this scheme is the Q-values related to four possible actions that are left, right, up (front) and down (back) and output of that is the best action to be taken by the UAV.

The exploration–exploitation trade-off becomes a problem during the UAV learning process. The exploration process is a way of taking as many actions as

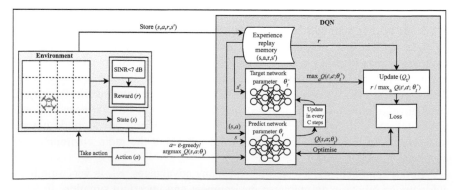

Figure 8.3 Graphical illustration of deep Q-network workflow for coverage hole detection in radio environment

possible to find the best strategy. On the other hand, the UAV can select actions with the largest Q-value in order to achieve the highest reward in the exploitation process. Exploration technique is very crucial because the best or optimal strategy can be achieved by exploring different states *s*. Having said that excessive exploration impacts the performance of UAV navigation as well as the learning rate. Thereby, a rational action selection technique needs to be employed in order to avoid the above-mentioned issues in the learning process which is a balanced exploration and exploitation.

In this work, the ε-greedy strategy has been used to complete the UAV action selection strategy. In ε-greedy scheme, a specific probability of random changes is calculated in the technique of action selection. The UAV will select random action with ε probability that encourages to explore all the state spaces and select the action $a_{\max}$ with the highest present Q-value to make use of the learnt knowledge wherever possible [14,23].

Reward: For UAV navigation and coverage hole detection, we have state space *s* to represent SINR strength at different positions under considered radio environment. Following the state space, we have action (that has been discussed earlier) and reward. The reward *r* has been defined as

$$r = \begin{cases} 1 & \text{Coverage Hole} \\ 0 & \text{No Coverage Hole} \end{cases}$$

The state–action or Q-function can be defined after action *a* in a state *s* at time *t* as

$$Q(s, a) = r + \gamma \max_{a \in A} Q(s', a) \tag{8.7}$$

where *r* is the immediate reward achieved while performing action *a* at state *s* and γ is the discount factor that determines the significance of the future reward value.

Experience replay: There is a special memory allocated for DQN to enhance the learning called experience replay. The main purpose of the experience replay is to store some transition such as (s, a, r, s') in memory for every step. During the training process, a sample of mini-batch is extracted from the memory pool so that the Q-network can learn from the previous experiences.

8.4.2 *DQN principles to detect coverage hole*

The purpose of the DQN method is to estimate the Q-function which presents the maximum accumulated reward in a particular state and action pair [24]. NN is applied in DQN method as a function approximator to achieve Q function [25].

The main principle of DQN to detect coverage hole can be divided into four steps as follows:

Step 1: This step is the prediction stage which is carried out by the Q-network that takes the latest state as input and gives an output of the predicted reward for particular actions. The action with the maximum Q_p value is the action which is $Q_p = \max_a Q(s, a : \theta)$. Here, it is to note that the actions are not always taken from Q-network in this step. A particular percentage of actions are randomly generated [26]. Again, the action selection strategy comes in to place in order to explore more geographical areas. The value of ε decays over time, and the ratio of exploration and exploitation is updated during the training period.

$$\text{Select action} = \begin{cases} \text{random action,} & \text{with } \varepsilon \text{ probability} \\ \arg\max_a Q(s, a; \theta_t), & \text{with } 1 - \varepsilon \text{ probability} \end{cases} \tag{8.8}$$

Step 2: This stage is handled by UAV in the considered radio environment. The UAV takes the predicted action as input and gives output as next state, reward comparing with SINR, and a terminal whether it is a coverage hole or not.

Step 3: In this step, the observations are pushed into the experience replay memory as an experience with (s, a, r, s').

Step 4: This step updates the Q-network by reducing loss between Q_p and Q_t using the following equation:

$$L(\theta_t) = \mathbb{E}_{(s,a,r,s') \sim ER}\left[\left(Q_t - Q_p\right)^2\right] \tag{8.9}$$

where $\mathbb{E}$ is the expectation, (s, a, r, s') are the random mini-batch samples from the experience replay ER. Then stochastic gradient descent is applied to optimise the loss function. In the previous equation, Q_t and Q_e can be, respectively, defined as

$$Q_t = (r + \gamma \max_{a'} Q(s', a'; \theta_t^-)) \tag{8.10}$$

$$Q_p = Q(s, a; \theta_t) \tag{8.11}$$

where parameters θ_t^- and θ_t are used as weight in the target network Q_t and prediction network Q_p, respectively, to stabilise the training where they are updated in every C steps (e.g. $C = 300$ in the simulation). When the quantity of the states becomes massive, it becomes difficult to maintain a look up table of state–action pairs in the memory. The standard solution of this problem is to employ function approximation. The weight θ_t is utilised as the function approximation to estimate the Q-value function such that $Q_p(s, a; \theta_t) \approx Q^*(s, a)$. This whole mechanism is provided in Algorithm 1.

Algorithm 1: Coverage hole detection exploiting DQN

    Input: Distributed BS, UAV as a user, initial policy parameters θ_t, empty replay   buffer M

    Output: $S(x_{UAV}, y_{UAV})$

1: Initialize the memory M with the size N
2: Initialize the network with Q_p random parameters θ_t (training network)
3: Initialize the network with Q_t random parameters $\theta_t^- = \theta_t$ (target network)
4: Start the simulation environment
5: **for** episode=$1, 2, \ldots, K$ **do**
6:     Observe the initial state from environment
7:     **for** time step=$1, 2, \ldots, T$ **do**
8:        Calculate SINR at the UAV
9:        Obtain reward r based on the SINR
10:      Select an action based on:

$$\text{Action } a = \begin{cases} \text{random action} & \text{with } \epsilon \text{ probability} \\ \arg\max_a Q(s, a; \theta_t) & \text{Otherwise} \end{cases}$$

11:      Perform the action a as well as scan SINR and observe reward r, next state s'
12:      Store the experience (s, a, r, s') in the memory M
13:      Sample random minibatch of experiences (s, a, r, s') from M
14:      Estimate the actual/targets Q_t for the experiences

$$\text{Set } Q_t = \begin{cases} r_j & \text{if episode terminates at} \\ & \text{step } j + 1 \\ r_j + \gamma \max_{a'} Q(s', a'; \theta_t^-) & \text{otherwise} \end{cases}$$

15:      Perform an optimization (gradient descent) algorithm step on $(Q_t - Q_p(s, a; \theta_t)^2)$ w.r.t. θ_t (network parameters)
16:      Every C steps reset $Q_t = Q_p$
17:      $s = s'$
18:    **end for**
19: **end for**

8.5 Simulation results and discussion

For simulation purposes, an open area has been considered which allows the UAV to stay line of sight with the MBS. Python platform has been used to execute the simulation. There are three MBSs in the considered radio environment with a transmission power of 43 dBm with the omnidirectional antenna as per system model [27]. The agent UAV that acts as UE receives the signal from these MBSs and calculates the SINR while moving along with the exploration strategy of the DQN. The UAV has four actions to perform which are left, right, up (front) and down (back). The reward has been defined as +1 for any poor coverage detection for every SINR value less than 7 dB. The simulation parameters are given in Table 8.2 for the considered radio environment as well as ML.

Figure 8.4 represents the simulation of the radio environment where UAV as red rectangle is moving grid by grid by following the DQN mechanism. Four actions can be taken in this mechanism at a constant height (1.5 m): left, right, up and down. The circles are representing the MBS in the grid. The search continues till UAV discovers the coverage hole which is shown as white square in Figure 8.4. It is obvious from the simulation results that UAV with DQN is more efficient in detecting coverage hole than the traditional DT and current MDT. The main reason for this effective detection

Table 8.2   Other simulation parameters

Parameter	Symbol	Value
Simulation environment	–	Rural
LTE Band	–	800 MHz
Bandwidth	–	20 MHz
Transmission power	P_t	43 dBm
Base Station Height	h_{MBS}	30 m
Noise	N	−130.92 dBm
UAV learning rate	α_Q	0.01
Discount factor	γ	0.9

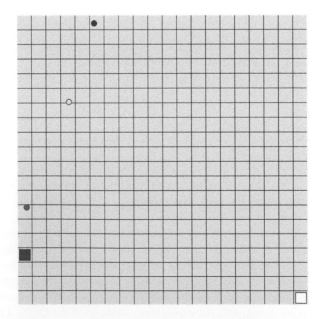

Figure 8.4   Coverage hole detection simulation by UAV

is the advantages of the UAV. Unlike MDT, UAV with DQN is free from any external intervention and can reach everywhere where other mechanisms cannot.

Figure 8.5 represents the heatmaps in different heights such as 1.5 m, 6 m, 30 m and 60 m, respectively. The heatmaps are generated to see the overall signal strength in different heights of the area. As the height increases, the signal becomes stronger due the to decay of PL exponent and shadowing components.

Figure 8.6(a) and (b) shows the performance comparison between Q-learning and DQN. Q-learning is a model-free RL that looks for the best action in a current state. During the time of Q-learning execution, a matrix or table of [state and action] is created. This table is updated over the training episodes. From the comparison, it can be seen that the episode length is slightly going shorter over the time while maintaining the exploration and exploitation strategy. The convergence of Q-learning takes some time in comparison with DQN. In DQN, the first few episodes are longer but converge quicker than Q-learning. However, there are some exploration strategies remains until the end of the training episodes. As a result, the learning curve of DQN is not as flat as the Q-learning. The accumulated reward in each episode has not been shown here because the reward has been defined as '1'. Thus, it is a straight line for both the algorithms.

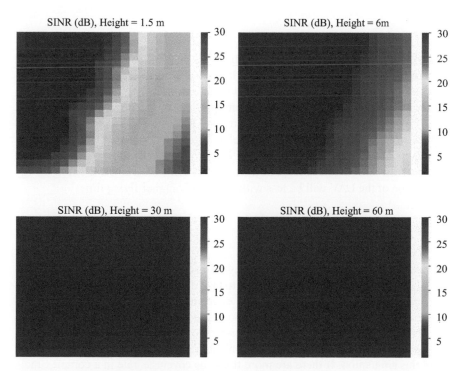

Figure 8.5 (a) Heatmap at height 1.5 m. (b) Heatmap at height 6 m. (c) Heatmap at height 30 m. (d) Heatmap at height 60 m

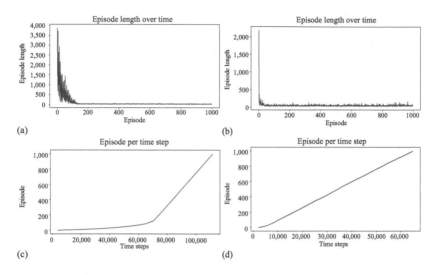

Figure 8.6   Performance evaluation comparison between Q-learning and DQN to detect coverage hole: (a) episode length for every episode in Q-learning, (b) episode length for every episode in DQN, (c) episode per time step in Q-learning and (d) episode per time step in DQN

Figure 8.6(c) and (d) shows time steps against episodes for both algorithms. The cumulative sum of time steps has been considered, which indicates that the running total time steps are growing in each episode. It can be seen from the graphs that the Q-learning algorithm converges around 70 thousands time steps. On the other hand, the convergence is taking place for DQN at approximately 5 thousands times steps. It has also been observed in the simulation that DQN is better in performance than the Q-learning in terms of random action selection and practical implementation. The UAV moves more steadily utilising the DQN algorithm than the Q-learning algorithm because of the action selection policy. Hence, it can be assumed that the energy consumption of the UAV will be less with potentially higher flying time.

8.6   Conclusions

In this chapter, we suggest an effective way of discovering a coverage hole with the help of UAV and ML. The main purpose is to take different parameters from the radio environment and detect the coverage hole efficiently and autonomously. The simulation results show that the proposed method is successful in detecting the coverage hole. Further research for this proposed method can be extended in to many directions. For example, the UAV has detected only a single objective or only one coverage hole in this simulation. If there are more than one coverage hole in a complex radio environment then we have to consider multi-objective RL and consider additional constraints such as UAV charging stations and obstacles, e.g., MBS, trees, buildings.

Also, the simulation of such complex radio environment needs to urban scenarios with multi obstacles avoidance techniques considering the speed of the UAV. Apart from these, we can also consider an on-demand UAV base station (tethered or untethered UAV) to provide coverage and capacity to a coverage hole or poor network service area. Based on the traffic requirement and available wireless backhaul, UAVs can act as a base station at the same time while flying to the coverage hole area in a shortest distance.

References

[1] Wang H, Raj B, and Xing EP. On the Origin of Deep Learning; 2017. Available from: http://arxiv.org/abs/1702.07800.

[2] Marr B. A Short History of Machine Learning – Every Manager Should Read. Forbes; 2016. http://tinyurl com/gslvr6k.

[3] Nunes DS, Zhang P, and Silva JS. A Survey on Human-in-the-Loop Applications Towards an Internet of All. IEEE Communications Surveys & Tutorials. 2015;17(2):944–965.

[4] Mozaffari M, Saad W, Bennis M, *et al*. A Tutorial on UAVs for Wireless Networks: Applications, Challenges, and Open Problems. IEEE Communications Surveys & Tutorials. 2019;21:2334–2360.

[5] Davidson J. Scottish Government Launches Procurement to Cover 4G Mobile 'Notspots'; 2018. Available from: https://www.holyrood.com/articles/news/scottish-government-launches-procurement-cover-4g-mobile-notspots.

[6] Scottish Government and Scottish Futures Trust. Scottish 4G Infill Programme Consultation: Request For Information. Edinburgh, UK: Scottish Government; 2018.

[7] Fernandes D, Ferreira LS, Nozari M, *et al*. Combining Drive Tests and Automatically Tuned Propagation Models in the Construction of Path Loss Grids. In: 2018 IEEE 29th Annual International Symposium on Personal, Indoor and Mobile Radio Communications (PIMRC). Bologna: IEEE; 2018. p. 1–2.

[8] Lin PC. Minimization of drive tests using measurement reports from user equipment. In: 2014 IEEE 3rd Global Conference on Consumer Electronics (GCCE). Tokyo: IEEE; 2014. p. 84–85.

[9] Akbari I, Onireti O, Imran A, *et al*. How reliable is MDT-based autonomous coverage estimation in the presence of user and BS positioning error? IEEE Wireless Communications Letters. 2016;5(2):196–199.

[10] Al-Ahmed SA, Shakir MZ, and Zaidi SAR. Optimal 3D UAV Base Station Placement by Considering Autonomous Coverage Hole Detection, Wireless Back-haul and User Demand. Journal of Communications and Networks. 2020 October; Manuscript under revision.

[11] Mahdavinejad MS, Rezvan M, Barekatain M, *et al*. Machine learning for Internet of Things data analysis: A survey. Digital Communications and Networks. 2018;4(3):161–175.

[12]   Ribeiro M, Grolinger K, and Capretz MA. MLaaS: Machine Learning as a Service. In: 2015 IEEE 14th International Conference on Machine Learning and Applications (ICMLA). Miami, FL: IEEE; 2015. p. 896–902.

[13]   Sharma K and Nandal R. A Literature Study On Machine Learning Fusion With IOT. In: 2019 3rd International Conference on Trends in Electronics and Informatics (ICOEI). Tirunelveli, India: IEEE; 2019. p. 1440–1445.

[14]   Sutton RS and Barto AG. Reinforcement learning: An introduction. Cambridge, MA: MIT Press; 2018.

[15]   Qiang W and Zhongli Z. Reinforcement learning model, algorithms and its application. In: 2011 International Conference on Mechatronic Science, Electric Engineering and Computer (MEC). Jilin: IEEE; 2011. p. 1143–1146.

[16]   François-Lavet V, Henderson P, Islam R, *et al.* An Introduction to Deep Reinforcement Learning; 2018. Available from: http://arxiv.org/abs/1811.12560.

[17]   Mnih V, Kavukcuoglu K, Silver D, *et al.* Playing Atari with Deep Reinforcement Learning; 2013. Available from: http://arxiv.org/abs/1312.5602

[18]   Amorim R, Nguyen H, Mogensen P, *et al.* Radio channel modeling for UAV communication over cellular networks. IEEE Wireless Communications Letters. 2017;6(4):514–517.

[19]   Rappaport TS. Wireless Communications: Principles and Practice. Prentice Hall communications engineering and emerging technologies series. Prentice Hall PTR New Jersey; 2002.

[20]   Al-Hourani A and Gomez K. Modeling Cellular-to-UAV Path-Loss for Suburban Environments. IEEE Wireless Communications Letters. 2018;7(1):82–85.

[21]   Ali NA, Mourad HAM, ElSayed HM, *et al.* General expressions for downlink signal to interference and noise ratio in homogeneous and heterogeneous LTE-Advanced networks. Journal of Advanced Research. 2016;7(6):923–929.

[22]   Rothschild J. Understanding LTE Signal Strength Values. USAT; 2017. Available from: https://usatcorp.com/faqs/understanding-lte-signal-strength-values/.

[23]   Xin J, Zhao H, Liu D, *et al.* Application of deep reinforcement learning in mobile robot path planning. In: 2017 Chinese Automation Congress (CAC). Jinan: IEEE; 2017. p. 7112–7116.

[24]   Arulkumaran K, Deisenroth MP, Brundage M, *et al.* Deep reinforcement learning: A brief survey. IEEE Signal Processing Magazine. 2017;34(6):26–38.

[25]   Lopez-Martin M, Carro B, and Sanchez-Esguevillas A. Application of deep reinforcement learning to intrusion detection for supervised problems. Expert Systems with Applications. 2020;141:112963.

[26]   Wang J, Gou L, Shen HW, *et al.* DQNViz: A Visual Analytics Approach to Understand Deep Q-Networks. IEEE Transactions on Visualization and Computer Graphics. 2018;25(1):288–298.

[27]   Holma H and Toskala A. WCDMA for UMTS: HSPA evolution and LTE. John Wiley & Sons; 2010.

Chapter 9

Artificial intelligence for localization of ultrawide bandwidth (UWB) sensor nodes

Fuhu Che[1], Abbas Ahmed[1], Qasim Zeeshan Ahmed[1], and Muhammad Zeeshan Shakir[2]

The application of position-awareness or location-awareness is becoming more and more prominent, and the demand for indoor positioning system (IPS) is urgent. Many different wireless technologies have been employed for the development of IPS, such as Bluetooth, radio-frequency identification (RFID), Zigbee, Ultrawide band (UWB), and Wi-Fi. Among these different technologies, UWB has a unique advantage in penetration ability, precise ranging, anti-multipath, and anti-interference due to its extremely large bandwidth. However, factors such as environmental noise, multipath effect, interference of nearby devices, and non-line of sight (NLOS) environment affect the accuracy of positioning and localization. Therefore, in this chapter, we attempt to enhance the indoor positioning accuracy of the UWB system by developing a Naïve Bayes (NB) classifier. Root-mean-square error (RMSE) criterion is selected to classify the received data into three different levels: low, medium, and high accuracy. After that, receiver operating characteristic (ROC) curves are plotted, and the area under the curves (AUC) enables us to visualize the accuracy of NB classifier. The developed technique is then tested and verified by two different indoor scenarios. The IPS is initially tested in a small-sized room having an area of around 16 m^2, followed by testing in a medium-sized room having an area of around 26 m^2. From our measurements, the NB classifier can achieve more than 90% of accuracy in the LOS environment and more than 87% of accuracy in a partial LOS environment.

9.1 Introduction

Positioning defines the ability to determine where an object or a person is located [1]. In recent years, the Global Positioning System (GPS) has brought great convenience to people's daily life, such as travel and navigation. In 2017, the US government claimed

[1]School of Computing and Engineering, University of Huddersfield, Huddersfield, UK
[2]School of Computing, Engineering and Physical Sciences, University of the West of Scotland, Paisley, UK

that with the help of GPS technology, the range of location error for an average user is within 7.8 m with 95% confidence interval [2]. However, this accuracy will not be suitable for an indoor localization application where the GPS signals are blocked. An IPS will continuously determine the position of a person or an object in real time with high accuracy [3]. Furthermore, the environment of indoor is challenging, because of different floor layout, nonavailability of LOS path, multipath due to the presence of different materials, and further complex and unknown environments. Ultra-wideband (UWB) is a suitable approach for IPS due to its extremely short radio pulses and wider frequency bandwidth that can facilitate the signal to pass through obstacles effectively and reduce infinite time resolution led by multipath effects [4]. UWB can provide centimeter-level positioning accuracy and can coexist with existing RF signals or external noise like Wi-Fi and Bluetooth Low Energy (BLE) due to the high data rate of communication.

There are several different positioning UWB algorithms; positioning can be classified into three main categorizations that are the time of arrival (TOA) [5], time difference of arrival (TDOA) [6], and two-way ranging (TWR) [7]. The principle is to install anchors or beacons at a known position and then to calculate the exchange of UWB signals between those known anchors and tags or agents with unknown position [8]. From this and the known positions of the anchors, the tag can then be localized by doing multilateration methods [9]. Each algorithm needs more than three anchors to locate the position of a tag in two-dimensional (2D) environment and more than four anchors to locate the tag in three-dimensional environment [10]. However, all these algorithms can detect within 10 cm of accuracy in LOS environment, which is superior to the other detection techniques such as Wi-Fi, BLE, and GPS.

This positioning accuracy within 10 cm is sufficient for general environments, but for some special occasions, like a moving forklift truck in a warehouse, this accuracy needs to be further improved as it may cause severe injury to the workers in the warehouse. Furthermore, UWB transmit power spectral density requirement is under -41.3 dB m/Hz, which limits the coverage distance [11]. The maximum distance with this power spectral density is generally less than 100 m [12]. As this coverage distance is a big problem so, when employing UWB systems for an indoor area such as airports, large factories, shopping malls, and stadiums, a large number of anchor nodes will be required; as a result, the cost of the deployed system will be increased. At present, most of the positioning accuracy algorithms require a clear LOS between the anchors and the tags. The accuracy of the algorithms is greatly reduced when this LOS is not there [13]. Therefore, maintaining high-precision positioning in NLOS will be an immense challenge [14]. Keeping these challenges in mind, localization algorithms are urgently required where the accuracy is still maintained when moving with fast speed, covering large distances and in NLOS environments.

Artificial intelligence (AI) is constantly evolving and currently knows no bounds. The power of machine learning (ML) is ensuring that the limits of AI bounds are extended, and the rules of traditional programming are broken. The deployment of AI and ML has already been proposed in various standards, including the 3rd Generation Partnership Project network data analytics (NWDA) [15], and the European

Telecommunications Standards Institute experimental network intelligence (ENI) [16]. NWDA utilizes the approach of slice and traffic steering and splitting, while ENI uses a cognitive network-management architecture and context aware-based approach [17]. This chapter employs a similar approach to AI and ML for improving the UWB positioning for LOS and NLOS environments. We propose a Naïve Bayes (NB) classifier that employs a probabilistic ML approach to the UWB positioning data. NB is preferred over other techniques because of its easy scalable quality and for the ability to respond to the request instantaneously. The collected data are classified into three different categories depending upon their distance from the exact location, which are low, medium, and high. The IPS is first tested in a small-sized room having an area of around 16 m^2, followed by testing in a medium-sized room having an area of around 26 m^2. From our measurements, the NB classifier can achieve more than 90% of accuracy in LOS environment and more than 87% of accuracy in partial LOS environment. ROCs are then employed to help one to visualize the proposed classifier and to evaluate the usefulness of the ML technique. The ROC curve indicates that the AUC is 96.2% and 93.1%, respectively, for high accurate samples when measurement is carried out in small-sized and medium-sized room.

This chapter contributes in the following two ways:

1. An ML-based NB classifier is developed to improve the positioning and localization capability of the IPS.
2. An extensive experiment is carried out based on using UWB sensor nodes for two different-sized rooms. Furthermore, LOS and partial LOS scenarios are studied in detail.

9.2 Indoor positioning system

Several technologies have been employed for IPS such as RFID, Wi-Fi, Bluetooth, UWB, and Zigbee [18, 19]. However, when deciding about the appropriate IPS technology, a judicious balance between the system complexity, cost, and accuracy is required. RFID, Wi-Fi, and Bluetooth have gained much attention due to their advantages in terms of low cost and ease of deployment. These techniques mainly employ the radio signal strength indicator (RSSI) to localize the target objects. The distance between the receiver and object is calculated through the attenuation of radio waves that are proportional to its distance. However, the main challenge is the performance in the presence of multipath propagation, interference, and localizing multiple objects, among others. Different approaches such as tag-based, reader-based, or hybrid-based have been incorporated for the purpose of localization and positioning. Table 9.1 summarizes the comparison of these different positioning technologies mentioned in terms of accuracy, coverage area, battery lifetime, number of tags required and price, and so on. However, as we are more focused toward localization, and accuracy is a key requirement, in this chapter our focus is toward UWB system for IPS.

9.2.1   UWB indoor positioning system

Different UWB positioning algorithms have been developed in the literature. These algorithms can be classified into three main categories that are TOA, TDOA, and TWR. Let us now discuss these algorithms in detail.

9.2.1.1   Time of arrival (TOA) positioning system

In TOA positioning system, the transmitter and the receiver are time synchronized. TOA or sometimes called as time of flight evaluates the travel time from the transmitted to a remote receiver. The distance is measured by using the round-trip time and then multiplying it by the speed of light. Now, trilateration techniques can be employed for determining the exact location of the tag. There are many algorithms for trilateration in literature such as [26–28] and references therein. Trilateration is a process of determining the relative position of the tag utilizing the geometry of triangles. In this method, two or more anchors are required to measure the distance between the tag and the anchors. Therefore, if we know the position of the anchors, the abovementioned method can help us to calculate distances d_1, d_2, and d_3 as depicted in Figure 9.1.

The distance in 2D between target and reference node d_i is calculated by the following formula:

$$d_i = \sqrt{(x - x_i)^2 + (y - y_i)^2} = c(t_i - t), \quad i = 1, 2, 3, \ldots, \tag{9.1}$$

where x and y are the coordinates of the target or tag and x_i and y_i are the coordinates of the reference node or anchor i. Therefore, the target can be uniquely localized at the intersecting point of these three circles as shown in Figure 9.1. The TOA algorithm requires accurate synchronization as a small-time error will have a devastating impact on the position accuracy. This project will use the TOA algorithm, as it is simple and the algorithm improves the battery life of the nodes. However, this algorithm requires all tags and anchors to have the same reference clock.

Table 9.1   Comparison of different positioning technologies

	RFID	Wi-Fi	Bluetooth	UWB
Accuracy (m)	<3 [20,21]	<15 [22]	<10 [23]	<0.1 [25,26]
Coverage area (m)	<100 [20,21]	<10 [22]	<50 [24]	<20 [25,26]
Battery lifetime	Years [18]	Weeks–months	Years	Days–months depending upon duty cycle
Number of tags	Low	High	High	Low–high
Stability of the large area	Medium	Medium	Medium	Complex
Cost	Low	Medium	Medium	High

9.2.1.2 Time difference of arrival (TDOA) positioning system

If the transmitter and the receiver cannot reach time synchronization, the TDOA algorithm is a better choice. This algorithm calculates the TDOA of a signal sent by an object and received by three or more anchors. The distance in 2D between target and reference node d_i is represented by the following equation:

$$t_{AB} \times c = d_1 - d_2 = d_3 - d_4$$

$$= \sqrt{(x - x_A)^2 + (y - y_A)^2} - \sqrt{(x - x_B)^2 - (y - y_B)^2} \qquad (9.2)$$

where t_{AB} represents the TDOA between reference anchors A and B as shown in Figure 9.2, c represents the speed of light, x and y are the coordinates of the target, (x_A, y_A) and (x_B, y_B) are the coordinates of reference anchors A and B, respectively. More than four reference anchors are required to estimate the target location in 2D environment.

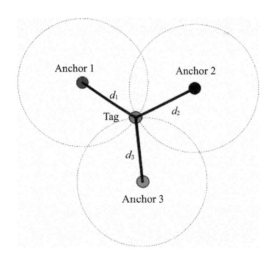

Figure 9.1 TOA positioning algorithm model

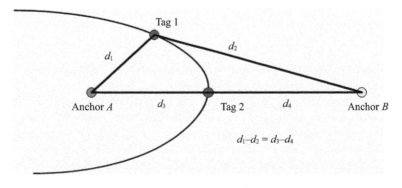

Figure 9.2 TDOA positioning algorithm model

The challenge of TDOA-based approaches is significant requirement of the bandwidth compared with other algorithms and at least four anchors.

9.2.1.3   Two-way ranging (TWR) positioning system

The distance between an anchor and a tag can be calculated by utilizing the TWR technique when there is no common clock among reference nodes. TWR technique algorithm utilizes bidirectional messages exchanged between a target and a reference node. Time elapse from transmitting a message to receiving its response is required for the TWR calculation. Apart from these algorithms, there are several other algorithms which use such as RSSI, angle of arrival, and hybrid algorithms. These algorithms need to be selected according to the design requirement and circumstances. However, developing algorithms which improves UWB positioning and localization capabilities is still an active area of research [29–33].

9.3   UWB ranging accuracy evaluation

As we discuss the positioning mentioned previously, all the algorithms are based on the measurement of time standards. In this case, there will be some time or frequency deviations caused by the radiator directly or by the multipath and NLOS scenarios. In this way, the calculated position will deviate from its true position, resulting in extremely low positioning accuracy at some time points that will greatly affect the accuracy of overall positioning. Therefore, the detection of outliers is the key to determine the accurate overall positioning system. Naïve Bayes can be used to evaluate the accuracy of system positioning, and the ROC curve can be used to visually observe the performance of the positioning. This section is going to analyze the characteristics of Naïve Bayes and the ROC curve.

9.3.1   Naïve Bayes (NB) classifier

Naïve Bayes (NB) classifier is one of the most popular and widely used classification algorithms in ML. In this method, Bayesian principle is employed which deploys probability statistics on the sample data set. From the probability perspective, according to Bayes Rule, the given probability $P(l|x)$ can be measured as

$$P(l|x) = \frac{P(x|l)P(l)}{P(x)}, \tag{9.3}$$

where $P(l|x)$ is the probability of location given the distance of the anchors, $P(l)$ is the prior probability of the location or position, $P(x|l)$ is the probability of the distance given location, and the $P(x)$ is the prior probability of the distance of the anchors.

As discussed previously, location-aware network has two types of sensor nodes. Anchors or beacons are nodes with known position, while tags or agents are nodes whose position is unknown. We focus on a network with total N number of anchor nodes and a tag position of which we want to determine. The Euclidean or the exact calculated distance between the tag and the ith anchor is given as d_i, $i = 1, 2, \ldots, N$ and the estimate distance between the ith anchor and the UWB tag is given as $\hat{d}_i$,

$i = 1, 2, \ldots, N$. Now NB can be used to classify the collected data that are received from the anchors. RMSE is the arithmetic square root of the MSE. The MSE is the average of the square of the difference between the measured distance and the actual distance. Therefore, RMSE is a measure of the deviation between the observed and the true values. The RMSE calculation formula is shown in the following:

$$RMSE = \frac{1}{N}\sqrt{(d_1 - \hat{d}_1)^2 + (d_2 - \hat{d}_2)^2 + \ldots + (d_N - \hat{d}_N)^2}. \tag{9.4}$$

Table 9.2 shows an IPS when four anchors and a tag are employed. However, it is difficult to intuitively evaluate the overall IPS because of a large data set. The three different levels of classifier are decided with the help of (9.4). If RMSE value is between $0 \leq RMSE < 0.03$, the data are classified as having high positioning accuracy, for an RMSE value of $0.03 \leq RMSE < 0.05$, the data are classified as having medium positioning accuracy, and finally, when the $RMSE \geq 0.05$, the data are classified as having low positioning accuracy. Keeping in view, with the previous threshold, data of Table 9.2 are classified as having low, medium, or high accuracy positioning information.

9.3.2 Receiver operating characteristic

While the Naïve Bayes (NB) algorithm is used to classify the results of the system, ROC enables a visual plot showing the performance of the classifier using a different threshold value. The ROC curve was initially used in World War II for evaluating the radar signals before deploying it in signal detection theory [14]. It is created by plotting the true-positive rate (TPR) against the false-positive rate (FPR) at numerous threshold settings. TPR determines how many correct positioning results occurred among all the positive positioning results available during the test, while FPR defines how many incorrect results have occurred among all negative positioning results available during the test.

The accuracy of the classifier can be measured by determining AUC. Generally, the more the AUC, the better the classifier. An area of 1 shows that the classifier has a perfect result, while an area of 0.5 represents a worse test that means the classifier cannot separate the samples for testing. Figure 9.3 illustrates the performance of the classifier and depending upon the AUC, it is classified into four different categories. The black curve indicates that the classifier does not have the ability to separate

Table 9.2   Classification of the IPS according to RMSE

Anchor 1		Anchor 2		Anchor 3		Anchor 4		RMSE	Classification level
d_1	$\hat{d}_1$	d_2	$\hat{d}_2$	d_3	$\hat{d}_3$	d_4	$\hat{d}_4$		
3.03	2.94	1.77	1.99	2.88	2.8	1.9	1.85	0.0639	Low
3.03	2.95	1.77	1.73	2.88	2.8	1.9	1.88	0.0304	Medium
3.03	3.04	1.77	1.77	2.88	2.84	1.9	1.89	0.0106	High

the samples, while the red curve indicates that the classifier is able to separate the samples accurately. Let us now proceed toward the implementation and evaluation of our UWB IPS.

9.4   Implementation and evaluation

In this section, we will mainly describe how the NB classifier algorithm and ROC curve are applied to the IPS to evaluate the system performance. Figure 9.4 illustrates the block diagram of the developed IPS. The system operates by employing two phases: off-line training and online testing. In the first phase, the IPS data are collected from the tag and preprocessed. The distance between the anchors and tags is calculated, followed by the RMSE as mentioned in (9.4). It is further used to produce

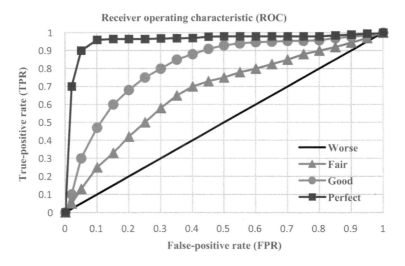

Figure 9.3   Receiver operating characteristic (ROC) curve

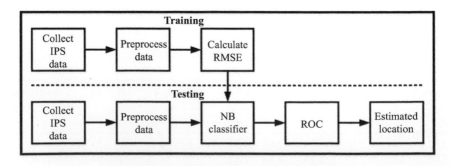

Figure 9.4   Block diagram of developed IPS

the fingerprint library. During the testing phase, the IPS data are calculated and pre-processed. They are then compared with the database utilizing an NB classifier as mentioned previously. The ROC is then plotted, and the confidence level is calculated which is utilized to improve the positioning results by deriving the final estimated location of the tag.

As mentioned previously there are two stages for the NB classifier, which are off-line training followed by online testing, respectively. As depicted in Algorithm (classifier: offline/online training stage), during the training phase, the data are collected, preprocessed, and then the distance between the tag and the anchors is estimated. As the position of the user is known, therefore, RMSE can be used to classify that data into three categories such as high, medium, and low accuracy. In this training stage, the original distances are classified and based on the subsequent fingerprints are collected and combined as a fingerprint.

Classifier: offline training stage:

Require: Dataset of the area
Require: Determine the distance
      for each location i
          calculate the distance of tag from each anchor
      end
Calculate **RMSE**

Classifier: online testing stage:

Require: The input containing all the information of distances
Require: L {Determine the location}
        for each location l_i
            calculate $P(l_i|x)$
      end
      argmax $P(l_i|x)$

In the testing phase, the corresponding fingerprints are collected and classified based on the feature. The probability of each location is measured, and the highest probability is selected for the estimated location which corresponds to the closest entry in the database. This is marked as the location of the tag. Based on Bayes theorem, the location is calculated as

$$P(L_i|x) = \frac{P(x|L_i)P(L_i)}{P(x)}, \tag{9.5}$$

where $P(L_i)$ is the location probability, and $P(x)$ is the probability of the observed features. $P(x|L_i)$ can be calculated from the training dataset and is assumed to follow a Gaussian distribution with variance, σ and mean, m.

9.4.1   Experiment setup and environment

Figure 9.5 shows two different indoor scenarios. As shown in Figure 9.5(a), the first testing location is a living room and kitchen together. The four anchors are placed in such a way that they have a complete LOS with the tag. The human wears the tag. The size of the room is 3.3×4.8 m^2.

The second testing location is another room as shown in Figure 9.5(b). The size of the room is 5.4×4.8 m^2, and the user can move freely within this room. However, the anchors are placed in such a way that they do not have a complete LOS with respect to tag as well as anchors. From the figure, it can be observed that anchors 2, 3, and 4 do not have a direct LOS as it is blocked by the room furniture.

In both the cases, the data are collected over one complete day. Furthermore, during the process of collecting data the human orientation and stance remained unchanged. However, after the training is carried out, the human can move freely within this room.

9.4.2   NB and ROC results

Figure 9.6 shows the summary of the result using the NB classifier, which is obtained by WEKA ML software. From this figure, it can be observed that out of 1,144 classified instances, 1,037 instances were classified correctly, resulting in an accuracy

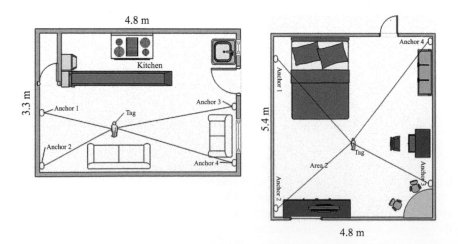

Figure 9.5   Data collecting and testing environments: (a) small-sized room and (b) medium-sized room

of 90.6469%. The reason for high accuracy is that the testing is carried out in a small-sized room having a complete LOS environment as mentioned in Figure 9.5(a). The remaining 107 instances cannot be correctly classified. As the classification results are compared with the actual locations, the confusion matrix can be developed which will assist us in analyzing the errors made by our NB classifier. From the generated confusion matrix, it can be observed that 185 samples (adding the elements in the third column) can be classified as highly accurate, 938 samples (adding the elements in the second column) are having medium level of accuracy, and 21 (adding the elements in the first column) samples have very low accuracy. Most errors occur when the sample is classified as a medium level instead of having a low level of accuracy.

Figure 9.7 shows the summary of the result using the NB classifier which is obtained by WEKA ML software. From this figure, it can be observed that out of 531 classified instances, 464 instances were classified correctly, resulting in an accuracy of 87.3823%. The reason for low accuracy is that the testing is carried out in a medium-sized room having partial LOS environment as mentioned in Figure 9.5(b). The remaining 67 instances cannot be classified correctly. As the classification results are compared with the actual locations, the confusion matrix can be developed which will assist us in analyzing the errors made by our NB classifier. From the generated confusion matrix, it can be observed that 18 samples (adding the elements in the third column) can be classified as highly accurate, 432 samples (adding the elements in the second column) are having medium level of accuracy, and 81 (adding the elements in the first column) samples have very low accuracy. Most errors occur when the sample is classified as medium level instead of having a low level of accuracy. Let us now calculate the ROC of these rooms.

```
=== Summary ===

Correctly classified instances        1,037              90.6469%
Incorrectly classified instances        107               9.3531%
Kappa statistic                           0.637
Mean absolute error                       0.0745
Root-mean-squared error                   0.2143
Relative absolute error                  53.7501%
Root relative squared error              81.6851%
Total number of instances             1,144

=== Detailed accuracy by class ===

              TP rate  FP rate  Precision  Recall  F-measure  MCC    ROC area  PRC area  Class
              0.615    0.011    0.381      0.615   0.471      0.477  0.990     0.531     Low
              0.911    0.121    0.983      0.911   0.946      0.657  0.947     0.990     Medium
              0.899    0.076    0.578      0.899   0.704      0.682  0.962     0.875     High
Weighted avg. 0.906    0.115    0.934      0.906   0.915      0.657  0.949     0.973

=== Confusion matric ===

   a   b   c    <-- classified as
   8   5   0     a = Low
  12 922  78     b = Medium
   1  11 107     c = High
```

Figure 9.6   Naïve Bayes classifier results for small-sized room

Finally, Figure 9.8 shows the ROC curve for a small-sized and a medium-sized room as mentioned in Figure 9.5. In this figure, TPR is plotted against the FPR. From this figure, it can be observed that AUC for the small-sized room is more than 0.94, which is an indication that the NB classifier for the UWB-based IPS performance is very good. The main reason for this good performance of the NB classifier is the presence of strong LOS and a small area of the room. This curve also indicates that most data can be classified correctly, and the distance and stability of UWB evaluation are relatively high. From Figure 9.8, it can be observed that AUC for the medium-sized room is more than 0.88, which is lower than the small-sized room. However,

```
=== Summary ===

Correctly classified instances          464            87.3823%
Incorrectly classified instances         67            12.6177%
Kappa statistic                         0.6416
Mean absolute error                     0.0881
Root-mean-squared error                 0.2659
Relative absolute error                34.3039%
Root relative squared error            74.3761%
Total number of instances               531

=== Detailed accuracy by class ===

              TP rate  FP rate  Precision  Recall  F-measure  MCC    ROC area  PRC area  Class
              0.602    0.031    0.840      0.602   0.701      0.650  0.972     0.778     Low
              0.960    0.362    0.891      0.960   0.924      0.661  0.987     0.947     Medium
              0.647    0.014    0.611      0.647   0.629      0.616  0.931     0.723     High
Weighted avg. 0.874    0.280    0.871      0.874   0.867      0.657  0.885     0.904

=== Confusion matric ===

  a    b   c   <-- classified as
 68   44   1   a = Low
 10  385   6   b = Medium
  3    3  11   c = High
```

Figure 9.7   Naïve Bayes classifier results for medium-sized room

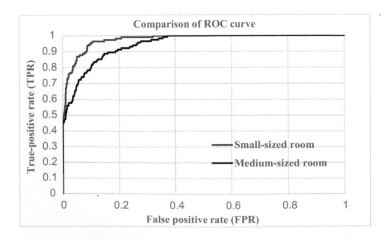

Figure 9.8   ROC curve of different areas

the AUC is still good enough despite the presence of NLOS. In the future, we will design stronger classifier algorithms that can improve the accuracy performance of the UWB system, especially in the NLOS environment.

9.5 Conclusion

In this chapter, we have designed an NB classifier for a UWB-based localization system. With the help of NB classifier and RMSE, the data are classified into three categories: high, medium, and low accuracy. ROCs are plotted to show the effectiveness of the NB classifier. As our developed technique obtains more than 90% classification accuracy, we have tested it into two different environments: LOS and partial NLOS conditions. Furthermore, to test the accuracy, small-sized and medium-sized rooms were used. From our measurements, it is observed that the accuracy of the developed NB classifier is dependent upon the environment. For LOS and NLOS environments, the accuracy are around 97% and 87.38%, respectively. Our future research will concentrate on technique that can further improve the localization classification and improve the positioning accuracy of the IPS.

References

[1] F. Zafari, A. Gkelias and K. K. Leung, "A Survey of Indoor Localization Systems and Technologies," in *IEEE Communications Surveys & Tutorials*, vol. 21, no. 3, pp. 2568–2599, Third Quarter 2019.

[2] B. A. Renfro, M. Stein, N. Boeker and A. Terry, An Analysis of Global Positioning System (GPS) Standard Positioning Service (SPS) Performance for 2017, 2018.

[3] Z. Wu, Q. Xu, J. Li, C. Fu, Q. Xuan and Y. Xiang, "Passive Indoor Localization Based on CSI and Naive Bayes Classification," in *IEEE Transactions on Systems, Man, and Cybernetics: Systems*, vol. 48, no. 9, pp. 1566–1577, 2018.

[4] Q. Z. Ahmed, K. Park and M. Alouini, "Ultrawide Bandwidth Receiver Based on a Multivariate Generalized Gaussian Distribution," in *IEEE Transactions on Wireless Communications*, vol. 14, no. 4, pp. 1800–1810, 2015.

[5] Y.-T. Chan, W.-Y. Tsui, H.-C. So and P.-C. Ching, "Time-of-Arrival Based Localization Under NLOS Conditions," in *IEEE Transactions on Vehicular Technology*, vol. 55, no. 1, pp. 17–24, 2006.

[6] H. Yu, G. Huang and J. Gao, "Constrained Total Least-Squares Localisation Algorithm Using Time Difference of Arrival and Frequency Difference of Arrival Measurements With Sensor Location Uncertainties," in *IET Radar, Sonar & Navigation*, vol. 6, no. 9, pp. 891–899, 2012.

[7] J.-Y. Lee and R. A. Scholtz, "Ranging in a Dense Multipath Environment Using an UWB Radio Link," in *IEEE Journal on Selected Areas in Communications*, vol. 20, no. 9, pp. 1677–1683, 2002.

[8]　D. Dardari, A. Conti, U. Ferner, A. Giorgetti and M. Z. Win, "Ranging With Ultrawide Bandwidth Signals in Multipath Environments," in *Proceedings of the IEEE*, vol. 97, no. 2, pp. 404–426, 2009.

[9]　H. Wymeersch, S. Marano, W. M. Gifford and M. Z. Win, "A Machine Learning Approach to Ranging Error Mitigation for UWB Localization," in *IEEE Transactions on Communications*, vol. 60, no. 6, pp. 1719–1728, 2012.

[10]　Y. Gu, A. Lo and I. Niemegeers, "A Survey of Indoor Positioning Systems for Wireless Personal Networks," in *IEEE Communications Surveys & Tutorials*, vol. 11, no. 1, pp. 13–32, First Quarter 2009.

[11]　Q. Z. Ahmed, L. Yang and S. Chen, "Reduced-Rank Adaptive Least Bit-Error-Rate Detection in Hybrid Direct-Sequence Time-Hopping Ultrawide Bandwidth Systems," in *IEEE Transactions on Vehicular Technology*, vol. 60, no. 3, pp. 849–857, 2011.

[12]　S. Maranò, W. M. Gifford, H. Wymeersch and M. Z. Win, "NLOS Identification and Mitigation for Localization Based on UWB Experimental Data," in *IEEE Journal on Selected Areas in Communications*, vol. 28, no. 7, pp. 1026–1035, 2010.

[13]　C. Huang, A. F. Molisch, R. He, *et al.*, "Machine Learning-Enabled LOS/NLOS Identification for MIMO System in Dynamic Environment," in *IEEE Transactions on Wireless Communications*, vol. 19, no. 6, pp. 3643–3657, 2020.

[14]　D. Feng, C. Wang, C. He, Y. Zhuang and X. Xia, "Kalman Filter Based Integration of IMU and UWB for High-Accuracy Indoor Positioning and Navigation," in *IEEE Internet of Things Journal*, vol. 7, no. 4, pp. 3133–3146, 2020.

[15]　3GPP, TS 29.520 Network Data Analytics Services for the 5G System; Stage 3 (Release 15), June 2018.

[16]　https://www.etsi.org/technologies-clusters/technologies/experiential-networked-intelligence.

[17]　C.-L. I, Q. Sun, Z. Liu, S. Zhang and S. Han, "The Big-Data-Driven Intelligent Wireless Network: Architecture, Use Cases, Solutions, and Future Trends," in *IEEE Vehicular Technology Magazine*, vol. 12, no. 4, pp. 20–29, 2017.

[18]　F. Gustafsson and F. Gunnarsson, "Mobile Positioning Using Wireless Networks: Possibilities and Fundamental Limitations Based on Available Wireless Network Measurements," in *IEEE Signal Processing Magazine*, vol. 22, no. 4, pp. 41–53, 2005.

[19]　L. M. Ni, D. Zhang and M. R. Souryal, "RFID-Based Localization and Tracking Technologies," in *IEEE Wireless Communications*, vol. 18, no. 2, pp. 45–51, 2011.

[20]　S. S. Saab and Z. S. Nakad, "A Standalone RFID Indoor Positioning System Using Passive Tags," in *IEEE Transactions on Industrial Electronics*, vol. 58, no. 5, pp. 1961–1970, 2011.

[21]　J. Niu, B. Wang, L. Shu, T. Q. Duong and Y. Chen, "ZIL: An Energy-Efficient Indoor Localization System Using ZigBee Radio to Detect WiFi Fingerprints," in *IEEE Journal on Selected Areas in Communications*, vol. 33, no. 7, pp. 1431–1442, 2015.

[22] Intel. Wireless LAN Standards Study. Accessed: Apr. 12, 2019.[Online]. Available: http://www.intel.com/content/dam/www/public/us/en/documents/case-studies/802-11-wireless-lan-standards-study.pdf.

[23] S. Alletto, R. Cucchiara, G. D. Fiore, *et al.*, "An Indoor Location-Aware System for an IoT-Based Smart Museum," in *IEEE Internet of Things Journal*, vol. 3, no. 2, pp. 244–253, 2016.

[24] S. C. Ergen, ZigBee/IEEE 802.15.4 Summary, UC Berkeley, Berkeley, CA, USA, p. 17, 2004.

[25] C. Huang, L. Lee, C. C. Ho, L. Wu and Z. Lai, "Real-Time RFID Indoor Positioning System Based on Kalman-Filter Drift Removal and Heron-Bilateration Location Estimation," in *IEEE Transactions on Instrumentation and Measurement*, vol. 64, no. 3, pp. 728–739, 2015.

[26] Z. Li, W. Dehaene, and G. Gielen, "A 3-Tier UWB-Based Indoor Localization System for Ultra-Low-Power Sensor Networks," in *IEEE Transactions on Wireless Communications*, vol. 8, no. 6, pp. 2813–2818, 2009.

[27] Kaiser, F. Zheng and E. Dimitrov, "An Overview of Ultra-Wide-Band Systems With MIMO,"ž in *Proceedings of the IEEE*, vol. 97, no. 2, pp. 285–312, 2009.

[28] S. Sadowski and P. Spachos, "RSSI-Based Indoor Localization With the Internet of Things," in *IEEE Access*, vol. 6, pp. 30149–30161, 2018.

[29] I. Guvenc and C. Chong, "A Survey on TOA Based Wireless Localization and NLOS Mitigation Techniques," in *IEEE Communications Surveys & Tutorials*, vol. 11, no. 3, pp. 107–124, Third Quarter 2009.

[30] H. Liu, H. Darabi, P. Banerjee and J. Liu, "Survey of Wireless Indoor Positioning Techniques and Systems," in *IEEE Transactions on Systems, Man, and Cybernetics, Part C (Applications and Reviews)*, vol. 37, no. 6, pp. 1067–1080, 2007.

[31] Q. Z. Ahmed and L. Yang, "Reduced-Rank Adaptive Multiuser Detection in Hybrid Direct-Sequence Time-Hopping Ultrawide Bandwidth Systems," in *IEEE Transactions on Wireless Communications*, vol. 9, no. 1, pp. 156–167, 2010.

[32] X. Bai, L. Dong, L. Ge, H. Xu, J. Zhang and J. Yan, "Robust Localization of Mobile Robot in Industrial Environments With Non-Line-of-Sight Situation," in *IEEE Access*, vol. 8, pp. 22537–22545, 2020.

[33] O. Alluhaibi, Q. Z. Ahmed, E. Kampert, M. D. Higgins and J. Wang, "Revisiting the Energy-Efficient Hybrid D-A Precoding and Combining Design For mm-Wave Systems," in *IEEE Transactions on Green Communications and Networking*, vol. 4, no. 2, pp. 340–354, 2020.

Chapter 10

A Cascaded Machine Learning Approach for indoor classification and localization using adaptive feature selection

Mohamed I. AlHajri[1], Nazar T. Ali[2], and Raed M. Shubair[1,3]

Sensor-based indoor tracking and positioning [1–8] facilitate evolving Internet-of-Things (IoT) applications [9–16], and their performance is significantly enhanced by identifying the indoor environment [17–25]. This identification is of paramount importance as it leads to efficient power consumption, when operating the deployed IoT sensors. This chapter presents an innovative cascaded two-stage machine learning approach for highly accurate and robust identification and localization in indoor environments using adaptive selection and combination of RF spatial signatures. The design of the machine learning algorithm is carried out with respect to a dataset constructed from practical measurements of the RF signal in various types of indoor environments. Several machine learning algorithms are explored, including decision tree (DT), support vector machine (SVM), and k-nearest neighbor (k-NN). In the proposed two-stage technique, machine learning is first used to identify the type of indoor environment. Second, machine learning is employed to identify the most appropriate selection and combination of RF signatures that result in the highest localization accuracy. Received signal strength (RSS), channel transfer function (CTF), and frequency coherence function (FCF) are the primary RF features being explored and combined.

The concept of indoor environment classification, although presented in this chapter for indoor localization, has several other important applications, including adaptive modulation and coding [26,27], indoor millimeter-wave [28–30], 5G waveform selection [31–33], visible light communication [34–36], energy harvesting, peak-average-power ratio (PAPR) [37–39], activity recognition [40], high-speed train [41–43], and Unmanned Aerial Vehicle (UAV)/robotics [44,45].

10.1 Introduction

The field of telecommunications was revolutionized by the advent of IoT that facilitated the development of unprecedented applications that are enabled through smart

[1]Department of Electrical Engineering and Computer Science, Massachusetts Institute of Technology, Cambridge, USA
[2]Department of Electrical and Computer Engineering, Khalifa University, Abu Dhabi, UAE
[3]Department of Electrical and Computer Engineering, New York University, NY, USA

sensors that cooperate efficiently to provide the desired service [9–15,46]. Successful deployment of IoT sensors is primarily dependent on the sensor to have the ability to adjust its power consumption according to the radio channel conditions that are formulated according to the type of the indoor environment.

Classification approaches in the literature have focused on categorizing environment into indoor and outdoor [17–25], rather than focusing on identifying the nature of the indoor environments. For example, the approach presented in [17] categorizes the surrounding environment into indoor, semi-outdoor, and outdoor. That approach is unpopular since it requires data collected from a large number of specially erected cell towers in a small proximity [17]. Other approaches for classifying environments into indoor/outdoor include cell identity maps [18] and chirp sound signals [19]. Finally, in [20], a semi-supervised machine learning method was introduced for indoor/outdoor classification.

The challenges associated with the indoor wireless channel, in the form of severe multipath effect and non-line-of-sight (NLOS), emphasize the need for a highly accurate and robust approach for indoor localization that can be deployed on the user device with minimum computation cost. The use of different RF features in various machine learning algorithms for location fingerprinting has been investigated in [1–8]. RF features included RSS, CTF, and FCF. Localization accuracy can be greatly enhanced if machine learning algorithms are implemented according to hybrid RF features that represent appropriate combination of the aforementioned primary features. This enhancement is due to the fact that with hybrid RF features, more information is available to the algorithm.

This chapter presents an innovative cascaded two-stage machine learning approach for highly accurate and robust identification and localization in indoor environments using adaptive selection and combination of RF spatial signatures. The design of the machine learning algorithm is carried out with respect to a dataset constructed from practical measurements of the RF signal in various types of indoor environments. Several machine learning algorithms are explored, including DT, SVM, and k-NN. In the proposed two-stage technique, and based on the authors prior work [47–50], machine learning is first used to identify the type of indoor environment. Second, machine learning is employed to identify the most appropriate selection and combination of RF signatures that result in the highest localization accuracy. RSS, CTF, and FCF are the primary RF features being explored and combined. Analysis is based on the k-NN machine learning algorithm applied on a dataset constructed from practical measurements of the RF signal in indoor environments. The primary RF signatures that are being explored and combined are RSS, CTF, and FCF.

10.2   Indoor radio propagation channel

10.2.1   Characteristics of RF indoor channel

Challenges associated with indoor localization are due to the nature of the indoor radio propagation channel that is characterized to be site specific, has severe multipath, and suffers from the lack of a LOS signal. The two primary reasons for inaccuracies encountered in indoor localization are multipath fading and NLOS conditions due to shadow fading. Radio propagation channel models are developed to provide a means to analyze the performance of a wireless receiver. Unlike telecommunication systems where performance criterion is the bit error rate, localization system performance is measured in terms of the accuracy of location estimation. The accuracy of location estimation is a function of the accuracy of location metrics and the complexity of localization algorithms. Models for localization application must reflect the effects of channel behavior on the estimated value of localization metrics at the receiver.

10.2.2 Design considerations for the RF indoor channel

It is important for any developed indoor localization method to take into consideration important factors that make the developed method viable and realizable on user devices in order to facilitate its wide-scale adoption of the localization technology. Power consumption is an important factor that needs to be taken into consideration when designing a localization algorithm because it is important to avoid techniques that cost a lot of energy and drains the user device battery. Computational complexity of the localization algorithm is also an important factor to be taken into consideration. Running a highly complex algorithm on the user device, though results in high accuracy, will unfavorably increase power consumption.

Indoor environments provide a challenging space for the localization system to operate in due to the presence of obstacles and multipath effects. This affects the accuracy with which the user/device position is obtained. Therefore, it is important for the localization method to incorporate multipath countermeasures within the developed algorithm in order to produce highly accurate results. Nevertheless, this often requires extensive signal processing and noise cancellation techniques that have, adversely, a negative impact on the computation cost.

10.3 Data collection phase: practical measurements campaign

The frequency domain CTF, $H(f)$, is obtained for four different environments. The floor plan of Figure 10.1 shows the following three indoor environments having boundaries: highly cluttered (Laboratory), medium cluttered (Narrow Corridor), and low cluttered (Lobby). In Figure 10.1, the red triangle represents the transmitter and the black asterisks represent the receiver positions at which measurements are taken. Besides the aforementioned environment of Figure 10.1, a fourth environment, open space (Sports Hall), has also been considered.

A square area within each environment was divided into uniform grids with a spacing of one wavelength ($\lambda = 12.5$ cm) at an operating frequency $f = 2.4$ GHz selected to examine the Wi-Fi bands associated with IEEE 802.11g standard. The physical arrangement resulted in a total of 196 positions so that small-scale variations can be better captured [51]. It should be pointed out that the real-time measurements were carried out under a stationary scenario with no movements around the transmitter and receiver.

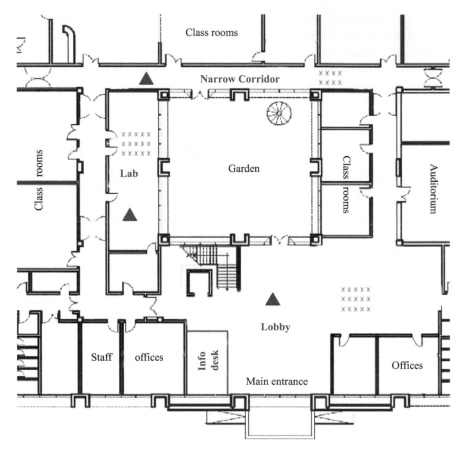

Figure 10.1   Floor plan

The measurement system consisted of low-loss RF cables, a ZVB14 vector network analyzer (VNA) used to measure the transmission coefficient S_{21}, and omni-directional antennas of equal heights 1.5 m at the transmitter and receiver ends. A program script was written for the VNA to run ten consecutive sweeps; each sweep covering a band of 100 MHz using 601 frequency points for which the frequency separation is 0.167 MHz. This means that the dataset generated for each environment consists of 196 × 10 samples. The dataset has been made available as open-access online so that it can be utilized for further explorations. It can be accessed online as per details in [52,53].

10.4   Signatures of indoor environment

10.4.1   *Primary RF features*

In a multipath rich indoor environment, the received signal $Y(f)$ contains replicas of the RF-transmitted signal $X(f)$. The ratio of $Y(f)$ to $X(f)$ defines the CTF, $H(f)$, that contains the multipath effects of the wireless channel. Hence, $H(f)$ can be represented as the superposition of the gains associated with the multipath components as follows [54]:

$$H(f) = \sum_{l=1}^{L} a_l \exp[-j(2\pi f \tau_l - \theta_l)] \qquad (10.1)$$

where a_f, τ_l, and θ_l are the amplitude, delay, and phase of the lth multipath component; L is the total number of multipath components; and f is a frequency within bandwidth of operation of the channel. The analysis in this chapter considers an indoor scenario with a high signal-to-noise ratio [55,56]. The CTF, $H(f)$, is considered as an RF feature that would be distinctively unique for every spatial position within the indoor environment. Under frequency-selective fading, this RF signature becomes more sensitive to channel variations due to the rapid fluctuations of the gains associated with its multipath components.

The complex autocorrelation of CTF, $H(f)$, defines another channel metric known as FCF, $R(f)$, given by:

$$R(f) = \int_{-\infty}^{\infty} H(\hat{f})H^*(\hat{f}+f)d\hat{f} \qquad (10.2)$$

FCF given in (10.2) represents the frequency domain coherence of the radio channel. It is interpreted as the autocorrelation of the CTF, $H(f)$, due to different frequency shifts. FCF is known for its slow varying nature in the spatial domain, which makes it a strong candidate as an RF signature.

10.4.2   Hybrid RF features

Characterizing the type of an indoor environment by a machine learning algorithm becomes a more accurate process when the algorithm makes decisions based on concatenation of primary RF features of the same environment. In such a way, the accuracy of prediction increases due to the wealth of information available to the algorithm from the multidimensional dataset constructed from the concatenation of the combined primary RF features of the same environment. Hence, the approach is based on *hybrid* features. The investigations were carried out using multidimensional information generated from various possible combinations of all or subset of RSS, CTF, and FCF which form the hybrid features. Results, presented in Section 10.5, based on these hybrid features show indeed a substantial improvement in the algorithm prediction resulting in a significant enhancement in environment separability and localization accuracy.

Uniform Manifold Approximation and Projection (UMAP) is a nonlinear dimensionality reduction technique that is well suited for embedding high-dimensional data for visualization in a low-dimensional space [57]. In this chapter, we mapped the 5-D hybrid RF feature vector (RSS+CTF+FCF) into 2-D, with results visualized in Figure 10.2. It should be noted that the hybrid RF feature vector (RSS+CTF+FCF) is 5-D, since it is the concatenation of the real-valued RSS followed by the real and

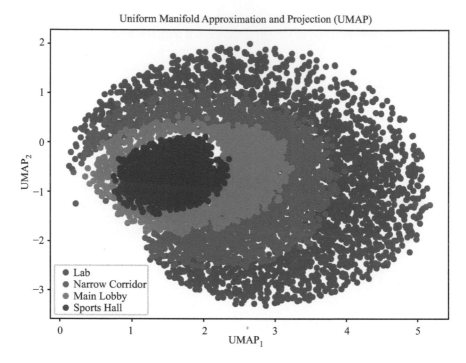

Figure 10.2   Using hybrid RF features in UMAP algorithm allowed different environments to be classified into distinctive clusters

imaginary parts of CTF and FCF, respectively. Figure 10.2 indicates that the resulting 2-D-mapped hybrid RF feature vector of the Sports Hall (open space) is closest to that of the Main Lobby (low cluttered). Figure 10.2 also indicates that the 2-D-mapped hybrid RF feature vector of the Narrow Corridor (medium cluttered) is surrounded by that from the Main Lobby (low cluttered) and Lab (highly cluttered). The 2-D embedding of the mapped RF features in Figure 10.2 shows that further insights can be gained from the UMAP visualization to confirm the advantage of using the concept of hybrid RF features.

10.5   Spatial correlation coefficient

The similarities between RF signatures can be assessed by computing the spatial correlation coefficient, $C^{(n)}$, given by [58]:

$$C^{(n)} = \left| \frac{\langle S_r, S^{(n)} \rangle}{\|S_r\| \, \|S^{(n)}\|} \right| \tag{10.3}$$

where S_r is the reference RF signature corresponding to CTF or FCF at a specific reference position, while $S^{(n)}$ is the RF signature at position n.

Small values of the spatial correlation coefficient, $C^{(n)}$, imply that there is a substantial difference between the RF signature at position n and the RF reference signature. In contrast, large values of the $C^{(n)}$ indicate that there is a high similarity between the RF signature at position n and the reference signature. The variation of spatial correlation coefficient, $C^{(n)}$, computed using CTF and FCF is shown in Figures 10.3 and 10.4, respectively.

In the first scenario, the spatial correlation coefficient in a highly cluttered environment using CTF and FCF is depicted in Figures 10.3(a) and 10.4(a), respectively. The high number of scatters causes the CTF to vary significantly. However, the correlation coefficient for FCF varies at a smaller rate when compared to the CTF.

In the second scenario, the spatial correlation coefficient in a medium-cluttered environment using CTF and FCF is depicted in Figures 10.3(b) and 10.4(b), respectively. The medium number of scatters also causes the CTF to vary significantly but at a lower rate than the highly cluttered scenario. Again, the correlation coefficient for FCF varies at a smaller rate when compared to the CTF.

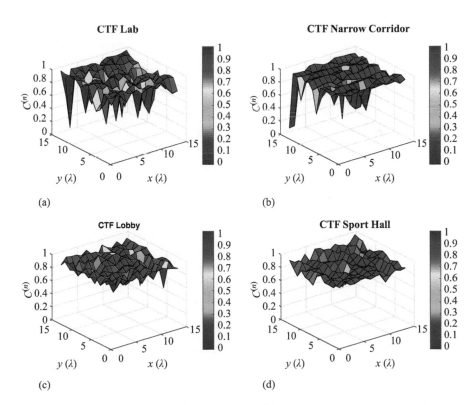

Figure 10.3   *Spatial correlation coefficient, $C^{(n)}$, based on CTF signatures for different environments: (a) highly cluttered, (b) medium cluttered, (c) low cluttered, and (d) open space*

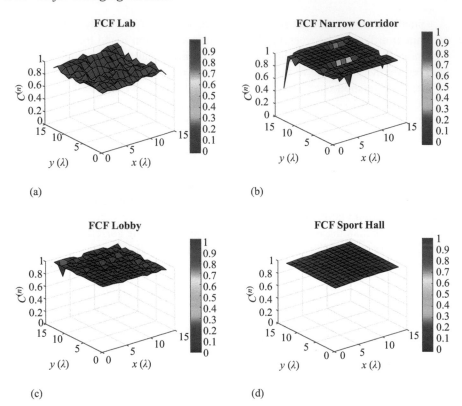

Figure 10.4   Spatial correlation coefficient, $C^{(n)}$, based on FCF signatures for different environments: (a) highly cluttered, (b) medium cluttered, (c) low cluttered, and (d) open space

In the third scenario, the spatial correlation coefficient in a low-cluttered environment using CTF and FCF is depicted in Figures 10.3(c) and 10.4(c), respectively. As expected, the low number of scatters would affect the CTF at a very low rate. It is interesting to observe, and unlike the former two scenarios, that the correlation coefficient for FCF is almost constant and does not change with position.

In the fourth scenario, the spatial correlation coefficient in an open-space environment using CTF and FCF is depicted in Figures 10.3(d) and 10.4(d), respectively. In this case, there are a very low number of scatters and therefore the CTF does not vary significantly. Similar to the third scenario, the correlation coefficient for FCF in this scenario is almost constant and does not change with position.

The previous results demonstrate that both CTF and FCF vary according to the environment which confirms that they are suitable candidates for environment classification.

10.6   Machine learning algorithms

Machine learning provides machines with the ability to learn autonomously based on experiences, observations, and analyzing patterns within a given dataset. In the following, we highlight the primary components of machine learning:

- Collecting and preparing data: The first step in machine learning is that we feed knowledge/data to the machine; these data are divided into two parts: training data and testing data. Usually, the dataset is split into 80/20 or 70/30 to make sure that the model once sufficiently trained can be tested later.
- Choosing and training a model: There are a variety of machine learning algorithms designed to solve a particular type of problem. It is important to choose and train a model depending on its suitability for the problem at hand.
- Evaluating a model: The machine learns the patterns and features from the training data and trains itself to take decisions like identifying, classifying, or predicting new data. To check how accurately the machine is able to take these decisions, the predictions are tested on the testing data. In this case, we will first work on the training data, and once the model is sufficiently trained, we use it on the testing data to understand how successful it is.

10.6.1   Decision trees

DT is a well-known and commonly used method in machine learning. A DT is a hierarchical structure, including decision (non-terminal) nodes, branches, and leaf (terminal) nodes, that represents attributes (features), conditions, and classes, respectively.

DTs are based on a binary DT that is constructed from the training data. The DT is constructed from three nodes: root, internal, and leaf. As described in [59,60], the root node has no incoming edges and just has outgoing edges. The internal node has exactly one incoming edge and two or more outgoing edges. The leaf node has one incoming edge and no outgoing edge and resembles a class label. The algorithm stops splitting into sub-trees when the uncertainty is minimum. The node data are split based on Gini diversity index [61]:

$$\text{Gini}(T) = \sum_{i=1}^{J} p_i(1 - p_i) = 1 - \sum_{i=1}^{J} p_i^2 \qquad (10.4)$$

where T is the training dataset, p_i is the probability of class i occurring at a certain node in the tree, and J is the total number of classes.

Three different types of DTs are used, simple, medium, and complex, based on the maximum number of splits 4, 20, and 100, respectively.

10.6.2   Support vector machine

SVM was initially defined by Vapnik [60,62] and is widely used for classification. The SVM algorithm processes a new data point by deciding, depending on the side on which it appears in. The classifier is based solely on the observation of samples of the form $\{(x_i, y_i), i=1,\ldots, n\}$, where x_i is the ith input and y_i is the corresponding label. The SVM finds the optimal margin classifier.

The solution to find the optimal classifier can be formulated as an optimization problem [62]:

$$\min_{\gamma,w,b} \quad \frac{1}{2}\|w^2\|$$
$$\text{subject to} \quad y^{(i)}(w^\mathsf{T} x^{(i)} + b) \geq 1, i = 1, \ldots, m \tag{10.5}$$

where w is the gradient of the linear classifier, and b is the y-intercept, and γ is

$$\gamma = \min_{i=1,\ldots,m} \gamma^{(i)} = \min_{i=1,\ldots,m} y^{(i)}\left(\left(\frac{w}{\|w\|}\right)^\mathsf{T} x(i) + \frac{b}{\|w\|}\right) \tag{10.6}$$

This optimization problem is a convex quadratic objective and has only linear constrains that can be solved using a quadratic program.

The dual problem is expressed as the following:

$$\max_{\alpha} \quad \sum_{i=1}^{m}\alpha_i - \frac{1}{2}\sum_{i,j=1}^{m} y^{(i)}y^{(j)}\alpha_i\alpha_j K(x_i, x_j)$$
$$\text{subject to} \quad \alpha_i \geq 0, i = 1, \ldots, m. \tag{10.7}$$
$$\sum_{i=1}^{m}\alpha_i y^{(i)} = 0.$$

where α_i is the Lagrange multiplier and $K(.,.)$ denotes the kernel function that measures the distance between the input vector x_i and the trained data x_j. Examples of kernel functions include linear kernel, Gaussian kernel, and polynomial kernel.

10.6.3 k-Nearest neighbor

k-NN algorithm is used to classify a set of data points into specific classes based on the similarities between the data points through examining the neighboring points according to the Euclidean distance calculated with respect to the classification feature. k-NN is a non-parametric method used for classification [60,63] in the k neighbors of each hybrid RF features vector will determine the type of environment. The k-neighbors are associated with the shortest k Euclidean distances, which are defined as follows:

$$d(\mathbf{s}_m, \mathbf{s}_n) = \|\mathbf{s}_m - \mathbf{s}_n\|_2 = \sqrt{\sum_{i=1}^{K} [s_m(i) - s_n(i)]^2} \tag{10.8}$$

where K is the length of the RF feature vector, $\mathbf{s}_m$ and $\mathbf{s}_n$ are the vectors of hybrid RF features at positions m and n, respectively.

10.7   Cascaded Machine Learning Approach

The Cascaded Machine Learning Approach is composed of two stages as shown in the flowchart of Figure 10.5. In the first stage, the indoor environment is identified using machine learning algorithms utilizing primary and hybrid RF features. The information obtained from the first stage is fed to the second stage in which an appropriate indoor localization model that is suitable for the environment type identified from the first stage is used to estimate the user position.

10.7.1   Machine learning for indoor environment classification

Table 10.1 shows that the classification accuracy using RSS can only reach up to 43.8%. When CTF is used, the classification accuracy improves and reaches up to 78.7% in the case of weighted k-NN ($k = 10$). The classification accuracy continues to improve when FCF is used and reaches up to 83.7%. Combing RSS with CTF

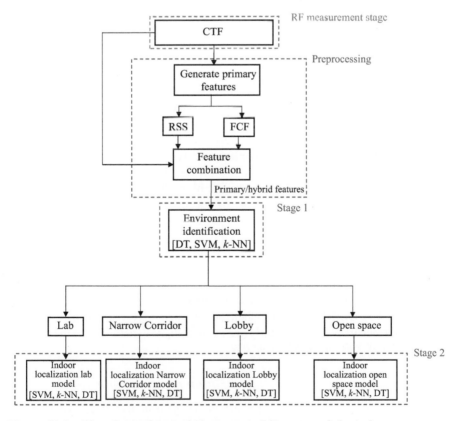

Figure 10.5   Flowchart of cascaded two-stage ML approach for indoor classification and localization

Table 10.1   Overall accuracy using different classifiers and RF features

| Features | Classifier | | | | | | |
	Simple DT (%)	Medium DT (%)	Complex DT (%)	Gaussian SVM (%)	k-NN $(k=1)$ (%)	k-NN $(k=10)$ (%)	Weighted k-NN $(k=10)$ (%)
RSS	41.5	43.3	42.6	43.8	34.7	39.5	35.1
CTF	42.6	48.6	57.8	61.1	77.1	77.4	78.7
FCF	52.8	59.1	65.1	60.5	83.6	75.6	83.7
RSS+CTF	47.1	51.2	56.6	62.3	77.0	76.5	78.3
RSS+FCF	53.8	60.4	67.2	73.2	92.4	83.7	91.9
CTF+FCF	55.8	63.3	73.6	89.3	**99.3**	94.2	99.1
RSS+CTF+FCF	56.5	62.8	74.7	91.2	**99.3**	94.2	98.9

The bold values represent the case which has the best performance.

improves the accuracy of classification compared to the individual performance, yet it does not exceed the accuracy attained using FCF. Unlike the combination with CTF, when RSS is combined with FCF, the classification accuracy exceeds that for FCF and can reach up to 92.4%. The combination of CTF and FCF was found to yield the highest classification accuracy of 99.3%, which is identically obtained as well when all three features are combined. Investigations indicated that adding RSS to the combination of CTF and FCF features does not have a noticeable improvement on the accuracy of classification. Hence, it can be concluded that a combination of CTF and FCF features is sufficient for an accurate classification on indoor environments. The accuracy of the adopted technique is represented in terms of the confusion matrix, shown in Figure 10.6, for which the diagonal elements represent the percentage of accurate prediction for each type of environment. The off-diagonal elements of the confusion matrix represent the percentage of misclassification. The results in Figure 10.6 have been obtained from 490 test cases per environment. The confusion matrix shows the four different environments denoted by 1 (no clutter), 2 (low clutter), 3 (medium clutter), and 4 (high clutter). It can be seen from Figure 10.6(c) that the overall classification accuracy is 99.3%, and the individual classification accuracy is above 98% for all different environments.

The performance of k-NN depends on the design parameter k. Figure 10.7 shows that the classification accuracy of k-NN degrades significantly and reaches almost 65.0% at $k = 100$. On the other hand, when the weighted k-NN is adopted, Figure 10.7 shows that the accuracy is significantly high with a slight variation, over the range of $1 \leq k \leq 100$ and does not go below 98.0%.

10.7.2   *Machine learning for localization position estimation*

Studies in the literature indicate that a substantial gain in accuracy is achieved by improving the construction of the RF signature, rather than the use of more complex algorithms [2,64–66]. As a result, in the second stage and after the type of indoor

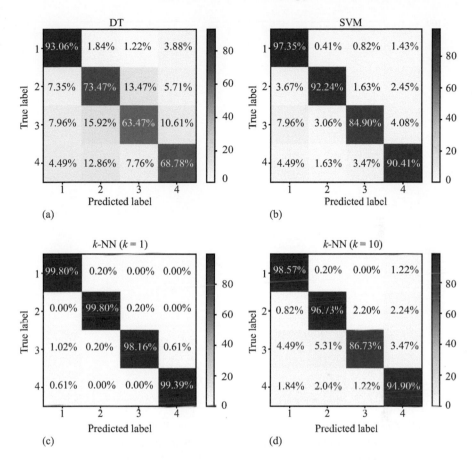

Figure 10.6 *Confusion matrix showing prediction accuracy of different methods for environment identification: (a) decision tree, (b) support vector machine, (c) k-NN (k = 1), and (d) k-NN (k = 10)*

environment has been identified, a specific selection and combination of RF features is utilized based on the identified indoor environment. We have adopted the k-NN algorithm again in the second stage in order to estimate the sensor position by comparing the testing RF feature to the training database of RF features, with the purpose of finding the best matching entry.

Table 10.2 shows the localization distance error, Root-Mean-Square Error (RMSE), using various primary and hybrid RF features. It can be seen that the choice of the best RF signature is dependent on the type of the indoor environment. In the case of the Lab, Narrow Corridor, and Lobby, a hybrid RF feature combining CTF+FCF produced the least error RMSE, whereas for the case of the Sports Hall, a primary RF feature based on FCF has the best performance. These findings clearly indicate

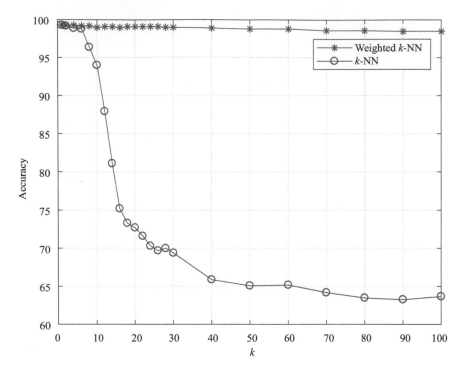

Figure 10.7   k-NN and weighted k-NN as a function of k

Table 10.2   Comparison of localization distance error, RMSE, for different types of indoor environments using k-NN algorithm based on various primary and hybrid RF features

	Primary RF features			Hybrid RF features				
	RSS (cm)	CTF (cm)	FCF (cm)	RSS+ CTF (cm)	RSS+ FCF (cm)	CTF+ FCF (cm)	RSS+ CTF+ FCF (cm)	α (%)
A: Lab	108.93	39.32	49.38	37.63	100.44	**36.95**	37.56	**66.0**
B: Narrow Corridor	102.93	28.60	45.28	30.11	97.22	**28.55**	30.06	**72.2**
C: Lobby	105.26	27.84	38.65	27.76	94.79	**27.56**	27.72	**73.8**
D: Sports Hall	109.03	60.85	**55.31**	61.55	103.17	60.84	61.55	**49.3**

The bold values represent the case which has the best performance.

the importance of incorporating information on the type of the indoor environment for improving location estimation.

In order to quantitatively assess the improvement in localization estimation, we define α (last column in Table 10.2) to represent the percentage reduction in

Table 10.3   Comparison of localization distance error, RMSE, for different types of indoor environments using Wk-NN algorithm based on various primary and hybrid RF features

	Primary RF features			Hybrid RF features				
	RSS (cm)	CTF (cm)	FCF (cm)	RSS+ CTF (cm)	RSS+ FCF (cm)	CTF+ FCF (cm)	RSS+ CTF+ FCF (cm)	α (%)
A: Lab	108.74	37.05	49.92	37.17	100.32	**36.98**	37.01	**66.0**
B: Narrow Corridor	103.9	28.9	45.52	29.75	96.96	**28.85**	29.65	**72.2**
C: Lobby	105.45	27.38	38.87	27.57	94.44	**27.08**	27.40	**74.3**
D: Sports Hall	111.01	60.39	**55.46**	60.45	102.80	60.36	60.44	**50.0**

The bold values represent the case which has the best performance.

localization distance error, RMSE, when the proposed method is used compared to the baseline method that uses RSS as the RF feature:

$$\alpha = \left(\frac{\text{RMSE}_{\text{RSS}} - \text{RMSE}_{\beta}}{\text{RMSE}_{\text{RSS}}} \right) \times 100\% \qquad (10.9)$$

where RMSE_{RSS} is the distance error due to RSS considered to be the baseline method, and RMSE_{β} is the distance error due to the RF feature that produces the lowest RMSE. It is evident from the computed values of α as given in the last column in Table 10.2 that the proposed method significantly reduces the percentage error in localization by at least 45% to more than 70% by using k-NN. In the case of Wk-NN, it is evident from the computed values of α as given in the last column in Table 10.3 that the proposed method significantly reduces the percentage error in localization by at least 50% to more than 70%.

10.8   Conclusion

This chapter developed a machine learning approach for indoor environment classification based on real-time measurements of the RF signal. Several machine learning classification methods were contemplated, including DTs, SVM, and k-NN, using different RF features. Results obtained show that a machine learning approach using k-NN method, utilizing CTF and FCF, outperforms the other methods in identifying the type of the indoor environment with a classification accuracy of 99.3%. The predication time was obtained to be less than 10 μs, which verifies that the embraced algorithm is successful for real-time deployment scenarios. The results of this chapter facilitate an efficient deployment of IoT applications in dynamic channels.

This chapter also developed a cascaded two-stage machine learning approach for highly accurate and robust indoor localization for IoT using the concept of hybrid RF features. In the first stage, k-NN algorithm was used to identify the type of indoor environment. In the second stage, k-NN algorithm was employed to identify the most appropriate selection and combination of RF features that yield the highest localization accuracy, based on the identified indoor environment. Investigations were contemplated using a genuine dataset produced from practical measurements of the RF signal in realistic indoor environments. Results show that the prediction of the algorithm based on the concatenation of primary RF features enhanced significantly as the localization accuracy improved by at least 50% to more than 70%. The noteworthy improvement in localization accuracy attained using the proposed two-stage machine learning method is attributed to the cascaded performance gains due to the identification of the type of environment and the concatenation of primary RF features.

The concept of indoor environment classification, although presented in this chapter for indoor localization, has several other important applications, including adaptive modulation and coding [26,27], indoor millimeter-wave [28–30], 5G waveform selection [31–33], visible light communication [34–36], energy harvesting, PAPR [37–39], activity recognition [40], high-speed train [41–43], and UAV/robotics [44,45].

References

[1]   Kushki A, Plataniotis KN, and Venetsanopoulos AN. Kernel-based positioning in wireless local area networks. IEEE Transactions on Mobile Computing. 200;(6):68–705.

[2]   Honkavirta V, Perala T, Ali-Loytty S, *et al.* A comparative survey of WLAN location fingerprinting methods. In: Positioning, Navigation and Communication, 2009. WPNC 2009. 6th Workshop on. Hannover, Germany: IEEE; 2009. p. 24–251.

[3]   Lin TN and Lin PC. Performance comparison of indoor positioning techniques based on location fingerprinting in wireless networks. In: Wireless Networks, Communications and Mobile Computing, 2005 International Conference on. vol. 2. Maui, HI, USA: IEEE; 2005. p. 1569–1574.

[4]   AlHajri MI, Alsindi N, Ali NT, *et al.* Classification of indoor environments based on spatial correlation of RF channel fingerprints. In: 2016 IEEE International Symposium on Antennas and Propagation (APSURSI). Fajardo, Puerto Rico: IEEE; 2016. p. 1447–1448.

[5]   Xie Y, Wang Y, Nallanathan A, *et al.* An improved K-nearest-neighbor indoor localization method based on spearman distance. IEEE Signal Processing Letters. 201;23(3):35–355.

[6]   Choi J, Kim J, and Kim NS. Robust time-delay estimation for acoustic indoor localization in reverberant environments. IEEE Signal Processing Letters. 2017;24(2):22–230.

[7]   Piciarelli C. Visual indoor localization in known environments. IEEE Signal Processing Letters. 2016;23(10):133–1334.

[8]   Tomic S and Beko M. A robust NLOS bias mitigation technique for RSSTOA-based target localization. IEEE Signal Processing Letters. 2019;26(1):64–68.

[9]   Zanella A, Bui N, Castellani A, *et al.* Internet of Things for smart cities. IEEE Internet of Things Journal. 201;1(1):2–32.

[10]   Al-Fuqaha A, Guizani M, Mohammadi M, *et al.* Internet of Things: A survey on enabling technologies, protocols, and applications. IEEE Communications Surveys Tutorials. 201;17(4):2347–2376.

[11]   Xu LD, He W, and Li S. Internet of Things in industries: A survey. IEEE Transactions on Industrial Informatics. 2014;10(4):2233–2243.

[12]   Palazzi V, Alimenti F, Kalialakis C, *et al.* Highly integrable paper-based harmonic transponder for low-power and long-range IoT applications. IEEE Antennas and Wireless Propagation Letters. 2017;16:319–3199.

[13]   Jha KR, Bukhari B, Singh C, *et al.* Compact planar multistandard MIMO antenna for IoT applications. IEEE Transactions on Antennas and Propagation. 2018;66(7):3327–3336.

[14]   AlHajri M, Goian A, Darweesh M, *et al.* Accurate and robust localization techniques for wireless sensor networks. June 2018, arXiv:180605765 [eessSP].

[15]   AlHajri M, Goian A, Darweesh M, *et al.* Hybrid RSS-DOA technique for enhanced WSN localization in a correlated environment. In: Information and Communication Technology Research (ICTRC), 2015 International Conference on. Abu Dhabi, UAE: IEEE; 2015. p. 23–241.

[16]   Goian A, AlHajri M, Shubair RM, *et al.* Fast detection of coherent signals using pre-conditioned root-MUSIC based on Toeplitz matrix reconstruction. In: 2015 IEEE 11th International Conference on Wireless and Mobile Computing, Networking and Communications (WiMob). Abu Dhabi, UAE: IEE; 2015. p. 16–174.

[17]   Zhou P, Zheng Y, Li Z, *et al.* IODetector: A generic service for indoor outdoor detection. In: Proceedings of the 10th ACM Conference on Embedded Network Sensor Systems. SenSy'12. New York, NY, USA: ACM; 2012. p. 11–126.

[18]   Liu Z, Park H, Chen Z, *et al.* An energy-efficient and robust indoor-outdoor detection method based on cell identity map. Procedia Computer Science. 2015;56:189–195.

[19]   Sung R, Jung S, and Han D. Sound based indoor and outdoor environment detection for seamless positioning handover. ICT Express. 2015;1(3): 106–109.

[20]   Radu V, Katsikouli P, Sarkar R, *et al.* A semi-supervised learning approach for robust indoor-outdoor detection with smartphones. In: Proceedings of the 12th ACM Conference on Embedded Network Sensor Systems. SenSys'14. New York, NY, USA: ACM; 2014. p. 28–294.

[21]   Park J, Curtis D, Teller S, *et al.* Implications of device diversity for organic localization. In: Proc. IEEE INFOCOM. Shanghai, China: IEEE; April 2011. p. 3182–3190

[22]   Ruiz-Ruiz AJ, Blunck H, Prentow TS, *et al.* Analysis methods for extracting knowledge from large-scale wifi monitoring to inform building facility

planning. In: Proc. IEEE Int. Conf. Pervasive Comput. Commun. Budapest, Hungary: IEEE; 2014. p. 13–138.

[23] Canovas O, Lopez-de Teruel PE, and Ruiz A. Detecting indoor/outdoor places using WiFi signals and AdaBoost. IEEE Sensors Journal. 2017;17(5): 1443–1453.

[24] Ali M, ElBatt T, and Youssef M. SenseIO: Realistic ubiquitous indoor outdoor detection system using smartphones. IEEE Sensors Journal. 201; 18(9):3684–3693.

[25] Zeng Q, Wang J, Meng Q, *et al.* Seamless pedestrian navigation methodology optimized for indoor/outdoor detection. IEEE Sensors Journal. 2018; 18(1):36–374.

[26] Zeng R, Liu T, Yu X, *et al.* Novel channel quality indicator prediction scheme for adaptive modulation and coding in high mobility environments. IEEE Access. 201;7:1154–11553.

[27] Lee H, Jung J, Baek C, *et al.* Adaptive modulation and coding for underwater acoustic communication. In: 2019 Eleventh International Conference on Ubiquitous and Future Networks (ICUFN). Zagreb, Croatia: IEEE; 2019. p. 54–56.

[28] Rappaport TS, Heath Jr RW, Daniels RC, *et al.* Millimeter wave wireless communications. USA: Pearson Education; 2015.

[29] Kanhere O and Rappaport TS. Position locationing for millimeter wave systems. In: 2018 IEEE Global Communications Conference (GLOBECOM). Abu Dhabi, UAE: IEE; 2018. p. 20–212.

[30] Xiao M, Mumtaz S, Huang Y, *et al.* Millimeter wave communications for future mobile networks. IEEE Journal on Selected Areas in Communications. 201;35(9):1909–1935.

[31] Gerzaguet R, Bartzoudis N, Baltar LG, *et al.* The 5G candidate waveform race: A comparison of complexity and performance. EURASIP Journal on Wireless Communications and Networking. 2017;2017(1):13.

[32] de Almeida IBF, Mendes LL, Rodrigues JJ, *et al.* 5G waveforms for IoT applications. IEEE Communications Surveys and Tutorials. 2019;21(3): 2554–2567.

[33] Kirev K and Schwarz S. Assessment and comparison of multicarrier waveforms under nonlinear conditions. In: WSA 201; 23rd International ITG Workshop on Smart Antennas. Vienna, Austria: VD; 2019. p. 1–5.

[34] Luo J, Fan L, and Li H. Indoor positioning systems based on visible light communication: State of the art. IEEE Communications Surveys and Tutorials. 2017;19(4):2871–2893.

[35] Jovicic A, Li J, and Richardson T. Visible light communication: Opportunities, challenges and the path to market. IEEE Communications Magazine. 2013;51(12):2–32.

[36] Pathak PH, Feng X, Hu P, *et al.* Visible light communication, networking, and sensing: A survey, potential and challenges. IEEE Communications Surveys and Tutorials. 201;17(4):2047–2077.

[37] Hou J, Ge J, Zhai D, *et al*. Peak-to-average power ratio reduction of OFDM signals with nonlinear companding scheme. IEEE Transactions on Broadcasting. 201;56(2):25–262.

[38] Kim KH. PAPR reduction in OFDM-IM using multilevel dither signals. IEEE Communications Letters. 2019;23(2):25–261.

[39] Tang B, Qin K, Zhang X, *et al*. A clipping-noise compression method to reduce PAPR of OFDM signals. IEEE Communications Letters. 2019;23:138–1392.

[40] Mannini A and Intille S. Classifier personalization for activity recognition using wrist accelerometers. IEEE Journal of Biomedical and Health Informatics. 2018;23:158–1594.

[41] He R, Ai B, Wang G, *et al*. High-speed railway communications: From GSM-R to LTE-R. IEEE Vehicular Technology Magazine. 201;11(3): 49–58.

[42] Zhou T, Tao C, Salous S, *et al*. Joint channel characteristics in high speed railway multi-link propagation scenarios: Measurement, analysis, and modeling. IEEE Transactions on Intelligent Transportation Systems. 2018;20(6):2367–2377.

[43] Zhou T, Tao C, Salous S, *et al*. Channel sounding for high-speed railway communication systems. IEEE Communications Magazine. 201;53(10): 7–77.

[44] Saska M, Krajnik T, and Pfeucil L. Cooperative μUAV-UGV autonomous indoor surveillance. In: International Multi-Conference on Systems, Signals and Devices. Chemnitz, Germany: IEEE; 2012. p. 1–6.

[45] Tomic T, Schmid K, Lutz P, *et al*. Toward a fully autonomous UAV: Research platform for indoor and outdoor urban search and rescue. IEEE Robotics and Automation Magazine. 2012;19(3):46–56.

[46] AlHajri MI, Shubair RM, Weruaga L, *et al*. Hybrid method for enhanced detection of coherent signals using circular antenna arrays. 2015 IEEE International Symposium on Antennas and Propagation & USNC/URSI National Radio Science Meeting, IEEE; 2015. p. 1810–1811.

[47] AlHajri MI, Ali NT, and Shubair RM. Classification of indoor environments for IoT applications: A machine learning approach. IEEE Antennas and Wireless Propagation Letters. 201;17(12):216–2168.

[48] AlHajri MI, Ali NT, and Shubair RM. A machine learning approach for the classification of indoor environments using RF signatures. In: Proc. IEEE Global Conf. Signal Inf. Proces. Anaheim, CA, USA: IEEE; 2018.

[49] AlHajri MI, Ali NT, and Shubair RM. Indoor localization for IoT using adaptive feature selection: A cascaded machine learning approach. IEEE Antennas and Wireless Propagation Letters. 2019.

[50] Chen Z, AlHajri MI, Wu M, Ali NT, and Shubair R. A Novel Real-Time Deep Learning Approach for Indoor Localization Based on RF Environment Identification. IEEE Sensors Letters, IEEE; 2020.

[51] Shu Y, Huang Y, Zhang J, *et al*. Gradient-based fingerprinting for indoor localization and tracking. IEEE Transactions on Industrial Electronics. 201;63(4):2424–2433.

[52] AlHajri MI, Ali NT, and Shubair RM. 2.4 GHZ indoor channel measurements data set. UCI Machine Learning Repositor; 2018. Available from: https://goo.gl/cTSF5j.

[53] AlHajri MI, Ali NT, and Shubair RM. 2.4 GHz Indoor Channel Measurements. IEEE DataPort; 2018. Available from: http://dx.doi.org/10.21227/ggh1-6j32.

[54] Nerguizian C, Despins C, and Affes S. Geolocation in mines with an impulse response fingerprinting technique and neural networks. In: Vehicular Technology Conference. Los Angeles, CA, USA: IEEE; 2004, VTC2004-Fall. 2004 IEEE 60th. vol. 5; 2004. p. 3589–3594.

[55] Alsindi N, Chaloupka Z, AlKhanbashi N, *et al.* An empirical evaluation of a probabilistic RF signature for WLAN location fingerprinting. IEEE Transactions on Wireless Communications. 2014;13(6):3257–3268.

[56] AlKhanbashi N, Alsindi N, Ali N, *et al.* Measurements and analysis of fingerprinting structures for WLAN localization systems. ETRI Journal. 2016;38(4):63–644.

[57] McInnes L, Healy J, and Melville J. UMAP: Uniform manifold approximation and projection for dimension reduction. 2018. arXiv preprint arXiv:180203426.

[58] Zhang J, Firooz MH, Patwari N, *et al.* Advancing wireless link signatures for location distinction. In: Proceedings of the 14th ACM International Conference on Mobile Computing and Networking. MobiCo'08. New York, NY, USA: ACM; 2008. p. 26–37.

[59] Quinlan JR. Learning efficient classification procedures and their application to chess end games. In: Machine learning. Berlin, Heidelberg: Springer; 1983. p. 46–482.

[60] Pedregosa F, Varoquaux G, Gramfort A, *et al.* Scikit-learn: Machine learning in python. Journal of Machine Learning Research. 201;12:282–2830.

[61] Raileanu LE and Stoffel K. Theoretical comparison between the Gini index and information gain criteria. Annals of Mathematics and Artificial Intelligence. 200;41(1):77–93.

[62] Cortes C and Vapnik V. Support-vector networks. Machine Learning. 1995;20(3):27–297.

[63] Altman NS. An introduction to kernel and nearest-neighbor nonparametric regression. The American Statistician. 199;46(3):17–185.

[64] Wang X, Gao L, and Mao S. CSI phase fingerprinting for indoor localization with a deep learning approach. IEEE Internet of Things Journal. 201;3(6):111–1123.

[65] Wang X, Gao L, Mao S, *et al.* CSI-based fingerprinting for indoor localization: A deep learning approach. IEEE Transactions on Vehicular Technology. 2017;66(1):76–776.

[66] Wang X, Gao L, and Mao S. PhaseFi: Phase fingerprinting for indoor localization with a deep learning approach. In: Global Communications Conference (GLOBECOM). San Diego, CA, USA: IEEE; 2015. p. 1–6.

Part III
Sensing

Chapter 11

EEG-based biometrics: effects of template ageing

*Pablo Arnau-González[1], Stamos Katsigiannis[1],
Miguel Arevalillo-Herraez[2] and Naeem Ramzan[1]*

This chapter discusses the effects of template ageing in electroencephalography (EEG)-based biometrics. This chapter also serves as an introduction to general biometrics and its main tasks: identification and verification. To do so, we investigate different characterisations of EEG signals and examine the difference of performance in subject identification between single-session and cross-session identification experiments. In order to do this, EEG signals are characterised with common state-of-the-art features, i.e. mel frequency cepstral coefficients (MFCCs), autoregression coefficients, and power-spectral-density (PSD)-derived features. The samples were later classified using various classifiers, including support vector machines and k-nearest neighbours (kNN) with different parametrisations. Results show that performance tends to be worse for cross-session identification compared to single-session identification. This finding suggests that temporal permanence of EEG signals is limited and thus more sophisticated methods are needed in order to characterise EEG signals for the task of subject identification.

11.1 Introduction

The ever increasing use of information systems and digital locking mechanisms that safeguard access to critical information and infrastructure requires the use of sophisticated security measures for restricting access to only authorised users. Techniques for authenticating users vary from the more traditional approaches of using usernames and passwords, to requiring specific hardware such as key passes or security tags, and to two-step authentication procedures and biometrics. The utilisation of biometric data has been broadly contemplated in the security domain, as an approach that meets the security requirements of such systems. Biometric modalities include fingerprints, iris, voice, face, or other physiological traits, such as the electrocardiogram [1,2].

[1]School of Computing, Engineering and Physical Sciences, University of the West of Scotland, Paisley, UK
[2]Departamento de Informatica, Universitat de Valencia, Valencia, Spain

Due to the already established connection between an EEG signal and the person, EEG-based subject identification has also attracted attention in the subject identification area over the past 10 years [3,4]. EEG signals encode information about the affective and mental state of a person and have therefore been widely studied in a multitude of applications, e.g. early diagnosis of Alzheimer's disease [5], detection of epilepsy episodes [6], assessment of user experience [7], and identification of individual emotional status and reactions [8–10].

Many studies in the field of EEG-based biometrics have been published lately; [11,12] provided a thorough overview of its opportunities and theoretical considerations. It is evident across the literature that the EEG signal procurement protocol is critical to the efficacy of an EEG-based biometric system, as the identification content within the brain signal may be influenced by the task in which the subjects are involved. Subjects are generally asked to conduct particular tasks or are subjected to predefined stimuli (e.g. pictures or videos). The use of different tasks, typically resting state, audio–visual impulses (sensory activity), or cognitive tasks that are frequently suggested in the literature [13], has been studied by Ruiz-Blondet *et al.* [3] and Maiorana and Campisi [14]. Imagined speech [15] and custom tasks [16], as well as the use of event-related potentials [17], were also used and resulted in increased accuracy and stability over time (increased permanence).

Attempts to identify individuals by only recording one session of data are commonly found in the literature [3,18–21]. These approaches typically have disregarded the issue of the permanence in EEG signals. Some studies have argued that there is not a significant decrease in performance; therefore, it is not necessary to record data in more than one session [4,21]. However, recent studies in the field have shown that these approaches are erroneous [14,22] and that there is a significant difference in performance when taking into account the degradation of the template quality over time. The effects of template ageing on EEG-based biometrics are examined in this chapter using a dataset created across various sessions spaced 1 week apart each.

The rest of this chapter is organised in five sections. General background in biometrics and EEG is provided in Section 11.2. The data acquisition protocol, the data preprocessing, the feature extraction, and the classification methodology are described in Section 11.3, while Section 11.4 provides the experimental procedure and acquired results. Finally, conclusions are drawn in Section 11.5.

11.2   Background

11.2.1   Biometrics

The ability to unequivocally identify individuals and associate personal traits with a subject has been of high relevance in history. Humans typically use corporal traits, such as face, voice, or gait, together with other contextual information in order to recognise others. The set of attributes associated with a person constitutes their personal identity.

The handling of personal identity plays a critical role in a variety of applications. Examples of such applications are border crossing management, physical access restrictions to certain facilities, such as power plants or airports, access control to shared resources, performing financial transactions, or others. The proliferation of web resources and the deployment of non-centralised services have highlighted the relevance of the risk of identity theft, now *vox populi*, becoming a topic of interest for users, increasing the demand for secure systems for the handling of personal identities.

A biometric system measures one or more physical or behavioural characteristics, including, but not limited to, fingerprint, face, iris, ear, voice, odour, or even the DNA of an individual, in order to determine their identity. These characteristics are referred to in different terms, for instance, traits, indicators, identifiers, or modalities. Biometric systems are usually employed for two distinct tasks: (a) verification/authentication and (b) identification.

11.2.1.1 Verification/authentication

In verification, the user takes an identity and the system verifies if the user is truly whoever they say they are. In this scenario, the query is compared only against the corresponding template of the requested identity. The identity is usually stored under a personal identification number, a username, or a token. If the user input matches or in some cases has a high enough similarity with the template of the requested identity, then the request and therefore the user, is considered legitimate and the user is verified/authenticated. Otherwise, if the samples are not similar enough, the request is rejected and the user is considered as an impostor. Verification is very frequent in applications whose goal is to stop unauthorised users from using a service or accessing a place.

Formally, verification can be posed as the following binary problem: let I be a requested identity and R be the user input during a request for the identity I. The decision that the system needs to take is that R is similar enough to I for the user to be considered either legitimate or an impostor. The decision rule will then be as the following:

$$D_{(I,R)} = \begin{cases} 1 & \text{if } s_{I,R} \leq \eta \\ 0 & \text{if } s_{I,R} > \eta \end{cases} \tag{11.1}$$

where $s_{I,R}$ is the similarity score and η the threshold for acceptance/rejection of the input.

11.2.1.2 Identification

Identification can be divided into positive and negative identifications. In positive identification, the user tries to identify himself in the system without explicitly assuming an identity. A positive identification system answers the question 'Are you someone known by the system?', obtaining the answer from a set of stored profiles. On the other hand, in negative identification, the user is assigned with an identity, and the system assumes it to be correct. The system then tries to determine whether the user is not the person whose identity has been assigned. The purpose of this kind of identification is to stop users from assuming multiple identities. A clear example of this application would be a system that decides if a certain person is presenting a false passport and the profile matches that stored in a watch list. Independently of the type of identification (positive or negative), the user input is compared with all the profiles stored in the database, and the system assigns an identity based on the similarity between the input and the template.

Formally, the problem of identification can be described as follows: let R be the user input during a request for identification. The system has to assign the identity I to the user, where $I \in \{I_1, I_2, \ldots, I_N, I_{N+1}\}$, with I_1 to I_N being the N identities known to the system and I_{N+1} corresponding to the unknown identity. The decision rule is

$$
R \in \begin{cases} I_{n_0} & \text{if } n_0 = \text{argmax } s_n \text{ and } s_{n_0} > \eta \\ I_{N+1} & \text{otherwise} \end{cases} \tag{11.2}
$$

11.2.1.3   Characteristics of biometric traits

Different biometric traits have been used in a number of applications, each of them having its own advantages and disadvantages. Therefore, the selection of a trait depends on the particular applications and their requirements, apart from performance or accuracy. In general, there are seven different facts that influence the selection of a biometric trait:

1. **Universality**: All the users must possess the trait.
2. **Uniqueness**: The trait should be sufficiently different across different subjects, being able to identify them unequivocally.
3. **Permanence**: The trait should have stability over a period of time. A trait that changes drastically over time is not useful for biometrics.
4. **Measurability**: It must be possible to acquire the biometric trait, using available hardware, without causing too much hustle to the users.
5. **Performance**: Besides recognition accuracy, the computational cost required for the matching algorithm and the throughput should meet the application restrictions.
6. **Acceptability**: The users of the application should be willing to present the trait.
7. **Circumvention**: The easiness with which a trait can be replicated or obfuscated by an attacker.

In any case, it is not expected for a single trait to match all the seven factors for all possible applications. In other words, there is no ideal trait but many are generally admissible. The relevance of a given trait to a specific application will depend upon how well the trait complies with the application requirements.

11.2.2   Electroencephalography

EEG is the recording of the electrical activity from the cerebral cortex, measured in microvolts (μV) [23]. The measured electrical potentials present in the scalp originate from the superposition of all the electrical fields generated by the dendrites during the synapses [24]. The recorded signals have been used in a number of applications, although mostly for medical purposes, such as seizure detection [25]. For the acquisition of conventional scalp EEG, electrodes are placed on the scalp of the person on locations specified by the *International 10–20 system*. The 10–20 system is the name given to the standardisation of the names of the electrodes and their placement on the scalp [26], as shown in Figure 11.1. The system gets its name from the separation of the adjacent electrodes that are separated by a 10% or 20% of the total front–back or right–left distance of the skull. The 10–20 system names the electrodes according to the positioning in the scalp, with the following naming system, *XXN*, where *XX* refers to the lobe, being Fp, F, C, O, T, P, referring to prefrontal, frontal, central, occipital, temporal, and parietal, respectively, and *N* referring to the positioning, where odd numbers refer to the left hemisphere and even numbers to the right hemisphere. It is also possible to find Z electrodes. In this case, the electrodes are placed on the central part of the scalp of their corresponding lobe. Typical reference electrodes are placed in Cz or Tz. The system has been extended for higher resolution strategies,

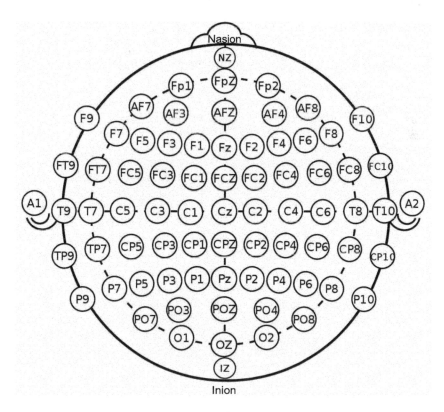

Figure 11.1   International 10–20 system for EEG electrode placement. Source: wikimedia.org. Published under the Creative Commons CC0 1.0 Universal Public Domain Dedication licence.

including the following regions, AF, FC, FT, CP, TP, PO, being those regions placed in the middle. For example according to that convention, AF would be placed between the anterior and frontal lobes.

11.2.3   EEG in biometrics

EEG signals have been traditionally restricted to the field of medicine. However, in recent years and with the use of machine learning technologies, EEG signals have been used for an ever-increasing pool of applications, mainly focused on brain–computer interfaces. More recently, researchers showed interest in the uniqueness of EEG for each individual and attempted to create biometric systems based on EEG signals [18,19,26]. Available works have typically disregarded the influence of the so-called *template ageing*, an effect that reflects how a given biometric trait changes over a period of time. However, as some studies suggest [14], EEG signals not only change with the passage of time, but the characterisations of said signals are also time dependent. In this chapter, we will compare both approaches and study how the systems behave in the case of single-session approaches vs multisession approaches, in order to examine the effects of template ageing in EEG-based biometrics.

11.3   Data acquisition and experimental protocol

A dataset with EEG recordings belonging to different people over a time period of 3 weeks was captured in order to test the temporal permanence of EEG signals. In order to do this, different classification experiments were designed with the aim to compare the accuracy of signals in a single-session acquisition vs a plausible scenario in which data from one or more sessions is used for enrolling users in the system and a recording from any other given day is used for validating these users.

11.3.1   Stimuli

Images with powerful emotional content were used to generate emotional responses to users, while recording EEG signals, according to recommendations of previous work [20]. The stimuli were acquired from two openly accessible picture datasets, i.e. the Geneva affective picture dataset (GAPED) [27] and the Open Affective Standardized Image Set (OASIS) [28]. The images of both datasets are annotated in terms of the emotional response they elicit to human viewers using Russell's *circumplex model of affect* [29] that considers emotion as being distributed in the two-dimensional valence/arousal space. Valence is a measure of the positiveness of an emotion, varying from negative to positive, while arousal is a measure of the excitement associated with an emotion, varying from low to high.

GAPED contains 730 different JPEG images. The pictures are annotated within the range [0, 100] in terms of arousal and valence. The pictures of the dataset belong to the following classifications: *snakes, spiders, natural problems (representing scenes that violate human rights), animal mistreatment (representing animal mistreatment scenes), neutral, and positive.* OASIS includes 900 distinct JPEG pictures. The pictures are annotated within the range [1, 7] in terms of arousal and valence. It also includes the median answers for each picture separated by gender. The OASIS dataset includes pictures from one of the following four mutually exclusive classifications: *animals, objects, people, and scenes.* It should be noted that some of the pictures contain explicit sexual material, leading to the removal of image #I537 from this research.

The two datasets contain a total of 1,630 images from which 48 were selected according to their associated valence/arousal ratings in order to obtain a representative set of images with an intense emotional content. To this end, each dataset's valence/arousal values were first standardised to the range $[-1, 1]$. The resulting valence/arousal space was then uniformly split into 12 regions of $\pi/6$ radians, as shown in Figure 11.2. Finally, four pictures were selected from each region, whose (valence, arousal) locations were farthest from the neutral emotion $(0, 0)$, as they contained the most intense emotional content in that region.

11.3.2 Experimental protocol

A total of 26 healthy subjects, aged between 23 and 55 years old ($\mu_{age} = 31.9$), were recruited as volunteers for data acquisition. The experiment took place inside a quiet room with ambient light and no physical supervision, in order to not alter the response of the participants and not introduce any artefacts related to stress or distractions.

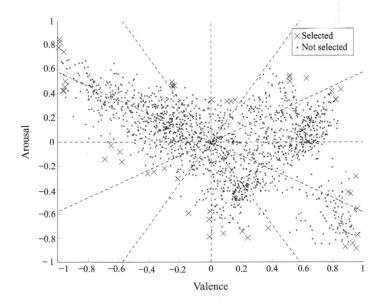

Figure 11.2   Images of the GAPED and OASIS datasets in valence/arousal space. Marked images were selected for this study.

Before starting the experiment, the experimental procedure and the used valence–arousal scale were explained, and participants were then asked to fill a consent form indicating that they agree to participate in the study and to the viewing of images that may depict strong emotional content.

Three sessions were recorded for each participant, each of them spaced 7 days apart. Out of the four images selected per region, one was randomly selected to be displayed in all the sessions as baseline, and each of the other three was assigned to one session, leading to a total of three sets of 24 images (12 repeated and 12 unique images per set). The selected images were presented to the participants for 5 s and immediately after seeing each image, the participants were asked to report the felt emotion using Self-Assessment Manikins [30] on a 9-point Likert scale. After the self-assessment, participants were asked to perform a simple mathematical operation and report the result, in order to reduce any effects of the emotional stimulus to their emotional state. The EEG activity was recorded during the whole session, using the 14-channel Emotiv EPOC+® wireless EEG device with a sampling rate of 256 Hz. Furthermore, timestamps with millisecond precision were used to synchronise the acquired EEG signals with the image stimuli viewing.

11.3.3 Data preparation and feature extraction

The recorded timestamps were used in order to divide the acquired EEG recordings into segments referring to specific images. Furthermore, the EEG segments were annotated with the ID of each respective participant, as well as with the valence and arousal values reported in the study by each respective participant. Then, the EEGLAB toolbox [31] was used to preprocess the EEG signals by applying the PREP pipeline for EEG data preprocessing as described in [32], in order to remove artefacts such as the ones stemming from muscle movement, jaw clenching, or eye blinking. Then, to create a machine learning model for subject identification from EEG signals, various features were extracted from the preprocessed EEG recordings, namely the MFCCs, PSD, and autoregression reflection coefficients (ARRCs).

11.3.3.1 Mel frequency cepstral coefficients

MFCCs are a parametric representation of the Fourier spectrum and have been commonly used in voice recognition [33,34] and more lately implemented to EEG-based person recognition [35,36]. In this work, MFCCs were computed using HTK-like filterbanks and the discrete cosine transform. MFCC features were computed using 18 filterbanks, as described in [35], generating a total of 12 cepstral coefficients per channel, after discarding the D_C coefficient. The feature vector was generated by concatenating each channel's cepstral coefficients, resulting in a total of 168 features (12 coefficients × 14 channels).

11.3.3.2 Power spectral density

PSD-based features have been frequently used to identify emotional states from EEG signals [37,43]. In this work, PSD features were calculated as described in [38]: First, on each channel, the PSD is calculated using Welch's algorithm. For each channel, the PSD is calculated using a 2 s Hamming window (512 samples) with a 75% overlap

(384 samples) and the FFT is generated over each of these windows and averaged across time. Finally, the feature vector was created by concatenating the resulting PSD values of the [1 − 40] Hz frequency band. This process resulted into a total of 38 features per channel, leading to a total of 532 features (38 features × 14 channels).

11.3.3.3 Autoregression reflection coefficients

ARRCs have been used extensively for EEG signal analysis [39]. Recently, various research works examined their effectiveness for EEG-based biometrics [22,35,40]. An EEG signal can be characterised as an output of a causal stable linear time-invariant stationary autoregressive (AR)(*P*th order) system based on the EEG spectrum's AR or all-pole model, with the AR parameters being estimated using the Yule–Walker equations [41]. Individual ARRCs were obtained by estimating an AR model of order 10 for each channel. Then, the feature vector was created by combining the 10 reflection coefficients of each channel, resulting to a total of 140 features (10 coefficients × 14 channels).

11.3.4 Classification

The acquired feature vectors were then used in order to create various supervised classification models for EEG-based subject identification, i.e. the prediction of the subject ID associated with a feature vector. The subject identification problem was thus modelled as a multi-class classification problem where each class referred to a specific subject's ID. The examined classification algorithms included the *k*NN for $k = 1, 3, 5, 7$, linear support vector machines (LSVM), SVM with the radial basis function kernel (RSVM), SVM with a second-order polynomial kernel (QSVM), and SVM with third-order polynomial kernel (CSVM).

11.4 Experimental results

In order to show the difference in performance that occurs when performing single-session or multiple-session identification tasks, two different experiments were considered, both using the same features and the same classifiers. The main difference between the two experiments is in the training and testing schemes. For the first experiment, samples from the same session were used for training and testing, following a *leave-one-out* cross validation strategy. In the second experiment, a cross-session subject identification task was examined by adopting a validation strategy that identifies the samples against samples collected in the past, e.g. training with samples from the first session and testing with samples from the second or third sessions. In this case, a single or more sessions were used for training the classifiers, and data from the remaining sessions were used for testing.

11.4.1 Single-session subject identification

Eight different classifiers were trained in order to evaluate the performance of the extracted features in a hypothetical identification system. The system in this case is trained and tested with samples extracted from the same recording session. In Table 11.1, the accuracy of the different classifiers is displayed for the different sessions recorded in this dataset and the different features computed. The highest accuracy of 0.885 was achieved using the LSVM classifier with the MFCC features. For all sessions, the combination of MFCC features and the LSVM classifier provided the highest classification accuracy. This shows that MFCC features provided the best characterisation of the individuals out of the three features examined. This fact is also supported by MFCC features achieving in general higher performance than the other features regardless of the classifier ($p < 0.05$), with the exception of the CSVM, where ARRC features performed considerably better than both MFCC and PSD features. The performance of the different classifiers seems more dependent on the features than on the training session, although, as can be seen in Table 11.1, CSVM was not capable of properly modelling the individuals with the exception of when the ARRC features were used.

11.4.2   Cross-session subject identification

Following a similar approach as in the previous experiment, the different classification algorithms were trained using the features extracted from one or more sessions. The difference in this case is that the trained models were tested against the samples from future acquisition sessions, i.e. sessions recorded later. This process led to a total of four possible experiments. Table 11.2 shows the identification accuracy achieved for the different classification experiments. The highest accuracy of 0.3370 was achieved using the MFCC features and the LSVM classifier when training with sessions 1 and 2 and testing with session 3. It is not clear why the accuracy increases so much in this case compared to when training with the first session and testing with the second or third sessions, or when training with the second session and testing with the third. It may be attributed to the different algorithms being able to generalise more knowledge, or simply because there are more data; therefore, the border between the different subjects is more defined. In general, MFCC features provided better accuracy than the other tested features regardless the time elapsed

Table 11.1   Classification accuracy for single-session subject identification

Session	Features	LSVM	RSVM	QSVM	CSVM	1-NN	3-NN	5-NN	7-NN
1	MFCC	0.885	0.848	0.868	0.052	0.855	0.835	0.798	0.756
	PSD	0.351	0.032	0.050	0.036	0.457	0.426	0.415	0.404
	ARRC	0.378	0.239	0.409	0.399	0.216	0.242	0.220	0.205
2	MFCC	0.849	0.817	0.778	0.047	0.833	0.806	0.768	0.754
	PSD	0.363	0.032	0.041	0.036	0.457	0.442	0.410	0.371
	ARRC	0.420	0.308	0.473	0.429	0.284	0.293	0.310	0.318
3	MFCC	0.750	0.742	0.689	0.040	0.717	0.683	0.661	0.645
	PSD	0.383	0.033	0.098	0.040	0.441	0.398	0.392	0.364
	ARRC	0.408	0.283	0.433	0.415	0.255	0.288	0.256	0.250

between the training and test session ($p < 0.05$). Regarding the performance of the different classifiers, as shown in Figure 11.3, the nearest neighbour classifiers provide generally better results compared to the performance of the SVM-based classifiers.

As previously noted in [42], the performance of the identification task is significantly increased when training with more than one session, an effect called *incremental learning*. The effects of incremental learning are displayed in Figure 11.4 where the maximum accuracy of the single-session training classification experiments is compared to the accuracy of the multiple-session classification experiments. As shown in that figure, the effects of incremental learning are evident regardless of the features employed, reinforcing the conclusions drawn in [42]. Moreover, in Figure 11.5, the distribution of results for the different classifiers in the case of the

Table 11.2 Classification accuracy for cross-session subject identification

Train session	Test session	Features	LSVM	RSVM	QSVM	CSVM	1-NN	3-NN	5-NN	7-NN
1	2	MFCC	0.112	0.130	0.110	0.037	0.130	0.144	0.151	0.146
		PSD	0.118	0.039	0.041	0.036	0.075	0.058	0.071	0.062
		ARRC	0.070	0.050	0.083	0.083	0.050	0.052	0.068	0.062
	3	MFCC	0.195	0.198	0.213	0.040	0.253	0.261	0.266	0.261
		PSD	0.132	0.040	0.063	0.040	0.116	0.144	0.134	0.126
		ARRC	0.102	0.078	0.119	0.111	0.060	0.074	0.119	0.122
2	3	MFCC	0.198	0.187	0.215	0.030	0.213	0.208	0.238	0.235
		PSD	0.132	0.031	0.046	0.040	0.107	0.126	0.137	0.131
		ARRC	0.091	0.066	0.091	0.091	0.078	0.078	0.079	0.081
1–2	3	MFCC	0.337	0.311	0.334	0.040	0.276	0.279	0.261	0.264
		PSD	0.071	0.040	0.015	0.040	0.147	0.164	0.174	0.167
		ARRC	0.136	0.111	0.154	0.149	0.081	0.089	0.096	0.106

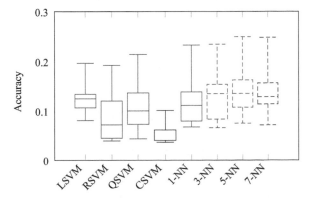

Figure 11.3 Distribution of classification accuracy for the different classifiers in the cross-session approach

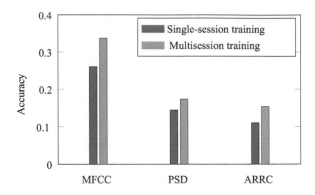

Figure 11.4   Maximum classification accuracy obtained for each of the studied features when using one session for training vs using multiple sessions for training

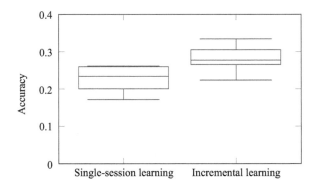

Figure 11.5   Mean classification accuracy using single-session learning vs incremental learning (multisession learning)

single-session learning is displayed against the case of incremental learning. That figure further demonstrates the potential benefits of incremental learning.

11.5   Conclusions

The correct identification of individuals from EEG signals is still a challenge that many researchers are working to solve. A good solution would provide a very convenient alternative for identifying individuals. Since EEG signals cannot be captured at a distance, it is extremely challenging to capture furtively the EEG of a given individual with malicious intentions. This trait is highly desired in critical applications involving very sensitive information. However, there is still much research to be done before this biometric modality can be exploited in practical applications. Typically, researchers have focused on identification in only one session. However, from the presented results it is clear that EEG signals are heavily affected by session-specific noise and phenomena. A number of artefacts are present in the EEG recordings, such as the precise electrode positioning (EEG signal caps are not always fitted in the exact same position), line, or other background-specific noises. The results provide evidence on why the developed methods should be tested in a multisession scenario, since it is not possible to generalise the results obtained from a single-session classification approach. Good performance in that scenario cannot guarantee good performance later in time. Moreover, the presented results show that the accuracy of the identification task will be worse in any given case in a multisession environment. Furthermore, results also show that from the examined representations, MFCC modelling of EEG signals performs consistently better in both scenarios regardless of the experimental setup, a finding that is consistent with similar studies [14,20], although the reported accuracy in those studies is considerably higher. This may be due to the different EEG-recording devices, since a consumer non-medical-grade device was used in this study, while the cited studies used medical-grade devices. The difference in performance between this and other works suggests that consumer-grade EEG devices have poorer quality compared to medical-grade devices; hence, robust features are necessary for lower quality devices. Nevertheless, the phenomenon of *incremental learning*, present in medical-grade recording devices, also appears in the proposed low-cost setup, showing that the development of more robust feature extraction approaches can potentially allow the use of consumer-grade EEG devices in practical EEG-based biometrics systems.

References

[1] Bowyer KW, Hollingsworth K, and Flynn PJ. Image understanding for iris biometrics: A survey. Computer Vision and Image Understanding. 2008;110(2):281–307.

[2] Louis W, Komeili M, and Hatzinakos D. Continuous authentication using one-dimensional multi-resolution local binary patterns (1DMRLBP) in ECG biometrics. IEEE Transactions on Information Forensics and Security. 2016;11(12):2818–2832.

[3] Ruiz-Blondet MV, Jin Z, and Laszlo S. CEREBRE: A novel method for very high accuracy event-related potential biometric identification. IEEE Transactions on Information Forensics and Security. 2016;11(7):1618–1629.

[4] Palaniappan R and Mandic DP. Biometrics from brain electrical activity: A machine learning approach. IEEE Transactions on Pattern Analysis and Machine Intelligence. 2007;29(4):738–742.

[5] Cichocki A, Shishkin SL, Musha T, et al. EEG filtering based on blind source separation (BSS) for early detection of Alzheimer's disease. Clinical Neurophysiology. 2005;116(3):729–737.

[6]   Kannathal N, Choo ML, Acharya UR, *et al.* Entropies for detection of epilepsy in EEG. Computer Methods and Programs in Biomedicine. 2005;80(3): 187–194.

[7]   Arnau-Gonzalez P, Althobaiti T, Katsigiannis S, *et al.* Perceptual video quality evaluation by means of physiological signals. In: Quality of Multimedia Experience (QoMEX), 2017 Ninth International Conference on. Piscataway, NJ, USA: IEEE; 2017. p. 1–6.

[8]   Arnau-González P, Arevalillo-Herráez M, and Ramzan N. Fusing highly dimensional energy and connectivity features to identify affective states from EEG signals. Neurocomputing. 2017;244:81–89.

[9]   Katsigiannis S and Ramzan N. DREAMER: A database for emotion recognition through EEG and ECG signals from wireless low-cost off-the-shelf devices. IEEE Journal of Biomedical and Health Informatics. 2018;22(1): 98–107.

[10] Koelstra S, Muhl C, Soleymani M, *et al.* DEAP: A database for emotion analysis; using physiological signals. IEEE Transactions on Affective Computing. 2012;3(1):18–31.

[11] Campisi P and La Rocca D. Brain waves for automatic biometric-based user recognition. IEEE Transactions on Information Forensics and Security. 2014;9(5):782–800.

[12] Abo-Zahhad M, Ahmed SM, and Abbas SN. State-of-the-art methods and future perspectives for personal recognition based on electroencephalogram signals. IET Biometrics. 2015;4(3):179–190.

[13] Yang S and Deravi F. On the usability of electroencephalographic signals for biometric recognition: A survey. IEEE Transactions on Human-Machine Systems. 2017;47(6):958–969.

[14] Maiorana E and Campisi P. Longitudinal evaluation of EEG-based biometric recognition. IEEE Transactions on Information Forensics and Security. 2018;13(5):1123–1138.

[15] Brigham K and Kumar BVKV. Subject identification from electroencephalogram (EEG) signals during imagined speech. In: 2010 Fourth IEEE International Conference on Biometrics: Theory, Applications and Systems (BTAS). Piscataway, NJ, USA: IEEE; 2010. p. 1–8.

[16] Chuang J, Nguyen H, Wang C, *et al.* I think, therefore I am: Usability and security of authentication using brainwaves. In: International Conference on Financial Cryptography and Data Security. Berlin, Heidelberg: Springer; 2013. p. 1–16.

[17] Armstrong BC, Ruiz-Blondet MV, Khalifian N, *et al.* Brainprint: Assessing the uniqueness, collectability, and permanence of a novel method for ERP biometrics. Neurocomputing. 2015;166:59–67.

[18] Arnau-Gonzalez P, Katsigiannis S, Ramzan N, *et al.* ES1D: A deep network for EEG-based subject identification. In: 2017 IEEE 17th International Conference on Bioinformatics and Bioengineering (BIBE). Piscataway, NJ, USA: IEEE; 2017. p. 81–85.

[19]   Thomas KP, Vinod AP, and Robinson N. Online biometric authentication using subject-specific band power features of EEG. In: Proceedings of the 2017 International Conference on Cryptography, Security and Privacy. New York City, NY, USA: ACM; 2017. p. 136–141.

[20]   Arnau-González P, Arevalillo-Herráez M, Katsigiannis S, *et al.* On the influence of affect in EEG-based subject identification. IEEE Transactions on Affective Computing. 2018; (Early access). DOI: 10.1109/TAFFC.2018. 2877986.

[21]   Chen Y, Atnafu AD, Schlattner I, *et al.* A high-security EEG-based login system with RSVP stimuli and dry electrodes. IEEE Transactions on Information Forensics and Security. 2016;11(12):2635–2647.

[22]   Maiorana E, Rocca DL, and Campisi P. On the permanence of EEG signals for biometric recognition. IEEE Transactions on Information Forensics and Security. 2016;11(1):163–175.

[23]   Marcuse LV, Fields MC, and Yoo JJ. Rowan's primer of EEG. Amsterdam, Netherlands: Elsevier Health Sciences; 2015.

[24]   Sanei S and Chambers JA. EEG signal processing. Hoboken, NJ, USA: Wiley Online Library; 2007.

[25]   Tzallas AT, Tsipouras MG, and Fotiadis DI. Epileptic seizure detection in EEGs using time–frequency analysis. IEEE Transactions on Information Technology in Biomedicine. 2009;13(5):703–710.

[26]   Homan RW, Herman J, and Purdy P. Cerebral location of international 10–20 system electrode placement. Electroencephalography and Clinical Neurophysiology. 1987;66(4):376–382.

[27]   Dan-Glauser ES and Scherer KR. The Geneva affective picture database (GAPED): A new 730-picture database focusing on valence and normative significance. Behavior Research Methods. 2011;43(2):468–477.

[28]   Kurdi B, Lozano S, and Banaji MR. Introducing the open affective standardized image set (OASIS). Behavior Research Methods. 2017;49(2): 457–470.

[29]   Russell J. A circumplex model of affect. Journal of Personality and Social Psychology. 1980;39:1161–1178.

[30]   Morris JD. Observations: SAM: The Self-Assessment Manikin; an efficient cross-cultural measurement of emotional response. Journal of Advertising Research. 1995;35(6):63–68.

[31]   Delorme A and Makeig S. EEGLAB: An open source toolbox for analysis of single-trial EEG dynamics including independent component analysis. Journal of Neuroscience Methods. 2004;134(1):9–21.

[32]   Bigdely-Shamlo N, Mullen T, Kothe C, *et al.* The PREP pipeline: Standardized preprocessing for large-scale EEG analysis. Frontiers in Neuroinformatics. 2015;9:16.

[33]   Ittichaichareon C, Suksri S, and Yingthawornsuk T. Speech recognition using MFCC. In: Proc. ICGSM. Pattaya, Thailand; 2012. p. 28–29.

[34]   Juvela L, Bollepalli B, Wang X, *et al.* Speech waveform synthesis from MFCC sequences with generative adversarial networks. In: Proc. ICASSP. Alberta, Canada; 2018. p. 5679–5683.

[35]   Piciucco E, Maiorana E, Falzon O, *et al.* Steady-state visual evoked potentials for EEG-based biometric identification. In: BIOSIG 2017. Piscataway, NJ, USA: IEEE; 2017.

[36]   Nguyen P, Tran D, Huang X, *et al.* A proposed feature extraction method for EEG-based person identification. In: Proc. ICAI. Las Vegas, NV, USA; 2012. p. 826–831.

[37]   Katsigiannis S and Ramzan N. DREAMER: A database for emotion recognition through EEG and ECG signals from wireless low-cost off-the-shelf devices. IEEE Journal of Biomedical and Health Informatics. 2017.

[38]   del Pozo-Banos M, Travieso CM, Alonso JB, *et al.* Evidence of a task-independent neural signature in the spectral shape of the electroencephalogram. International Journal of Neural Systems. 2018;28(01):1750035.

[39]   Rahman MM, Chowdhury MA, and Fattah SA. An efficient scheme for mental task classification utilizing reflection coefficients obtained from autocorrelation function of EEG signal. Brain Informatics. 2018;5(1):1.

[40]   Hine GE, Maiorana E, and Campisi P. Resting-state EEG: A study on its non-stationarity for biometric applications. In: Proc. BIOSIG. Darmstadt, Germany; 2017.

[41]   Kay SM. Modern spectral estimation. Noida, Uttar Pradesh, India: Pearson Education India; 1988.

[42]   Marcel S and Millan JDR. Person authentication using brainwaves (EEG) and maximum a posteriori model adaptation. IEEE Transactions on Pattern Analysis and Machine Intelligence. 2007;29(4):743–752.

[43]   Arnau-Gonzalez P, Ramzan N, Arevalillo-Herrraez M. A method to identify affect levels from EEG signals using two dimensional emotional models. In: 30th European Simulation and Modelling Conference (ESM'2016); 2016. p. 1–5.

Chapter 12

A machine-learning-driven solution to the problem of perceptual video quality metrics

Stamos Katsigiannis[1], Hassan Rabah[2], and Naeem Ramzan[1]

The advent of high-speed internet connections, advanced video coding algorithms, and consumer-grade computers with high computational capabilities has led video-streaming-over-the-internet to make up the majority of network traffic. This effect has led to a continuously expanding video streaming industry that seeks to offer enhanced quality-of-experience (QoE) to its users at the lowest cost possible. Video streaming services are now able to adapt to the hardware and network restrictions that each user faces and thus provide the best experience possible under those restrictions. The most common way to adapt to network bandwidth restrictions is to offer a video stream at the highest possible visual quality, for the maximum achievable bitrate under the network connection in use. This is achieved by storing various pre-encoded versions of the video content with different bitrate and visual quality settings. Visual quality is measured by means of objective quality metrics, such as the mean squared error (MSE), peak signal-to-noise ratio (PSNR), structural similarity (SSIM) index, visual information fidelity (VIF), and others, which can be easily computed analytically. Nevertheless, it is widely accepted that although these metrics provide an accurate estimate of the statistical quality degradation, they do not reflect the viewer's perception of visual quality accurately. As a result, the acquisition of user ratings in the form of mean opinion scores (MOSs) remains the most accurate depiction of human-perceived video quality, albeit very costly and time consuming, and thus cannot be practically employed by video streaming providers that have hundreds or thousands of videos in their catalogues. A recent very promising approach for addressing this limitation is the use of machine learning techniques in order to train models that represent human video quality perception more accurately. To this end, regression techniques are used in order to map objective quality metrics to human video quality ratings, acquired for a large number of diverse video sequences. Results have been very promising, with approaches like the Video Multimethod Assessment

[1]School of Computing, Engineering and Physical Sciences, University of the West of Scotland, Paisley, UK
[2]Institut Jean Lamour, University of Lorraine, Nancy, France

Fusion (VMAF) metric achieving higher correlations to user-acquired MOS ratings compared to traditional widely used objective quality metrics. In this chapter, we examine the performance of VMAF and its potential as a replacement for common objective video quality metrics.

12.1 Introduction

The last decade saw an explosion in the use of video streaming platforms, with predictions estimating that video streaming will account to 82% of global IP traffic by 2022, up from 75% in 2017 [1]. Available network capacity keeps increasing both for the traditional, wired land-based networks and for the wireless mobile networks. Optic fibre-based networks can offer bandwidths in the range of Gbps, while next-generation 5G mobile networks promise speeds up to 10 Gbps and latency of less than 1 ms. Despite the phenomenal increase in network capacity, demand for bandwidth continues to increase as video content of higher resolutions becomes available. Streaming raw video is unpractical due to extremely high bandwidth requirements. For example streaming 1 s of a 1,920 × 1,080 video sequence at 30 fps with 24 bit colour depth would require the transmission of approximately 178 MB of data, without including protocol overheads and audio. Furthermore, network capacity and latency have large variations depending on the user, the location, the time within the day, and overall network congestion, while the capability of end-user devices to play the transmitted videos depends on their hardware specifications. Sophisticated video compression and transmission algorithms are used in order to address these issues and facilitate the streaming of high-quality video in practice.

The most common approach for achieving flexible and uninterrupted video streaming under variable network conditions is to offer to the users the highest quality video stream possible under the specific conditions and constraints of each user. To achieve this, video sequences are compressed using various bit rates and/or spatial resolutions, and each version is divided in smaller segments that are typically a few seconds long. Then, these video segments are made available via a web server and are accessed by video player software using standard HyperText Transfer Protocol (HTTP) GET requests. A manifest file containing information about all the available versions of the video is created and used by the client in order to request the segments that fit its requirements. Requirements depend on bandwidth, latency, hardware capabilities, etc. and can vary during playback. As a result, adaptation to different versions is achieved by requesting different segments of a video, thus increasing or decreasing the received quality as seen fit. While various video streaming protocols exist, the most dominant are Apple HTTP Live Streaming [2] and MPEG Dynamic Adaptive Streaming over HTTP [3].

Although video compression allows the transmission or storage of video content in a practical and cost-effective manner, it suffers from an important side effect. The reduction in bit rate or in spatial resolution used for the compressed sequences leads to a reduction in visual quality. The compressed video sequences can suffer from loss of fidelity, compression artefacts, colour fading, and blur among others. Considering that video streaming systems aim to stream to the users the highest quality video possible, the accurate evaluation of the visual quality of each compressed version of the video becomes crucial, especially the perceptual quality as experienced by the human visual system [4]. Video quality assessment (VQA) techniques can be divided into two categories, depending on how the quality evaluation is achieved: (a) objective VQA approaches and (b) subjective VQA approaches.

Objective video quality models consist of mathematical models that measure the differences between the original and the distorted video sequences and deterministically output the same quality score when the same video sequences are compared under the same parameters. Objective VQA approaches are further divided into three categories, depending on the amount of information they require regarding the original video sequence:

1. **Full reference (FR)**. FR approaches require full access to the reference video sequence in order to estimate the quality of the examined version.
2. **Reduced reference (RR)**. RR approaches require only a set of features extracted from the reference video sequence in order to estimate the quality of the examined version.
3. **No reference (NR)**. NR approaches require no information regarding the reference video sequence.

Subjective VQA approaches measure video quality as perceived by humans. Video quality scores are computed by conducting experiments where users are asked to watch and rate the quality of various video sequences. The acquired ratings are then averaged in order to compute the final video quality rating, as perceived by the human viewers, in the form of a MOS. Subjective VQA approaches can be divided into two categories, depending on how the quality rating experiments are conducted:

1. **Single-stimulus**. In single-stimulus experiments, viewers are requested to rate the quality of single video sequences, without having access to the reference video sequences.
2. **Double/multiple-stimulus**. In double/multiple-stimulus experiments, viewers watch both the reference and distorted versions of the video sequences and provide ratings in relation to the reference.

It is well accepted in the literature that objective quality metrics fail to accurately model video quality as perceived by human viewers. To this end, subjective video quality ratings provide the most accurate measurement of video quality. However, conducting subjective video quality rating experiments to acquire MOS ratings is a time-consuming, expensive, and arduous task; thus, it cannot be practically employed by video streaming providers that have hundreds or thousands of videos in their catalogues. Researchers have tried to bridge the gap between objective and subjective VQAs by training machine learning models in order to map objective quality metrics to subjective quality ratings (MOS), effectively using the easy to compute deterministic objective metrics to predict ratings subjectively decided by human viewers. This chapter examines the performance of one of the most promising machine-learning-based VQA metrics, the VMAF [5].

12.2 Objective video quality assessment methods

Various FR, RR, and NR VQA methods that do not rely on machine learning have been proposed in the literature across the years, with some, like the PSNR and the SSIM, being extensively used by the industry and the research community in production systems and as benchmarks. An overview of some of these traditional metrics is provided in this section.

12.2.1 Full-reference metrics

Some of the most commonly used FR VQA methods were originally used for the quality assessment of images and were extended for use in video by being applied to each frame of the videos. Methods like that include the MSE-based PSNR, the VIF [6], the SSIM index in its various forms [7], and the visual signal-to-noise ratio (VSNR) [8]. However, it is well established that such metrics fail sometimes in characterising the perceptual quality of the video sequences depending on the types of the distortion and the content of the video [9–11]. Various other FR metrics have been proposed in the literature [12]. Aabed *et al.* [13] proposed a perceptual quality metric that utilises low-complexity power spectral features in the frequency domain, while Manasa and Channappayya [14] proposed the use of optical flow statistics, such as the minimum eigenvalue of the local flow patches, the mean, the standard deviation, and the coefficient of variation in order to estimate temporal quality and the use of SSIM for spatial quality estimation, combining both for computing the final quality score. Seshadrinathan and Bovik [15] proposed the MOVIE index that examines temporal, spatial, and spatiotemporal characteristics of distortion in order to estimate video quality. Various works also examined video quality in relation to motion [15], in relation to the frame rate and quantisation [16], and in relation to network QoS and application QoS within the context of web streaming [17].

12.2.2 Reduced-reference metrics

The biggest difficulty in designing RR metrics is the extraction of suitable and descriptive features from the reference video sequence in order to have sufficient data for an accurate video quality prediction [18]. Tao *et al.* [19] proposed a relative video quality metric, rPSNR, that can be computed without parsing or decoding the transmitted video, and without any knowledge of video characteristics. Piamrat *et al.* [20] proposed the Pseudo Subjective Quality Assessment metric, a hybrid metric that makes the use of objective and subjective features to evaluate QoE for video streaming in wireless networks. Entropic differences and wavelet-based natural video statistics were utilised by Soundararajan and Bovik [21] for their RR video quality metric, while Baik *et al.* [22] used a machine learning model to estimate the effect of spatial distortions, types of buffering, and resolution changes in quality degradation.

12.2.3   *No-reference metrics*

Various NR metrics have been proposed in the literature following different approaches [9,23]. The NORM algorithm by Naccari *et al.* [24] uses macroblock information at the decoder level in order to evaluate distortions on H.264/AVC streamed videos. Wu *et al.* [25] used local texture and global intensity features extracted from the decoded video to evaluate the quality of stalled streaming video. Pixel-based features and bitstream information were used by Winkler and Mohandas [12] for real-time video quality estimation, while a combination of a spatio-temporal natural scene statistics model for videos and a motion model that quantifies motion coherency in video scenes were proposed by Saad *et al.* [26]. Mittal *et al.* [27] exploited the intrinsic statistical regularities observed in natural videos to achieve NR quality assessment, while features based on a 3D shearlet transform were used by Li *et al.* [28].

12.3   The video multimethod assessment fusion (VMAF) metric

Expanding on previous work by Liu *et al.* [29] and Liu *et al.* [30], researchers developed the VMAF [5] FR VQA metric that employs a machine learning approach in order to map multiple elementary objective quality metrics to subjective quality ratings (MOS). The rationale behind this approach is that although each individual objective metric cannot fully capture the perceptual quality of the video, as it has its respective drawbacks and advantages, 'fusing' multiple metrics together by assigning weights to each through a machine learning algorithm could potentially preserve the advantages of each metric and deliver a more accurate final video quality score. Furthermore, since these weights would be trained for optimising the accuracy of predicting subjective ratings provided by actual viewers, it is expected that such a metric would be more accurate in predicting perceptual video quality. The VMAF metric was originally trained on the NFLX video dataset [5], while a newer subjective dataset with a broadened scope was used for recent releases [31] that included more diverse content and source artefacts such as film grain and camera noise, and a larger range of encoding resolutions and compression parameters.

VMAF uses support vector machine regression [32] to map the combination of the following three elementary metrics to subjective video quality ratings [5]:

- **Visual information fidelity (VIF)** [6], which is a widely used image quality metric. The original VIF metric measures quality by determining the loss of fidelity in four scales. VMAF used a modified version of VIF where the loss of fidelity at each of the four scales is considered as an elementary metric instead of the combined VIF score.
- **Detail loss measure (DLM)** [33], which is an image quality metric that measures the loss of details that affect content visibility. Although originally proposed to be used in combination with the additive impairment measure, VMAF uses only DLM as an elementary metric.
- **Motion** [5], which is a simple temporal feature that measures the average low-pass-filtered differences between consecutive frames.

VMAF scores are computed for each frame of a video sequence, and the final VMAF score for a video sequence is computed through simple temporal pooling by computing the arithmetic mean of the VMAF scores across all frames, as experiments showed that the arithmetic mean yields the highest correlation with subjective scores.

Experiments on various subjective video quality datasets showed that VMAF scores were better correlated to MOS ratings compared to traditional quality metrics [5], and the VMAF metric has now been adopted widely by industry and researchers [31]. VMAF scores have a range from 0 to 100, with 0 being the lowest and 100 the highest quality. The current default VMAF model (v0.6.1) has been trained using subjective ratings acquired using a 1,080p display with a viewing distance of 3H, H being the height of the screen, and following an absolute category rating (ACR) methodology were viewers rated the quality of the video sequences on the scale of 'bad', 'poor', 'fair', 'good', and 'excellent'. Under the specific viewing conditions that the subjective quality tests were conducted, a VMAF score of 20 maps the 'bad' quality, a score of 100 the 'excellent' quality, and a score of 70 would be between 'good' and 'fair' [31]. As a result, when applying the default VMAF model to video sequences of different spatial resolution than 1,080p, then the VMAF scores refer to ratings at different viewing conditions. Considering that the default model measures quality at the critical angular frequency of 1/60 degree/pixel, this geometry applies to 1,080p at 3H, to 720p at 4.5H, to 480p at 6.75H, etc. As a result, the application of the default model to a 480p video sequence would yield a quality rating referring to a viewing distance of 6.75H [31]. When computing VMAF on down-sampled video sequences, VMAF developers suggest the up-sampling of the sequence to the resolution of the reference sequence before VMAF application as otherwise the obtained VMAF score will fail to capture scaling artefacts [31].

12.4   Experimental evaluation

To evaluate the performance of VMAF under various settings, VMAF (v0.6.1), Y-PSNR, SSIM, and MS-SSIM quality scores were computed for the video sequences of three publicly available video datasets and their Pearson's correlation coefficient (ρ) with the available MOS ratings, as well as the R^2 for the linear fit were computed.

12.4.1   Datasets

12.4.1.1   MPEG-JVET2018 video sequences dataset

The MPEG-JVET2018 [45] test video sequences contained five test sequences at a resolution of 1,080p (1,920 × 1,080), progressively scanned using 4:2:0 colour sampling, with a duration of 10 s. Two sequences had a frame rate of 50 fps and 8 bits per sample, one sequence 60 fps and 8 bits per sample, and two sequences 60 fps and 10 bits per sample. Details of the test sequences are provided in Table 12.1. The video sequences were encoded using two software packages, the HM 16.16 and the Joint Exploration Test Model (JEM) 7.0 software package [34]. The Joint Video Exploration Team (JVET) maintains the JEM software package in order to study

Table 12.1 Details of the MPEG-JVET2018 dataset's video sequences and the resolution for all sequences is 1,920 × 1,080

Name	Frame rate	Bit depth	Source	Target bit rate (kbit/s)			
				Rate 1	Rate 2	Rate 3	Rate 4
BQTerrace	60	8	NTT DOCOMO Inc.	400	600	1,000	1,500
RitualDance	60	10	Netflix	900	1,500	2,300	3,800
MarketPlace	60	10	Netflix	500	800	1,200	2,000
BasketballDrive	50	8	NTT DOCOMO Inc.	800	1,200	2,000	3,500
Cactus	50	8	EBU/RAI	500	800	1,200	2,000

coding tools in a coordinated test model [35]. The purpose of this datasets was to facilitate testing in accordance with BT.500 [36] in order to examine the proposals from 24 proponents. As a result, the MPEG-JVET2018 dataset contained (4 rates × 2 encoders × 24 proponents) × 5 sequences + 5 reference sequences = 965 video sequences in total. The MOS ratings were acquired using a degradation category rating (DCR) [37] method, leading to a quality rating scale with values in the range between 0 (lowest quality) and 10 (highest quality). Since all the video sequences in the MPEG-JVET2018 dataset are 1,080p, they adhere to the specifications of the default VMAF model.

12.4.1.2 HEVC verification dataset (Tan *et al.* [38])

Twenty video sequences that have been used in [38] for the evaluation of video quality and compression performance of the H.265/HEVC [39] standard were used for the evaluation of the VMAF metric. Four categories of spatial resolutions were included in the experimental evaluation: UHD (3,840 × 2,160 except for one sequence that was 4,096 × 2,048), 1,080p (1,920 × 1,080), 720p (1,280 × 720), and 480p (832 × 480), with five video sequences per resolution. These sequences were selected from different sources so as to have different spatio-temporal characteristics, leading to differences in the behaviour of the compression algorithms utilised. Furthermore, the frame rate of the sequences spans from 30 to 60 frames per second, while all the sequences are in the $Y'C_BC_R$ colour space (as defined by ITU-R Rec. BT.709 [40]), with 8 bits per sample of each component. The video sequences were compressed using the AVC (JM-18.5, High profile [41]) and HEVC (HM-12.1, Main profile [42]) compression standards. For each sequence and each compression standard, four different fixed quantisation parameter settings were selected for compression so that the resulting bit rates for the respective HEVC-encoded sequences would be approximately half the bit rate of the AVC-encoded sequences, as well as so that their subjective quality would span a wide range of MOS values. Following this procedure, 8 test sequences were created from each of the 15 initial sequences resulting to a total of 160 test sequences. Furthermore, the quality of the created video sequences in terms of average MOS was subjectively evaluated in [38] at two test sites, under a controlled laboratory environment. The MOS scores were recorded using a DCR [37] method, leading to a quality rating scale with values in the range between 0 (lowest quality) and 10 (highest quality). Only the 1,080p sequences of the Tan *et al.* dataset adhere to the specifications of the default VMAF model. Nevertheless, it is interesting to examine VMAF's default model's performance against other metrics that are not constrained by resolution for video sequences of various resolutions.

12.4.1.3   ITS4S dataset

The ITS4S dataset [43] was primarily designed for the evaluation of NR video quality metrics and adheres to the following two factors: (a) the metric performance must degrade gracefully in response to new content (i.e. subject matter, camera, and editing) and (b) the metric must accurately predict the quality of original videos (e.g. broadcast quality, contribution quality, professional cameras, and prosumer cameras). It contains 813 video sequences from which 35% contain no compression artefacts, while the rest 65% contain simple impairments, in order to minimise the confounding factor of coding impairments on the original video's quality as the coding bitrate is reduced. The video content was selected out of a pool of HDTV and 4K videos [44] that were recorded using various resolutions and frame rates. The video sequences included in the ITS4S have been converted to 720p ($1,280 \times 720$) at 24 fps and were coded using H.264 high profile VBR 2-pass coding at bitrates spanning from 0.512 to 2.340 Mbps, while 20 Mbps were used for the reference sequences. MOS ratings were acquired using the ACR method, leading to a quality rating scale with values in the range between 1 (lowest quality) and 5 (highest quality). Since VMAF is designed with coding and down-sampling-related distortions in mind, its performance on the ITS4S dataset is expected to suffer, since ITS4S contains numerous sequences with impairments that are unrelated to coding. Furthermore, although the resolution of the video sequences is not 1,080p, both the reference and the impaired sequences have the same resolution (720p) thus no up-scaling is required. Nevertheless, as explained in Section 12.3, the acquired VMAF scores will refer to a viewing condition of 4.5H distance from the screen.

12.4.2   Video quality scores

It must be noted that although MOS ratings were available for the reference sequences of the three datasets, the reference sequences were not included in the experimental comparison of the VMAF (v0.6.1), Y-PSNR, SSIM, and MS-SSIM metrics, since the Y-PSNR value for reference sequences is infinite; thus the correlation could not be established properly.

The performance of VMAF (v0.6.1), Y-PSNR, SSIM, and MS-SSIM in terms of Pearson's correlation coefficient (ρ) and the R^2 in relation to the available MOS ratings for each dataset are provided in Table 12.2. Furthermore, Figures 12.1–12.3 provide scatter plots showing the observers' MOS on the *x*-axis and the predicted score from the examined quality metrics on the *y*-axis. From Table 12.2, it is evident that VMAF achieved the best correlation with viewers' quality ratings for all the examined datasets. The performance of MS-SSIM was similar to VMAF for the MPEG-JVET2018 dataset ($\rho = 0.90$) and marginally worse for the 1,080p sequences of the Tan *et al.* dataset ($\rho_{VMAF} = 0.72$ vs $\rho_{MS-SSIM} = 0.71$).

Table 12.2 *Pearson's correlation coefficient (ρ) and R^2 between the VMAF (v0.6.1), Y-PSNR, SSIM, and MS-SSIM scores and the available MOS for each dataset*

Dataset	VMAF		Y-PSNR		SSIM		MS-SSIM	
	ρ	R^2	ρ	R^2	ρ	R^2	ρ	R^2
MPEG-JVET2018	**0.90**	0.816	0.70	0.492	0.89	0.792	**0.90**	0.807
Tan *et al.*	**0.66**	0.435	0.48	0.234	0.42	0.179	0.57	0.327
Tan *et al.* (1,080p)	**0.72**	0.519	0.67	0.445	0.68	0.457	0.71	0.509
ITS4S	**0.34**	0.112	0.31	0.099	0.26	0.067	0.26	0.066

Note: Results in bold indicate the highest linear correlation for each dataset.

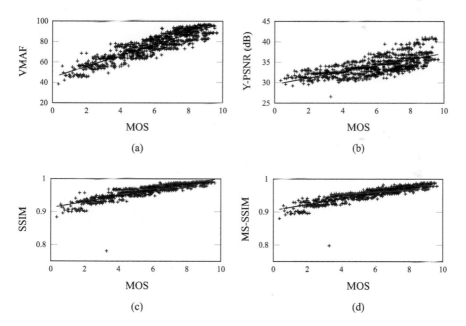

Figure 12.1 *Acquired quality scores for the MPEG-JVET2018 dataset in relation to MOS, using (a) VMAF, (b) Y-PSNR, (c) SSIM, and (d) MS-SSIM*

Regarding the MPEG-JVET2018 dataset, the correlation between VMAF scores and MOS was the highest among the three examined datasets (0.90). The video sequences in the dataset fully complied with the VMAF guidelines and model used (1,080p with video-coding-related distortions) and the accompanying MOS were relative to the reference video sequences. As expected, VMAF performed very well. Regarding the Tan *et al.* dataset, the correlation between VMAF and MOS was significantly lower (0.66) than the one achieved for the MPEG-JVET2018 dataset. Although

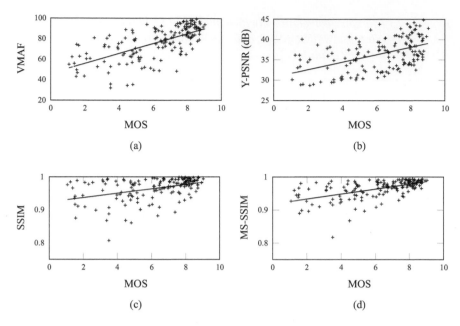

Figure 12.2   Acquired quality scores for the Tan et al. [38] dataset in relation to MOS, using (a) VMAF, (b) Y-PSNR, (c) SSIM, and (d) MS-SSIM

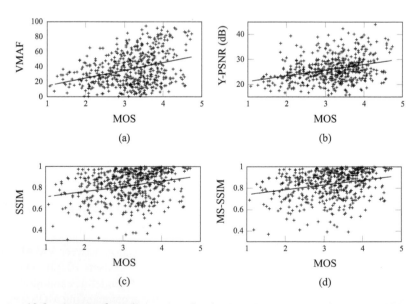

Figure 12.3   Acquired quality scores for the ITS4S dataset in relation to MOS, using (a) VMAF, (b) Y-PSNR, (c) SSIM, and (d) MS-SSIM

the distortions in the video sequences were related to H264/AVC and H265/HEVC coding and the accompanying MOSs were relative to the reference video sequences, the resolutions of the video sequences varied (UHD, 1,080p, 720p, 480p). VMAF guidelines state that the default VMAF model is trained and optimised for 1,080p video. When only the 1,080p sequences of the Tan *et al.* dataset were examined, VMAF's correlation to MOS improved, albeit only slightly (0.72), with MS-SSIM achieving a marginally worse correlation of 0.71. Regarding the ITS4S dataset, as expected due to the type of distortions included, the correlation between VMAF and MOS was the lowest among the examined datasets at 0.34, slightly better than the correlation with Y-PSNR which was 0.31. It seems that when MOS is not relative to the reference sequence and the scores do not scale similarly across different sequences, VMAF is not working well and Y-PSNR provides comparable performance as a quality metric. Interestingly, SSIM and MS-SSIM performed the worst for this dataset, achieving a correlation of 0.26. A larger and even more diverse dataset could help one to establish this argument more definitely, but still the evidence points towards that direction.

12.5 Conclusion

Examining the quality ratings achieved by VMAF, it is evident that VMAF scores are more aligned to viewer quality ratings compared to Y-PSNR, SSIM, and MS-SSIM, with MS-SSIM achieving the second best results. The very strong correlation of 0.90 achieved for the MPEG-JVET dataset shows that VMAF performs very well when the examined video sequences follow the default VMAF model's guidelines in terms of resolution, and when the impairments are related to coding impairments that VMAF was originally designed for. Similarly, good results were achieved for the 1,080p sequences of the Tan *et al.* dataset, which included video-coding-related impairments only, considering that the nominal correlation values for all metrics were lower than the ones achieved for the MPEG-JVET. While correlations to MOS ratings were significantly low for the ITS4S dataset, VMAF still achieved the highest correlation to viewer-perceived quality. However, it is evident that the design constraints of VMAF, as well as of the other metrics, lead to significant differences between viewer-perceived quality scores and the computed scores. Our experimental evaluation showed that machine learning approaches for mapping objective video quality metrics to human-perceived video quality scores have great potential for providing perceptually accurate objective video quality metrics. However, more work is needed in order to provide metrics that would be suitable for a wide range of impairment types and would not be limited to specific usage scenarios.

References

[1]   Barnett T, Jain S, Andra U, *et al.* Cisco Visual Networking Index (VNI) Complete Forecast Update, 2017–2022; 2018. APJC Cisco Knowledge Network (CKN) Presentation.

[2]   RFC 8216. HTTP Live Streaming; 2017. Apple Inc.

[3]   ISO/IEC 23009-1. Dynamic Adaptive Streaming Over HTTP (DASH) – Part 1: Media Presentation Description and Segment Formats; 2017.

[4]   Aabed MA and AlRegib G. PeQASO: Perceptual Quality Assessment of Streamed Videos Using Optical Flow Features. IEEE Transactions on Broadcasting. 2019;65(3):534–545.

[5]   Li Z, Aaron A, Katsavounidis I, *et al.* Toward A Practical Perceptual Video Quality Metric; 2016. Accessed: 2019-11-08. https://medium.com/netflix-techblog/toward-a-practical-perceptual-video-quality-metric-653f208b9652.

[6]   Sheikh HR and Bovik AC. Image Information and Visual Quality. IEEE Transactions on Image Processing. 2006;15(2):430–444.

[7]   Zhou Wang, Bovik AC, Sheikh HR, *et al.* Image Quality Assessment: From Error Visibility to Structural Similarity. IEEE Transactions on Image Processing. 2004;13(4):600–612.

[8]   Chandler DM and Hemami SS. VSNR: A Wavelet-Based Visual Signal-to-Noise Ratio for Natural Images. IEEE Transactions on Image Processing. 2007;16(9):2284–2298.

[9]   Hemami SS and Reibman AR. No-Reference Image and Video Quality Estimation: Applications and Human-Motivated Design. Signal Processing: Image Communication. 2010;25(7):469–481. Special Issue on Image and Video Quality Assessment.

[10]   Chikkerur S, Sundaram V, Reisslein M, *et al.* Objective Video Quality Assessment Methods: A Classification, Review, and Performance Comparison. IEEE Transactions on Broadcasting. 2011;57(2):165–182.

[11]   Murroni M, Rassool R, Song L, *et al.* Guest Editorial Special Issue on Quality of Experience for Advanced Broadcast Services. IEEE Transactions on Broadcasting. 2018;64(2):335–340.

[12]   Winkler S and Mohandas P. The Evolution of Video Quality Measurement: From PSNR to Hybrid Metrics. IEEE Transactions on Broadcasting. 2008;54(3):660–668.

[13]   Aabed MA, Kwon G, and AlRegib G. Power of tempospatially unified spectral density for perceptual video quality assessment. In: 2017 IEEE International Conference on Multimedia and Expo (ICME). Piscataway, NJ, USA: IEEE; 2017. p. 1476–1481.

[14]   Manasa K and Channappayya SS. An Optical Flow-Based Full Reference Video Quality Assessment Algorithm. IEEE Transactions on Image Processing. 2016;25(6):2480–2492.

[15]   Seshadrinathan K and Bovik AC. Motion Tuned Spatio-Temporal Quality Assessment of Natural Videos. IEEE Transactions on Image Processing. 2010;19(2):335–350.

[16]   Ou Y, Ma Z, Liu T, *et al.* Perceptual Quality Assessment of Video Considering Both Frame Rate and Quantization Artifacts. IEEE Transactions on Circuits and Systems for Video Technology. 2011;21(3):286–298.

[17]   Mok RKP, Chan EWW, and Chang RKC. Measuring the quality of experience of HTTP video streaming. In: 12th IFIP/IEEE International Symposium on

Integrated Network Management (IM 2011) and Workshops. Piscataway, NJ, USA: IEEE; 2011. p. 485–492.

[18] Nauge M, Larabi M, and Fernandez C. A reduced-reference metric based on the interest points in color images. In: 28th Picture Coding Symposium. Piscataway, NJ, USA: IEEE; 2010. p. 610–613.

[19] Tao S, Apostolopoulos J, and Guerin R. Real-Time Monitoring of Video Quality in IP Networks. IEEE/ACM Transactions on Networking. 2008;16(5): 1052–1065.

[20] Piamrat K, Viho C, Bonnin J, *et al.* Quality of experience measurements for video streaming over wireless networks. In: 2009 Sixth International Conference on Information Technology: New Generations. Piscataway, NJ, USA: IEEE; 2009. p. 1184–1189.

[21] Soundararajan R and Bovik AC. Video Quality Assessment by Reduced Reference Spatio-Temporal Entropic Differencing. IEEE Transactions on Circuits and Systems for Video Technology. 2013;23(4):684–694.

[22] Baik E, Pande A, Stover C, *et al.* Video acuity assessment in mobile devices. In: 2015 IEEE Conference on Computer Communications (INFOCOM). Piscataway, NJ, USA: IEEE; 2015. p. 1–9.

[23] Shahid M, Rossholm A, Lövström B, *et al.* No-Reference Image and Video Quality Assessment: A Classification and Review of Recent Approaches. EURASIP Journal on Image and Video Processing. 2014;2014 (1):40.

[24] Naccari M, Tagliasacchi M, and Tubaro S. No-Reference Video Quality Monitoring for H.264/AVC Coded Video. IEEE Transactions on Multimedia. 2009;11(5):932–946.

[25] Wu Q, Li H, Meng F, *et al.* Toward a Blind Quality Metric for Temporally Distorted Streaming Video. IEEE Transactions on Broadcasting. 2018;64(2):367–378.

[26] Saad MA, Bovik AC, and Charrier C. Blind Prediction of Natural Video Quality. IEEE Transactions on Image Processing. 2014;23(3):1352–1365.

[27] Mittal A, Saad MA, and Bovik AC. A Completely Blind Video Integrity Oracle. IEEE Transactions on Image Processing. 2016;25(1):289–300.

[28] Li Y, Po L, Cheung C, *et al.* No-Reference Video Quality Assessment With 3D Shearlet Transform and Convolutional Neural Networks. IEEE Transactions on Circuits and Systems for Video Technology. 2016;26(6):1044–1057.

[29] Liu TJ, Lin YC, Lin W, *et al.* Visual Quality Assessment: Recent Developments, Coding Applications and Future Trends. APSIPA Transactions on Signal and Information Processing. 2013;2:e4.

[30] Lin JY, Liu T, Wu EC, *et al.* A fusion-based video quality assessment (FVQA) index. In: Signal and Information Processing Association Annual Summit and Conference (APSIPA), 2014 Asia-Pacific. Piscataway, NJ, USA: IEEE; 2014. p. 1–5.

[31] Li Z, Bampis C, Novak J, *et al.*. VMAF: The Journey Continues; 2018. Accessed: 2019-11-08. https://medium.com/netflix-techblog/vmaf-the-journey-continues-44b51ee9ed12.

[32] Cortes C and Vapnik V. Support-Vector Networks. Machine Learning. 1995;20(3):273–297.

[33] Li S, Zhang F, Ma L, *et al.* Image Quality Assessment by Separately Evaluating Detail Losses and Additive Impairments. IEEE Transactions on Multimedia. 2011;13(5):935–949.

[34] Joint Video Exploration Team. Joint Exploration Model (JEM); 2019. Available from: https://jvet.hhi.fraunhofer.de/svn/svn_HMJEMSoftware/.

[35] Joint Video Exploration Team (JVET) of ITU-T VCEG (Q6/16) and ISO/IEC MPEG (JTC 1/SC 29/WG 11). Algorithm Description of Joint Exploration Test Model 7 (JEM7); 2017. Doc. JVET-G1001. Available from: http://phenix.it-sudparis.eu/jvet/.

[36] ITU-R. Methodology for the Subjective Assessment of the Quality of Television Pictures; 2012. Recommendation ITU-R BT.500-13. Available from: https://www.itu.int/rec/R-REC-BT.500.

[37] ITU-T. Subjective Video Quality Assessment Methods for Multimedia Applications; 2008. ITU-T Rec. P.910.

[38] Tan TK, Weerakkody R, Mrak M, *et al.* Video Quality Evaluation Methodology and Verification Testing of HEVC Compression Performance. IEEE Transactions on Circuits and Systems for Video Technology. 2016;26(1):76–90.

[39] ITU-T. H.265: High Efficiency Video Coding; 2016. ITU-T Rec. H.265.

[40] ITU-R. Parameter Values for the HDTV Standards for Production and International Programme Exchange; 2002. ITU-R Rec. BT.709.

[41] JVT of ITU-T SG16/Q6 and ISO/IEC JTC1/SC29/WG11. AVC JM Reference Software Codebase, Version 18.5; 2013. Available from: http://iphome.hhi.de/suehring/tml/.

[42] JCT-VC of ITU-T SG16/Q6 and ISO/IEC JTC1/SC29/WG11. HEVC HM Reference Software Codebase, Version 12.1; 2013. Available from: http://hevc.hhi.fraunhofer.de/svn/svn_HEVCSoftware/.

[43] Pinson MH. ITS4S: A Video Quality Dataset With Four-Second Unrepeated Scenes; 2018. NTIA Technical Memo TM-18-532. Available from: https://www.its.bldrdoc.gov/publications/details.aspx?pub=3194.

[44] Pinson MH and Janowski L. AGH/NTIA: A Video Quality Subjective Test with Repeated Sequences; 2014. NTIA Technical Memo TM-14-505. Available from: https://www.its.bldrdoc.gov/publications/details.aspx?pub=2758.

[45] Segall C, Baroncini V, Boyce J, Chen J, and T. Suzuki, JVET-H1002: Joint Call for Proposals on Video Compression with Capability Beyond HEVC, JVET-H1002 (v6), July 2018.

Chapter 13

Multitask learning for autonomous driving

Murtaza Taj[1] and Waseem Abbas[2]

Every instant the decision that an autonomous vehicle has to make depends upon a large number of measured and estimated parameters. These include those related to driving control (steering angle, acceleration, braking, etc.) as well as scene information (number of lanes, current lane, drivable area, etc.). Thus, autonomous driving is inherently a multitask learning (MTL) problem. Furthermore, some tasks may depend upon one another and can benefit from a joint learning scheme, while others may be unrelated. In the current work, we propose a generalized MTL framework for the estimation of various parameters needed for autonomous driving. This framework generates different networks for the estimation of a different set of tasks based on their relationship. The relationship among tasks to be learned is handled by including shared layers in the architecture. Later, the network separates into different branches to handle the difference in the behavior of each task. More specifically, we provide a solution for the estimation of driving control parameters as well as those related to scene information. We demonstrated the performance of the proposed solution on four publicly available benchmark datasets: Comma.ai, Udacity, Berkeley Deep Drive (BDD) and Sully Chen. A synthetic dataset GTA-V for autonomous driving research has also been proposed to further evaluate the proposed approach.

13.1 Introduction

The idea of self-driving cars goes back to the 1920s, while the first autonomous car appeared in the 1980s when researchers at Carnegie Mellon University launched their Navlab project [1]. This success and then declining interest of the research community in the self-driving car can be related directly with the progress in artificial intelligence research particularly Neural Networks. Again in 2012, with the success of AlexNet [2], neural networks or more specifically convolutional neural networks reappeared as the mainstream research topic in machine learning research. This marked the beginning of a new era for the century-old idea of self-driving cars. However, this time

[1]Department of Computer Science, Syed Babar Ali School of Science and Engineering, Lahore University of Management Sciences, Lahore, Pakistan
[2]Cloud Application Solutions Division, Mentor—A Siemens Business, Lahore, Pakistan

around both the academic community and industry are heavily invested in achieving this goal.

Autonomous navigation requires effective digital control of steering, acceleration and braking systems. It also requires an understanding of the surrounding world to ensure safe coexistence with other vehicles and objects [3]. Safe coexistence with other static and dynamic objects is a very challenging task, and most existing prototypes address these concerns by using a wide variety of sensors such as an array of cameras, LIDARs and radars. This makes them infeasible for the consumer market, and the researchers are trying to gain as much information as possible with just a single camera.

End-to-end deep learning is among the most widely used approaches [4–6] that utilizes a single-camera view. Many proposed end-to-end deep learning methods estimate a single parameter such as only steering angle from one or more images [4,7]. Efforts have been made to simultaneously estimate multiple parameters from a single camera only. This makes the task of autonomous driving an MTL problem. In this chapter, we propose a deep-learning-based MTL approach using a single-camera view to estimate driving control parameters as well as scene understanding needed to navigate through the dense traffic. As an example, we estimate steering angle, acceleration and brake pressure among driving control parameters and information about road extent, lanes and drivable area as scene information [8–10].

13.2 Related work

The existing literature on camera-based autonomous vehicles can be broadly categorized into three groups: end-to-end only, end-to-end with temporal information and end-to-end with reward/penalty as summarized in Table 13.1. A more detailed coverage may be found in Janai *et al.* [11].

13.2.1 Feed-forward end-to-end learning

The feed-forward end-to-end learning approach that includes mapping raw input images to steering angles was first successfully demonstrated by LeCun *et al.* [16] and then by Bojarski *et al.* [4], and many variants of these networks have been proposed afterward to further improve the accuracy. Their architecture consisted of only five convolutional layers and three fully connected (FC) layers, which makes it suitable for real-time applications for the estimation of the only single driving parameter, the steering angle. Chen and Huang [18] proposed a simpler variant consisting of only three convolutional layers and two FC layers so that the network can be trained on smaller datasets as well.

Inspired by the promising results of GoogleLeNet [31] on ImageNet challenge, Chen *et al.* [7] and Al-Qizwini *et al.* [19] proposed a hybrid approach that used a convolutional neural network (CNN) to extract affordance indicators (such as lane and object distances) that were then used to extract vehicle control parameters, such as steering angle and speed. Since affordance parameters are difficult to obtain in

Table 13.1   Summary of related work (Key terms: S, Steering angle; B, brake; A, acceleration/speed; L, lane information; T, TORCS [12]; C, Comma.ai [13]; U, Udacity; C, CARLA [13]; S, Sumo [14]; Y, Sulley Chen [15]; BDD, Berkeley Deep Drive; O, others; FF, feed forward; R/P, reward/penalty; T, temporal; Syn., synthetic)

Cat.	Ref.	Datasets			Output			
		Real	Syn.	DS	S	A	B	L
FF	[16]	✓		O	✓			
	[7]		✓	T	✓			✓
	[4,17]	✓	✓	O	✓			
	[18]	✓		C	✓			
	[19]		✓	T	✓			✓
R/P	[20]		✓	T	✓	✓	✓	
	[21]			T	✓	✓	✓	
	[22]		✓	S	✓	✓	✓	
	[23]	✓	✓	C,O	✓	✓	✓	
	[24]	✓	✓	O	✓			
T	[25]		✓	BDD	✓			
	[26]		✓	U	✓			
	[27]	✓		O	✓			
	[6]	✓		C	✓			
	[28]	✓		O			✓	✓
	[29]	✓	✓	U,O	✓	✓		
	[5]	✓	✓	U,G,O	✓			
	[30]	✓		C	✓			

real-life scenarios, they trained their architecture on TORCS [12] simulator. All these architectures use one or more FC layers, as done in seminal work by LeCun *et al.* [32], which significantly increased their parameters. However, the analysis of internal layers of end-to-end models suggests that the driving control information can be extracted without incorporating global information flow [17]. Thus, in our work, we show that the requirement of FC layers can be relaxed without compromising accuracy.

13.2.2   Reward-based/penalty-based end-to-end learning

Reward-based learning or reinforcement learning is an alternative paradigm that has received significant attention in estimating driving controls [20–24,33]. In this paradigm, an agent takes actions to maximize a cumulative reward based on its actions in a controlled environment. These approaches are based on online learning from mistakes and their applicability, in real-life self-driving scenarios, is not feasible, as these approaches require controlled environments, with predefined policies or rewards/penalty values; thus, most of the literature is based on simulators such as SUMO [14], CARLA [13], GTA [34], Udacity [35] and TORCS [12].

13.2.3   End-to-end with temporal information

Sequential information is commonly used in CNNs using long short-term memory (LSTM) [36] layers that are building blocks of recurrent neural networks (RNNs), in which connections, between units, form a directed cycle, thus it allows exhibiting dynamic temporal behavior. A wide-spread use of temporal sequence information, using recurrent neural networks, can be found in existing approaches. Xu *et al.* [25] incorporated temporal information using both temporal convolutions, and LSTM, to predict both discrete (straight, stop, left turn and right turn) and continuous (angular speed) driving actions. John *et al.* [27] used particle filters, whose proposal distributions were learned using LSTM.

Chi and Mu [26] proposed to use two subnetworks; one for feature extraction and other for steering angle prediction, both incorporate LSTM layers. Similarly, gated recurrent unit (GRU) [28] and delta networks (DNs) [6] are also used to estimate driving control parameters. LSTM units are fundamentally gating units that allow the flow of information to memory units for storing temporal information. Variants such as gated recurrent units (GRU) [28] and delta networks (DN) [6] allow update of information in memory cells as well as control of information to memory cells, respectively. Since these networks provide robustness against vanishing gradients, they have been used by the self-driving community to predict discrete [28] as well as continuous driving actions [6].

Visual saliency is another cue that is commonly used in perception as it relates to machine-made decisions with human behavior. In [5], first, using LSTM, spatiotemporal attention blobs were generated, which were, in turn, used to predict steering angles. Similarly, He *et al.* [29] used LSTM to feedback for computation of speed along with steering angle, while Du *et al.* [30] used residual blocks with LSTM. In our work instead, we obtained a reduction in error just by careful redesigning feed-forward end-to-end network [4,16], and these results can be further improved using temporal and other cues.

13.3   Problem formulation

The main focus of this research is to measure the quality of the learned models for driving parameter estimation. Although the proposed method is generic, we experimented with the estimation of steering angle, acceleration, brake and lane information (number of lanes on the left and the right of the vehicle). For driving parameter estimation, following the methodologies in prior studies [37,38], normal behavior and decisions taken by human drivers on the road are selected as reference. In other words, we tried to mimic human driving decisions for driving parameters while driving on roads and understanding available space (lanes) for overtaking or lane changing tasks. In a nutshell, these problems can be stated as follows:

- Driving parameters: Let x denote the current frame of driver view and has ground truths $\mathbf{y_D} \in \{\theta, a, b\}$ that denote the steering angle, acceleration and brake, respectively. Deep learning feature mapping function can be defined as $D_{driving} : R^{w \times h \times c}$ where w, h and c are the input width, height and the number of channels, respectively. Function $D_{driving}$ is required to predict $\hat{\mathbf{y}}_{\mathbf{D}} \in \hat{\theta}, \hat{a}, \hat{b}$ causally by minimizing the loss function. Where $\hat{\theta}$, $\hat{a}$, $\hat{b}$ are predicted values of steering angle, acceleration and brake, respectively.

• Scene understanding (lane information): The input image x, captured from the driver view, is labeled with ground truth $\mathbf{y}_{\mathbf{L}} \in \{l_L, l_R\}$ where l_L and l_R denote the number of lanes on the left and the right side of the vehicle, respectively. A function (D_{Lanes}) can be defined as $D_{Lanes} : x^{w \times h \times c}$ where w, h and c denote image width, height and number of channels, respectively, and map the input image x to output predictions $\hat{y}_L \in \{\hat{l}_L, \hat{l}_R\}$, where $\hat{l}_L$ and $\hat{l}_R$ are predicted numbers of lanes on the right and the left of the vehicle.

Frequently used variables that are used in this chapter are given in Table 13.2.

13.4 Driving parameter estimation

Primary driving commands or driving parameters include the steering angle, speed, acceleration and brake. Seminal work related to driving parameter estimation had been reported in the literature by proposing classical computer vision algorithms and deep learning models. Using the standard motion model and computer vision techniques, it is possible to get a closed-form solution like [39–42]. However, it has been noted that the deep learning [2,43,44], or generically the machine learning techniques, outperforms the conventional computer vision and image processing techniques [45].

Table 13.2   Commonly used variables

$x, \mathbf{x}$	Single and a vector of inputs
$\theta, \hat{\theta}$	Actual and predicted steering angle
$\theta_\tau, \hat{\theta}_\tau$	Actual and predicted steering torque
$\theta_v, \hat{\theta}_v$	Actual and predicted steering speed
$v, \hat{v}$	Actual and predicted speed
$a, \hat{a}$	Actual and predicted acceleration
$b, \hat{b}$	Actual and predicted brake
$l_L, \hat{l}_L$	Actual and predicted lanes on left
$l_R, \hat{l}_R$	Actual and predicted lanes on right
l_T, l_C	Total lane count and current lane
$\mathbf{y}_{\mathbf{D}}, \hat{\mathbf{y}}_{\mathbf{D}}$	Actual and predicted driving parameters
$\mathbf{y}_{\mathbf{L}}, \hat{\mathbf{y}}_{\mathbf{L}}$	Actual and predicted lane parameters
n	number of samples for SGD
$\mathbf{h}_{L+1}$	Regression layer
$\mathbf{h}_L$	Feature layer
$\mathbf{h}_l$	Intermediate layer
∇	Gradient
$\mathbf{W}, \mathbf{B}$	Weights and bias
$a_{i,j,k}, g_{i,j,k}$	Output and input of an activation function
k	Learning rate decaying factor
$\mathbf{p}$	Input to residual connection
u_t	Inverse of the steering angle (θ)

Since driving parameters include estimating multiple tasks (steering angle, acceleration, braking, etc.), it is useful to model it as an MTL problem. Given multiple tasks to learn where all or subset of these tasks is related, the MTL models aim to learn each task by consuming the information from the related subset of tasks. To achieve the MTL aims for a unified model by sharing inter-task information, there are two questions to be addressed: what to share and how to share.

What information needs to be shared covers parameters, instance and feature sharing. Parameter-based MTL scheme aims to help the model in learning a task by providing model parameters of other tasks. The instance-based MTL scheme focuses on the identification of meaningful data instances for each task and shares the identified data instances to learn a task. The feature-based MTL schemes aim to learn the common features among the given tasks.

How to share the information given that what information is required to be shared provides the concrete ways to achieve the MTL goals using knowledge sharing. In the area of autonomous driving, MTL can be categorized into two groups: (i) feature-based and (ii) parameter-based [46]. In feature-based, the same features are learned for the estimation of various tasks, whereas in a parameter-based approach various tasks are linked together to achieve knowledge transfer among tasks.

We implemented three variants of the MTL model shown in Figure 13.1. Depending upon the structure and information sharing, we named these models as early separation (ES), early separation with attention (ESA) and no separation (NS). Vanishing gradient is a challenging problem that can overfit a model. To address this challenge, residual connections are added to train the models on large datasets. Fully convolutional blocks are used with ReLU activation functions, and tanh activation layer is used in the last layer to handle both positive and negative values in predictions. The same environments and configuration parameters are used for training and evaluation of the proposed model and its variants. Network architecture and design choices are discussed in the following subsections.

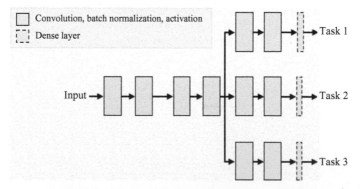

Figure 13.1   *Proposed model for the multitask learning of statistically driving parameters consists of some shared convolutional layers followed by task-independent branches where each branch contains one or more convolutional blocks*

13.4.1 Early separation (ES) network

To analyze the information-sharing scheme, the ES model is designed in a way such that low-level features are shared in early stages (first two convolutional blocks), and the high-level features are learned in separate branches dedicated to each task. ES model is shown in Figure 13.3 (row 1) which is inspired from Inception [47] and ResNet [48] models. Each separate branch consists of seven layers and residual connections. The first residual connection is formed as a shortcut connection and the second residual connection contains a convolutional layer to reduce feature size. The last layer comprises three single neurons for regression. The residual connection is shown in Figure 13.2 and can be defined as

$$\mathbf{r} = F(\mathbf{p}, W_i) + \mathbf{p} \tag{13.1}$$

where $\mathbf{p}$ is the input to the residual connection, and $F(\mathbf{p}, W_i)$ is the residual mapping to be learned. The dimensions of $\mathbf{p}$ and F must be equal. If this is not the case, we used residual connection: $\mathbf{r} = F(\mathbf{p}, W_i) + W_j\mathbf{p}$ where W_j is a matrix formed using convolution to match the size.

ReLU maps data on a range of zero to infinity, whereas *tanh* maps between -1 and $+1$. Hence, in our case, input image (x_i) is mapped to steering command ($\hat{y}$) which may contain both negative and positive angles.

13.4.2 Early separation with attention

Attention mechanisms in deep learning allow the models to focus on the information that provides strong features [17]. Using attention mechanisms, the convergence of a deep learning model can be enhanced which motivated us to use the attention layer with ES model and named the model ESA which is shown in Figure 13.3 (row 1). The core function of attention mechanism is to assign a probability to the areas of images by using the Markov assumption and guides the network to focus on the important areas of the input image. To visualize the significance of the attention layer, the regions of interest are highlighted and shown in Figure 13.4. These highlighted areas are the features that the model focused on more comparatively.

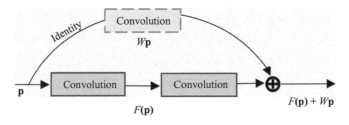

*Figure 13.2   Residual connection used in all variants as short skip connection.
Convolution layer (dotted) is optional which is used to change the
dimension of features*

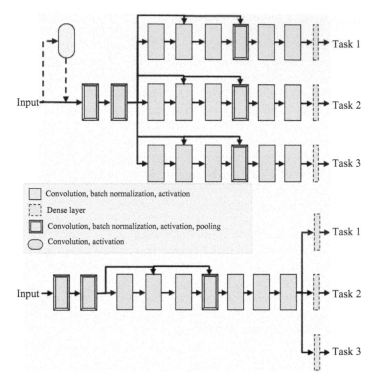

Figure 13.3   Multitask learning schemes: (row 1) early separation and early separation with attention (dotted connection is for only attention block); (row 2) no separation

Figure 13.4   Visualization of activation of attention layer from ESA (early separation with attention) model where green color represents the lowest to highest concentration on different spatial locations (best viewed in color)

13.4.3 No separation

This variant of the proposed model has been carried out to analyze the impact of feature sharing such that learning common features for multiple tasks using a unified branch. In contrast to other variants, the NS model contains only a single branch (middle branch) of ES with an additional two convolutional blocks where all the layers learn the common features. The model architecture is shown in Figure 13.3 (row 2). The first two convolution blocks are used to learn low-level features, and these features are fed to another series of convolutional and residual connections. The output from two of these convolutional blocks is added to the output of residual connections, and the resulted output is provided to four convolutional blocks. for a fear comparison, the configurations of residual connections and activation functions are the same as used in the ES model. The output of the final convolution block is separated and provided to three regression layers to generate predictions for all three tasks simultaneously.

13.5 Scene understanding

In computer vision, scene understanding covers a wide spectrum; however, in the case of autonomous vehicles, we are not interested in understanding everything about the scene. Instead, we are interested in information about the road and the objects occupying the road. This includes road boundaries, number of lanes, various lane markings, road conditions, etc. Although the interaction with objects sharing the road is very important, since knowing the intent of these objects is very difficult, the task can be simplified to quantifying the effect that they produce on the scene structure, i.e., the area left available to drive after sharing the road with other objects. More specifically in this chapter, we aim to answer the following questions: (i) how many lanes are present on each side of the vehicle? (ii) what are the boundaries of each of these lanes? and (iii) how much area is available in these lanes for driving?

13.5.1 Lane marking and lane(s) count

The modern navigation systems and GPS maps such as Google Maps, Bing Maps and Apple Maps have simplified the task of finding a route from one point to another. Most of the roads particularly highways and those within urban centers are already marked in these maps. Many human drivers are heavily relying on these maps for their daily driving needs. Human drivers need to constantly look at the windscreen, this limits there capabilities in analyzing this rich information. However, autonomous vehicles can fuse information from a large number of sources, including various maps as well as active sensors (cameras, lidar, radar, etc.). The real challenge now is navigation through traffic; this requires an understanding of road structure as well as obstacles present on the road. Both the lane markings as well as traffic flow can provide this crucial information.

Lane markings: The medium through road planners communicate with the drivers is road markings. These markings provide information about what is allowed and disallowed, and the various options are available to the drivers to safely achieve their goal of rapid navigation. Road markings can be divided into two categories: (i) lane markings (see Figure 13.5) and (ii) other road markings. Lane markings provide information crucial for navigation, while the other road markings provide additional information such as left turn, bicycle lane and allowed speed.

The lane marking can be divided into *across the carriageway* and *along the carriageway*. They are also referred to as parallel lane markings and vertical lane markings (see Figure 13.5). For tasks such as continue in the current lane, lane change and overtake, vertical lane markings play a critical role and are important in the case of a highway or expressway scenarios, whereas the horizontal lane marking is more common in dense urban lanes. Furthermore, in many underdeveloped countries and remote locations, lane markings may not be present or disappear over time. Thus, in our work instead of annotating and identifying lane markings, we introduced the task of counting lanes on both sides of the vehicles.

Lane count: We annotated five datasets: Comma.ai [50], Udacity [35], BDD [51], Sully Chen's [15], GTA-V for lane information. These annotations include the number of lanes on the left of the vehicle and the number of lanes on the right of the vehicle. Using perception of road width, lane count, traffic width and the type of lanes we came up with 110,000, 40,000, 100,000, 40,000 and 70,000 annotated images of Comma.ai [50], Udacity [35], BDD [51], Sully Chen's [15] and $GTA - V$ dataset, respectively. Annotated data contain different challenging scenarios that include lighting conditions, road visibility, poor lane marking, differentiation

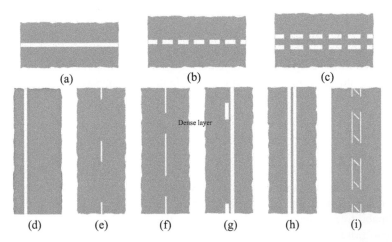

Figure 13.5   *Commonly present lane markings: (row 1) across the carriage way or parallel markings: (a) stop line at signal or stop sign, (b) stop line for pedestrians at level crossing, (c) give way to traffic on major road; (row 2) along the carriage way or vertical markings: (d) edge line, (e) center line, (f) hazard warning, (g) overtake allowed, (h) must not cross, (i) should not enter [49]*

between highway lanes and side trip lanes. A comparison of the proposed annotations as with existing datasets is shown in Table 13.3. Some challenging scenarios are shown in Figure 13.6, and a map of the simulated city is shown in Figure 13.7. With traditional computer vision and image processing techniques, it is very hard to identify lanes on underexposed (D) or overexposed images (E). We also annotated such images for both training and testing samples to train and test the proposed model for challenging lighting scenarios. Summary of lane annotation in multiple scenarios is enlisted next:

- Emergency lanes: Left and right emergency lanes, marked with a continuous line, are not counted as available lanes in the annotation.
- Side trip lanes: We included side trip lanes (entrance and departure of the highways) in lane counting.
- Invisible lanes: We included the images where visibility of lane marking was very poor or invisible due to traffic congestion.

Table 13.3   Comparisons with other lane marking datasets

Dataset	Training frames	Total frames	Hours	Attributes
Caltech Lanes [52]	–	1,224	1	2
Road Marking [53]	–	1,443	3	10
KITTI-ROAD [54]	289	579	1	2
VPGNct [55]	14,783	21,097	2	17
BDD100K [56]	70,000	100,000	3	11
Ours	288,000	360,000	5	4

Figure 13.6   Challenging scenarios in the Comma.ai dataset [50] for lane positioning estimation with prediction (green) and ground truth (blue): (a) an emergency lane on left, (b) side trip lane on the right, (c) poor lane marking, (d, e) bad lighting and (f) shadow in the lane. l_L, left lanes; l_R, right lanes. Total number of lanes = $l_L + l_R + 1$, current lane = $l_L + 1$

- Traffic signals: In this particular scenario, the difference in road width and unavailability of lane markings could contribute as artifacts. We excluded such images from training and testing dataset.

Lane position and count estimation: The estimation of the number of lanes on the left and the right of the vehicles and eventually the current lane of the vehicles is also an MTL problem. Thus, for the estimation of lane information parameters, we used the model that we proposed for the estimation of driving control parameters (steering angle, acceleration, brake). We trained our model for two parameters (lanes on the left and right of the vehicle) with the same proposed network for two tasks as shown in Figure 13.1. As a regression problem, the model results continuous values as predictions that are mapped to the nearest integer.

Evaluation of the proposed model for the estimation of lane parameters has been conducted on all five datasets. Percent accuracy is used as the evaluation metric, and the results of the proposed model are summarized in Table 13.4. We also trained the Autopilot [50] and PilotNet [4] for a single-task problem to estimate lane information in such a way that a model can predict only a single parameter, as these models were proposed for a single task. It can be seen that Autopilot [50] and PilotNet performed quite well on the estimation of lane information. On the other hand, the proposed model is trained for multitask problems and can predict both tasks at a time. Sharing the basic features of road and lanes has increased the performance of the proposed model, and it surpasses all model tasks for the single parameter. We

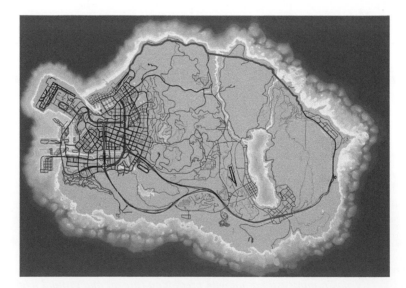

Figure 13.7   Map of GTA-V simulation environment. A vehicle is driven in this city on the road, marked with a red line. Both left and right turns are present in the route with random traffic moving on the road (best viewed in color)

obtained 100% accuracy on GTA-V and Sully Chen's dataset [15] for both lanes (l_L, l_R) and more than 99.9% accuracy on Comma.ai [50] and Udacity [35] dataset, as summarized in Table 13.4. BDD dataset [51] contains images of a highway as well as street roads with challenging scenarios that make this dataset challenging for the estimation of lane parameters. We obtained 97.4% and 96.6% accuracy on the BDD dataset as a multitasking problem. Current position of the vehicle can be calculated by as $l_C = l_L + 1$ and adding this information to the l_R resulted the total number of lanes ($l_T = l_C + l_R + 1$). Some challenging scenarios and the predictions are shown in Figure 13.6. An algorithm is derived in Algorithm 13.1 that exploits the lane localization information and driving parameter (steering angle) to generate direct control commands.

13.5.2 Drivable area segmentation

The task of everyday driving is to navigate through the busy road and reach the desired destination. While pursuing this goal at every timestamp the human drivers, as well as autonomous vehicles, need to estimate whether they can continue going in the current lane or do they have to switch to another lane to reach their desired goal. If we assume that we have complete information about all the information present in the scene as well as road structure, the goal for autonomous vehicles can be restated to develop an algorithm to drive a vehicle as fast as possible through dense traffic [57]. In real scenarios, it is very difficult to detect and recognize all the objects present in the scene and requires a very high level of computation and that too using a large array of sensors. So far it has been demonstrated only in simulated environments such as DeepTraffic [57].

Table 13.4　Evaluation for lane position estimation on Comma.ai [50], Udacity [35], BDD [51], Sully Chen's [15] and GTA-V dataset where percent accuracy is used as evaluation metric (Key terms: l_L, lanes on the left of the vehicle; l_R, lanes on the right of the vehicle)

Dataset	Parameter	Multitask model		
		Autopilot [50]	PilotNet [4]	Proposed
Comma.ai	l_L	99.4	99.6	99.9
	l_R	99.3	99.5	99.8
Udacity	l_L	97.23	98.4	99.4
	l_R	98.8	99.2	99.7
BDD	l_L	87.2	92.7	97.4
	l_R	88.4	89.1	96.6
Sully Chen	l_L	98.9	99.5	100
	l_R	99.4	99.2	100
GTA-V	l_L	98.9	99.4	100
	l_R	99.4	99.1	100

Table 13.5 Comparison of training and testing complexity of the experimented models, including proposed model, its variants, PilotNet [4] and Autopilot [50] on all five datasets (Comma.ai [50], Udacity [35], BDD [51], Sully Chen's [15] and GTA-V). Single-task and multitasks models trained for driving parameters and lane information are evaluated. (Key terms: ES, early separation; ESA, early separation with attention; NS, no separation; l_L, the total number of lanes on left of the vehicle; l_R, the total number of lanes on the right of the vehicle)

Dataset	Outputs	Model	Task	Epochs	Training time (h)	Throughput (Hz)	Network parameters	MAE
Comma.ai [50]	Single task	PilotNet [4]	θ	16	10	29	46,814,583	0.140
			a	18	11			0.625
			b	21	12			62.943
		Autopilot [50]	θ	31	13	40	8,456,817	0.149
			a	32	15			0.480
			b	31	17			74.136
		Proposed	θ	28	14	41	8,389,633	0.023
			a	32	16			0.059
			b	34	18			41.900
	Multitasks	ES	θ, a, b	44	28	23	19,110,659	28.876
		ESA		47	22	24	19,113,213	29.928
		NS		36	18	27	9,006,723	3.877
		Proposed	l_L, l_R	22	10	26	16,846,450	13.994
			θ, a, b	34	13	26	25,236,083	
Udacity [35]	Single task	PilotNet [4]	θ	16	10	29	46,814,583	0.098
			θ_τ	18	11			1.144
			θ_ν	21	12			2.560
		Autopilot [50]	θ	31	13	40	8,456,817	0.106
			θ_τ	32	15			1.120
			θ_ν	31	17			2.578
		Proposed	θ	28	14	41	8,389,633	0.074
			θ_τ	32	16			1.106
			θ_ν	34	18			2.449

Dataset	Type	Method	Outputs				Parameters	
	Multitasks	ES	θ, θτ, θv	44	28	23	19,110,659	1.518
		ESA		47	22	24	19,113,213	1.569
		NS		36	18	27	9,006,723	1.486
		Proposed	lL, lR	22	10	26	16,846,450	1.802
BDD [51]	Multitasks	ES	θ, θτ, θv	34	13	26	25,236,083	
		ESA	lL, lR	22	03	29	46,814,583	
		NS		18	03	26	16,846,450	
		Proposed		18	03	40	8,456,817	
Chen's [15]	Single task	PilotNet[4]	θ	20	04	26	16,846,450	0.235
		Autopilot[50]		22	03	29	46,814,583	0.093
		Proposed		18	03	40	8,456,817	0.056
	Multitasks	Proposed	lL, lR	20	04	41	8,389,633	
GTA-V			θ	22	03	26	16,846,450	
	Single task	PilotNet	θ	09	24	29	46,814,583	0.011
			ν	11	26			10.091
			b	12	29			0.078
		Autopilot	θ	10	25	40	8,456,817	0.012
			ν	12	27			12.763
			b	14	30			0.088
		Proposed	θ	13	27	41	8,389,633	0.009
			ν	12	26			9.239
			b	14	28			0.042
	Multitasks	ES	lL, lR	14	28	25	16,846,450	4.649
			θ, ν, b	18	30	23	19,110,659	
		ESA	lL, lR	15	27	26	16,846,450	4.481
			θ, ν, b	18	30	24	19,113,213	
		NS	lL, lR	14	22	26	16,846,450	4.526
			θ, ν, b	16	24	27	9,006,723	
		Proposed	lL, lR	14	25	26	16,846,450	3.065
			θ, ν, b	15	27	26	25,236,083	

Algorithm 13.1: Driving control logic for lane change

Input: image data x_i, size *width, height, channels*
while Autonomous mode = True **do**
  estimate steering angle $\hat{\theta}$
  estimate lane information $\hat{l}_L, \hat{l}_R$
  find other parameters: $\hat{l}_C = \hat{l}_L + 1, \hat{l}_T = \hat{l}_C + \hat{l}_R$
  if lane change = left **then**
    if $l_L > 0$ **and** $\hat{\theta} < 0$ **then**
      $l_C = l_C + 1$
    else
      if $l_L =< 0$ **and** $\hat{\theta} < 0$ **then**
        keep going in current lane
        $l_C = l_C$
      end if
    end if
    if lane change = right **then**
      if $l_R > 0$ **and** $\hat{\theta} > 0$ **then**
        $l_C = l_C - 1$
      else
        if $l_R =< 0$ **and** $\hat{\theta} > 0$ **then**
          keep going in current lane
          $l_R = l_R$
        end if
      end if
    end if
  end if
end while

In March 2018, Uber's self-driving Volvo SUV hit and killed a woman while trying to recognize the already detected object present on the road. Since then the task of self-driving has been redefined to that of identifying the drivable area, i.e., to the segment which part of the current and adjacent lanes are available to drive without detecting and identifying the neighboring object. This allows vehicles to decide whether they can continue in the current lane or do they require to find an alternate path to drive through the busy traffic. More specifically, the goal is to identify *direct drivable* and *alternative drivable* segments. The direct drivable as defined in BDD100K [51] means that the ego vehicle has the road priority and can keep driving in that area (see Figure 13.8). Similarly, the alternate drivable includes the lanes where the road priority potentially belongs to other vehicles and so the vehicle can drive in the area but has to be cautious [51] (see Figure 13.8).

From the machine learning viewpoint, the task is to classify each pixel on an image into three classes: direct drivable, alternate drivable and others. Several semantic segmentation algorithms can segment an image into several categories including road. However, the task of drivable area segmentation is an extension of road segmentation as it requires the road segment to be further subsegment into three classes, two

Figure 13.8   Sample results of drivable area segmentation using multitask U-Net

of which are visually similar and only differ in their spatial configuration. Several semantic segmentation algorithms have been proposed to achieve this goal [58–61]. Our proposed solution is based on Multitask U-Net [58] as it requires only coarse data label for training. Multitask U-Net [58] is a multi-class segmentation approach that involves three connected tasks: (i) rough detection of class instances, (ii) separation of wrongly connected objects without a clear boundary and (iii) pixel-wise segmentation to find the accurate boundaries of each object. These three tasks are trained in an end-to-end learning framework similar to the architecture presented in this chapter. Figure 13.8 shows some of the results obtained using this approach. These results can be further improved by introducing point-wise spatial attention to relax the local neighborhood constraint [61].

13.6   Computational complexity

Table 13.5 shows a complexity analysis of the proposed model, its variants and compared state-of-the-art models. The number of epochs and network parameters shows the training complexity of a model, whereas the testing rate shows the total number of frames tested in a second. We used the same environment for the training and testing of all models. The computational complexity of a deep learning model can be computed by counting the total number of network parameters as

$$Complexity = 2HC + H^2 \tag{13.2}$$

where H is the number of total hidden neurons and C is the total number of identical values.

It can be seen that the proposed model has the smallest number of training parameters for a single-task problem. In addition to the comparatively small number of parameters, the proposed model has the highest throughput rate of value 41 Hz (frames/s). On the other hand, for the multitasking problem, the proposed model has a throughput value of 26 frames/s. Another very apparent thing is that PilotNet [4], even though it has a throughput of 29 Hz, is by far the most expensive model in terms of the number of parameters.

13.6.1   Error vs. throughput

In addition to computational complexity, we present an analysis of the error, through-put and the number of model parameters of experimented models. Figure 13.9 illustrates this analysis, where the x-axis, y-axis, and circle size show the steering angle error (MAE), throughput (images per second) and the number of model parameters respectively. The analysis is conducted for the models trained for driving parameters which include ES, ESA, NS and the proposed model on three datasets namely Comma.ai [57], Udacity [28] and GTA-V. An ideal model should result in a minimum error while having a small number of parameters with the highest throughput.

For Comma.ai dataset [50] (Figure 13.9(a)), we note that all the variants of the proposed model have a larger error as compared to the proposed model with a notice-able margin. ES model has the largest throughput (27 Hz) among all the models but the proposed model is close enough with a throughput of 26 frames/s. Similarly, on Udacity [35] and GTA-V datasets, the proposed model sustains the performance in terms of error and throughput by having the lowest error value. Accuracy and

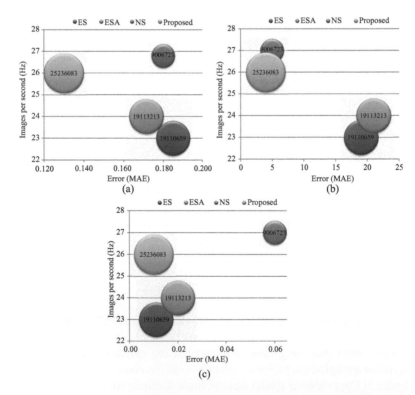

Figure 13.9   Comparison of inference per second vs. mean absolute error of the proposed model and its variants, where the size of circles shows the total number of trainable parameters: (a) Analysis on Comma.ai dataset [50], (b) analysis on Udacity dataset [35], (c) analysis on GTA-V dataset (best viewed in color)

throughput, both parameters have their significance to control an autonomous vehicle precisely with minimum time head. The proposed model shows its credibility to control the autonomous vehicle by achieving lower error without affecting the throughput.

13.7 Summary

In this chapter, we propose a simpler yet effective method for driving control estimation. We trained our model individually on steering angle, brake and acceleration and compared it with state-of-the-art approaches. We further trained the same model to estimate steering angle, brake and acceleration and showed that our method outperformed state-of-the-art approaches in both individuals and combined tasks. We argued that information available in a single image has not been completely utilized in the existing literature and provided evidence using a benchmark test set. Additionally, we provided annotations for lane information for benchmark datasets that we aim to release along with our proposed solution that obtained over 99% accuracy for lane information task. Our work has led us to conclude that the proposed approach has been able to predict driving primary parameters and vehicle localization on the road regardless of road conditions.

References

[1] Kanade T, Thorpe C, and Whittaker W. Autonomous Land Vehicle Project at CMU. In: Proceedings of the 1986 ACM Fourteenth Annual Conference on Computer Science. CSC'86. New York, NY, USA: ACM; 1986. p. 71–80. Available from: http://doi.acm.org/10.1145/324634.325197.

[2] Krizhevsky A, Sutskever I, and Hinton GE. ImageNet Classification with Deep Convolutional Neural Networks. In: Advances in Neural Information Processing Systems. Lake Tahoe, USA: Harrahs and Harveys; 2012. p. 1097–1105.

[3] Lio MD, Mazzalai A, Gurney K, *et al.* Biologically Guided Driver Modeling: the Stop Behavior of Human Car Drivers. IEEE Transactions on Intelligent Transportation Systems. 2018;19(8):2454–2469.

[4] Bojarski M, Del Testa D, Dworakowski D, *et al.* End to End Learning for Self-Driving Cars. arXiv preprint arXiv:160407316. 2016.

[5] Kim J and Canny J. Interpretable Learning for Self-Driving Cars by Visualizing Causal Attention. In: Int. Conf. on Computer Vision. Venice, Italy: IEEE; 2017.

[6] Neil D, Lee JH, Delbruck T, and Liu SC. Delta Networks for Optimized Recurrent Network Computation. In: Int. Conf. on Machine Learning Sydney, Australia; 2017.

[7] Chen C, Seff A, Kornhauser A, and Xiao J. DeepDriving: Learning Affordance for Direct Perception in Autonomous Driving. In: Int. Conf. on Computer Vision. Araucano Park, Las Condes, Chile: IEEE; 2015.

[8] Menéndez-Romero C, Winkler F, Dornhege C, *et al.* Maneuver Planning for Highly Automated Vehicles. In: Intelligent Vehicles Symposium. Los Angeles, CA, USA: IEEE; 2017. p. 1458–1464.

[9]   Jiang J and Astolfi A. A Lateral Control Assistant for the Dynamic Model of Vehicles Subject to State Constraints. In: Conf. on Decision and Control. Melbourne, Australia: IEEE; 2017. p. 244–249.

[10]   Wu Y, Chen Z, Liu R, *et al.* Lane Departure Avoidance Control for Electric Vehicle Using Torque Allocation. Mathematical Problems in Engineering. 2018; 2018.

[11]   Janai J, Güney F, Behl A, *et al.* Computer Vision for Autonomous Vehicles: Problems, Datasets and State-of-the-Art. arXiv:170405519. 2017.

[12]   Wymann B, Dimitrakakis C, Sumner A, *et al.* TORCS, The Open Racing Car Simulator, v1.3.5, http://torcs.sourceforge.net last accessed: 10 Jul 2020.

[13]   Dosovitskiy A, Ros G, Codevilla F, *et al.* CARLA: An Open Urban Driving Simulator. last accessed: 07 Dec 2018. 2017.

[14]   Krajzewicz D, Erdmann J, Behrisch M, *et al.* Recent Development and Applications of SUMO – Simulation of Urban MObility. International Journal on Advances in Systems and Measurements. 2012;5(3&4):128–138.

[15]   Chen S. https://goo.gl/5Wq7fe. last accessed: 10 Jul 2020.

[16]   LeCun Y, Muller U, Ben J, *et al.* Off-Road Obstacle Avoidance through End-to-End Learning. In: Advances in Neural Information Processing Systems. British Columbia, Canada: Vancouver; 2005. p. 739–746.

[17]   Bojarski M, Yeres P, Choromanska A, *et al.* Explaining How a Deep Neural Network Trained with End-to-End Learning Steers a Car. arXiv:170407911. 2017.

[18]   Chen Z and Huang X. End-to-End Learning for Lane Keeping of Self-Driving Cars. In: Intelligent Vehicles Symposium. Los Angeles, CA, USA: IEEE; 2017. p. 1856–1860.

[19]   Al-Qizwini M, Barjasteh I, Al-Qassab H, *et al.* Deep Learning Algorithm for Autonomous Driving Using GoogLeNet. In: Intelligent Vehicles Symposium. Los Angeles, CA, USA: IEEE; 2017. p. 89–96.

[20]   Sallab AE, Abdou M, Perot E, *et al.* Deep Reinforcement Learning framework for Autonomous Driving. arXiv 170402532. 2017.

[21]   Lillicrap TP, Hunt JJ, Pritzel A, *et al.* Continuous Control With Deep Reinforcement Learning. arXiv:150902971. 2015.

[22]   Isele D, Cosgun A, Fujimura K. Analyzing Knowledge Transfer in Deep Q-Networks for Autonomously Handling Multiple Intersections. arXiv:170501197. 2017.

[23]   Codevilla F, Müller M, López A, Koltun V, and Dosovitskiy A End-to-end Driving via Conditional Imitation Learning. In: Int. Conf. on Robotics and Automation. Brisbane, Australia; 2018.

[24]   Innocenti C, Lindén H, Panahandeh G, *et al.* Imitation Learning for Vision-based Lane Keeping Assistance. In: Int. Conf. on Intel. Trans. Sys. Yokohama, Japan: IEEE; 2017. p. 425–430.

[25]   Xu H, Gao Y, Yu F, *et al.* End-to-End Learning of Driving Models From Large-Scale Video Datasets. In: Conf. on Computer Vision and Pattern Recognition. Honolulu, Hawaii, USA: IEEE; 2017. p. 3530–3538.

[26] Chi L and Mu Y. Learning End-to-End Autonomous Steering Model from Spatial and Temporal Visual Cues. In: Workshop on Visual Analysis in Smart and Connected Communities, Mountain View, California, USA; 2017. p. 9–16.

[27] John V, Mita S, Tehrani H, *et al.* Automated Driving by Monocular Camera Using Deep Mixture of Experts. In: Intelligent Vehicles Symposium. Los Angeles, CA, USA: IEEE; 2017. p. 127–134.

[28] Olabiyi O, Martinson E, Chintalapudi V, *et al.* Driver Action Prediction Using Deep (Bidirectional) Recurrent Neural Network. arXiv:170602257. 2017.

[29] Yang Z, Zhang Y, Yu J, *et al.* End-to-End Multi-Modal Multi-Task Vehicle Control for Self-Driving Cars with Visual Perception. International Conference on Pattern Recognition, Beijing, China; 2018

[30] Du S, Guo H, and Simpson A. Self-Driving Car Steering Angle Prediction Based on Image Recognition. Santa Clara County, California: Stanford; 2017. CS231 course project.

[31] Szegedy C, Liu W, Jia Y, *et al.* Going Deeper With Convolutions. In: Conf. on Computer Vision and Pattern Recognition. Boston, MA, USA: IEEE; 2015.

[32] LeCun Y, Boser BE, Denker JS, *et al.* Handwritten Digit Recognition With a Back-Propagation Network. In: Advances in Neural Information Processing Systems. Denver, Colorado, USA; 1990. p. 396–404.

[33] Wolf P, Hubschneider C, Weber M, *et al.* Learning How to Drive in a Real World Simulation With Deep Q-Networks. In: Intelligent Vehicles Symposium. Los Angeles, CA, USA: IEEE; 2017. p. 244–250.

[34] Richter SR, Vineet V, Roth S, and Koltun V. Playing for Data: Ground Truth From Computer Games. In: European Conf. on Computer Vision. Amsterdam, Netherlands; 2016.

[35] Udacity. https://github.com/udacity/self-driving-car, last accessed: 10 Jul 2020.

[36] Hochreiter S and Schmidhuber J. Long Short-Term Memory. Neural Computation. 1997;9(8):1735–1780.

[37] Schmidhuber J. Deep Learning in Neural Networks: An Overview. Neural Networks. 2015;61:85–117.

[38] Muller U, Ben J, Cosatto E, *et al.* Off-Road Obstacle Avoidance Through End-to-End Learning. In: Advances in Neural Information Processing Systems. British Columbia, Canada: Vancouver; 2006. p. 739–746.

[39] Hee Lee G, Faundorfer F, and Pollefeys M. Motion Estimation for Self-Driving Cars With a Generalized Camera. In: The Conference on Computer Vision and Pattern Recognition. Portland, Oregon, USA: IEEE; 2013.

[40] Levinson J, Askeland J, Becker J, *et al.* Towards Fully Autonomous Driving: Systems and Algorithms. In: Intelligent Vehicles Symposium 2011 IEEE. Baden-Baden, Germany: IEEE; 2011. p. 163–168.

[41] Li TH, Chang SJ, and Chen YX. Implementation of Human-Like Driving Skills by Autonomous Fuzzy Behavior Control on an FPGA-Based Car-Like Mobile Robot. IEEE Transactions on Industrial Electronics. 2003;50(5):867–880.

[42] Falcone P, Borrelli F, Asgari J, *et al.* Predictive Active Steering Control for Autonomous Vehicle Systems. IEEE Transactions on Control Systems Technology. 2007;15(3):566–580.

[43]   Girshick R, Donahue J, Darrell T, *et al.* Rich Feature Hierarchies for Accurate Object Detection and Semantic Segmentation. In: Proceedings of the IEEE Conference on Computer Vision and Pattern Recognition. Columbus, Ohio, USA; 2014. p. 580–587.

[44]   Erhan D, Szegedy C, Toshev A, *et al.* Scalable Object Detection Using Deep Neural Networks. In: Proceedings of the IEEE Conference on Computer Vision and Pattern Recognition. Columbus, Ohio, USA; 2014. p. 2147–2154.

[45]   Oliva A and Torralba A. Modeling the Shape of the Scene: A Holistic Representation of the Spatial Envelope. International Journal of Computer Vision. 2001;42(3):145–175.

[46]   Zhang Y, Wei Y, and Yang Q. Learning to Multitask. In: Bengio S, Wallach H, Larochelle H, *et al.*, editors. Advances in Neural Information Processing Systems 31. Curran Associates, Inc.; 2018. p. 5771–5782. Available from: http://papers.nips.cc/paper/7819-learning-to-multitask.pdf.

[47]   Szegedy C, Ioffe S, Vanhoucke V, *et al.* Inception-v4, Inception-ResNet and the Impact of Residual Connections on Learning. In: AAAI Conf. on Artificial Intelligence. vol. 4. San Francisco, California, USA; 2017. p. 12.

[48]   He K, Zhang X, Ren S, *et al.* Deep Residual Learning for Image Recognition. In: Conf. on Computer Vision and Pattern Recognition. Las Vegas, Nevada, USA: IEEE; 2016. p. 770–778.

[49]   Highway Code Road Markings T. https://www.highwaycodeuk.co.uk/road-markings.html. last accessed: 13 Jul 2020.

[50]   Santana E and Hotz G. Learning a Driving Simulator. arXiv preprint arXiv:160801230. 2016.

[51]   Xu H, Gao Y, Yu F, *et al.* End-to-End Learning of Driving Models From Large-Scale Video Datasets. In: Conf. on Computer Vision and Pattern Recognition. Honolulu, Hawaii, USA: IEEE; 2017. p. 3530–3538.

[52]   Aly M. Real Time Detection of Lane Markers in Urban Streets. In: Intelligent Vehicles Symposium, 2008 IEEE. Eindhoven, Netherlands: IEEE; 2008. p. 7–12.

[53]   Wu T and Ranganathan A. A Practical System for Road Marking Detection and Recognition. In: 2012 IEEE Intelligent Vehicles Symposium. Alcala de Henares, Spain: IEEE; 2012. p. 25–30.

[54]   Fritsch J, Kuehnl T, and Geiger A. A New Performance Measure and Evaluation Benchmark for Road Detection Algorithms. In: 16th International IEEE Conference on Intelligent Transportation Systems (ITSC 2013). The Hague, Netherlands: IEEE; 2013. p. 1693–1700.

[55]   Lee S, Kim J, Shin Yoon J, *et al.* VPGNet: Vanishing Point Guided Network for Lane and Road Marking Detection and Recognition. In: Proceedings of the IEEE International Conference on Computer Vision. Venice, Italy; 2017. p. 1947–1955.

[56]   Yu F, Xian W, Chen Y, *et al.* BDD100K: A Diverse Driving Video Database With Scalable Annotation Tooling. arXiv preprint arXiv:180504687. 2018.

[57]   Traffic D. https://github.com/lexfridman/deeptraffic. last accessed: 13 Jul 2020.

[58] Ke R, Bugeau A, Papadakis N, *et al.* A Multi-Task U-Net for Segmentation With Lazy Labels. CoRR. 2019;abs/1906.12177. Available from: http://arxiv.org/abs/1906.12177.

[59] Roberts B, Kaltwang S, Samangooei S, *et al.* A Dataset for Lane Instance Segmentation in Urban Environments. In: European Conf. on Computer Vision. Munich, Germany; 2018.

[60] Abbas W and Taj M. Adaptively Weighted Multi-task Learning Using Inverse Validation Loss. In: Int. Conf. on Acoustics, Speech and Signal Processing. Brighton, UK: IEEE; 2019.

[61] Zhao H, Zhang Y, Liu S, *et al.* PSANet: Point-Wise Spatial Attention Network for Scene Parsing. In: European Conf. on Computer Vision. Munich, Germany; 2018.

Chapter 14

Machine-learning-enabled ECG monitoring for early detection of hyperkalaemia

Constance Farrell[1] and Muhammad Zeeshan Shakir[1]

Hyperkalaemia is the medical terminology for a blood potassium level above normal parameters (greater than 5.5 mmol). This can have a variety of causes; however, patients with significant renal impairment/disease are particularly at a high risk as their kidneys are compromised and unable to filter out excess potassium from the bloodstream. Hyperkalaemia is a medical emergency and requires urgent medical intervention; if left untreated, there is an extremely high risk of cardiac arrest and death as high potassium levels directly affect the electrical activity of the heart. Cardiac activity can be observed by performing an electrocardiogram (ECG) test that is routinely used in all clinical areas worldwide. This research investigates the use of ECG tests as a diagnostic tool for the early detection of hyperkalaemia, and the role of machine learning in the prediction of blood potassium levels from ECG data alone. Support vector machines (SVMs), k-nearest neighbour (k-NN), decision tree and Gaussian Naïve Bayes classifiers were used comparatively to classify ECG data as either 'normokalaemia' or 'hyperkalaemia'. Results showed that the decision tree model performed the best, achieving a 90.9 per cent predictive accuracy.

14.1 Introduction

Current research from Kidney Care UK [1] approximates there to be around 3 million people in the United Kingdom (UK) living with renal/kidney disease at varying degrees of severity. All of whom are considered to be at a high risk of developing hyperkalaemia and would benefit greatly from remote testing and early diagnosis. Patients with renal impairment also have a highly increased risk of developing other additional health problems in other anatomical systems, including heart failure, high blood pressure, electrolyte imbalance and metabolic acidosis [2]. Certain individuals may also develop hyperkalaemia without the presence of renal impairment; however, those with kidney disease are the most at risk due to the high incidence of occurrence and the difficulty of managing fluctuating potassium levels in renal patients [3].

[1]School of Computing, Engineering and Physical Sciences, University of the West of Scotland, Paisley, Scotland, UK

Potassium plays a vital role in maintaining electrical charge within the heart which is essential for the heart to beat regularly. Fluctuations in blood potassium levels cause disruption to the timing and rhythm of contractions within the heart which has a detrimental effect, resulting in arrhythmias and irregularities. The severity and risk of sudden cardiac arrest progressively worsen as the potassium level increases, hospital admission and urgent treatment is required for hyperkalaemia.

At present, the only way to detect and diagnose hyperkalaemia is by obtaining venous (or arterial) blood and performing a laboratory test which can only be done by suitably qualified professionals in a healthcare environment. By the time, patients decide to seek medical attention, symptoms tend to have developed and progressed significantly with potassium levels dangerously high [4]. This explains the high number of instances of cardiac arrests associated with hyperkalaemia as symptoms are not always present, especially in mild–moderate stages. A method of remote testing potassium levels would enable earlier detection of hyperkalaemia which means patients could seek treatment sooner, maximising the chances of a good outcome and reducing the risk of sudden cardiac arrest [5].

Remote patient monitoring is an emerging field of technologies that are currently being developed to support the management of chronic health conditions in the community. ECG tests are traditionally performed in a clinical setting by a clinician who is able to interpret the findings of the test. Advancements in technology have enabled the development of mobile sensors that are capable of capturing an ECG from a handheld smartphone device [6]. The data from the ECG is then stored on the device awaiting review from a clinician. An application that is able to interpret the ECG results almost instantaneously through machine learning would enable the patient to seek treatment faster and improve patient safety.

Blood potassium levels cannot be diagnosed from an ECG test alone at present; however, with the aid of technology, there is huge potential for this to be developed. Certain ECG trends and changes are exhibited and associated with varying stages of hyperkalaemia; thus, an estimate of blood potassium level can be derived from an ECG test [7].

This research investigates the possible uses of machine learning in the identification of hyperkalaemia-related changes to electrical activity within the heart and its accuracy in predicting blood potassium values from ECG test output. Machine learning expands on existing statistical techniques and can accommodate a broad array of data types enabling the production of results in more complex situations [8]. It is a rapidly expanding field and is already being used in many areas within the healthcare sector. Modern electronic health records generate a vast amount of data, and machine learning can assist in making sense of this data by identifying patterns and producing clinically valuable statistical information. This research will focus on exploring supervised learning techniques using existing ECG data which is publicly available online.

Early identification and diagnosis of hyperkalaemia is imperative for the timely initiation of treatment and is essential for the prevention of sudden cardiac arrest. The mortality rate is heightened in patients with pre-existing kidney disease and other co-morbidities. Long *et al.* [9] emphasise the importance of rapid diagnosis and management of hyperkalaemia as the rate at which it accrues impacts the severity of negative effects on the physiological systems of the body.

A blood test is currently the gold standard of clinical test for blood potassium level detection [10]. However, this requires laboratory testing which is invasive for the patient, time consuming and can result in a delay in treatment. There is a definite need for remote-monitoring methodologies capable of detecting abnormal potassium levels before the patient becomes symptomatic [11]. The potential of ECG testing for potassium level detection in the community setting has attracted attention from researchers, from both technological and clinical backgrounds.

14.1.1   ECG for chronic kidney disease

ECG tests are traditionally performed in a clinical setting by a suitably qualified professional using 12 adhesive electrodes and 12 leads which connect to a portable machine that displays and prints the output. Sabiullah *et al.* [12] found hyperkalaemia to be a major threat to patient safety in chronic kidney disease (CKD), with the severity of threat increasing as kidney function deteriorates. They found that the mortality rate due to cardiac arrest was significantly higher in CKD patients. They examined the ECG changes that occur as blood potassium levels increase and found a distinctive correlating pattern. Research by Viera and Wouk [13] observed similar ECG patterns in patients as potassium levels increased. The earliest initial sign is peaked T waves, followed by loss of P waves and then widening of the QRS complex and sine waves [14]. Typical hyperkalaemia-induced arrhythmias include sinus bradycardia, sinus arrest, ventricular tachycardia and ventricular fibrillation [15].

There have been recent developments in the design of ECG capturing technologies. Attia *et al.* [16] conducted research in to the abilities of a single-lead ECG to calculate blood potassium values without requiring a blood and laboratory test. Their study used a population of haemodialysis patients of which 66 per cent were men and 34 per cent were female, a fairly even distribution. A data-processing algorithm was created using the MATLAB® environment (MathWorks) to estimate potassium levels based on T-wave characteristics present on the single-lead ECG test. Calculated potassium values from the ECG were then compared with actual values from patients' blood tests which was found to have a high level of accuracy with a mean absolute error of 10 per cent. This research was highly significant in identifying the potential of remote ECG testing as a method of calculating blood potassium levels.

Yasin *et al.* [17] further expanded on this concept and tested the potassium-detection abilities of a single-lead ECG using electrodes attached to a handheld smartphone. They also compared the results with potassium values from blood tests taken at the same time and achieved a high level of accuracy with a reduction in the mean absolute error to 9 per cent. Although their algorithm can be considered as successful in their research, the population used to test it only consisted of 18 patients all with potassium levels in the normal range (3.5–5.5 mmol). Therefore, this cannot presently be applied in the detection of hypo/hyperkalaemia as there is no evidence to suggest or prove that the algorithm is capable of detecting values lower or greater than the normal range.

A breakthrough in the real-life implementation of mobile healthcare technologies was made in 2012 when the American Food and Drug Administration approved the use of the Kardia smartphone case with ECG capturing sensors by medical device and artificial intelligence company, AliveCor. This works by the user placing their fingers on the sensors attached to the smartphone case which obtains an ECG, the data is then stored offline on an application installed on the mobile device [18]. Various tests showed the smartphone ECG performed excellently and had a strong correlation with the traditional 12-lead ECG used in hospitals making it a viable option for remote monitoring [19].

Since 2012, many developments have been made to AliveCor's mobile ECG. It is currently compatible with most iPhones and Android smartphones [20] that ECG data is available for clinical practitioners to review at the users request with data being transmitted over Wi-Fi, LTE or 4G connectivity [21]. The mobile ECG has been shown to produce highly accurate results but still requires analysis and interpretation by a clinician for the detection of abnormalities [22]. However, research into the interpretative and diagnostic potential of remote ECG applications is ongoing.

14.1.2   Non-invasive methods for potassium detection

Advances in healthcare designed to assist in the remote monitoring of physiological signs include wearable sensor technologies and mobile devices that generate large amounts of data [23]. Machine learning has the potential to revolutionise the way in which the data contained in these devices is analysed and used by clinicians. Several machine learning algorithms have been used for ECG classification such as artificial neural networks (ANNs), SVMs, Naïve Bayes and k-NN models [24–27]. The vast majority of current research into ECG data analysis and classification tends to focus on the identification and/or prediction of cardiac abnormalities and disease.

Although indicative of the potential diagnostic role machine learning can play with ECG data, the technological techniques used for the detection of cardiac issues cannot automatically be applied to the detection of hyperkalaemia as parameters differ greatly. ECG changes specifically related to high potassium levels require a unique model designed exactly for that purpose such as the algorithm proposed by Attia *et al.* [16]. Their algorithm was able to detect potassium levels with a 12-per cent mean error (approximately 0.5 mmol) in a small sample of stable haemodialysis patients. Their ECG analysis focused solely on T-wave peak and amplitude changes with varying potassium levels at different periods of time. Findings suggest that further research is required to improve the level of accuracy and generalisability, as the algorithm is unable to work for anyone with any form of cardiac disease which is very common among renal patients. Hadjem and Naït-Abdesselam [28] tested the accuracy of seven different supervised learning classification models in detecting T-wave changes in ECG test data. Results showed that the decision tree model performed best with high accuracy (92.5 per cent) and low error rate (7.4 per cent).

Galloway *et al.* [29] investigated the abilities of ECG tests to detect hyperkalaemia but used a different method of testing, a deep-learning classification model and found results which contrasted the findings by Rafique *et al.* [30]. In this research, 1.5

million ECGs from around 450,000 patients were used to train a deep neural network. Results were promising as they showed that the deep learning model was able to detect hyperkalaemia with a high sensitivity and a high area under the curve (between 0.853 and 0.901). This highlights the potential effective use of applying machine learning and artificial intelligence in the identification of hyperkalaemia by ECG data analysis and requires further investigation.

Research by Velagapudi *et al.* [31] found that incorporation of the QRS complex as well as T-wave analytics improved the diagnostic performance of their classification model in the identification of hyperkalaemia from raw ECG data. The data used in the study was obtained from 12-lead ECGs and while their model may be useful in a clinical setting, it cannot be applied to the single-lead ECGs used in remote health monitoring without further research. However, other researchers such as Littmann and Gibbs have also found that QRS widening and axis shift is highly indicative of extreme hyperkalaemia and should be included in diagnostic modelling [32].

A non-invasive method for potassium detection was proposed by Dillon *et al.* [33], in which they developed a mathematical formula to calculate blood potassium levels from ECG data. The formula was based on signal-averaged T-wave characteristics identified from extracting features. The features extracted were all T-wave data, and no other peaks in the signals were included in the development of the formula. A very small sample of participants was used (12), and the researchers found that even small changes were detectable. Yasin *et al.* [17] used a linear regression model to calculate blood potassium values from raw ECG data; however, their model is person specific and must be altered for each individual so therefore cannot be generalised. A summary of key research in this field is provided in Table 14.1.

Pilia *et al.* highlighted the potential abilities of an ANN to predict blood potassium concentrations from ECG features [34]. The neural network consisted of one layer and six neurons, and the researchers state that a small predictive error margin was achieved. However, this research is completely theoretical with the ECG data simulated in a laboratory setting thus making it vulnerable to researcher bias. The model has not been tested with any real clinical data and lacks ecological validity. Neural networks have been found to perform well in the detection and diagnosis of cardiac abnormalities/arrhythmias [25,35] and could be a potentially useful method for the detection of hyperkalaemia from ECG data. This is currently an under-developed area and may benefit from further research in future.

Table 14.1   Normal ECG feature parameters

Signal feature	Duration (s)	Cardiac function
PR interval	0.12–0.20	Atrial depolarisation
QRS complex	0.08–0.10	Ventricular depolarisation
ST segment	0.08–0.12	Complete ventricular depolarisation
QT interval	<0.44	Total duration of depolarisation and repolarisation
T wave	0.10–0.25	Ventricular repolarisation
R–R interval	0.6–1.2	Ventricular rhythm (duration per heartbeat)

This research differs from existing bloodless potassium-predicting technologies in that it incorporates all PQRST peak patterns and changes in the classification stage, whereas the current methodologies are largely solely focused on T waves only. Some of the current proposed methods involve deriving mathematical equations on an individual patient-to-patient basis [16,17]. An algorithm can therefore not be generalised, and individualised programmes for each patient would be largely time consuming and unrealistic. This research aims to develop a model that can be applied to all patients, is non-specific and can be used remotely by all.

14.2   ECG signal analysis

ECG tests produce sensor-based data which exists in waveforms; this is significantly more complex to analyse compared with standard numerical or image data. The typical signal produced by a standard heartbeat viewed as normal exhibits a waveform consisting of several peaks identified as 'PQRST' complex. The ECG signal depicted in Figure 14.1 displays the expected pattern of a normally functioning heart. Previous research has shown that every interval and duration of the signal produced by the ECG must be in a very specific range to be considered normal [36]. The typical duration and associated function of each interval are given in Table 14.1. Any disturbance to the electrical conduction of the heart will alter the heartbeat's pathway and timing.

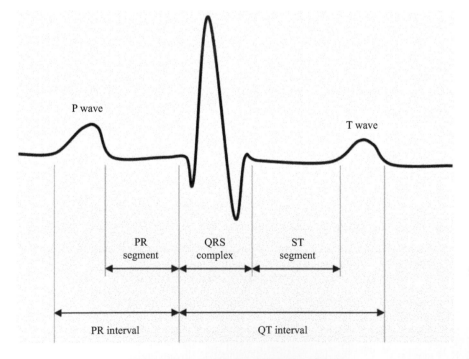

Figure 14.1   A regular ECG signal [41]

Resultingly, any defect will cause a change in signal produced by the ECG with features out-with the normal PQRST pattern.

MATLAB appears to be the most popular programming language and environment used in ECG analysis and modelling research as it has multiple application–programming interfaces specifically designed for working with sensor-based data [37]. Azariadi *et al.* [38] successfully developed an algorithm in MATLAB for ECG signal analysis and cardiac arrhythmia detection. They used discrete wavelet transform (DWT) for analysis and an SVM classifier, a binary classifier to label each heartbeat as 'Normal' or 'Abnormal'. The model was trained and tested, producing a 98.9 per cent accuracy which suggests that this is a highly suitable method for ECG abnormality detection.

Feature extraction is an important aspect of machine learning in the predictive modelling of ECG data, as 'normal' peaks must first be identified, from which a rule base can then be established to determine boundaries between normal and abnormal outputs [36]. The detection of the PQRST peak is an important first step in ECG feature extraction as highlighted by Reddy *et al.* [39]. In their research, MATLAB functions are used to derive normal parameter values for PQRST waves which must be precise as any values out-with these are then classified as abnormal. Feature extraction provides the foundation for successful algorithm building in machine learning [40].

14.2.1 ECG abnormalities caused by hyperkalaemia

Potassium plays a vital role in maintaining regular electrical charge and contributing to calcium release within the heart, causing it to beat and pump blood around the body. A constant safe level of potassium is required in the blood serum in order to maintain homeostasis within the body. Disruptions to blood potassium levels affect the timing and rhythm of cardiac muscle contractions which can be observed in the signals emitted from an ECG test.

Research has found that hyperkalaemia causes a pattern of distinct ECG abnormalities to occur which progressively worsen in severity as potassium levels increase [12]. The first indication is peaked T waves which are a clear indication of hyperkalaemia. Previous studies have solely used a change in T waves as an estimation of potassium level and produced fairly accurate results [16]. However, as potassium levels become further elevated, more life-threatening abnormalities occur which should also be recognisable by any classification model. A prolonged P–R segment is also another indication of mild hyperkalaemia. P-wave flattening and a prolonged QRS complex are indicative that potassium levels are largely elevated. Progressive QRS widening can be seen as levels increase, signals resembling a mathematical sine wave are representative of extreme hyperkalaemia with heart failure imminent without urgent medical attention. These effects are depicted in Figure 14.2.

14.2.2 Feature extraction and peak detection algorithm

The extraction of 'PQRST' features from raw ECG data is an important task as it provides the basis for quantification and modelling. Different feature extraction methodologies used in previous research as detailed in the literature review section include genetic algorithms, wavelet transform and non-linear transformation. There have been many 'QRS' detection algorithms successfully developed and implemented in real-world applications. The creation of such algorithms tends to be very complex due to the variability of normal QRS intervals and the presence of different types of noise, such as artefacts resulting from electrode motion, muscle noise and power-line interference.

An algorithm for feature extraction was developed in MATLAB-computing environment due to its capabilities in working with quantitative data and was deemed suitable for the analysis of raw ECG data. This was based upon the same basic principles as Pan–Tompkins algorithm for QRS detection [43]. This is a real-time algorithm that consists of band-pass filter, differentiator, integrator and moving-window [42]. Adaptations have been made, and a prototype of the algorithm has been developed to include P-wave and T-wave detections, which is highly important in the detection of hyperkalaemia.

A simplified prototype algorithm has been developed to detect PQRST peaks as accurately as possible from raw ECG signal data. Band-pass filtering is used for preprocessing, including high-pass and low-pass filters which only allow a certain frequency band to pass through thus helping to eliminate the effects of movement-induced noise. MATLAB code is used to calculate and display original signal, signal with low-pass filter, signal with high-pass filter and the derivative base filter. The

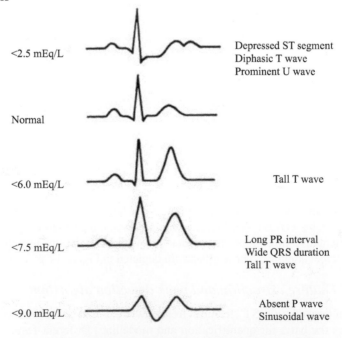

Figure 14.2   Hyperkalaemia-related ECG changes [42]

output is displayed in Figure 14.3. Signal filtering at varying frequencies is used to produce a windowed estimate of energy in QRS frequency band and optimise accuracy of peak selection. The imaginary parts in Figure 14.3 illustrate the process of Fourier Analysis – breaking down the signal into individual sine waves for each of the filters used.

The filtered signal is derived using a derivative base filter to highlight the PQRST features. The decision rule uses a first derivative-based squaring function of the filtered ECG signal to extract features P, Q, R, S and T as can be observed in Figure 14.4. Heart rate can also be calculated by measuring the R–R intervals.

14.3 ECG data collection and preprocessing

To investigate the performance of machine learning models in the prediction of blood potassium levels, a suitable dataset was identified and used as further detailed next. This was done using Python, a high-level programming language and a suitable IDE chosen for its statistical tools and good graphical/visual tools. The data was explored to check for outliers, missing values and irregularities, which is fundamental in any data science task to avoid obscure results being produced [44].

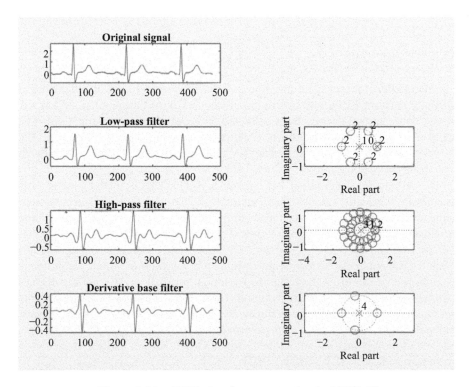

Figure 14.3   ECG signal preprocessing in MATLAB

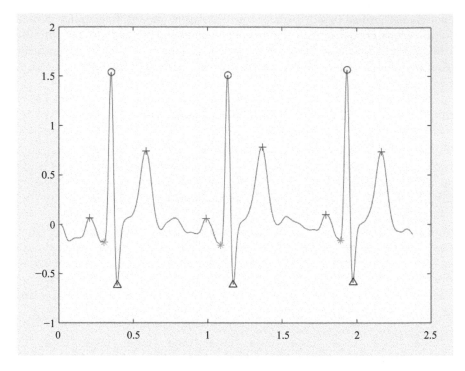

Figure 14.4   PQRST features

Due to ethical reasons and the timescale for the research, it was unfeasible to physically perform ECGs and obtain blood samples from the population. Instead, relevant data that had already been collected for research purposes was used. The dataset used was obtained from the 'Electrocardiographic abnormalities and QTc interval in patients undergoing hemodialysis' study by Nie *et al.* and is freely available online from the public library of science [45].

The participants consisted of 141 haemodialysis patients of mixed gender. Various clinical information were obtained, including ECG test data and blood potassium results, which were of particular interest for the purpose of this research. After some participants were excluded from the original study due to known severe cardiac disease, the final dataset published contained 109 rows and 73 columns. A new subset of this dataset was created for the purpose of this research in which the columns were narrowed down to 19 and excluded irrelevant information, the number of rows remained the same as in the original dataset. The numerical data of ECG components after feature extraction had been performed such as P wave, QRS complex, T wave and the duration between each, were present in the columns as well as; gender, age, heart rate, blood potassium values both pre and post dialysis and the presence of known cardiac defects (RBBB and LBBB).

Data was checked for outliers using scatter plots and any missing values were removed using .dropna() function. The .info() and .describe() functions were used to gain a further insight into the dataset and identify the type of data (e.g. integers and floats). A subset of the original dataset was created as outlined earlier, containing only data which was directly relevant to this research. Columns were renamed accordingly, and a correlation table was used to identify significant relationships between variables.

14.4   Machine learning classification models

A comparison of machine learning supervised classification models was made to investigate the suitability of their use in predicting hyperkalaemia from ECG data alone. Python programming language and PyCharm IDE were used due to its extensive selection of libraries and evidenced proficiency in machine learning [46]. Models used include SVM, k-NN, decision tree and Gaussian Naïve Bayes. These models were chosen as they have all been successfully used in previous research involving the prediction of cardiac disease from ECG data. Although a different medical condition, the findings are transferable due to similarities in identifying/classifying patterns and trends in ECG data.

After data preprocessing and visualisation have been performed, the data was then split into training and testing data. This is a method of cross-validation, a statistical technique that is used to test the performance of the machine learning model and is important in the reduction of selection bias and avoidance of overfitting. The function, 'X train,X test,Y train,Y test=traintestsplit', was used to split data into training and testing sets. The X variable consisted of a combination of attributes attained from ECG analysis, including heart rate, P-wave height, P–R duration, QRS complex, QT duration and QTc. Data was then normalised to enable comparison of data from multiple columns within the dataset. The Y variable was the blood potassium level which the model is aiming to predict based on the independent variables listed previously. The data was split into 80 per cent training and 20 per cent for testing.

14.4.1   Support vector machines

SVMs are a supervised learning technique capable of both classification and regression. It attempts to classify data by finding a hyperplane that linearly separates data from different classes [47]. The algorithm is given labelled training data and then outputs an optimal plane which categorises new examples. It finds a line/hyperplane in multidimensional space that separates out classes. Linear algebra is used to transform the problem and establish a suitably positioned hyperplane. Different kernel functions use algebraic equations for predicting new inputs. For the linear kernel which was used in this research, the prediction of a new input is made by using the dot product between the input x and each support vector x_i and is calculated with the following equation:

$$f(x) = B(0) + \text{sum}(a_i \times (x, x_i)) \tag{14.1}$$

This equation involves calculating the inner products of a new input vector x with all of the support vectors in the training dataset. $B(0)$ and a_i are coefficients that must be estimated by the learning algorithm, for each input from the training data. The 'C' parameter from the sklearn library is also known as the regularisation parameter. This informs the SVM optimisation how much to avoid misclassifying each training sample [48]. Higher values tend to produce a decreased occurrence in the instances of misclassification. The SVM algorithm from sklearn library was used with the training and testing data to predict a value for the blood potassium level.

14.4.2   k-Nearest neighbour

k-NN is another, simpler supervised machine learning algorithm that can be used in both classification and regression problems [49]. This algorithm involves the assumption that similar things exist in close proximity to one another and bases its classification method around the mathematical calculation of distance between points. It is a non-parametric learning algorithm that separates data points into different classes with the aim of predicting the class of a new sample point. A simplified step-by-step process of the k-NN algorithm is as follows:

Hu *et al.* [50] found k-NN to be useful in their research with EEG signal data; their findings can be applied in this research as the raw data is similar. The k-NN algorithm was imported from the sklearn library and training/testing data used to classify new input values as either being hypokalaemia, normokalaemia or hyperkalaemia.

14.4.3   Decision tree model

In computational complexity theories, the decision tree model is a model that essentially incorporates a sequence of branching operations based upon comparisons of some quantities which are assigned to the unit computational cost. They develop classification systems that are capable of forecasting future observations based on a set of pre-determined decision rules. The decision tree model is composed of nodes and edges, starting from a root node with no incoming edge. Instances are navigated from the root of the tree according to the decisions made by internal nodes and then classified [51] (Figure 14.5).

Algorithm 1: k-NN classifier

Require: training data (T) and testing data (D)
Ensure: $k \geq 1$ where $k \leftarrow 1, 2, 3, \ldots, n$
   Initialise the value of k
   for each data point d in D **do**
      calculate distance (Euclidean/Manhattan) (e) between d and all data point $t \in T$
      store e in list and sort in ascending order based on the distance values
      select k-nearest points according to k minimum distances.
   end for
   take the commonest class
   return the anticipated class

Verma *et al.* [53] successfully used a decision tree classifier in the prediction of cardiac arrhythmias using ECG signal data similar to that used in this research. Results showed the model to have an average predictive accuracy of 88.4 per cent which is significant enough to suggest potential usage in real-life implementation. Kasar and Joshi [54] also found that characteristics extracted from raw ECG signal data and feature vectors were compatible for use with their decision tree algorithm in the identification of cardiac disease. Evaluation showed their algorithm to have an average classification accuracy of 92.5 per cent which is relatively high, especially when compared with other classification models.

Existing research that uses decision tree models to classify ECG signal data is largely focused on the identification/prediction of cardiac disease/abnormalities; there is little application in the diagnosis of hyperkalaemia from ECG data alone. As discussed in the literature review, Hadjem and Naït-Abdesselam [28] used a decision tree technique to identify T-wave ECG abnormalities from ECG data after feature extraction had been performed. Results showed the decision tree model to have an overall accuracy of 92.5 per cent and a 7.5 per cent error rate. These findings are applicable to this research as the detection of T waves is highly significant in the identification of hyperkalaemia. Expanding on this, the pre-designed decision tree classifier was imported from the sklearn library using Python and used with multiple ECG features to enable a more precise prediction.

The use of T waves alone as an indicator of blood potassium level can lead to error and misdiagnosis as there are other possible causes for T-wave distortion/

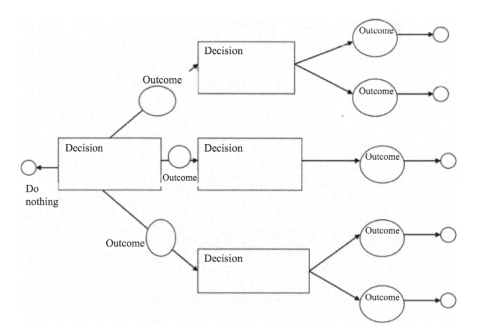

Figure 14.5   Decision tree model [52]

elevation [55]. Additional ECG changes indicative of hyperkalaemia were included in this research as well as T-wave peak height to enable a more accurate prediction and avoid misdiagnosis. The decision tree model was able to accommodate for the additional variables.

14.4.4   Gaussian Naïve Bayes model

Naïve Bayes is a probabilistic machine learning algorithm that is based on Bayes Theorem (Equation (14.2)) and can be used in multi-class classification problems. This approach is based on the simplistic hypothesis in that it assumes the presence/absence of a particular feature of a class is unrelated to the presence/absence of any of the other features involved, it follows the principle of conditional probability.

$$P(A|B) = \frac{P(B|A)P(A)}{P(B)} \tag{14.2}$$

where $P(A|B)$ denotes the probability of A given B, $P(B|A)$ denotes the probability of B given A, $P(A)$ denotes the probability of A occurring and $P(B)$ denotes the probability of A occurring. The Gaussian Naïve Bayes model is the simplest Naïve Bayes classifier with the assumption that the features in the dataset are normally distributed. The mean μ and standard deviation σ are estimated from the training data input values x for each class to summarise the distribution. Probabilities of new input x values are then calculated by using the Gaussian probability density function:

$$f(x, \mu, \sigma) = \frac{1}{\sigma\sqrt{2\pi}} \exp -\frac{x - \mu^2}{2\sigma^2} \tag{14.3}$$

Naïve Bayes classifiers have been used in previous research involving automated ECG data interpretation and abnormality detection like that used by Bayasi *et al.* [56] when they looked at predicting ventricular arrhythmias from ECG signal data. They used a Naïve Bayes classifier after feature selection had been performed, results showed the model to have an overall accuracy of 86 per cent when trained and tested. Sannino and De Pietro [57] also found a Naïve Bayes classifier to perform well in their research which was heartbeat detection and classification from ECG data which could be transferable in the diagnosis of hyperkalaemia due to similarities. As with the previous algorithms, Python was used again with the Gaussian Naïve Bayes model from the sklearn library.

14.5   Results

The prototype algorithm developed in MATLAB for PQRST feature extraction from raw ECG data successfully identified all peaks from the signals successfully. After the moving average filter, threshold signals and derivative base filter were applied, peaks were accurately found at the relevant points in the sample data. The algorithm was tested with the sample ECG data and performed well for all of the samples; an example is given of the output from one of the dataset samples in Figure 14.6.

Multiple machine learning models (SVM, k-NN, decision tree and Gaussian Naïve Bayes) were used with training and testing data, and accuracy used as a measure of classifier performance. Based solely on ECG data, the aim was for the models to distinguish between normokalaemia and hyperkalaemia. There were some instances of hypokalaemia in the sample data set but not enough to eliminate the issue of overfitting; this is something that could be explored further in future research. The decision tree model performed the best with 90.9 per cent predictive accuracy, k-NN achieved 77.3 per cent accuracy, SVM and Gaussian Naïve Bayes performed the worst as they both had approximately 72 per cent of accuracy. Kasar and Joshi [54] found the decision tree model to have 92.5 per cent of accuracy in a similar study; however, their goal was to identify cardiac disease from ECG data, specifically myocardial infarction in which ECG feature changes are much more distinguishable and intensified. Hyperkalaemia ECG changes vary between levels of serum potassium elevation which explains why a lower predictive accuracy was achieved in this instance.

Normal ECG parameters are given in Figure 14.1. Features extracted during peak analysis within these ranges can be classified as normokalaemia. Specific parameters leading to the classification of hyperkalaemia were identified as follows:

- T-wave amplitude greater than 0.53 mV
- QRS duration greater than 0.12 s
- PR interval greater than 0.22 s
- P-wave amplitude less than 0.04 mV

The presence of one or a combination of features found to be in the threshold/s listed earlier during peak analysis is highly likely to be classified as hyperkalaemia. This is very generalised and does not account for any cardiac abnormalities which should be considered and thresholds adapted accordingly.

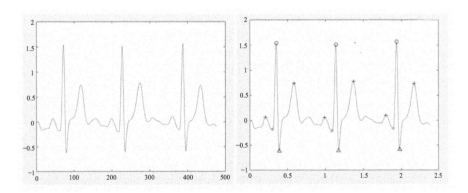

Figure 14.6   Sample ECG data before and after feature extraction

14.6   Conclusions and recommendations

This research has successfully produced a prototype of an algorithm for the feature extraction of PQRST peaks in MATLAB. Alternative existing algorithms such as the Pan–Tompkins algorithm [43] focus on identifying the QRS complex which alone is unsuitable in the diagnosis of hyperkalaemia as P and T waves are fundamentally affected by alterations in blood potassium levels. DWT is another frequently used method in feature extraction from ECG signals [38]. However, DWT uses kernels which can bias the shape of the signal to be similar to that of an arbitrary, preselected shape which could negatively impact on the accuracy of estimated potassium level.

Results showed that out of the four machine learning classification models tested (SVM, k-NN, decision tree and Gaussian Naïve Bayes), the decision tree model performed the best with 90.9 per cent of accuracy. This indicates that the decision tree model is the most suitable out of all of the models tested, in the identification of hyperkalaemia from ECG data. There is definite potential for the use of machine learning in recognising ECG changes associated with raised blood potassium levels.

This research has highlighted that machine learning has the potential to be hugely beneficial to people living with kidney disease and/or on dialysis. The early identification of hyperkalaemia will prevent symptoms, reduce the negative effects and decrease the risk of mortality as seeking treatment sooner is linked to a highly improved outcome for the individual [58]. The proposed prototype algorithms for hyperkalaemia detection have been designed separately on different platforms (MATLAB and Python). Future recommendations would be to merge and fully automate the algorithms enabling compatibility with mobile devices.

Further testing is also recommended with real-world testing involving a sample of patients from a population of people with kidney disease. Testing should be carried out thoroughly with ECGs from all participants obtained from the same mobile sensors in a controlled environment to exclude any bias or interference and maintain consistency. Blood samples should be collected from participants by a suitable qualified clinician to compare the actual value with that predicted by the machine learning model.

Existing literature suggests that mixed models which incorporate multiple algorithms into a combined model (e.g. deep learning and SVM) have performed very well in the identification of cardiac disease from raw ECG data. This has the potential to be useful in the detection of hyperkalaemia due to similarities in identifying trends and patterns in ECG signals. Combined classifiers should be further explored to ensure that the best possible model is developed.

References

[1]   Kidney Care UK. Facts and Stats; 2019. Available from: https://www.kidneycareuk.org/news-and-campaigns/facts-and-stats.

[2]   Kurniawan A and Hsu C. Association of kidney function-related dietary pattern, weight status, and cardiovascular risk factors with severity of impaired kidney

function in middle-aged and older adults with chronic kidney disease: a cross-sectional population study. Nutrition Journal. 2019;18(1):27.

[3] Montford J and Linus S. How dangerous is hyperkalemia? Journal of the American Society of Nephrology. 2017;28(11):3155–3165.

[4] Albright RC. Water and electrolyte disturbances in acute renal failure. Critical Care Nephrology. 2019;3:645–649.

[5] Noah B, Keller M, Stein L, *et al.* Impact of remote patient monitoring on clinical outcomes: an updated meta-analysis of randomized controlled trials. Digital Medicine. 2018;1(1):20172.

[6] Vashist SK and Luong JH. Wearable technologies for personalized mobile healthcare monitoring and management. Raymond Kai-Yu Tong (Ed.), In Wearable Technology in Medicine and Health Care. 2018;235–259.

[7] Corsi C, Cortesi M, Callisesi G, *et al.* Noninvasive quantification of blood potassium concentration from ECG in hemodialysis patients. Scientific Reports. 2017;7(1):42492. doi: 10.1038/srep42492.

[8] Beam A and Kohane I. Big data and machine learning in health care. JAMA. 2018;319(13):1317.

[9] Long B, Warix JR, and Koyfman A. Controversies in management of hyperkalemia. The Journal of Emergency Medicine. 2018;55(2):192–205.

[10] Opoku-Okrah C, Safo B, and Dogbe E. Changes in potassium and sodium concentrations in stored blood. Pan African Medical Journal. 2015;20:236.

[11] Núñez J, Bayés-Genís A, Zannad F, *et al.* Long-term potassium monitoring and dynamics in heart failure and risk of mortality. Circulation. 2018;137(13): 1320–1330.

[12] Sabiullah M, Rahmathunnisa R, and Veeramalla V. Fatal effects of hyper-kalemia. Journal of Evolution of Medical and Dental Sciences. 2015;4(76): 13267–13273.

[13] Viera AJ and Wouk N. Potassium disorders: hypokalemia and hyperkalemia. American Family Physician. 2015;92(6):487–495.

[14] Panneerselvam A. ECG in hyperkalaemia. Postgraduate Medical Journal. 2018;94(1115):537.

[15] Varga C, Kálmán Z, Szakáll A, *et al.* ECG alterations suggestive of hyper-kalemia in normokalemic versus hyperkalemic patients. BMC Emergency Medicine. 2019;19(1):33.

[16] Attia Z, DeSimone C, Dillon J, *et al.* Novel bloodless potassium determina-tion using a signal-processed single-lead ECG. Journal of the American Heart Association. 2016;5(1):e002746.

[17] Yasin O, Attia Z, Dillon J, *et al.* Noninvasive blood potassium measure-ment using signal-processed, single-lead ECG acquired from a handheld smartphone. Journal of Electrocardiology. 2017;50(5):620–625.

[18] Walker A and Muhlestein J. Smartphone electrocardiogram monitoring: current perspectives. Advanced Health Care Technologies. 2018;4:15–24.

[19] Waks J, Fein A, and Das S. Wide complex tachycardia recorded with a smart-phone cardiac rhythm monitor. JAMA Internal Medicine. 2015;175(3):437.

[20]   Rahman T and Amirfar V. AliveCor mobile ECG: a smartphone with heart. Pharmacy Today. 2016;22(3):56.

[21]   Kanchi S, Sabela M, Mdluli P, *et al.* Smartphone based bioanalytical and diagnosis applications: a review. Biosensors and Bioelectronics. 2018;102: 136–149.

[22]   Guzik P and Malik M. ECG by mobile technologies. Journal of Electrocardiology. 2016;49(6):894–901.

[23]   Majumder S, Mondal T, and Deen M. Wearable sensors for remote health monitoring. Sensors. 2017;17(1):130.

[24]   Luz E, Schwartz W, Cámara-Chávez G, *et al.* ECG-based heartbeat classification for arrhythmia detection: a survey. Computer Methods and Programs in Biomedicine. 2016;127:144–164.

[25]   Patro KK and Kumar PR. Effective feature extraction of ECG for biometric application. Procedia Computer Science. 2017;115(1):296–306.

[26]   Diker A, Avci E, Cömert Z, *et al.* Classification of ECG signal by using machine learning methods. In 2018 26th Signal Processing and Communications Applications Conference. Izmir Turkey: IEEE. 2018;p. 1–4.

[27]   Celin S and Vasanth K. ECG signal classification using various machine learning techniques. Journal of Medical Systems. 2018;42(12):241.

[28]   Hadjem M and Naït-Abdesselam F. An ECG T-wave anomalies detection using a lightweight classification model for wireless body sensors. In 2015 IEEE International Conference on Communication Workshop (ICCW). London, UK: IEEE. 2015; p. 278–283.

[29]   Galloway C, Valys A, Shreibati J, *et al.* Development and validation of a deep-learning model to screen for hyperkalemia from the electrocardiogram. JAMA Cardiology. 2019;4(5):428.

[30]   Rafique Z, Aceves J, Espina I, *et al.* Can physicians detect hyperkalemia based on the electrocardiogram? The American Journal of Emergency Medicine. 2020;38(1):105–108.

[31]   Velagapudi V, O'Horo JC, Vellanki A, *et al.* Computer-assisted image processing 12 lead ECG model to diagnose hyperkalemia. Journal of Electrocardiology. 2017;50(1):131–138.

[32]   Littmann L and Gibbs M. Electrocardiographic manifestations of severe hyperkalemia. Journal of Electrocardiology. 2018;51(5):814–817.

[33]   Dillon J, DeSimone C, Sapir Y, *et al.* Noninvasive potassium determination using a mathematically processed ECG: proof of concept for a novel "bloodless, blood test". Journal of Electrocardiology. 2015;48(1):12–18.

[34]   Pilia N, Dössel O, Lenis G, *et al.* ECG as a tool to estimate potassium and calcium concentrations in the extracellular space. In 2017 Computing in Cardiology. Rennes France: IEEE. 2017;p. 1–4.

[35]   Abdalla F, Wu L, Ullah H, *et al.* ECG arrhythmia classification using artificial intelligence and nonlinear and nonstationary decomposition. Signal, Image and Video Processing. 2019;13(7):1283–1291.

[36]   Gandham S and Bhuma A. ECG feature extraction and parameter evaluation for detection of heart arrhythmias. Journal on Digital Signal Processing. 2017;5(1):29.

[37] Demski A and Soria ML. ecg-kit: a Matlab toolbox for cardiovascular signal processing. Journal of Open Research Software. 2016;4(1):e8.

[38] Azariadi D, Tsoutsouras V, Xydis S, *et al.* ECG signal analysis and arrhythmia detection on IoT wearable medical devices. In 2016 5th International Conference on Modern Circuits and Systems Technologies (MOCAST). Thessaloniki Greece: IEEE. 2016; p. 1–4.

[39] Reddy KG, Vijaya PA, and Suhasini S. ECG signal characterization and correlation to heart abnormalities. International Research Journal of Engineering and Technology. 2017;4(5):1212–1216.

[40] Savalia S, Acosta E, and Emamian V. Classification of cardiovascular disease using feature extraction and artificial neural networks. Journal of Biosciences and Medicines. 2017;5(11):64.

[41] Malasri K and Wang L. Design and implementation of a secure wireless mote-based medical sensor network. Sensors (Basel, Switzerland). 2009;9:6273–6297. Available from: https://creativecommons.org/licenses/by/3.0/legalcode.

[42] Serum Potassium effects on ECG. Available from: https://nursekey.com/wp-content/uploads/2016/12/B9780323020404000134_f12-03-978032302040 4.jpg.

[43] Pan J and Tompkins W. A real-time QRS detection algorithm. IEEE Transactions on Biomedical Engineering. 1985;32(3):230–236.

[44] Lee C and Yoon H. Medical big data: promise and challenges. Kidney Research and Clinical Practice. 2017;36(1):3–11.

[45] Nie Y, Zou J, Liang Y, *et al.* Electrocardiographic abnormalities and QTc interval in patients undergoing hemodialysis. PLoS One. 2016;11(5): e0155445.

[46] Raschka S and Mirjalili V. Python Machine Learning. Birmingham, UK: Packt Publishing Ltd. 2017.

[47] Suthaharan S. Support vector machine. Machine Learning Models and Algorithms for Big Data Classification. USA: Springer. 2016;p. 207–235.

[48] Chapter 2: SVM (Support Vector Machine). Available from: https://medium.com/machine-learning-101/chapter-2-svm-support-vector-machine-theory-f0 812effc72.

[49] Zhang S, Li X, Zong M, *et al.* Efficient *k*-NN classification with different numbers of nearest neighbors. IEEE Transactions on Neural Networks and Learning Systems. 2017;29(5):1774–1785.

[50] Hu B, Li X, Sun S, *et al.* Attention recognition in EEG-based affective learning research using CFS+ *k*NN algorithm. IEEE/ACM Transactions on Computational Biology and Bioinformatics. 2016;15(1):38–45.

[51] Afkhami RG, Azarnia G, and Tinati MA. Cardiac arrhythmia classification using statistical and mixture modeling features of ECG signals. Pattern Recognition Letters. 2016;70:45–51.

[52] Decision Tree Model Template. Available from: https://www.wordtemplates online.net/wp-content/uploads/Decision-Tree-Example-650x452.png.

[53] Verma L, Srivastava S, and Negi PC. A hybrid data mining model to predict coronary artery disease cases using non-invasive clinical data. Journal of Medical Systems. 2016;40(7):178.

[54]   Kasar SL and Joshi MS. Analysis of multi-lead ECG signals using decision tree algorithms. International Journal of Computer Applications. 2016;134(16):27–30.

[55]   Jalanko M, Heliö T, Mustonen P, *et al.* Novel electrocardiographic features in carriers of hypertrophic cardiomyopathy causing sarcomeric mutations. Journal of Electrocardiology. 2018;51(76):983–989.

[56]   Bayasi N, Tekeste T, Saleh H, *et al.* Low-power ECG-based processor for predicting ventricular arrhythmia. IEEE Transactions on Very Large Scale Integration (VLSI) Systems. 1974;24(5):1962–1974.

[57]   Sannino G and De Pietro G. A deep learning approach for ECG-based heartbeat classification for arrhythmia detection. Future Generation Computer Systems. 2018;86:446–455.

[58]   Sterns RH, Grieff M, and Bernstein PL. Treatment of hyperkalemia: something old, something new. Kidney International. 2016;89(3):546–554.

Chapter 15

Combining deterministic compressed sensing and machine learning for data reduction in connected health

Hassan Rabah[1], Slavisa Jovanovic[1] and Naeem Ramzan[2]

Connected health is continuously developing, particularly with the advent of the Internet of Things (IoT) interconnecting various sensing nodes capable of measuring a person's vital signs such as electrocardiogram (ECG). In the years to come, the current forecasts indicate a significant increase in demand of such devices, especially among a currently underserved but significant population. Most of the existing devices performing measurement and data transmission require significant effort to integrate more intelligent processing or even decision-making, at least for data reduction and more autonomy. In this chapter, we propose to combine a simple compressed sensing (CS) measurement technique with a machine learning classification, both for data reduction and low power consumption. The classification is performed on compressed data, whereas the transmission is achieved only for warnings, by sending classification information in the case of a probable pathology detection, and if necessary the compressed data for further analysis. For data acquisition, we utilize a simple deterministic measurement matrix that facilitates the hardware implementation. The performance of the proposed approach is demonstrated using ECG recordings from three PhysioNet databases: MIT–BIH Arrhythmia Database, MIT–BIH Normal Sinus Rhythm Database and The BIDMC Congestive Heart Failure Database.

15.1 Introduction

The early and rapid detection of heart disorders is a very important act of surveillance, and even more critical than treatment to follow. These disorders can be diagnosed by real-time analysis of ECG signal. Continuous monitoring of cardiac health is possible and well approved thanks to the wireless body sensor network devices (WBSN) connected to the monitoring center via wireless links [1]. The challenges in such networks are mainly: limited available bandwidth, low memory capability, reduced

[1]Université de Lorraine, CNRS, IJL, Nancy, France
[2]School of Computing, Engineering and Physical Sciences, University of the West of Scotland, Paisley, UK

computational power and limited energy due to the use of small battery [2]. Research has shown that most of the power in a wireless biosensor is consumed by the radio transceiver during the data transmission [3]. Therefore, compressing data can reduce the power consumption of the wireless biosensors during transmission but requires sufficient computation power to perform compression.

CS is a technique suitable for compressing and recovering signals having sparse representations in certain bases [4]. CS has been widely used to compress the data while sensing the signal in the wireless biosensors because most of the bio-signals such as ECG have sparse representation in time domain or a given transform domain [5]. The main advantage with CS is that its acquisition process requires less computational power and addresses the constraints of the wireless biosensors. The complexity of the CS encoder depends on the description of the measurement matrix. Initially, random matrices were commonly used. However, they are difficult to implement in hardware. Recently, deterministic measurement matrices have been proposed to facilitate the hardware implementation [6,7]. On the other hand, the recovery process of CS is also computationally complex; and it is generally performed on a distant computer or in the cloud. Thus, even if there exist efficient algorithms and acceleration techniques, it is not suitable to use them for the real-time diagnosis.

From the detection point of view, machine learning algorithms for automatic classification of ECG signal have gained recently an increasing attention [8]. In this area, the focus is done on feature selection and extraction [9], and robustness of the machine learning classifiers [10]. In this chapter, we exploit the combination of CS and machine learning for data reduction, power consumption and real-time detection with respect to some features, instead of a full signal reconstruction. For the CS part, we propose the utilization of an encoder based on deterministic measurement matrix of our previous work, in association with machine learning to increase the capacity of a WBSN and to reduce the energy consumption of the wireless biosensors. The remainder of this chapter is organized as follows. Section 15.2 introduces the basics of CS, the proposed measurement matrix and the principle of classification in compressed domain. Detailed methods for compressive sensing, feature extraction and classification in the compressed domain are given in Section 15.3. The obtained results are provided in Section 15.4 and conclusions are given in Section 15.5.

15.2   Background and related work

15.2.1   Compressive sensing

Compressive sensing is a sensing procedure that compresses a signal at the time of acquisition. This technique relies on the sparsity of the signal of interest either in the time domain, in a transform basis or in a learned basis. A signal $\mathbf{x} \in \mathbb{R}^N$ is said to be K-sparse or compressible in a basis $\mathbf{\Psi} \in \mathbb{R}^{N \times N}$ if its transform $\alpha \in \mathbb{R}^N$ ($\mathbf{x} = \mathbf{\Psi}\alpha$) contains at most K nonzero or significant elements such that the remaining $(N - K)$ elements can be discarded without perceptible loss.

The K-sparse signal $\mathbf{x} \in \mathbb{R}^N$ is compressively sensed by multiplying it by a rectangular matrix $\mathbf{\Phi} \in \mathbb{R}^{M \times N}$ during the *acquisition process*, where $K < M < N$. The resulting vector $\mathbf{y} \in \mathbb{R}^M$ is called the measurement vector and $\mathbf{\Phi}$ is called the measurement or sensing matrix. Since $\mathbf{x}$ is sparse in a basis $\mathbf{\Psi}$, $\mathbf{y}$ is expressed as follows:

$$\mathbf{y} = \mathbf{\Phi}\mathbf{x} = \mathbf{\Phi}\mathbf{\Psi}\alpha \tag{15.1}$$

The *recovery process* reconstructs the original signal $\mathbf{x}$ from the measurement vector $\mathbf{y}$ by solving (15.1). Since $\mathbf{\Phi} \in \mathbb{R}^{M \times N}$ is a rectangular matrix ($M < N$), the problem formulated in (15.1) is ill posed and has infinite solutions. However, based on the knowledge that $\mathbf{x}$ is sparse in a basis $\mathbf{\Psi}$, the recovery process can be performed in two steps.

The first step finds the sparse vector $\tilde{\alpha}$ by solving the following minimization problem:

$$\min_{\tilde{\alpha}} \|\tilde{\alpha}\|_0 \text{ such that } \mathbf{\Phi}\mathbf{\Psi}\tilde{\alpha} = \mathbf{y} \tag{15.2}$$

Once the vector $\tilde{\alpha}$ has been obtained, the second step reconstructs the original signal as follows:

$$\tilde{\mathbf{x}} = \mathbf{\Psi}\tilde{\alpha} \tag{15.3}$$

The appropriate solution to (15.2) is generally computed by using convex relaxation-based and greedy-pursuits-based algorithms such as the orthogonal matching pursuit. In order to find the unique solution of (15.2), the measurement matrix $\mathbf{\Phi}$ must satisfy the restricted isometry property (RIP) condition [11]. $\mathbf{\Phi}$ is said to satisfy the K-RIP if there exists a restricted isometry constant δ_K, $0 < \delta_K < 1$ such that

$$(1 - \delta_K)\|\alpha\|_2^2 \leq \|\mathbf{\Phi}\mathbf{\Psi}\alpha\|_2^2 \leq (1 + \delta_K)\|\alpha\|_2^2 \tag{15.4}$$

for all K-sparse vectors α. In general, it is difficult to evaluate the RIP of a given matrix [12,13]. A sufficient condition used in CS literature is the incoherence between the measurement matrix $\mathbf{\Phi}$ and the sparsity basis $\mathbf{\Psi}$ [14]. The coherence μ between the two matrices is expressed as follows:

$$\mu(\mathbf{\Phi}, \mathbf{\Psi}) = \max_{i,j} \frac{|\langle \phi_i, \psi_j \rangle|}{\|\phi_i\|_2 \|\psi_j\|_2} \tag{15.5}$$

where $\phi_{i \in \{1,...,M\}}$ and $\psi_{j \in \{1,...,N\}}$, respectively, represent the row vectors of $\mathbf{\Phi}$ and the column vectors of $\mathbf{\Psi}$. The matrices $\mathbf{\Phi}$ and $\mathbf{\Psi}$ are incoherent if μ is small enough.

Initially random matrices, where the entries are generated by an independent and identically distributed Gaussian or Bernoulli process, are commonly used since they satisfy the RIP and low coherence with high probability [15]. Recently, more attention has been paid to deterministic measurement matrices [6,7,16]. Indeed, the hardware implementation of deterministic measurement matrix is simple. However, the reconstruction of signal $\tilde{\mathbf{x}}$ can be very costly especially in the case of IoT with limited computational resources and energy. Therefore, computing in a compressed domain can achieve good results, very reduced data communication and thus low power.

15.2.2   *Classification in compressed domain*

The last decade had witnessed an important activity in the area of processing in the compressed domain. The first research addressed the problem of efficient feature extraction from compressed video and audio data bases [17]. In the particular case of CS, where the measurements are obtained by projecting signal on random vectors, it was mathematically proven that CS measurement can be effectively used in signal classification [18]. In [19], Davenport *et al.* demonstrated that small numbers of nonadaptive compressive measurements can suffice to capture the relevant information required for accurate classification. They proposed a *smashed filter* that is based on a matched filter while stressing its compressive nature. Learning directly in the compressed domain has also been demonstrated in [20]. In [21], the authors exploited the discriminative nature of sparse representation to perform classification. CS has been combined with support vector machines (SVMs) in [20,22] and least squares regression [23]; it was shown that training based on the compressed data performs almost as well the best possible SVM classifier in the data domain. In [24], the authors presented novel approaches that can deal with complex machine learning problems. In particular, they show how to reduce the time needed to train feed-forward neural networks, considering only multilayer perceptrons. CS was also associated with deep learning in [25] for image classification. Random Gaussian measurement matrix and discrete cosine transform (DCT) matrix were applied to images and block-wise histograms used as a feature extractor. A convolutional CS framework was proposed in [26] by associating CS and CNN along with convolutional filters for image classification. Signal processing operations are applied directly to compressively sensed signal for classification by using discrete wavelet transform for feature extraction and K-means for clustering [27]. In [28], an end-to-end deep learning approach for CS is presented, in which a network composed of fully connected layers followed by convolutional layers performs the linear sensing and nonlinear inference stages. During the training phase, the sensing matrix and the nonlinear inference operator are jointly optimized, and the proposed approach outperforms state-of-the-art works for the task of image classification. In [29], the authors investigated the application of CS in planar tactile arrays. For the measurement matrix, the scrambled block Hadamard ensemble (SBHE) is used. SBHE is a partial block Hadamard transform with randomly permuted columns. The full signal is compressed using the SBHE matrix to generate the compressed signal of a single time instance of contact with an object. Soft-margin SVM is used for classification. Most of the existing works have focused on the image classification applications, and to the best of our knowledge most of the measurement matrices utilized for CS are random Gaussian. In this work, we propose the association of a simple deterministic measurement matrix associated to SVM classifier for ECG classification in the compressed domain. The following section gives the details of the proposed method.

15.3   Method

The proposed structure for real-time ECG monitoring is shown in Figure 15.1. This structure consists of three main operations: compressive sensing acquisition, feature extraction and classification. In the first operation, the signal $\mathbf{X} = \{\mathbf{x} \in \mathbb{R}^N\}$ is compressively sensed and provides the measurement data $\mathbf{Y} = \{\mathbf{y} \in \mathbb{R}^M\}$. The second operation generates the features $\mathbf{F}$ from the measurement vectors. The final operation, after training, classifies the features into different classes $\mathbf{C}$. The details of different operation are given in the following.

15.3.1   Compressive sensing acquisition

In most published papers on classification in the CS domain, the utilized matrices are randomly generated. The complexity of the CS acquisition depends on the description of the measurement matrix $\mathbf{\Phi}$. To facilitate the implementation of CS acquisition, particularly for low resource nodes, we utilize a deterministic binary block diagonal (DBBD) matrix developed in our previous work [7], which is described as follows:

$$\mathbf{\Phi}_{\text{DBBD}} = \begin{bmatrix} [1\dots1] & 0 & 0 & 0 \\ 0 & [1\dots1] & 0 & 0 \\ 0 & 0 & \ddots & 0 \\ 0 & 0 & 0 & [1\dots1] \end{bmatrix} \tag{15.6}$$

- $\mathbf{\Phi}_{\text{DBBD}}$ is binary since its elements belong to $\{0, 1\}$ set.
- $\mathbf{\Phi}_{\text{DBBD}}$ is block diagonal.
- Each block that composes the diagonal of $\mathbf{\Phi}_{\text{DBBD}}$ has a fixed length $m = N/M$ and can be viewed as a vector $\mathscr{B} \in \mathbb{R}^m$. We set all the elements of $\mathscr{B}$ to "1" as shown in (15.6).

In order to compare the performance of the *DBBD* matrix and the generally used matrix (random matrix), we evaluated the coherence between the inverse DCT (IDCT) matrix and these two matrices versus compression ratio (CR) defined as

$$CR(\%) = \frac{N - M}{N} \times 100;$$

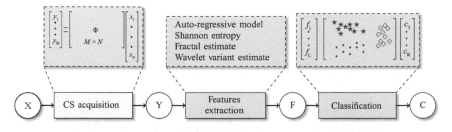

Figure 15.1   General structure of the proposed framework

where N and M are, respectively, the lengths of the vectors $\mathbf{x} \subset \mathbf{X}$ and $\mathbf{y} \subset \mathbf{Y}$. The results are shown in Figure 15.2.

Regardless the measurement matrix, we obtain a lower coherence μ by increasing the value of N. Notice that if CR is less than or equal to 80%, $\mu(\mathbf{\Phi}_{DBBD}, \mathbf{\Psi}_{IDCT})$ is lower than $\mu(\mathbf{\Phi}_{Gaussian}, \mathbf{\Psi}_{IDCT})$. For a CR of 90%, we obtain a slightly higher coherence μ with $\mathbf{\Phi}_{DBBD}$. However, there is no significant difference between them since the deviation is 0.06, which is much less than the upper boundary of μ.

15.3.2   Feature extraction

Feature extraction is an important part of the classification chain. The role of this part is not only to reduce data but also to extract relevant information for the classifier. For ECG signal, there are various features that are used to characterize the signal. In this work, we will utilize three kernels: auto-regressive (AR) model, Shannon entropy and fractal estimates. The feature extraction operation will generate the features vector $\mathbf{F} = \{f_1, f_2, \ldots, f_L\}$ consisting of concatenation of the outputs of the next detailed kernels.

15.3.2.1   Auto-regressive (AR) model

The AR model is applied to obtain the temporal structures of ECG waveforms. The AR model of order p consists of representing the signal y_m at a time instant m as a linear combination of p previous values of the same signal. Specifically, the process is modeled as $y_m = \sum_{i=1}^{p} a_i y_{m-i} + e_m$, where a_i is the ith coefficient of the model and e_m is a white noise with mean zero, and p the AR order. In our study, we choose $p = 4$ as in [30] where the authors used model order selection methods to determine that a fourth-order model provided the best fit for ECG waveforms; the features are noted $\{ar_1, ar_2, ar_3, ar_4\}$.

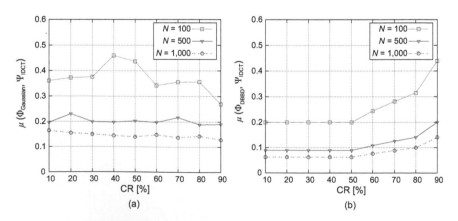

Figure 15.2   Coherence between measurement matrices, (a) $\mathbf{\Phi}_{Gaussian}$ and (b) $\mathbf{\Phi}_{DBBD}$, and transform domain $\mathbf{\Psi}_{IDCT}$ as a function of CR

15.3.2.2   Shannon entropy

In [31], the authors considered the separation of training and testing samples from the same set of patients. To this end, they proposed a method to classify ECG signals using the Shannon entropy computed on the terminal nodes of a wavelet packet. Shannon wavelet packet entropy is a powerful tool for transient signal analysis, which gives information on stroke evaluation. The wavelets are computed down to level 4 using maximal overlap discrete wavelet packet transform, thus giving 16 features $\{se_1, se_2, \ldots, se_{16}\}$.

15.3.2.3   Multifractal (MF) wavelet

Alterations to the control system of the heart are reflected in changes in the complex and irregular fluctuations of the ECG signal. Multifractal (MF) analysis is a tool suited for the analysis of this kind of fluctuations, since it gives a description of the singular behavior of a signal. Recently, a new approach for MF analysis was proposed, the wavelet leaders, which shows remarkable improvements over previous methods. In [32], the authors propose the application of wavelet-leader-based MF analysis in short-time windows with the aim of characterizing and detecting ischemic episodes. Two fractal measures computed by MF 1-D wavelet leader estimates are used as features. These features are a singularity spectrum, which is a measure of the MF nature of the ECG signal, and the holder exponent describes power-law behavior in the signal at different resolutions. These two features are denoted $\{mf_1, mf_2\}$.

15.3.2.4   Feature vector

Compressive sensing is applied to ECG data ($\mathbf{x} \in \mathbb{R}^N$). The compressively sensed data ($\mathbf{y} \in \mathbb{R}^M$) is fed to the feature extraction operation. The ration $R = N/M$ is utilized to define the size of time window for feature extraction. We define T as the total size of noncompressed data $\mathbf{X} = \{\mathbf{x}\}$ and T_W as a time window for feature extraction from noncompressed data. In this case, the number of features extracted for each window T_W is 22 (4 AR features, 16 Shannon entropy features and 2 MF wavelet features). The total number of features for noncompressed data is $L = 22 \, T/T_W$. All these features are concatenated to construct the feature vector $\mathbf{F} = \{ar_1, \ldots, ar_4, se_1, \ldots se_{16}, mf_1, mf_2\}$.

   When the feature extraction is applied to the compressively sensed data $\mathbf{Y}$, the size of the processing window is reduced with the same factor R as the total data. Thus, the number of features remains the same while processing a reduced number of data.

15.3.3   Classification

For the classification of ECG signal in the compressed domain, we use SVM; more details can be found, for example in [33]. SVMs were originally developed for binary classification. For a binary problem, given a set of l data elements $\mathbf{x}_i$ and their corresponding class y_i: $\{(\mathbf{x}_1, y_1), (\mathbf{x}_2, y_2), \ldots, (\mathbf{x}_l, y_l)\}$ where $\mathbf{x}_i \in \mathbb{R}^n$ and $y_i = \pm 1$ the training step consists of resolving the following quadratic programming problem with linear restrictions (note that here **x** and y are not the same as in the previous sections).

$$maximize : \sum_{i=1}^{l} \alpha_i - \frac{1}{2} \sum_{i,j=1}^{n} \alpha_i \alpha_j y_i y_j K(x_i, x_j),$$ (15.7)

$$subject\ to : 0 \leq \alpha_i \leq C\ (i = 1, \ldots, l), \sum_{i=1}^{l} \alpha_i y_i = 0$$ (15.8)

where $\alpha > 0$ are Lagrange multipliers. When the optimization problem is solved, many α_i will be equal to 0, and the others will be support vectors. C is positive constant that expresses degree of losing constraint and is empirically chosen by the user. A large C can classify training examples more correctly. $K(x_i, x_j)$ is the kernel function. In our case, a multi-class SVM with a quadratic kernel is used.

15.4   Experimental results and discussion

In this section, we present the experimental results for performing the feature extraction and classification in the compressively sensed data. We compare obtained results for random measurement matrix and proposed deterministic matrix. We also compare the obtained results for different compressing rates with no compression case.

15.4.1 Datasets

In the numerical experiments, we have used the ECG data from the MIT–BIH Arrhythmia Database corresponding to the normal heartbeat and two types of arrhythmia [34,35]. Each type of heartbeat was extracted from the record that contained most beats of this type. In this work, we utilized the available dataset in [36] where there are 96 recordings from persons with arrhythmia, 30 recordings from persons with congestive heart failures and 36 recordings from persons with normal sinus rhythms.

15.4.2 Training and validation results

The ECG dataset described previously uses 162 measurements sampled at 128 Hz. Each measurement has a size of 2^{16} samples. The measurements are labeled: *ARR* (arrhythmia), *CHF* (congestive heart failure) and *NSR* (normal sinus rhythm). The classifier is trained to distinguish among *ARR*, *CHF* and *NSR* in two cases: noncompressed data and compressively sensed data. In the two cases, 70% of dataset is used for training and the rest for validation. Features are extracted from the two subsets: features for training and features for validation. The feature vectors are composed of 22 features, as described earlier. In the case of noncompressed data, a time window of size 8, 192 is utilized to extract 22 features, thus giving a total of 176 features for each ECG signal. The same number of features is also extracted from the compressively sensed data. However, the size of time window is divided by the sensing rate thanks to the compression obtained by CS operation. The procedure is applied to each sensing rate and for the two types of measurement matrices: random Gaussian matrix Φ_{Gaussian} and deterministic matrix Φ_{DBBD}.

The performance of classifier in classifying the features extracted from original signal as well as from compressive measurements is compared using the standard metrics, i.e., accuracy, precision, recall (or sensitivity) and $F1$-score (weighted average of precision and recall). These are calculated from the parameters true positive (TP), true negative (TN), false positive (FP) and false negative (FN) as follows:

$$Accuracy = \frac{TP + TN}{TP + FP + FN + TN} \qquad Precision = \frac{TP}{TP + FP}$$

$$Recall = \frac{TP}{TP + FN} \qquad F1\text{-}score = 2 \times \frac{Recall \times Precision}{Recall + Precision}$$

Figures 15.3 and 15.4 show the values of these parameters in the confusion matrices for the deterministic measurement matrix and Gaussian matrix, with sampling rate varying from 1 to 16. The confusion matrices summarize the distributions for elements belonging to a given class (one per row: ARR, CHF or NSR) being assigned a given class label (one per column: ARR, CHF or NSR). The diagonal elements show the number of correct classification for each of the classes. The matrices show that performance is almost stable as R increases for Φ_{DBBD} matrix except for CHF class for $R = 16$, compared to the noncompressed data. However, the performance is degrading with increase of R especially for CHF class. These figures show that the proposed matrix performs better than Gaussian matrix.

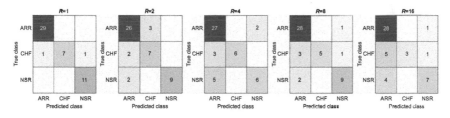

Figure 15.3 Confusion matrices of classification results by SVM classifier sensing matrix Φ_{DBBD} with sampling rates varying from $R = 1$ to 16

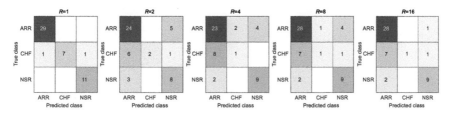

Figure 15.4 Confusion matrices of classification results by SVM classifier sensing matrix $\Phi_{Gaussian}$ with sampling rates varying from $R = 1$ to 16

Table 15.1 compares the accuracies obtained using original signal and the compressively sensed signal for different sensing rates and for the Gaussian and deterministic measurements matrices. The CS method with the proposed deterministic matrix Φ_{DBBD} is able to achieve better accuracies than the random Gaussian matrix $\Phi_{Gaussian}$. Precision, recall and $F1$ score are also used for the evaluation of the classifier. These metrics are shown, respectively, in Figures 15.5, 15.6 and 15.7

Table 15.1   Accuracies of SVM applied to the original signal and compressive measurements for Gaussian matrix and deterministic matrix for different sampling rates $R = N/M$

Sensing rate	CS signal dimension	$\Phi_{Gaussian}$ accuracy (%)	Φ_{DBBD} accuracy (%)
1 (no CS)	8,192	95.91	95.91
2	4,096	69.38	85.71
4	2,048	67.34	79.59
8	1,024	69.38	85.71
16	512	77.55	77.55

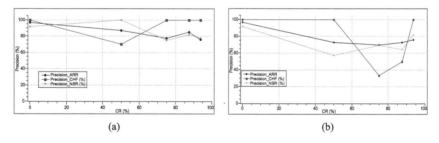

(a)   (b)

Figure 15.5   Precision for ARR, CHF and NSR as a function of CR: (a) Φ_{DBBD} sensing matrix and (b) $\Phi_{Gaussian}$ sensing matrix

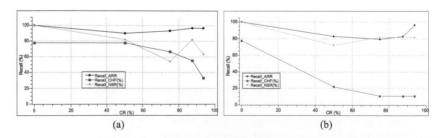

(a)   (b)

Figure 15.6   Recall for ARR, CHF and NSR as a function of CR: (a) Φ_{DBBD} sensing matrix and (b) $\Phi_{Gaussian}$ sensing matrix

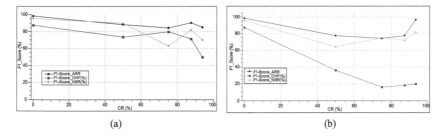

(a)   (b)

Figure 15.7   F1-Score for ARR, CHF and NSR as a function of CR: (a) Φ_{DBBD} sensing matrix and (b) $\Phi_{Gaussian}$ sensing matrix

demonstrating again that the proposed Φ_{DBBD} matrix is capable of not only preserving information on ECG classes but also performing better than widely user random measurement matrix.

15.5   Conclusion

The Nyquist sampling technique has shown its limitation due to the huge data that can be generated. Compressive sampling has demonstrated to be very efficient in data reductions, but to the detriment of expensive deported processing, which is not suitable for continuous monitoring and real-time decision-making in low power and low resources wireless devices. In this chapter, we have presented a method based on a combination of deterministic CS and machine learning for data reduction in connected health. The method is applied to ECG signal classification in the compressed domains without reconstructing the signal. We demonstrate that is possible to capture the difference between the normal heartbeat and two types of arrhythmia by the performance of the SVM classifier on the test set. We also compared the performances of a simple deterministic measurement matrix with random Gaussian measurement matrix. The obtained results, particularly precision and accuracy, of the deterministic matrix are far superior to that of random Gaussian matrix.

References

[1]   Pantelopoulos A and Bourbakis N. A Survey on Wearable Sensor-Based Systems for Health Monitoring and Prognosis. IEEE Transactions on Systems, Man, and Cybernetics, Part C: Applications and Reviews. 2010;40(1):1–12.

[2]   Pal R, Gupta B, Prasad N, Prasad R. Efficient data processing in ultra low power wireless networks: Ideas from compressed sensing. In: 2nd International Symposium on Applied Sciences in Biomedical and Communication Technologies, 2009. ISABEL 2009; 2009. p. 1–2. Available from: https://doi.org/10.1109/ISABEL.2009.5373662.

[3]   Chen F, Chandrakasan A, and Stojanovic V. Design and Analysis of a Hardware-Efficient Compressed Sensing Architecture for Data Compression in Wireless Sensors. IEEE Journal of Solid-State Circuits. 2012;47(3):744–756.

[4]   Donoho D. Compressed Sensing. IEEE Transactions on Information Theory. 2006;52(4):1289–1306.

[5]   Ciocoiu I. Foveated Compressed Sensing. Circuits, Systems, and Signal Processing. 2014:1–15. Available from: http://dx.doi.org/10.1007/s00034-014-9878-2.

[6]   Zeng L, Zhang X, Chen L, *et al.* Deterministic Construction of Toeplitzed Structurally Chaotic Matrix for Compressed Sensing. Circuits, Systems, and Signal Processing. 2014:1–17. Available from: http://dx.doi.org/10.1007/s00034-014-9873-7.

[7]   Ravelomanantsoa A, Rabah H, and Rouane A. Compressed Sensing: A Simple Deterministic Measurement Matrix and a Fast Recovery Algorithm. IEEE Transactions on Instrumentation and Measurement. 2015;64(12):3405–3413.

[8]   Mustaqeem A, Anwar SM, and Majid M. Multiclass Classification of Cardiac Arrhythmia Using Improved Feature Selection and SVM Invariants. Computational and Mathematical Methods in Medicine. 2018;2018:1–10.

[9]   de Chazal P, O'Dwyer M, and Reilly RB. Automatic Classification of Heartbeats Using ECG Morphology and Heartbeat Interval Features. IEEE Transactions on Biomedical Engineering. 2004;51(7):1196–1206.

[10] Ince T, Kiranyaz S, and Gabbouj M. A Generic and Robust System for Automated Patient-Specific Classification of ECG Signals. IEEE Transactions on Biomedical Engineering. 2009;56(5):1415–1426.

[11] Candès EJ. The Restricted Isometry Property and Its Implications for Compressed Sensing. Comptes Rendus Mathematique. 2008;346(9):589–592. Available from: http://www.sciencedirect.com/science/article/pii/S163 1073X08000964.

[12] Ben-Romdhane M, Rebai C, Desgreys P, Ghazel A, and Loumeau P. Flexible baseband analog front-end for NUS based multistandard receiver. In: Joint IEEE North-East Workshop on Circuits and Systems and TAISA Conference, Toulouse; 2009. p. 1–4. Available from: http://10.1109/NEWCAS.2009.5290417.

[13] Bandeira A, Dobriban E, Mixon DG, *et al.* Certifying the Restricted Isometry Property Is Hard. IEEE Transactions on Information Theory. 2013;59(6):3448–3450.

[14] Gangopadhyay D, Allstot E, Dixon A, *et al.* Compressed Sensing Analog Front-End for Bio-Sensor Applications. IEEE Journal of Solid-State Circuits. 2014;49(2):426–438.

[15] Baraniuk R. Compressive Sensing [Lecture Notes]. IEEE Signal Processing Magazine. 2007;24(4):118–121.

[16] Tang Y, Lv G, and Yin K. Deterministic Sensing Matrices Based on Multidimensional Pseudo-Random Sequences. Circuits, Systems, and Signal Processing. 2014;33(5):1597–1610. Available from: http://dx.doi.org/10.1007/s00034-013-9701-5.

[17]   Wang H, Divakaran A, Vetro A, *et al.* Survey of Compressed-Domain Features Used in Audio-Visual Indexing and Analysis. Journal of Visual Communication and Image Representation. 2003;14(2):150–183.

[18]   Haupt J, Castro R, Nowak R, *et al.* Compressive sampling for signal classification. In: 2006 Fortieth Asilomar Conference on Signals, Systems and Computers. Pacific Grove, CA, USA: IEEE; 2006.

[19]   Davenport MA, Duarte MF, Wakin MB, *et al.* The smashed filter for compressive classification and target recognition. In: Bouman CA, Miller EL, and Pollak I, editors. Proceedings Volume 6498, Computational Imaging V; 64980H, San Jose, CA, USA; 2007. https://doi.org/10.1117/12.714460

[20]   Calderbank R, Jafarpour S, and Schapire R. Compressed Learning: Universal Sparse Dimensionality Reduction and Learning in the Measurement Domain. Princeton University; 2009. Available from: http://dsp.rice.edu/files/cs/cl.pdf.

[21]   Wright J, Yang AY, Ganesh A, *et al.* Robust Face Recognition via Sparse Representation. IEEE Transactions on Pattern Analysis and Machine Intelligence. 2008;31(2):210–227.

[22]   Calderbank R and Jafarpour S. Finding needles in compressed haystacks. In: INSPEC Accession Number: 12966276. IEEE, Kyoto, Japan; 2012. DOI: 10.1109/ICASSP.2012.6288656.

[23]   Maillard OA and Munos R. Compressed least-squares regression. In: NIPS 2009. Vancouver, Canada; 2009. Available from: https://hal.inria.fr/inria-00419210.

[24]   Fabisch A, Kassahun Y, Wöhrle H, *et al.* Learning in Compressed Space. Neural Networks. 2013;42:83–93.

[25]   Gan Y, Zhuo T, and He C. Image classification with a deep network model based on compressive sensing. In: 2014 12th International Conference on Signal Processing (ICSP). IEEE, Hangzhou, China; 2014. DOI: 10.1109/ICOSP.2014.7015204.

[26]   Snoek J, Rippel O, Swersky K, *et al.* Scalable Bayesian optimization using deep neural networks. In: Bach F and Blei D, editors. Proceedings of the 32nd International Conference on Machine Learning. vol. 37 of Proceedings of Machine Learning Research. Lille, France: PMLR; 2015. p. 2171–2180. Available from: http://proceedings.mlr.press/v37/snoek15.html.

[27]   Shoaib M, Jha NK, and Verma N. Signal Processing With Direct Computations on Compressively Sensed Data. IEEE Transactions on Very Large Scale Integration (VLSI) Systems. 2015;23(1):30–43.

[28]   Adler A, Elad M, and Zibulevsky M. Compressed Learning: A Deep Neural Network Approach. ArXiv. 2016;abs/1610.09615.

[29]   Hollis B, Patterson S, and Trinkle J. Compressed Learning for Tactile Object Recognition. IEEE Robotics and Automation Letters. 2018;3(3):1616–1623.

[30]   Zhao Q and Zhang L. ECG feature extraction and classification using wavelet transform and support vector machines. In: 2005 International Conference on Neural Networks and Brain. IEEE, Beijing, China; 2005. DOI: 10.1109/ICNNB.2005.1614807.

[31]   Li T and Zhou M. ECG Classification Using Wavelet Packet Entropy and Random Forests. Entropy. 2016;18(8):285.

[32]   Leonarduzzi RF, Schlotthauer G, and Torres ME. Wavelet leader based multifractal analysis of heart rate variability during myocardial ischaemia. In: 2010 Annual International Conference of the IEEE Engineering in Medicine and Biology. IEEE, Buenos Aires, Argentina; 2010. DOI: 10.1109/IEMBS.2010.5626091.

[33]   Cristianini N and Shawe-Taylor J. An Introduction to Support Vector Machines and Other Kernel-Based Learning Methods. Cambridge University Press; 2000. DOI: https://doi.org/10.1017/CBO9780511801389.

[34]   Goldberger AL, Amaral LAN, Glass L, *et al.* PhysioBank, PhysioToolkit, and PhysioNet. Circulation. 2000;101(23):e215–e220.

[35]   Moody GB and Mark RG. The Impact of the MIT-BIH Arrhythmia Database. IEEE Engineering in Medicine and Biology Magazine. 2001;20:45–50.

[36]   MATLAB, editor. Signal Classification Using Wavelet-Based Features and Support Vector Machines; 2019.

Chapter 16

Large-scale distributed and scalable SOM-based architecture for high-dimensional data reduction

Slavisa Jovanovic[1], Hassan Rabah[1], and Serge Weber[1]

The Internet of Things (IoT) is generating and collecting a huge amount of data of different types by distributed sensing nodes over time. The acquisition, aggregation and processing of these data strain the overall data chain at all levels: first, at the sensing node level where very limited power budgets constrain their computation capabilities; and second, at the cloud level where decision should be made within tight and often hard timing requirements based on the received data which, prior to sending back the decision to IoT nodes, undergo aggregation and processing. On the other hand, these hard timing constraints direct the initial IoT paradigm of a myriad of highly connected nodes and centralized cloud computing for decision-making to edge computing, where a part of the centralized computation and processing is pushed away from cloud to distributed nodes making them more autonomous and less dependent on the centralized decision and bandwidth bottlenecks. Even though the distributed nodes are gaining more computation power, a huge amount of data collected over time by a node are often difficult or even impossible to process at the edge level. In order to extract useful information needed for prediction purposes or control decisions, due to the redundancy of the collected data streams, a common solution is to reduce their dimensionality before their further processing by the means of clustering, vector quantization, compression, etc. Machine learning such as self-organizing feature maps (SOMs) is a commonly used technique for clustering and data dimensionality reduction. In fact, their inherent property of topology preservation and unsupervised learning of processed data put them in the front of candidates for data reduction. However, the high computational cost of SOMs limits their use to offline approaches and makes the on-line real-time high-performance SOM processing more challenging. In this chapter, we focus on the large-scale distributed and scalable SOM model adapted for distributed computing nodes and present the main challenges for its adoption in the resources limited environments.

[1]Université de Lorraine, CNRS, IJL, Nancy, France

16.1　Introduction

In the era of IoT and Big Data, a huge amount of data of all types are continuously produced at high-speed rates by highly connected and distributed nodes employed in many application fields [1]. Even though the distributed nodes have higher computation capabilities, it is often difficult or even impossible to process all collected data at the sensor and/or edge level. In order to extract useful information from acquired data needed for prediction purposes or control decisions at the sensor or edge level, due to the redundancy of the collected data streams, a common solution is to reduce data dimensionality before further processing. The techniques and tools for data reduction allowing to considerably reduce the amount of data before their processing without losing the most relevant information are gaining more attention in the recent years [1–3]. Data mining techniques allowing to reduce the data dimensionality, to cluster or fusion data and thus reduce their quantity are commonly used for this purpose [3]. These techniques, belonging to the broader group of tools and techniques called Big Data analytics, especially address the preprocessing steps in the Big Data chain such as clustering, vector quantization, compression, etc. [4]. In the literature, different methods such as hierarchical [5], squared error-based [6], graph theory-based [7], fuzzy systems [8], neural networks-based [9] and data visualization [10,11] can be found. They can be [2] parametric or nonparametric, based on the use of linear or nonlinear kernels for data projection, with different times and computational complexities, using vectorial or distance-based data types, suited or not for large input data sets, supervised or unsupervised. Among these techniques, we find some machine-learning approaches such as SOMs. They are parametric, nonlinear, unsupervised, suitable for large data sets and data visualization. Moreover, their inherent property of topology preservation and unsupervised learning of processed data with a linear time and computational complexity put them in the front of candidates for data reduction. However, the high computational cost of SOMs limits their use to offline approaches and makes the online real-time high-performance SOM processing more challenging.

Different implementations of SOMs can be found in the literature [12–22]. They can be in software (SW) programable platforms (CPU and/or GPU), in dedicated hardware, field programable gate array (FPGA) or application-specific integrated circuit (ASIC), or in mixed HW/SW platforms. The SW programable SOMs have more flexibility, especially in terms of SOM network parameters which can be easily adapted to satisfy different application needs. However, these implementations are often strayed from embedded and power-constrained environments due to their high power consumption and unsuitability to respect tight real-time constraints found in some application domains. Unlike SW SOMs, SOM implementations in dedicated hardware offer a high performance per watt ratio and may be preferred in hard real-time environments. On the downside, their limited flexibility confines their use to application-specific domains, where all parameters (vector dimension, network size, timing and memory constraints) are predefined in advance in the design phase. In order to use SOMs in hard real-time application-agnostic embedded environments, both the high flexibility allowing to adapt the SOM parameters to any application needs and high performances to process continuously arriving data streams are needed. In the present study, the main focus is on the model of large-scale, distributed, highly configurable and scalable HW SOMs based on the recent works in the field, allowing one to provide new insights and orientations in the design of future HW SOMs.

The rest of this chapter is organized as follows: Section 16.2 presents the state-of-the-art SOM implementations. The SOM algorithm is described in Section 16.3. The proposed large-scale SOM HW model is presented in Section 16.4. The results of validation of the proposed model as well as the obtained results for different parameters are all shown and discussed in Section 16.5. Finally, Section 16.6 gives the concluding remarks and the future outlook of this work.

16.2 Related work

The SW programable SOM implementations mainly depend on the type of the used hardware support. In [12], Chen *et al.* proposed a novel SW CPU-based SOM implementation with the possibility of dynamically modifying the number of learning iterations depending on the nature of input data. A color quantization application was used for validation purpose of the proposed implementation where some improvements were observed at the quantization level due to the proposed configurability, but at the expense of the overall performances. Kuremoto *et al.* in [13] proposed a flexible and adaptable SW programable CPU-based SOM architecture with capabilities of additional learning, optimal neighborhood preservation and automatic tuning of paramcters through growing of the initial SOM structure during the learning phase. However, the gained flexibility is obtained to the detriment of poor timing performances. A multi-GPU-based SOM implementation was proposed by De *et al.* [14], which provides much better timing performances compared to thc existing CPU-based implementations but remains still inadequate for real-time applications due to the limited performances expressed in millions of connection updates per second (MCUPS) per consumed watt.

Dedicated hardware for SOM implementations provide real-time capabilities and good performances per watt ratio compared to the CPU- or GPU-based solutions previously presented. Such SOM implementations are commonly emulated in FPGAs or manufactured as customized ASICs. Hikawa and Maeda proposed an FPGA-based hardware SOM in [20]. The SOM algorithm is implemented in a fully parallel manner on a network of 16×16 SOM neurons with an improved neighborhood function. The obtained MCUPS performances are the best among those reported in the literature, but to the detriment of the flexibility: no parameter change is possible during the SOM operation. In [19], Tamukoh and Sekine proposed a dynamically reconfigurable HW SOM where the flexibility is introduced by exploiting the dynamic reconfiguration of FPGAs at the expense of limited timing performances. A multi-FPGA-based hardware implementation of SOM is proposed by Lachmair *et al.* in [23]. The proposed scalable architecture is reconfigurable and adaptable to different applications and was validated on hyperspectral imaging data sets on the large SOM networks connected between multiple FPGAs through bus-based communication approach. The obtained performances are also among the best ones reported in the literature. In [22,24], Abadi *et al.* were among the first who addressed the problem of scalability and flexibility of the HW SOMs. They proposed a layered architecture where the computation layer composed of neurons is completely decoupled from the communication one implemented with a network-on-chip (NoC) approach. Consequently, more flexibility has been given to the whole architecture, but to the detriment of the overall system performances. The proposed approach has been used to propose a novel HW SOM architecture capable of processing multiple data sets by the means of simple reconfiguration [25]. As a result, different applications characterized with different needs (and SOM parameters) can be processed simultaneously within the same HW SOM architecture. Moreover, the same idea was exploited in [26] to propose an HW SOM architecture having, to the best of our knowledge, the best performances in terms of MCUPS reported in the literature so far.

From the presented literature survey, it can be noticed that in the field of SOM implementations, the ultimate objective is to have both the high flexibility and scalability of SW SOMs, and the high performances and low power consumption of HW SOMs. The recent works in the field of SOM implementations showed that very promising solutions are the ones based on the distribution of the SOM operation over a highly connected network of routers called *network-of-chip* [22,24–26]. The work presented in this chapter follows these ultimate guidelines and presents a realistic model of such HW SOM architectures allowing future exploration of possible architectural choices to take in their design.

16.3 Background

The original SOM algorithm proposed by Kohonen is presented in Algorithm 1 [27]. A set G of neurons, each one characterized by its own weight $\vec{w}$ randomly initialized, goes iteratively through two phases: learning and recall. In each iteration, carried out in both learning and recall phases, an input vector $\vec{\xi}$ from input space X of the same size as $\vec{w}$ is presented and compared to the latter. The metric used to compare these two vectors ($\vec{\xi}$ and $\vec{w}$) is usually the Euclidean distance (see lines 5–7 of Algorithm 1). Once these distances d_n ($n \in G$) are calculated for all neurons, the best matching unit (BMU) or the winning neuron n_c, which is the neuron having the weights closest to the input vector, has to be identified (line 8 of Algorithm 1). If the network is in the recall phase (all neurons previously trained), the algorithm ends up with the identification of the BMU. On the other hand, if the network is in the learning phase, at the end of each iteration after identifying the BMU, the weights of all neurons in its vicinity ($n \in G_c \subset G$) should be adapted (see lines 9–13 of Algorithm 1). The neurons whose weights will be adapted are identified by their relative position with respect to the BMU. If a position of a given neuron with respect to the BMU's one is below or equal to N_R, where N_R is the neighboring ratio, its weights will be adapted, otherwise no. The adaptation of neurons' weights is expressed by lines 14–17 of Algorithm 1, where

---

Algorithm 1: SOM algorithm [27]

---

1 **SOM** (G, X)

> **inputs :** The set G of neurons with weights $\vec{w}$; The set X of input vectors $\vec{\xi}$
> **output:** The set G of trained neurons

2   initialize h_ε parameters, N_R, i_t

3   **foreach** $n \in G$ **do**

4       $\vec{w_n} \leftarrow$ random vector

5   **for** i_t *random* $\vec{\xi}$ **do**

6   **foreach** $n \in G$ **do**

7          $d_n \leftarrow \| \vec{\xi} - \vec{w_n} \|_2$

8       $c = \underset{n \in G}{argmin}(d_n)$

9   **if** *learning* **then**

10          $G_c \leftarrow \emptyset$

11   **foreach** $n \in G$ **do**

12   **if** $\|r_n - r_c\| \le N_R$ **then**

13                $G_c \leftarrow G_c \cup \{n\}$

14   **foreach** $n \in G_c$ **do**

15             $\varepsilon_n \leftarrow h_\varepsilon(n, n_c)$

16             $\vec{w_n} \leftarrow \vec{w_n} + \varepsilon_n(\vec{\xi} - \vec{w_n})$

17   update h_ε parameters, N_R

18   **return** G;

ε_n is the neighborhood function used to define the degree of learning of a neuron and is often defined by

$$\varepsilon_n = \alpha \times \exp\left(-\frac{\| \vec{r}_n - \vec{r}_c \|}{2\sigma^2}\right) \tag{16.1}$$

with α, σ, $\vec{r}_c$ and $\vec{r}_n$ representing, respectively, learning and neighborhood rate, BMU's position and position of the neuron n. The parameters α and σ are the parameters of the neighboring function ε_n. On the other hand, the neurons of the SOM are often organized in a mesh rectangular grid $L \times K$ and the neighboring ratio N_R is in that case initialized to $(L + K)/2$.

16.4 Proposed SOM model

The architecture of the proposed SOM model is presented in Figure 16.1(a), where $L \times K$ clusters of neurons are interconnected via the same number of NoC routers.

Each cluster is composed of a 2D mesh of $M \times N$ neurons, all connected to a common module called cluster winner search (CWS). The clusters exchange data via NoC routers to which they are connected through a network interface (NI) module. The NI ensures all communication tasks of a cluster: reception of input data vectors and identities of local BMUs during the BMU search operation, and the identity of the global BMU at each iteration; and the sending of the local cluster BMU to other clusters of the network. In the next sections, the behavioral models of all blocks of the presented SOM architecture are detailed.

16.4.1   NoC router model

The synoptic scheme of the NoC router used in this SOM architecture is presented in Figure 16.1(c). Each router has five bidirectional links allowing one to connect it to four direct neighboring routers in a 2D mesh grid in directions called West (W), South (S), East (E) and North (N) (see Figure 16.1(c)), and to the processing element directly attached to the router, the direction called Local (L). A pair of FIFO buffers

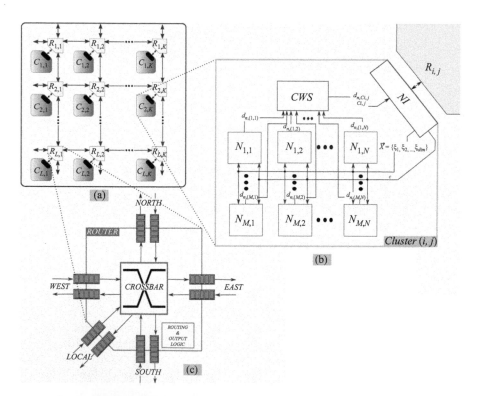

Figure 16.1   *Proposed SOM architecture: (a) $L \times K$ neurons interconnected with a 2D network-on-chip of the same size, (b) neuron's synoptic scheme architecture, (c) NoC router internal architecture and (d) an example of message exchange taking place in the proposed architecture*

per input/output port at each side (W, S, E, N and L) is used to store temporarily the incoming data before their routing through output ports to final destination. The NoC router used in this SOM model employs the wormhole switching technique, where a message carrying data to transport between source and destination is decomposed in the smallest data units called flits. There are two types of messages used in this architecture: one-flit messages or header messages, and more-than-one flit messages. Each message starts with a *header*, which carries out the routing information (the destination address) for the whole message. In the case of more-than-one flit messages, each message contains two other flits: *body* flit containing the data payload and *tail* flit which is the last body flit of a message. Each of these flits has its own code allowing the router receiving them to manage the established connection between its input and output ports without interruption.

The state diagram of the input/output function of the proposed NoC router model is presented in Figure 16.2. The proposed router implements five input/output functions, one per input port. The main goal of this function is to read the incoming data, to decode each flit type and to transfer them finally to the corresponding output port according to the destination address carried out in their header flit. The input/output function starts with the reading of the header flit of the first message (state *readh* in Figure 16.2). This state is reading the data stored in the input FIFO buffer. If no data

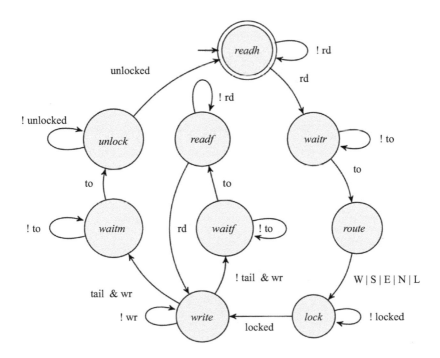

Figure 16.2   State diagram of the input/output function of the proposed router model

are stored in this buffer, no read operation will be executed (rd low), the input/output function remains blocked in this state. The move to the *waitr* state is achieved upon the reception of a header flit, or after the read operation of the input FIFO buffer (rd high). The *waitr* state models the NoC router latency. The move to the next is possible when the timeout signal to of this waiting period is generated. After being delayed by the router latency, the header flit of the incoming data is used to find the output port of the router through which the data will leave the router. This is done in the *route* state. The result of this operation is the name of one of the five output ports: W, S, E, N or L. The identified output port should be locked before its use by an input/output function. The output port locking is done in *lock* state where a fair mutex mechanism is used to handle multiple accesses to the same output port. If the output port identified in the *route* state is unavailable, the signal locked will be set to low and the input/output function will be blocked in the *lock* state; otherwise it will be set to high and will allow one to move to the next write state. In the *write* state, the data are written to the output port (wr high) if the corresponding output buffer is not full; otherwise the function will be blocked (wr low) in this state until the availability of free slots in the output buffer. Depending on the type of data message that is received, the input/output function will leave the *write* state toward inner state loop *waitf*-*readf*-*write* for more-than-one flit messages (tail high), or toward *waitm* for one flit messages (tail low). In the former case, all following flits (body and tail flits) will be written on the same reserved output port as they arrive. The state *waitf* ensures the respect of the flit latency between all written flits, whereas the state *readf* allows one to read all remaining flits one by one in the loop and to write them in the write state. In the one-flit message case, from the *write* state the input/output function moves to the *waitm* state, where the inter-message latency waiting is produced. Before joining the initial *readh* state, the input/output function passes through

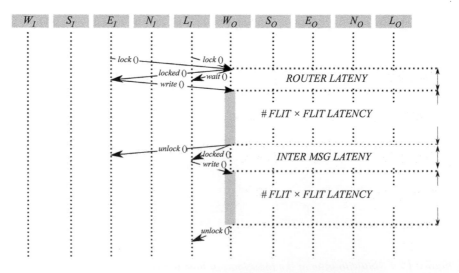

Figure 16.3   Synoptic scheme of sharing the same output port

unlock state where the previously reserved output port is released (unlocked high). Figure 16.3 illustrates an example of managing writing to the same output port by two input/output functions. Both functions try to lock the same output port at the same time. In this case, one of them will be randomly chosen to access the requested output port, while the other will remain locked at the time of writing the whole data message by the first one. The fair mutex mechanism used in this model allows one to avoid starvation situations where an output port is monopolized by some input ports. Table 16.1 summarizes the main parameters and properties of the presented NoC router model.

16.4.2   Neuron model

The smallest processing unit in the SOM algorithm is called neuron. It ensures the calculation of the Euclidean distance and the update of its weights in each iteration (lines 7 and 16 in Algorithm 1, respectively). The behavior of the neuron model used in this architecture is described with the state diagrams of distance and update functions presented, respectively, in Figure 16.4(a) and (b). Although these two functions are

Table 16.1   NoC router model properties

	Number	Type	Description
Inputs	5	FIFO	Inputs toward W, S, E, N and L side
Outputs	5	FIFO	Outputs toward W, S, E, N and L side
Parameters	4	–	Router, flit, inter message latency; data type

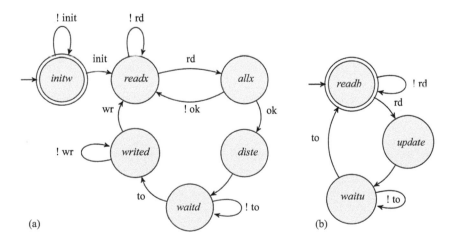

Figure 16.4   State diagrams of the main functions in the proposed neuron model: (a) distance calculation function and (b) weights update function

implemented in parallel in the presented model, they are executed sequentially in the SOM algorithm because the update of the neuron's weights is done at the end of each iteration, which starts with the distance calculation. The presented neuron model has three inputs (see Table 16.2), of which two are used to supply weights and input vectors to the neuron and its distance calculation function. The weights vector input is used only in the initialization phase, depicted with *initw* in the state diagram from Figure 16.4(a). In this state, the weights of a neuron are initialized with the random values supplied by the user. The weight vector supplying as well as the input vector supplying (described later) are done sequentially by reading at one time a chunk of vector elements, whose size is also configurable with the used data type. For instance, if the size of the chunk is configured to one vector element, an N-element vector will be read sequentially in N cycles. When the initialization phase is done (`init` high), the distance calculation function moves to the *readx* state, where the input vector is acquired before Euclidean distance calculation. In the *readx* state, the input vector is read sequentially, one chunk by chunk (`rd` high), and the `allx` states ensure that the whole input vector is read before distance calculation (`ok` high). Once the input vector is entirely acquired by the neuron, the distance calculation function moves to *diste* state where the Euclidean distance between the input vector and neuron's weights is computed. To model the distance calculation time, the state *waitd* is used. After the distance calculation elapsed time (`to` high), the computed distance and the id of the neuron are written on the outputs of the neurons. The id of the neuron is needed because the neurons are organized in clusters (see Figure 16.1). The writing of the computed distance and the neuron's id on the neuron's outputs (`wr` high) allows one to go back to the *readx* state and to prepare the neuron for the next iteration.

The weights update function, whose state diagram is presented in Figure 16.4(b), starts with the reception of the identity of the BMU at the end of each iteration. This is depicted with the state *readb*. By knowing the BMU's id, the neuron starts the updating of its weights if its relative position with the respect to the BMU's one is in the neighboring radius N_R (see Algorithm 1). The state *waitu* models the duration of this update procedure.

16.4.3   CWS model

The finite state diagram of the CWS model is presented in Figure 16.5. Its main function is to find, in each iteration for a given input vector, the local BMU among

Table 16.2   Neuron model properties

	Number	Type	Description
Inputs	3	FIFO	Input and weights vector; BMU's id
Outputs	2	FIFO	Computed distance and the neuron's id
Parameters	4	–	Distance calculation and weights update latency; vector dimension, data type

the neurons belonging to the same cluster. The number of inputs of the proposed CWS model depends on the number of neurons used in a cluster (see Table 16.3). If a cluster is of $M \times N$ size, the number of inputs is equal to $M \times N \times 2 + 2$, where not only the neurons' distances will be used as inputs but also their corresponding identities. Two additional inputs are from the two neighboring clusters because the global BMU search operation is carried out in a systolic manner as described in [22]. The CWS main function starts with the reading of all inputs. This is depicted with the states *readd* and *alldist* in Figure 16.5. All inputs are read one by one (rd is

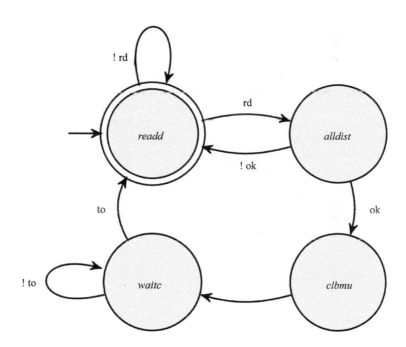

Figure 16.5 *State diagram of the input/output function of the proposed router model*

Table 16.3 *CWS model properties*

	Number	Type	Description
Inputs	$N \times M \times 2 + 2$	FIFO	Neurons' distances and their identities; neighboring clusters' distances
Outputs	1	FIFO	Cluster BMU's identity
Parameters	3	–	Input number; CWS latency; data type

high after a successful read of an input), until the successful reading of all inputs (ok high). By modeling the readd state as a blocking state and using FIFO-based inputs, the cluster BMU search cannot start until all inputs have been read. Therefore, if the distance calculation of the neurons belonging to different neighboring clusters is not done synchronously, this asynchronous positioning of the inputs will not perturb the CWS model operation. The cluster BMU operation is modeled with the *clbmu* state and its duration with the *waitc* state. The duration of the cluster BMU operation is cluster size dependent. It is assumed that the CWS search operation is done in $\lceil \log_2 (N \times M) \rceil$ cycles, where $N \times M$ is the number of neurons in a cluster. The cycle duration T_{cycle} is configurable by the user, thus giving the overall CWS latency equal to $\lceil \log_2 (N \times M) \rceil \times T_{\text{cycle}}$.

16.4.4   NI model

The NI is the module whose main function is to ensure the communication tasks between clusters of the network, and indirectly the distribution of the SOM operation. The encoding of data to exchange between clusters in the form of NoC understandable messages and decoding of the received messages are the main functions of this module. The NI model proposed in this architecture has two main functions, reception and transmission, whose state diagrams are depicted in Figures 16.6 and 16.7, respectively. As stated in Section 16.4.1, there are two types of messages circulating in the proposed architecture: one and more-than-one flit messages. Depending on the type of the received messages, their processing will be different. The reception function of the NI starts in the blocking *readh* state, where the arrival of all sort of messages is waited. The state diagram shown in Figure 16.6 depicts the reception of messages at a flit

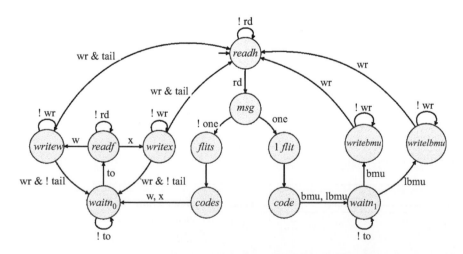

Figure 16.6   State diagram of the reception function of the NI module

level. Upon the reception of the header flit of an incoming message (rd high), the
type of received message is determined in the state *msg*. In the case of more-than-
one flit messages (one set to low), the reception function moves to the *flits* state,
thus indicating that other incoming flits of the same message are to come. In the
state *codes*, the received header flit is decoded to know what type of information
the incoming message is carrying: the weights for initialization (w set to high) or
the input vector (x set to high) for learning or recall phases. After extracting the type
of the data the corresponding cluster will receive, the reception function moves to
one of the two inner state loops: *waitn₀–readf–writex* for input vector reception or
waitn₀–readf–writew for weight vector reception.

In both inner state loops, the vectors (weights or inputs) are received flit by flit
(rd is set high after a successful reception of one flit) and written to the corresponding output of the NI module (weights or input vector outputs, see Table 16.4). In

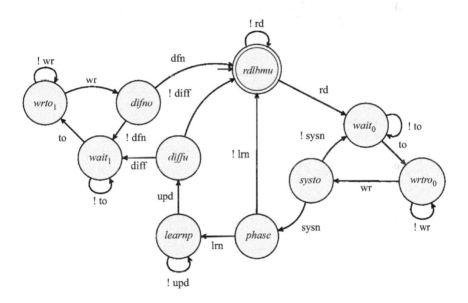

Figure 16.7   State diagram of the transmission function of the NI module

Table 16.4   NI model properties

	Number	Type	Description
Inputs	3	FIFO	Router; local BMU's distance and ID
Outputs	6	FIFO	Router; weight and input vector links to cluster local BMU's distance and ID; BMU's ID
Parameters	2	–	NI latency; data type

addition, the both inner state loops have a common waiting state *waitn*$_0$ introducing the additional NI latency during the processing of each flit. Both inner state loops finish once the tail flit of the incoming messages is received (`tail` set to high) and move to the initial *readh* state. On the other hand, in the case of one-flit messages, the reception function moves from *msg* state to *1-flit* state (`one` is set to high). The *1-flit* state indicates that no more flits are waited for this message and moves to the *code* state where the type of the one-flit message should be identified. The one-flit messages can contain the BMU's identity of the whole network (`bmu` set to high) or the local BMU's identities received from neighboring clusters during the global BMU search (`lbmu` set to high). After the NI latency elapsed time in *waitn*$_1$ state, the NI reception function moves, depending on the type of one-flit message, either to *wrtbmu* or *wrtlbmu* state. In both states, the received data are written on the corresponding outputs (see Table 16.4), thus engaging the CWS operation (write in *wrtlbmu*) or the update of the weights of the cluster's neurons (write in *wrtbmu*).

The state diagram of the NI transmission function is shown in Figure 16.7. It starts from the state *rdlbmu* where the local BMU of the corresponding cluster is waited. Once this value is supplied by the corresponding cluster (`rd` set to high), the transmission function moves to the inner state loop *wait*$_0$–*wrto*$_0$–*systo* where the received local BMU from clusters is sent to neighboring clusters in a systolic manner described previously. The state *wrto*$_0$, *wait*$_0$ and *systo* ensure, respectively, the writing of data to the output link connected to the router, waiting the NI latency before sending and the verification if the number of clusters to which the data should be sent is respected (`sysn` is set to high where this number is achieved). After sending the local BMU value to all neighboring clusters (defined by the systolic rule detailed in [22]), if the SOM network is in recall phase (no weights update) it moves to the initial *rdlbmu* state (`lrn` set to low). Otherwise, it moves to the *learnp* state where it waits for the update signal `upd` to start updating of the weights of all neurons belonging to the corresponding cluster. This update signal is provided by the NI reception function upon reception of the global BMU identity (state *wrtbmu*, Figure 16.7). The systolic manner of data exchange imposes some rules especially on the NIs positioned on the rightmost column of the network during the diffusion of the global BMU identity (see [22] for more details). Upon its reception, they need to send it to all clusters belonging to the same row. The NIs belonging to this rightmost column are specified with the signal `diff`: if `diff` is set to high, the corresponding NI has this "diffusion role," otherwise no. Therefore, the transmission of the NIs having this "diffusion role" moves to the second inner state loop of this state diagram *wait*$_1$–*wrto*$_1$–*diffno*. The role of this second inner state loop is similar to the first one. The main difference is in the data that are to be sent, the global BMU identity in this case, and in the number of clusters to which these data should be sent. The latter is controlled with the *difno* state that moves to the initial state *rdlmbu* when the total number of sending, defined by the systolic way of data exchange, is completed (`dfn` is set to high).

16.5 Results and discussion

The proposed SOM model of a distributed hardware NoC-based architecture has been described with SystemC 2.3 language. All input/output ports and communication links were described by using `sc_fifo` primitive channel, whose role is to model the behavior of an FIFO model along all communication links. The parameters used in this experimental part are summarized in Table 16.5. All router's, NI's and neuron's parameters have been extracted from an HW SOM architecture described in [26]. First, the proposed SOM model has been validated at a functional level on an image quantization application. These results are presented in Figure 16.8 for different sizes of SOM networks: from 2×2 to 15×15 neurons, the top image represents the extracted color palette for a given SOM size whereas the bottom image shows the quantized image obtained by using the extracted color palette. It can be noticed that by increasing the number of neurons in a SOM network (network size), the total number of colors used to represent the observed image increases, thus giving better results in terms of quantization. This is also confirmed with the results shown in Figure 16.9(a), where average quantization error (AQE) is shown for each SOM network size as a function of iteration number. The final AQE, which is the AQE at the end of learning phase, is also presented as a function of the SOM network size in Figure 16.9(b). Moreover, Figure 16.9(c) shows the evolution of the peak-signal-to-noise ratio (PSNR), computed between the quantized and original image, with the SOM network size. It also confirms the previous statements that the image quantization performances increase with the number of used neurons. Second, the proposed SOM model has been used to evaluate the performances of the modeled distributed hardware SOM architecture from [26] for different architectural choices. Thus, the size of clusters has been varied with the size of the NoC, and these results are presented in Figures 16.10–16.12, respectively. Figure 16.10 shows the values of

Table 16.5 SOM model parameters

	Value	Description
Network size	2×2 to 32×32	4 to 1,024 NoC routers
Cluster size	2×2 to 10×10	4 to 100 neurons per cluster
Vector dimension	3	Adapted to image quantization
Distance latency	4	Vector dimension + 1 [26]
Weights update latency	4	Vector dimension + 1 [26]
CWS latency	1	Latency per comparison stage [26]
Router latency	2	[26]
Flit latency	1	[26]
Inter message latency	0	[26]
NI tx latency	1	[26]
NI rx latency	1	[26]
Data type	54 bit	Flit type (2), distance (24), address (12) BMU ID (12), code (4)

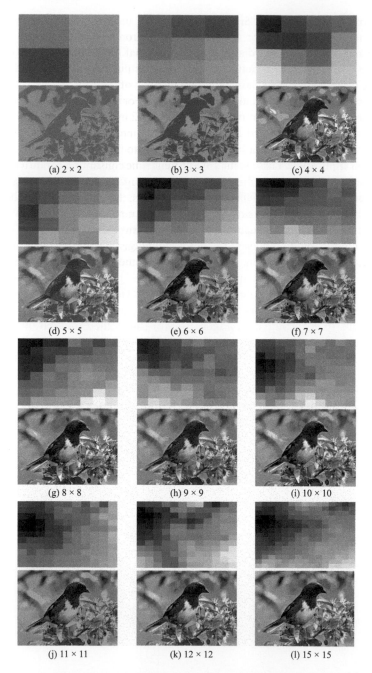

*Figure 16.8   Image quantization results obtained with the proposed SOM model:
from (a) 2 × 2 to (l) 15 × 15 SOM networks with extracted color
palette (top image) and corresponding quantized image (bottom
image)*

total learning time needed for different sizes of NoC network and associated clusters. For instance, for a cluster size 1 × 1, only one neuron is associated with each NoC router. Consequently, the number of neurons is equal to the number of NoC routers and these results are shown in the topmost curve of Figure 16.10. By increasing the size of clusters, to achieve the same total number of neurons in the SOM model, the network of NoC routers should be decreased. For instance, in the case of 2 × 2 clusters, the total learning time is almost divided by 2 in comparison to the initial case corresponding to the 1 × 1 cluster. By continuing to increase the size of clusters (from 1 × 1 to 10 × 10), the total learning time continues to fall. These results are expected because, as it has been identified in [26], the most time consuming part in a distributed NoC-based SOM operation is the data exchange through the network. Thus, for a given number of neurons, by increasing the size of clusters, the total number of routers will decrease. Therefore, the data exchange through the network during the BMU search operation will be limited and less time-consuming, thus giving a smaller total learning time. In addition, by increasing the number of neurons in a cluster, the cluster BMU operation will be increased because of greater number of local comparisons to do.

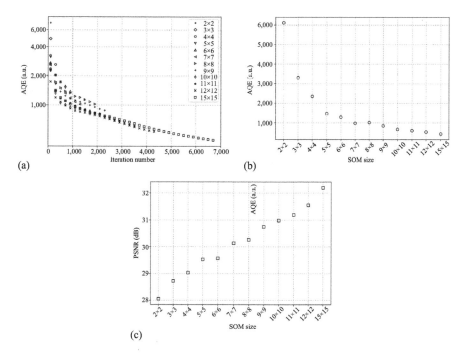

Figure 16.9   Image quantization performances in terms of (a) evolution of AQE for different SOM networks (from 2 × 2 to 15 × 15) as a function of iteration size, (b) evolution of the final AQE with the SOM network size and (c) PSNR with respect to the original image

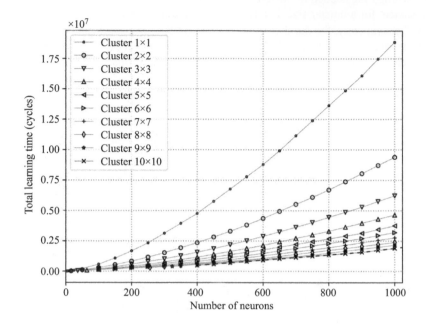

Figure 16.10   Total learning time

However, the increase in the cluster processing time is less significant compared to the data exchange over the NoC network that remains the most time-consuming operation. These conclusions are also confirmed with the results presented in Figure 16.11 where the evolution of the time of one iteration is presented as a function of number of neurons. With the bigger NoC and smaller cluster, the time of one learning iteration is more significant. For instance, it can be noticed that the same NoC size, presented with red horizontal lines in Figure 16.11(a) and (b), gives a smaller value of the learning iteration time with the cluster size increasing. It does mean that, when a large number of neuron is needed, the bigger clusters should be privileged. On the other hand, Figure 16.11(c) shows that the cluster size with the minimal NoC size of 2×2 also imposes the minimal number of neurons. For instance, for 5×5 clusters connected with a 2×2 NoC network, the number of neurons is equal to 100. Moreover, the proposed distributed SOM model has been evaluated in terms of performances. These results are presented in Figure 16.12 in terms of MCUPS. The value of MCUPS is related to the operating frequency of the hardware architecture. Thus, these performances have been shown in Figure 16.12(a) in terms of $MCUPS \times 10^{-6}/f$, where f is the hardware operating frequency. On the other hand, the same results have been presented for the operating frequency $f = 250$ MHz, extracted from the modeled hardware architecture in [26].

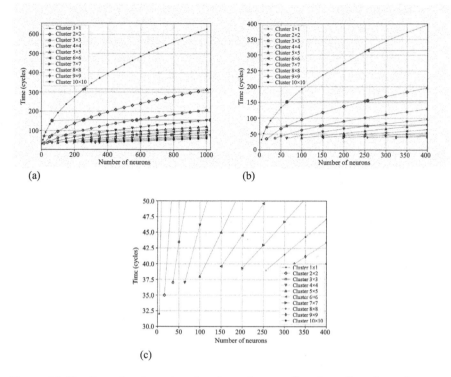

Figure 16.11   *Learning iteration time in cycles as a function of number of neurons (up to 1,000) for different size of clusters (from 1 × 1 to 10 × 10): (a) up to 1,000 neurons; red lines show the same NoC size for different clusters: 16 × 16, 8 × 8 and 4 × 4 from top to bottom, respectively; (b) up to 400 neurons; red lines show the same NoC size for different clusters: 16 × 16, 8 × 8 and 4 × 4 from top to bottom, respectively; (c) up to 400 neurons; zoom on the 2 × 2 NoC network with different sizes of clusters*

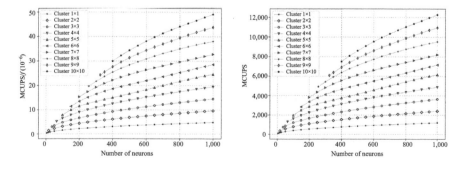

Figure 16.12   *Performance evaluation of the distributed SOM architecture in terms of MCUPS as a function of the number of neurons and cluster sizes: (a) MCUPS per f, where f is the cycle frequency and (b) MCUPS for f = 250 MHz [26]*

16.6   Conclusion

In this work, a SystemC model of a hardware, scalable and distributed SOM architecture is presented and evaluated. The main goal of this modeling approach is to provide a realistic model of such HW SOM architectures allowing future exploration of possible architectural choices to take in their design. The presented model has been validated functionally on an image quantization application. Moreover, the timing performances of the proposed model have been evaluated for different networks and cluster sizes. Therefore, by varying the number of neurons grouped in clusters and connected to NoC routers, the time of one learning iteration decreases considerably as well as the overall learning time. Moreover, the overall performances of the SOM increase in terms of MCUPS as it is inversely proportional to the learning iteration time. Consequently, the proposed SOM model provides us new insights and orientations in the design of future large-scale HW SOMs, where cluster-oriented neurons should be privileged for large-scale networks in order to obtain the optimal temporal performances.

References

[1]   Ur Rehman MH, Yaqoob I, Salah K, *et al.* The role of big data analytics in industrial Internet of Things. Future Generation Computer Systems. 2019;99:247–259.

[2]   Gisbrecht A and Hammer B. Data visualization by nonlinear dimensionality reduction. Wiley Interdisciplinary Reviews: Data Mining and Knowledge Discovery. 2015;5(2):51–73.

[3]   Xu R and Wunsch II D. Survey of clustering algorithms. IEEE Transactions on Neural Networks. 2005;16(3):645–678.

[4]   Kambatla K, Kollias G, Kumar V, *et al.* Trends in big data analytics. Journal of Parallel and Distributed Computing. 2014;74(7):2561–2573.

[5]   Bouguettaya A, Yu Q, Liu X, *et al.* Efficient agglomerative hierarchical clustering. Expert Systems with Applications. 2015;42(5):2785–2797.

[6]   Arora P. and Varshney S. Analysis of k-means and k-medoids algorithm for big data. Procedia Computer Science. 2016;78:507–512.

[7]   Yin H, Benson AR, Leskovec J, *et al.* Local higher-order graph clustering. In: Proceedings of the 23rd ACM SIGKDD International Conference on Knowledge Discovery and Data Mining. Halifax, NS, Canada: ACM; 2017. p. 555–564.

[8]   Bodyanskiy YV, Tyshchenko OK, and Kopaliani DS. An evolving connectionist system for data stream fuzzy clustering and its online learning. Neurocomputing. 2017;262:41–56.

[9]   Liu H and Ban X. Clustering by growing incremental self-organizing neural network. Expert Systems with Applications. 2015;42(11):4965–4981.

[10] Arias-Castro E, Lerman G, and Zhang T. Spectral clustering based on local PCA. The Journal of Machine Learning Research. 2017;18(1):253–309.

[11]   Naik GR, Al-Timemy AH, and Nguyen HT. Transradial amputee gesture classification using an optimal number of sEMG sensors: an approach using ICA clustering. IEEE Transactions on Neural Systems and Rehabilitation Engineering. 2015;24(8):837–846.

[12]   Chen L, Liu Y, Huang Z, *et al*. An improved SOM algorithm and its application to color feature extraction. Journal of Neural Computing and Applications. 2013;24:1759–1770.

[13]   Kuremoto T, Komoto T, Kobayashi K, *et al*. Parameterless-growing-SOM and its application to a voice instruction learning system. Journal of Robotics. 2010;2010:9.

[14]   De A, Zhang Y, and Guo C. A parallel adaptive segmentation method based on SOM and GPU with application to MRI image processing. Journal of Robotics. 2016;198:180–189.

[15]   Tamukoh H, Aso T, Horio K, *et al*. Self-organizing map hardware accelerator system and its application to realtime image enlargement. In: 2004 IEEE International Joint Conference on Neural Networks (IEEE Cat. No. 04CH37541). vol. 4. Budapest, Hungary: IEEE; 2004. p. 2683–2687.

[16]   Porrmann M, Witkowski U, and Ruckert U. Implementation of Self Organizing Feature Maps in Reconfigurable Hardware. In: Omondi AR and Rajapakse JC, editors. FPGA Implementations of Neural Networks. 1st ed. Boston, MA: Springer US; 2006. p. 247–269.

[17]   Manolakos I and Logaras E. High throughput systolic SOM IP core for FPGAs. In: Proceedings of the 2007 IEEE International Conference on Acoustics, Speech and Signal Processing (ICASSP'07), vol. 2, Honolulu, HI, USA; 2007. p. 61–64.

[18]   Ramirez-Agundis A, Gadea-Girones R, and Colom-Palero R. A hardware design of a massive-parallel, modular NN-based vector quantizer for real-time video coding. Microprocessors and Microsystems. 2008;32:33–44.

[19]   Tamukoh H and Sekine M. A dynamically reconfigurable platform for self-organizing neural network hardware. In: International Conference on Neural Information Processing. Sydney, Australia: Springer; 2010. p. 439–446.

[20]   Hikawa H and Maeda Y. Improved learning performance of hardware self-organizing map using a novel neighborhood function. IEEE Transactions on Neural Networks and Learning Systems. 2015;26:2861–2873.

[21]   Abadi M, Jovanovic S, Ben Khalifa K, *et al*. A hardware configurable self-organizing map for real-time color quantization. In: 2016 IEEE International Conference on Electronics, Circuits and Systems (ICECS). Monte Carlo, Monaco; 2016. p. 336–339.

[22]   Abadi M, Jovanovic S, Khalifa KB, *et al*. A scalable and adaptable hardware NoC-based self organizing map. Microprocessors and Microsystems. 2018;57:1–14. Available from: http://www.sciencedirect.com/science/article/pii/S0141933117301916.

[23]   Lachmair J, Merenyi E, Porrmann M, *et al*. A reconfigurable neuroprocessor for self-organizing feature maps. Journal of Neurocomputing. 2013;112: 189–199.

[24]   Abadi M, Jovanovic S, Ben Khalifa K, *et al.* A Scalable Flexible SOM NoC-Based Hardware Architecture. In: Merényi E, Mendenhall MJ, and O'Driscoll P, editors. Advances in Self-Organizing Maps and Learning Vector Quantization. Cham: Springer International Publishing; 2016. p. 165–175.

[25]   Abadi M, Jovanovic S, Khalifa KB, *et al.* A multi-application, scalable and adaptable hardware SOM architecture. In: 2019 International Joint Conference on Neural Networks (IJCNN). Budapest, Hungary: IEEE; 2019. p. 1–8.

[26]   Jovanovic S, Rabah H, and Weber S. High performance scalable hardware SOM architecture for real-time vector quantization. In: 2018 IEEE International Conference on Image Processing, Applications and Systems (IPAS). Sophia-Antipolis, France: IEEE; 2018. p. 256–261.

[27]   Kohonen T. Self-Organizing Maps. 3rd ed. Berlin, Heidelberg: Springer-Verlag; 2001. p. 29.

Chapter 17

Surface water pollution monitoring using the Internet of Things (IoT) and machine learning

Hamza Khurshid[1], Rafia Mumtaz[1], Noor Alvi[1],
Faisal Shafait[1], Sheraz Ahmed[2], Muhammad Imran Malik[1],
Andreas Dengel[2], and Quanita Kiran[1]

Water is one of the basic resources required for human survival. However, pollution of water has become a global problem. 2.4 billion people worldwide live without any form of water sanitation. This work focuses on case study of water pollution in Pakistan where only 20% of the population has an access to good-quality water. Drinking bad-quality water causes diseases such as hepatitis, diarrhea and typhoid. Moreover, people living close to the industrial areas are more prone to drinking polluted water and catching diseases as a result. Yet, there is no system that can monitor the quality of water or help in disease prevention. In this work, an Internet of Things (IoT)-enabled water quality monitoring system is developed that works as a stand-alone portable solution for monitoring water quality accurately and in real time. The real-time results are stored in a cloud database. The public web portal shows these results in the form of data sheets, maps and charts for analyzing data. Further, this data along with the collected data of past water quality is used to generate machine learning (ML) models for prediction of water quality. As a consequence, a model for prediction of water quality is trained and tested on a test set. The predictions on the test set resulted in a mean squared error (MSE) of 0.264.

17.1 Introduction

Water is a vital requisite for existence of life on the Earth; however, this vital resource is in danger. One out of nine people worldwide uses drinking water from unsafe sources [1], while 2.4 billion people live without any form of sanitation [1]. In this work, a case study of water pollution of Pakistan is presented. Water is of utmost importance in Pakistan due to its agronomic nature and due to unavailability of drinkable water

[1]School of Electrical Engineering and Computer Science (SEECS), National University of Sciences and Technology (NUST), Islamabad, Pakistan
[2]Deutsches Forschungszentrum für Künstliche Intelligenz GmbH (DFKI), Forschungsbereich Smarte Daten & Wissensdienste, Kaiserslautern, Germany

to more than 80% of its population [2]. So the majority of the population remain oblivious to the consequences of drinking polluted water, i.e., development of diseases such as hepatitis, diarrhea and typhoid. People living close to the industrial areas are more prone to drink polluted water and catch diseases as a result [3,4]. Pakistan is the seventeenth country across the globe facing acute water crisis. Despite of all the efforts made by government, there has been no solution that could decrease the rate of mortality due to water pollution. In today's world of smart cities and advanced technologies that can solve most complex problems, this basic problem still remains unresolved in Pakistan. The laboratories set up by the government of Pakistan log water quality data manually and perform tests on it in chemical labs. These labs are very few and the data they produce is not used for effective analysis. This monitoring process is also expensive, non-real time and unavailable in majority of the cities of Pakistan.

To solve this problem, an IoT-enabled solution for real-time monitoring of water quality parameters is developed. It can monitor temperature, pH, dissolved oxygen (DO), conductivity and turbidity. These parameters are used to calculate water quality index (WQI) [5] that is an international unit for measuring water quality. These IoT nodes can be deployed in the form of a network at a water reservoir or any source of water for urban areas. This IoT network of water quality monitoring nodes is connected to the internet in a way that the data is continuously synchronized with the back-end web server. The users of the system can browse the website to analyze and monitor the quality of water at various source points. Meanwhile, past data of water quality is used to generate ML model for prediction of future water quality data.

17.2 Literature review

This section contains review of related literature. In [6], a system for monitoring water quality is developed. It monitors parameters such as pH and turbidity. It also uses a cloud back end to store the data. In [7], a case study is presented on the monitoring of the water quality parameters such as turbidity, total dissolved solids (TDSs) and pH. Daud *et al.* in [2] collected water quality samples from all over Pakistan. They compared different parameters of water quality against NEQS (National Environmental Quality Standards) and WHO (World Health Organization) standards. Majority of the samples indicated the presence of high total *coliform, fecal coliform, Escherichia coli (E. coli)* primarily due to the mix of sewerage water and secondarily due to the disposal of industrial wastes. It was recommended to install and maintain the treatment plants and ensure regular enforcement of NEQS. In [8], 46 piped water samples were collected across different places of Orangi Town, Karachi and tested for bacteriological and physiochemical analyses using WHO standards and National Standards for Drinking Water Quality that are considered to be the benchmark of comparative analysis. The statistical analysis for each of the parameters was performed and it was found that physiochemical parameters were well in limits except sulfates. However, bacteriological parameters such as total *fecal coliform* and total *coliform* counts were critically high, reflecting poor hygienic and sewerage conditions. Another research on the data set of river Ravi by sampling its data for 3 years, from Jan 2005 to Mar

2007, from 14 sampling stations is presented in [9]. In this study, 12 parameters, *COD (chemical oxygen demand), suspended solids, phosphorus, BOD (biochemical oxygen demand), DO, chloride, total nitrogen, sodium, nitrate, oil and grease, nitrite and total coliforms*, were tested.

There are several studies that used ML approaches. In [10], a research is described which is conducted on Rawal watershed, situated in Islamabad. A total of 663 water samples have been collected from 13 different stations and tested for *appearance, temperature, turbidity, pH, alkalinity, hardness as CaCO₃, conductance, calcium, TDSs, chlorides, nitrates and fecal coliforms* against WHO standards. A correlation analysis was performed to draw out the correlation among the parameters. In [11], research is conducted on the data set of 47 wells and springs (2006–13) acquired from the Ministry of Iran. The study considered 16 water quality parameters. The method used in this study was proposed by Horton (1965) to calculate WQI. There were three methodologies that were employed: artificial neural network (ANN) with early stopping, ANN with ensemble averaging and ANN with Bayesian regularization. The correlations were computed between the observed and the predicted values of WQI and were found to be 0.94 and 0.77.

Some studies used IoT-enabled systems. In [12], a generic IoT system for real-time water quality monitoring is discussed. It comprises sensors that read parameter readings, then those parameter readings are transmitted to a controller through wireless communication devices attached with sensors. The controllers, through some wireless communication technology, store those sensor readings to a data storage that are reflected in some customized application. In [13], authors proposed a general framework for IoT system for real-time water quality monitoring, demand forecasting and anomaly detection. For an IoT system, they have considered the parameters *turbidity, chlorine, ORP, nitrates, pH, conductivity and temperature* and used their sensors. Their proposed system is quite a general one and no data-set has been used to test it. In 2015, authors developed a real-time IoT-based water quality monitoring system using different water quality sensors [14]. They connected it to the Raspberry Pi minicomputer. However, the proposed system is not feasible and cost effective for large systems. In addition to that it only provides the feature of monitoring.

17.3 Methodology

In this section, we will discuss the methodology which was followed to conduct this study. The methodology can also be seen as a flow-chart in Figure 17.1.

17.3.1 Development of water quality monitoring IoT nodes

In this section, the development of the IoT nodes and all of its components is explained.

17.3.1.1 Selected parameters

Following parameters were chosen to be monitored by the system.

1. **Temperature:** Most of the water quality parameters are related to temperature; so when it is paired with other parameters, true values of these parameters can be found which are affected by temperature. In this way, it helps in WQI calculations.

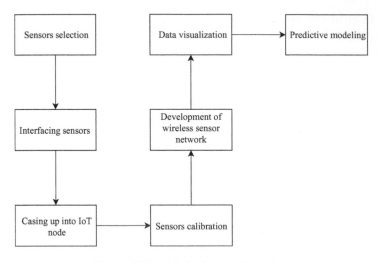

Figure 17.1   Methodology flow chart

2. **Dissolved oxygen:** It determines the health of water. Fish and aquatic animals cannot survive in water with low DO. So, it contributes to the overall WQI. It is monitored in mg/L, percent DO or ppm.
3. **Conductivity:** It measures the ability of water to conduct electricity through it. This depends upon the presence of certain ions present in the water. Pure water has poor conductivity due to the absence of impurities and ions. It is also used to calculate TDSs. It is monitored in μS/cm.
4. **pH:** It is a measure of how acidic or alkaline the water is. It can range from 0 to 14 with 0 being maximum acidic and 14 being maximum alkaline. Normal pH of drinking water lies in the range of 6–8.
5. **Turbidity:** It is the measure of haziness or cloudiness of water. Hazy or cloudy water is considered impure, so it contributes toward overall WQI. It is measured in NTU (nephelometric turbidity unit).

17.3.1.2   Sensors

Sensors are the most important part for any IoT-enabled monitoring system, as they influence the cost-effectiveness of the project. Also, the quality of sensors determines the quality of data generated by the system. Usually, there is a trade-off between the quality of sensor and its cost-effectiveness. The lower quality sensors are very cost-effective but the data they generate is not accurate. Also, these sensors are more prone to early retirement. On the other hand, the sensors from good brands are costlier, but the data they generate is highly accurate and reliable.

Research about various brands providing sensors for water quality monitoring was done for finding the perfect combination of cost-effectiveness and data accuracy. The search narrowed down to three options at the end, which were Libelium sensors, vernier sensors and locally available sensors. Libelium sensors were highly accurate but costly. On the other hand, local sensors were easily available and cheaper but they were inaccurate and unreliable. It is also found that these sensors were prone to early retirement. However, vernier sensors offered a perfect blend of accuracy and cost-effectiveness. They were accurate in readings and their error rates were comparable to that of Libelium. So, vernier sensors were chosen for this system. A brief detail of each of the sensors used is provided next.

17.3.1.3   Temperature sensor

Vernier temperature sensor monitors temperature of water in degree Celsius. The sensor as can be seen in Figure 17.2 has a probe made of steel which can be dipped in water. When powered, it generates a signal with readings of temperature in real time.

17.3.1.4   Dissolved oxygen sensor

Vernier DO sensor monitors the concentration of oxygen dissolved in water in mg/L. Similar to the temperature sensor, it is also a probe that can be dipped into water to generate readings. However, this probe has a membrane cap at the end which is filled with an electrode filling solution. The sensor can be seen in Figure 17.3.

17.3.1.5   Conductivity sensor

Vernier conductivity sensor monitors the conductivity of water in μS/cm. As can be seen in Figure 17.4, it also has a probe. The probe can be dipped into water to make the sensor generate readings. The sensor can be configured to work with different ranges of conductivity. There are three ranges of operation, thus the sensor can have three levels of sensitivity, which can be used in different types of situations. An

Figure 17.2   Vernier temperature sensor

Figure 17.3   Vernier dissolved oxygen sensor

Figure 17.4   Vernier conductivity sensor

Figure 17.5   Vernier pH sensor

important reason for monitoring conductivity is to calculate TDS contents in water as conductivity can be converted to TDS units quite easily.

17.3.1.6   pH sensor

Vernier pH sensor (Figure 17.5) monitors the pH level of water. It is also a probe that is dipped into water for the purpose of taking readings. The probe is stored in a 10% KCl solution. The storage solution keeps the sensor healthy and ready for instant use when it is not being used.

17.3.1.7   Turbidity sensor

Vernier turbidity sensor (Figure 17.6) monitors the turbidity of water in the range of 0–200 NTU. It has a closed chamber that contains a bottle. When the bottle inside is filled with water and the chamber is closed, the sensor monitors turbidity of this water by monitoring dispersion of light in the water.

17.3.1.8   Interfacing sensors

The sensors used here are generic sensors intended for use in laboratories. So, an interface had to be created between these sensors and the system. Arduino was used

Figure 17.6 Vernier turbidity sensor

Figure 17.7 British telecom plug

Figure 17.8 SparkFun Vernier Arduino Interface Shield

as the development platform, thus they had to be interfaced with Arduino board. All of the vernier sensors listed previously come with a British telecom plug for connection, which can be seen in Figure 17.7.

To create an interface between the Arduino and British telecom plugs of vernier sensors, SparkFun's Vernier Arduino Interface Shield was used (Figure 17.8). The shield has four British telecom sockets for vernier sensors. Two of the sockets support digital sensors, while the remaining two support analog sensors. The shield converts the readings from sensors to analog voltages ranging from 0 to 5 V. This output of shield is connected to analog ports on Arduino to record this voltage for each sensor connected to shield. As all of the sensors were analog sensors, three interface shields were needed for each node to create interface for five sensors.

17.3.1.9   Design of water quality monitoring IoT nodes

All the five sensors were connected to interface shields, and these shields were connected to Arduino. The Arduino microcontroller was programmed to calculate sensor readings from all the sensor voltages using calibration equations (explained later in the chapter). Also, ESP8266 was used as Wi-Fi module to send these values to web server. Later, the whole node was cased up for better portability. The final node after the design completion can be seen in Figure 17.9.

17.3.1.10   Sensors calibration

Now that the node is up and running, there was a need to verify and ensure that the sensors are properly configured to give accurate readings. For this purpose, the process of linear calibration was used. Vernier describes this process in its user manual for analog sensors calibration [15]. It is also explained in detail next.

For sensors provided, the values are mapped linearly from voltage values to sensor outputs using a line in XY-plane where sensor voltages are plotted on x-axis and actual parameter readings on y-axis. So, each voltage value maps to an actual parameter reading directly using this linear relation. This means that the equation of line can be used to translate between voltages and actual readings of parameters. The equation of line is

$$y = mx + c \tag{17.1}$$

where y is value with respect to y-axis, x is value with respect to x-axis, m is slope and c is intercept. Now, this equation for sensors can be rewritten as following:

$$actual\ reading = slope \times sensor\ voltage + intercept \tag{17.2}$$

Here, slope and intercept are fixed values for a sensor, as they define the line for relationship of that sensor's values with its voltage. These two values for each sensor need to be found for further evaluation of actual sensor readings (parameter

Figure 17.9   Design of water quality monitoring node

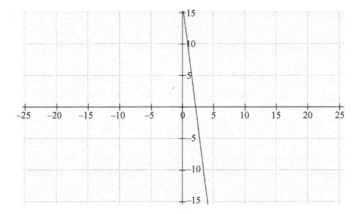

Figure 17.10   Linear calibration plot for pH

readings). For this purpose, two standard solutions are obtained whose readings are known. Then, sensor voltages are taken for these two solutions using sensors. Using these two (x, y) pairs with equation of two-variables, the system of two equations is then solved simultaneously. Hence, the values of slope and intercept for each sensor are obtained.

For example, for calibrating the pH sensor, solutions with pH 7 and 4.2 were used. Voltages of pH sensor for these two solutions were found and then the pairs of values were used to find slope and intercept of the calibration line. The calculated line for pH sensor after calibration can be seen in Figure 17.10.

It should be noted that it has to be done for each sensor unit and for each new IoT node as sensors are not sold pre-calibrated. Also, this ensures that the readings generated from all the sensors are accurate.

Linear calibration is a pre-built mechanism in monitors sold by vernier, with which sensors are attached and readings are obtained on-the-go. However, it was interfaced with an Arduino, so it had to be done separately. Two standard solutions for each parameter were used and the linear calibration equations were solved for each sensor. These equations were then programmed into Arduino. Now, it had the ability to calculate sensor readings on-the-go.

17.3.2   Development of wireless sensor network

After the development of IoT nodes, the back end to complete the wireless sensor network was created. This network of nodes followed the client–server model. The details of implementation are provided next.

17.3.2.1   Cloud back end

For any IoT system, internet connectivity is a crucial part. A cloud back end is deployed to complete the internet side of the IoT system. A PHP-enabled and MySQL-enabled web hosting server is used and an online database on the MySQL server is created. The structure of database is created in an order to support storing of all the parameters of water quality for any number of nodes simultaneously. The scripts in PHP are developed to create a RESTful API (application programming interface) on the server. The API provides data storage and data retrieval functions. The Arduino boards in the developed nodes are programmed to access this API over the internet and send sensor values to them. Thus, each node creates a packet containing values from every sensor and sends it to the API hosted at the server along with its node identification number. The API stores this data into the MySQL database. When a network of IoT nodes is deployed over a geographic area and each node has connectivity to the internet, the entire system is centralized using the web server as the common contact point. Also, the web server can be accessed anywhere in world to observe and analyze the stored data. This completes the loop of IoT-enabled monitoring. A website is also developed to display the data stored at the server. The services of this website are explained in more detail in later part of this chapter.

17.3.3　Data visualization

As the wireless sensor part is completed, there is a need to visualize the data and made it available to general public. For this purpose, a web portal is developed.

17.3.3.1　Web portal development

The web portal is developed with the following features:

1.　Display **Data Sheets** for showing all the data stored at the server in tabular form. Users can access the data by node ID and see individual records.
2.　Display **Maps** showing data geographically. Water quality by areas can be seen clearly in this view.
3.　Display **Charts** for analyzing trend of data generated over time.

Some screenshots from the website can be seen in Figures 17.11 and 17.12.

Data Table

10 ▾ records per page					Search
Time/Date ▲	Turbidity	pH	Disolved Oxygen	Conductivity	Temperature
2019-06-20 11:24:57	201.35	2.31	9.31	909.32	29.67
2019-06-20 11:24:57	201.35	2.31	9.31	909.32	29.67
2019-06-20 11:27:50	126.68	2.35	10.10	1022.98	29.48
2019-06-20 11:27:50	126.68	2.35	10.10	1022.98	29.48
2019-06-20 11:28:56	107.67	2.42	9.05	795.65	29.67
2019-06-20 11:28:56	107.67	2.42	9.05	795.65	29.67
2019-06-20 11:29:44	238.68	2.35	9.24	833.54	29.67
2019-06-20 11:29:44	238.68	2.35	9.24	833.54	29.67
2019-06-20 11:30:25	204.74	1.74	9.39	1136.65	29.48
2019-06-20 11:30:25	204.74	1.74	9.39	1136.65	29.48

Figure 17.11　Website snippet showing a data sheet

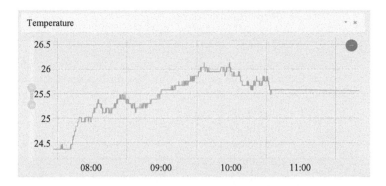

Figure 17.12   Website snippet showing a data chart for temperature

Figure 17.13   Data collection points on Rawal Dam

17.3.4   Prediction of water quality using machine learning

The prime objective of predictive modeling is to use the data generated by IoT nodes, as well as historic data from other sources to forecast the future trends of water quality. For predictive modeling, there must be an adequate size of data to be fed into the ML algorithms. For this purpose, following data was collected:

- Real-time data of water quality of 4 months (from September to December 2019) from Rawal Dam was collected. Rawal Dam is the main source of water supply to the city of Rawalpindi. This data was collected at regular intervals using the IoT nodes. The data collection points can be seen in Figure 17.13.
- The historic data of past 4 years (2015–19) of water quality was collected from Rawal Lake filtration plant. This data was combined with the IoT nodes data to make its size suitable for predictive modeling.

Table 17.1   Water quality classes

Quality class	WQI range	Description
Class 1	100–95	Excellent water quality
Class 2	94–90	Very good water quality
Class 3	89–80	Good water quality
Class 4	79–65	Medium water quality
Class 5	64–45	Polluted water
Class 6	44–0	Very polluted water

Table 17.2   Predictive model results

Error type	Error
Mean absolute error	0.276
Mean squared error	0.264

17.4   Results and discussion

The data from Rawal Dam was collected at its three inlet streams and one outlet stream for 4 months starting from September 2019. WQI of this data was calculated and it is classified according to the classes of WQI specified in literature [5]. As per the results of this classification, 0.0049% of the data lies in Class 5, while the remaining 99.9951% of data lies in Class 6 which is the poorest quality class as can be seen in Table 17.1. The average WQI is 22.99 with standard deviation of 8.52, while maximum and minimum are 61 and 6, respectively. This tells us that the quality of water that is being supplied from Rawal Dam is of extremely bad quality.

The data is then digitized and preprocessed in order to feed it into a long short-term memory (LSTM) neural network. LSTM is a recurrent-neural-network-based architecture, which has feedback points for processing the complete sequences of data instead of just one data point. LSTMs are used mainly for context-based or sequence-based data. The choice of LSTMs is due to two major reasons:

1. LSTMs are capable of finding trends in time series data. So, they have the ability to predict future values based on past data.
2. LSTMs perform better on sequential data as compared to conventional neural networks.

The neural network architecture had three layers. The first layer being the input layer contained 155 neurons, the second layer contained 200 LSTM units, while the third layer had 5 neurons. For each training iteration, data of last 31 days was fed to model for output of each day's data. So for each iteration, five parameters for

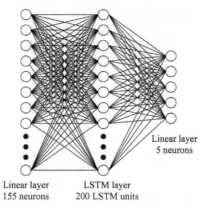

Figure 17.14   Neural network architecture

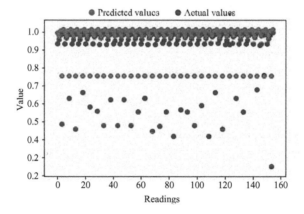

Figure 17.15   Ground truth and predicted values

31 days were used as input to forecast next day's data. This makes number of input parameters equal to 155 thus input layer's size and output parameters equal to 5 that was output layer's size. The network was not made deep to avoid over-fitting due to the low number of records in the data-set. The architecture of our network can be seen in Figure 17.14.

The framework used for training was PyTorch. For optimization, Adam optimizer was used with MSE loss function. To avoid the risks of over-fitting, the training was done only for 15 epochs. Out of the 48-month data records, the data of 47 months was used for training, while the remaining 1 month was used for testing. As per the results, the mean average error is 0.276, R-squared is 0.112, while MSE is 0.264 (Table 17.2). Also, the correlation between scaled actual and predicted values can be seen in Figure 17.15.

Neural networks always perform better with comparatively bigger data-sets than the one used here. However, in the absence of large amounts of data, the results produced are promising and can be used to predict water quality with good accuracy.

17.5   Conclusion and future work

The low adoption of modern techniques due to the lack of literacy, institutional capability to deliver technology and economic constraints has made Pakistan reliant on traditional system. The traditional tools for water quality monitoring are manually controlled, based on human intervention, rather than technology. Quality assessments are usually carried out in research laboratories where data is processed in non-real time. Toward such end, the development of an IoT-based system to monitor the quality of water in Pakistan is a promising alternative to traditional complex and ineffective approaches, thus providing a proper and near real-time assessment of water to the community. In order to ensure an accurate and reliable analysis in monitoring water quality, we need a large number of water samples where IoT resolves such issues of data collection, analysis and communication. The major outcomes of this research work are the development of low-cost indigenous solution based on latest technology, a system that offers near real-time water quality status by monitoring parameters such as pH level, turbidity, temperature, conductivity and DO, as well as the development of a state-of-the-art apparatus that provides water quality data with high temporal resolution through effective data communication. Such a system is beneficial not only for the water regulating and environment protection authorities but also for the research community and public at large.

An extension and future work of this research is predictive healthcare. For this purpose, the data of patients suffering from water borne diseases will be acquired. This data will be collected from a government hospital, where this data will help us to identify regions of poor water quality. It will also support us to get an insight of the seasonal variations affecting the water quality, the surroundings of the patient residence degrading the water quality and the time period when more cases with water borne diseases are reported to the local hospital. For predictive modeling, ML algorithms will be applied. The selection of the algorithm will be part of the research.

Acknowledgment

This research was funded by DAAD, Germany and was conducted in IoT Lab of NUST-SEECS, Islamabad, Pakistan.

References

[1]   WHO/UNICEF Joint Water Supply, Sanitation Monitoring Programme, and World Health Organization. (2015). Progress on sanitation and drinking water: 2015 update and MDG assessment. World Health Organization.

[2]   Daud, M. K., Nafees, M., Ali, S., *et al.* (2017). Drinking water quality status and contamination in Pakistan. BioMed Research International.

[3]   Draft South Asia. (2000). Water vision 2025, country report, Pakistan.

[4]   Kahlown, M. A., Tahir, M. A., Rasheed, H., and Bhatti, K. P. (2006). "Water quality status, national water quality monitoring programme." Fourth Technical Report PCRWR, 5.

[5]   Dascalescu, I. G., Morosanu, I., Ungureanu, F., Musteret, C. P., Minea, M., and Teodosiu, C. (2017). Development of a versatile water quality index for water supply applications. Environmental Engineering and Management Journal, 16(3), 525–534.

[6]   Shafi, U., Mumtaz, R., Anwar, H., Qamar, A. M., and Khurshid, H. (2018, October). Surface water pollution detection using internet of things. In 2018 15th International Conference on Smart Cities: Improving Quality of Life Using ICT & IoT (HONET-ICT), Islamabad: IEEE. (pp. 92–96).

[7]   Haydar, S., Arshad, M., and Aziz, J. A. (2016). Evaluation of drinking water quality in urban areas of Pakistan: A case study of Southern Lahore. Pakistan Journal of Engineering and Applied Sciences, 5, 16–23.

[8]   Alamgir, A., Khan, M. A., Hany, O. E., *et al.* (2015). Public health quality of drinking water supply in Orangi Town, Karachi, Pakistan. Bulletin of Environment, Pharmacology and Life Sciences, 4(11), 88–094.

[9]   Ejaz, N. A. E. E. M., Hashmi, H. N., and Ghumman, A. R. (2011). Water quality assessment of effluent receiving streams in Pakistan: A case study of Ravi River. Mehran University Research Journal of Engineering & Technology, 30(3), 383–396.

[10] Ali, M., and Qamar, A. M. (2013, September). Data analysis, quality indexing and prediction of water quality for the management of Rawal watershed in Pakistan. In Eighth International Conference on Digital Information Management (ICDIM 2013), Islamabad: IEEE. (pp. 108–113).

[11] Sakizadeh, M. (2016). Artificial intelligence for the prediction of water quality index in groundwater systems. Modeling Earth Systems and Environment, 2(1), 8.

[12] Geetha, S., and Gouthami, S. (2016). Internet of things enabled real time water quality monitoring system. Smart Water, 2(1), 1.

[13] Vijai, P., and Sivakumar, P. B. (2016). Design of IoT systems and analytics in the context of smart city initiatives in India. Procedia Computer Science, 92, 583–588.

[14] Vijayakumar, N., and Ramya, A. R. (2015, March). The real time monitoring of water quality in IoT environment. In 2015 International Conference on Innovations in Information, Embedded and Communication Systems (ICIIECS), Nagercoil: IEEE. (pp. 1–5).

[15] Vernier Software & Technology. (2013). Calibrate an analog sensor. Retrieved February 28, 2020, from https://www.vernier.com/files/sample_labs/VST_STEM_PROJECT-calibrate_analog_sensor.pdf.

Conclusions

Artificial intelligence and machine-learning field have continuously been expanding their applications into various domains, some of which have the potential to revolutionise people's daily lives. Ever-increasing importance of automation in the digital transformation of our society, economy and industry have necessitated the use of artificial intelligence, machine learning for robotics, sensing and networking. Artificial intelligence and machine learning enabled mobile networks, including infrastructure and user services, can observe, learn and adapt their operations according to environment and user requirement. This book presents use cases where artificial intelligence and machine learning have been integrated in the field of complex wireless networks, allowing accuracy in indoor positioning and localisation for improved user services, managing mobility of users and design intelligent handover mechanism, detect poor coverage holes in the wireless networks and facilitate the network densification, designing and developing intelligent resource allocation schemes, improving spectral efficiency and integrating intelligent spectrum access and sharing schemes for improved spectrum efficiency.

Similarly, artificial intelligence and machine learning have been successfully applied in the field of robotics, allowing robotic hands to operate similar to human hands via learning by example (machine learning), in the field of human–computer interaction, allowing the translation of bio-signals to affective or emotional states of the users, in the field of autonomous vehicles, allowing for efficient object tracking from drones and for efficient translation of visual inputs to driving parameters for autonomous cars, in the field of biometrics, facilitating the use of brain signals as a biometric modality, in the field of video quality assessment, assisting the mapping of elementary objective quality metrics to visual quality ratings provided by human viewers, in the field of connected health, applied for the detection of diagnosis of pathological situations and remote condition monitoring based on compressed electrocardiography (ECG) signals, in the field of Internet-of-Things (IoT) networks for dimensionality reduction in collections of huge amounts of data.

Despite the outstanding advances that artificial intelligence and machine learning have brought to all these fields, there is still work to be done. In the case of robotic hands operation, the proposed solution has to be integrated into existing solutions, as well as be tested with larger data sets. In the case of affective computing and emotion recognition, the proposed solutions require field testing in real environments, as well as integration in real systems in order to examine their suitability for non-controlled environments. The proposed approach for object tracking in drones has to be studied using a variety of visual features to be tracked, as well as targets of different shapes.

In the case of autonomous cars, the presented solution has to be integrated and tested in a real autonomous car, since it was evaluated on public data sets. Furthermore, the use of brain signals as a biometrics modality is still in its infancy and more work is needed in order to be exploited in practical applications, as higher accuracy and more practical signal acquisition devices are needed. In the case of visual quality assessment metrics, machine-learning-based methods demonstrate great potential, but more work is needed in order to provide metrics that would be suitable for a wide range of impairment types and would not be limited to specific usage scenarios.

In the connected health case, more sophisticated machine-learning algorithms could be potentially explored for the task of detecting pathological situations or remote monitoring of the patients based on ECG data or mobile ECG, whereas in the case of dimensionality reduction in collections of huge amounts of data for IoT network applications, integration and deployment in large-scale real and complex systems with real live traffic could further demonstrate the potential of the proposed approaches. Artificial intelligence and machine-learning algorithms can facilitate the optimisation of large-scale complex systems considering the stringent requirements such as reliability and latency via ultra-reliable and low-latent communication. For example, high-precision robot controls, factory automation, real-time human–machine interactions and intelligent system for autonomous cars, etc. can be considered as potential applications; however, the importance of understanding the data and feeding the meaningful training set to the specific artificial intelligence and machine-learning algorithms for these future applications have not fully been recognised and considered as one of the open challenges.

Index